The Trial of Bhagat Singh

The Trial of Bhagat Singh

Politics of Justice

NEW EDITION

A.G. Noorani

OXFORD
UNIVERSITY PRESS

OXFORD
UNIVERSITY PRESS

Oxford University Press is a department of the University of Oxford.
It furthers the University's objective of excellence in research, scholarship,
and education by publishing worldwide. Oxford is a registered trademark of
Oxford University Press in the UK and in certain other countries

Published in India by
Oxford University Press
22 Workspace, 2nd Floor, 1/22 Asaf Ali Road, New Delhi 110002, India

© A.G. Noorani 1996

The moral rights of the author have been asserted

Originally Published by Konark Publishers Pvt. Ltd., Delhi 1996
Published by Oxford University Press, Karachi 2001
This Edition is reprinted with permission from Oxford University Press, Karachi
Oxford India Paperbacks 2005
28th impression 2024

ISBN-13: 978-0-19-567817-8
ISBN-10: 0-19-567817-6

Printed in India by Replika Press Pvt. Ltd

To Ammajan who is no more

Contents

Preface

This book was written as a study in the politics of justice. Bhagat Singh's trial falls in the same gory tradition as Maharaja Nanda Kumar's in 1775 and Bahadur Shah Zafar's in 1858. In each case, the stakes were too high for the British rulers to permit their opponent to remain free. The last Moghul Emperor was spared a death sentence only because it would have aroused deep resentment; the Raj was none too secure; and he was too frail to pose a challenge. The other two had to be put out of harm's reach.

Early this year, the publishers of this edition published the author's book *Indian Political Trials 1775–1947* in which the theme—politics of justice—was fully discussed in the Introduction. Bhagat Singh's trial was excluded because it had been covered separately in the previous edition of this book. The Introduction to the present paperback edition is written anew, excluding analyses of politics of justice. But it reproduces for the first time excerpts from Bhagat Singh's notebook which he maintained while under sentence of death and which provides much insight into his political outlook.

I incurred many a debt in what proved to be a very fascinating study. The late Ali Sardar Jafri gave a lot of his time for discussions which provided useful insights. It is to him that I owe discovery of the last and priceless letter which Bhagat Singh wrote in Urdu, in his own hand, to his youngest brother Kultar immediately after their last meeting. It figures in Part III of the film *Literary Storm* which he produced and directed for the Films Division of India. He also wrote its script. The Chief Producer of the Films Division Mr D. Gautaman, and his staff helped enormously to secure a copy of the letter which is printed in the book.

Dr Bipan Chandra provided some useful material. Dr Kamlesh Mohan answered queries besides according permission for reproduction of the site map attached to the First Information Report, which she improved for publication in her able work *Militant Nationalism in Punjab*.

Mr V.N. Narayanan, then editor of the *Tribune*, kindly permitted me to consult old files of the paper. Mr A.K. Avasthi, Senior Reprography Officer of the Nehru Memorial Museum and Library, New Delhi, helped to fill the gaps of references not always precise. His assistance was unfailing and invaluable. I owe a lot to him and to the Library as, indeed, I do to the National Archives of India, New Delhi and its then Director-General Mr S. Sarkar, and his colleagues, especially Mr T.V. Haranthe Babu, a Deputy Director-General. I wish to thank Dr P.C. Rao, then Law Secretary, Government of India, for his help. Thanks are also due to Dr S.R. Gunpule, Librarian, Bombay University Library, and his staff and to Mr Govind B. Kadam, Librarian, High Court Library, Bombay for their invaluable assistance.

Mr Sumit Chakravarthy, editor of *Mainstream*, was kind to permit reproduction of D.P. Das's article 'Gandhi and Bhagat Singh'. Syed Rahat Hasan then Information Officer, British High Commission, New Delhi, provided biodata of British mandarins of the late 1920s whose ghosts, largely exorcised from North Block, still stalk the corridors of South Block, not without providing occasional help to its present occupants. None of them, of course, is in any way responsible for the contents of the book.

Last, Mr Anil Joseph Chandy, my editor at Oxford University Press, New Delhi for his invaluable assistance in procuring Bhagat Singh's notebook from the Nehru Memorial Museum and Library. This edition draws on it for the first time. Three others deserve my grateful thanks.

Mrs Ameena Saiyyid, Managing Editor of Oxford University Press, Karachi, which had published the book in 2002, readily accorded her permission for this paperback edition. It is to Mr Indrajit Hazra, Assistant Editor of the *Hindustan Times* and an accomplished novelist, that I owe the idea of this edition in India. He had found it hard to get a copy in India, obtained one eventually, and suggested a reprint. I am grateful to Mr Manzar Khan, Managing Director of Oxford University Press, New Delhi for accepting my proposal for a paperback edition.

April 2005   A.G. Noorani
                                                             Mumbai

Introduction

B hagat Singh's trial is one of those episodes in the history of India's struggle for freedom of which little is known. Historians and his contemporaries' writings have thrown light on facets of his personality and his outlook which his amazing courage and deep commitment tended to overshadow. A man of intense feeling, he was also a man of remarkable intellectual qualities who was ever ready to learn and unlearn.

But far less is known of some dark aspects of the trial. This book seeks to explore them. It raises certain issues which have not received the attention they deserve. The farcical character of the trial was not studied in depth, perhaps because Bhagat Singh's culpability in the murder of John Saunders, Assistant Superintendent of Police, was not in question. But the Lahore conspiracy case merits study for its own sake as a classic case of abuse of the judicial process for political ends. On 1 May 1930 the Governor-General promulgated an Ordinance establishing a Special Tribunal to try the case while taking good care to deprive the accused of the right of appeal to the High Court. The law requires confirmation of death sentences by the High Court. The Ordinance robbed them of this precious right.

A little over six months later, the Punjab Government got enacted a special statute to set up a Commission to try certain persons on charges as grave and the same Governor-General secured enactment of a central law conferring on the accused those very rights of appeal to and confirmation of sentences by the High Court. The animus against Bhagat Singh and his comrades could not have been demonstrated more brazenly.

Nor is that all. The Ordinance expired after six months. This was a unique trial by a Tribunal which was itself under a death sentence, suspended for six months. It, therefore, sacrificed justice to despatch. There was another unique feature which was even more revolting. Half way through the trial, a member of the Tribunal, Justice Sayad Agha Haider, was unceremoniously removed from it. He was then a sitting judge of the Lahore High Court. His objection to the use of violence by the police on Bhagat Singh and his associates and his close questioning of the prosecution witnesses had alarmed the authorities. They had decided that Bhagat Singh should not be left alive, not even in prison serving a long sentence. It would have been embarrassing to carry out this design if the Tribunal were to split two to one. The Judge hailed from Saharanpur in Uttar Pradesh.

S.M.A. Kazmi, Dehra Dun correspondent of the *Indian Express* reported his relatives' resentment at the films which romanticized that sordid episode very much as Richard Attenborough projected a varnished version of the Hunter Commission on the Jalianwala Bagh massacre in his film *Gandhi*. It was not the Commission's English members who grilled the official witnesses; on the contrary, they tried to protect them. The honour of subjecting those witnesses to a searing cross-examination belongs to Sir Chimanlal Setalvad, one of the greatest Indian advocates of all time. He clashed repeatedly with the English members. Independent India ignores him because, unlike the other Liberals, he was too proud to pay homage to popular heroes.

Justice Agha Haider's relatives revealed to Kazmi that the President of the Tribunal, Justice John Coldstream, an ICS Judge of the Lahore High Court, informed the Governor of Punjab about his colleague's 'non-co-operative' attitude. The Government Advocate, Carden Noad, was sent to Justice Haider's home 'to pacify him, but the latter turned him out, saying "I am a judge, not a butcher"' (The *Indian Express*, 19 June 2002). The Judge was removed from the Tribunal.

Ironically, though Bhagat Singh had shot Saunders in broad day light, it was on the solitary testimony of a witness, who happened to be there by sheer chance, that his conviction at the trial rested. The other witnesses had collapsed. Continuous legal assistance would have made a difference. But the defendants had little interest in their acquittal.

One hopes that the National Archives of India would publish a full account of the trial. Besides the official record, the editor of the work would do well to draw on Sukh Dev's copy of the transcript lodged in the Private Collection of the National Archives because he made some revealing disclosures and comments in his marginal notes. A man facing certain death, as he did, would not lie. The*Tribune* covered the trial fully and reported incidents and exchanges in court which no official record would report. A full report of Bhagat Singh's trial must draw on all these three sources. I have reproduced some of the comments Sukh Dev inscribed on his copy of the trial transcript.

Reading old newspapers and records evokes in one's mind the atmosphere of a bygone era. One is struck by several features of those times that bear recalling today. Debates in the Central Assembly were of a remarkably high quality. That breed of parliamentarians is now extinct. Then, as now, Lahore served as a centre of intellectual ferment and political protest. But it has lost its old composite culture, as have many Indian cities. Yet, it is in Lahore that most of the few adherents to the credo of secularism in Pakistan reside today. Morarji Desai and Charan Singh never tired to saying that Urdu was the language of the Pakistan movement. The records show that it was very much the language of revolution ('Inquilab Zindabad') and of most revolutionaries in Northern India, not least Bhagat Singh's.

Bhagat Singh's life and thinking hold lessons for the terrorist and the state alike. He grew up in an atmosphere in which, disillusioned with the moderates' politics, many a patriot took to revolutionary politics. We owe to Professors Malwinder Jit Singh and Harinder Singh a full account of the Ghadr movement of 1914–15 based on the judgements delivered by the Special Tribunal in what were truly the first Lahore Conspiracy Cases (*War Against King Emperor: Ghadr of 1914–15: A Verdict by Special Tribunal* , Bhai Sahib Randhir Singh Trust, Ludhiana, 2001).

Bhagat Singh was seven then. He was twenty-three when he was executed on 23 March 1931. The notebook testifies to his vast reading and to his readiness to learn. He was a blind follower of no leader and an uncritical supporter of no ideology. He was no terrorist. It is not possible to say in what direction his study and reflection would have taken him over the years, had he but lived. The notebook is very catholic in its selection of quotations. These few reproductions that follow from the notebook provide a flavour of the whole.

King's Salary

It is inhuman to talk of a million sterling a year, paid out of the public taxes of any country, for the support of an individual, whilst thousands who are forced to contribute thereto, are pining with want and struggling with misery. Govt. does not consist in a contrast between prisons and palaces, between poverty and pomp; it is not instituted to rob the needy of his mite and increase the worthlessness of the wretched.

P. 204

: .o. .

"Give me liberty or death"

It is in vain, Sir, to extenuate the matter. Gentlemen, may cry, peace, peace — but there is no peace. The war is actually begun. The next gale that sweeps from the North to our ears the clash of resounding arms. Our brethren are already in the field. Why stand we here idle? What is it that gentlemen wish? What would they have? Is life so dear or peace so sweet as to be purchased at the price of chains and slavery. Forbid it, almighty God! I know not what course other may take, as for me, give me liberty or death.

Patrick Henry.

: .o. .

Right of labour "Whoever produces anything by weary labour, does not need a revelation from heaven to teach him that he has a right to the thing produced."

Robert G. Ingersoll

"We consider it horrible that people should
have their heads cut off, but we have not
been taught to see the horror of life-long
death which is inflicted upon a whole population
by poverty and tyranny." *Mark Twain*

Anarchists:

" . . . . The Anarchists and the apostles of
insurrection are also represented; and if some
of the things seem to the reader the mere
unchaining of furies, I would say, let him not
blame the faithful anthologist, let him not
blame even the writer — let him blame
himself, who has acquiesced in the existence
of conditions which have driven his fellowmen
to extremes of madness and despair."
                    Upton Sinclair. Preface 19
                    Cry for Justice

The old labourer:

" . . . . He (the old labourer out of employment)
was struggling against age, against nature, against
circumstances; the entire weight of society, law
and order pressed upon him to force him to lose
his self-respect and liberty. . . . He knocked
at the doors of the farms and found good in
man only — not in law and order, but
in individual man alone. "
                    Richard Jefferies. 80:

Sir Henry Maine has said,

"That most of the land of England has passed to its present owners by the mistake of lawyers — mistakes that in lesser criminals were punished by hanging."

"The law convicts the man or woman
Who steals the goose from off to Common,
But lets the greater felon loose
Who steals the Common from the goose."

Constitution of Labour and State : —

"Not only the ancient and feudal, but also
the representative State of today is an instrument of
exploitation of wage-labour by capital." Engels.

Dictatorship : —

"Since the state is only a temporary institution
which is to be made use of in revolution in order
forcibly to suppress the opponents. it is perfectly absurd
to talk of about a free popular State; so long as
the proletariate still needs the state it needs it not
in the interest of freedom, but in order to suppress
its opponents, and when it becomes possible to speak
of freedom the state, as such, ceases to exist."
                    Engels in his letter to Bebel March 28th 1875.

The impatient idealists : —

            The impatient idealists — and without some
impatience a man will rarely prove effective —
is almost sure to be led into hatred by the oppositions
and disappointments which he encounters in his
endeavour to bring happiness to the world.
                    Bertrand Russell.

Autograph
of Mr. BK Dutt
taken on 12th July '30
in Cell No: 137
Central Jail Lahore,
four days before his final
departure from this jail.
Bhagat Singh.

Aim of Communists :

"The Communists disdain to conceal their ~~views~~ views and ~~and~~ aim. They openly declare that their ends can be attained only by the forcible overthrow of all existing social conditions. Let the ruling classes tremble at a Communist revolution. The proletarians have nothing to lose but their chains. They have a world to win. Working men of all countries, unite!

Aim of Communist Revolution :

"We have seen above, that the first step in the revolution by the working class, is to raise the proletariat to the position of ruling class, to win the battle of democracy, to wrest, by degrees, all capital from the bourgeoisie, to centralize all instruments of production in the hands of the State, i.e. of the proletariat organized as the ruling class; and to increase the total of productive forces as rapidly as possible.

"Communist Manifesto"

Law :—

" We term any kind of rule or canon whereby actions are framed, a law ". [Hooker]

" Law in its most general sense signifies a rule of action, and is indiscriminately to all kinds of action whether rational or irrational, animate or inanimate. Thus we say, the Laws of motion, of gravitation, of optics of nature and of nations." {Blackstone}.

Kinds of Laws :—

1. Imperative Law
2. Physical Law or Scientific Law
3. Natural or Moral Law
4. Conventional Law
5. Customary Law
6. Practical or Technical Law
7. International Law
8. Civil Law or the Law of the State.

Punishment :—

Political Crimes :—

We agree with the great body of legislators in thinking, that though, in general a person who has been a party to a criminal design, which has not been carried into effect,* yet an exception to this rule must be made with respect to high offences against the State; for State Crimes, and especially the most heinous and formidable State crimes, have this peculiarity, that, if they are successfully committed, the criminal is almost always secure from punishment. The murderer is in greater danger after his victim is despatched than before. The thief is in greater danger after the purse is taken than before. But the rebel is out of danger as soon as he has subverted the Govt. As the penal law is impotent against a successful rebel, it is consequently necessary that it should be made strong and sharp against the first beginning of rebellion …."

[I. L.C.C. Judgement 186]
PP 120.

*
[be not
dealt
with
severely
dealt with]

Bhagat Singh was secular to the core and parted company with his mentor, Lala Lajpat Rai, when his politics increasingly assumed a communal colour. He wielded the gun himself, consciously, not through another. Unlike such, he never sought clemency and never gave assurances of good behaviour. His letter to Sukh Dev sternly rebuked him for entertaining thoughts of suicide.

No. Being progressive and giving up life for great and inspiring ideals can never be termed as suicide. The death of our friend (Yatindranath Das, who fasted for 64 days and died protesting against jail conditions) is unforgettable. Would you call it suicide?

Our suffering has brought positive results. A revolution is going on throughout our country. Our objective has been attained. Deaths in such kind of struggles are the best way to leave this world. Those of us who feel that they would be given a death sentence should patiently wait for that day. This death would still be very beautiful. But to give up life just to avoid the troubles would be very shameful...

We have discussed it many a times that the originality which is omnipresent in Russian literature isn't visible in our literature at all. We used to praise the pains and sorrows depicted in Russian literature. But we could not feel the agony from the core of the heart. We praise their extrovert character that scale new heights but never ever did we think as to why they are ahead of us. Our situation becomes pitiable and laughable when we allow mysticism to enter our life. People like us who call themselves revolutionaries should always be prepared for all the sorrows which we ourselves invite through struggles and that allows us to call ourselves revolutionaries.

...The opportunity to study some big social issues like crime and sin can be availed only in jails. I have studied some literature on this topic, and jail is the best place for self-study. The best part of self-study is—you should yourself bear the pain...

I would also like to say that the father of socialism, 'Marx,' was not its originator in reality. In fact, Europe's industrial revolution had produced a host of people with the same vision, and Marx was one of them. Though Marx had, undoubtedly, been helpful in giving a push to the time circle to some extent.

Neither I nor you are the fathers of socialism in this country. It is a result of time and circumstances. Undoubtedly, we have done some ordinary and small things to promote this thought. That is why I say that having taken the responsibility of such an important deed, we must continue it and keep moving.

Committing suicide just to get rid of sorrows will not guide the public, rather this will be assumed as a reactive act. We have worked under testing conditions to oppose pressure, depression and violence prevalent in the jail—that too without breaking its norms. When we were doing our jobs we were targeted in various ways... The pain was so much that even those who called themselves 'great revolutionaries' left us all alone. Were not those conditions highly testing? Then what was the logic... behind continuing our efforts and revolution? Doesn't this logic, alone empower our thoughts? And don't we have examples of those revolutionaries who are still active even after returning from jail? Had Bakunin thought the way you did, he would have committed suicide at the very outset. Today, you can see infinite numbers of Russian revolutionaries who have spent most of their lives in prisons, yet they are holding responsible positions. Humans must always stick to their beliefs. Nobody can predict the future...

...I have no doubt whatsoever that I would be sentenced for death. I am not expecting any sort of complete pardon for decent behaviour. Even if there is any kind of relaxation, it won't be complete pardon. Whatever relaxation provided, it would be very limited and complicated. There will be no forgiveness for us... I wish our freedom... becomes an integrated and global issue, and just as our revolution reaches the peak when we get hanged... When the fate of a country is at stake, an individual's fate should be completely overlooked.

(Excerpted from *Main Bhagat Singh Bol Raha Hoon* by Raj Shekhar Vyas, reproduced in *Tehelka*, 2 April 2005).

In a real sense, Bhagat Singh's intellectual life properly began only when he entered the prison. He had, of course, read avidly before. But the activist had little time for intellectual pursuits. They came to a tragic and abrupt end with his death.

1

The Man and the Phenomenon

"**I**T is very easy and very fatuous to condemn persons or acts without seeking to understand the springs of action, the causes that underlie them. Bhagat Singh was not previously well known, he did not become popular because of an act of violence, an act of terrorism. Terrorists have flourished in India, off and on, for nearly thirty years, and at no time, except in the early days of Bengal, did any of them attain a fraction of that popularity which came to Bhagat Singh. That is a patent fact which cannot be denied; it has to be admitted."

This passage in Jawahar Lal Nehru's *Autobiography* has been quoted often and reveals a characteristic blend of mixed feelings of admiration, disapproval and a hesitation in expressing either without qualification.[1] The *Autobiography* was published in 1936, five years after Bhagat Singh was executed. On October 7, 1930, he and two others, Shivram Rajguru and Sukh Dev, were sentenced to be hanged by the neck by a Special Tribunal for the murder, in Lahore on December 17, 1928, of an Assistant Superintendent of Police, John Poyantz Saunders, as part of a conspiracy to wage war against the Government of India. Bhagat Singh was 23 when he forfeited his life, Saunders was 21.

It was a tragic case of mistaken identity. They had intended to kill the Superintendent of Police, J.A. Scott, who, they believed, had struck the blows on Lala Lajpat Rai during a procession in Lahore on October 30, 1928. The entire country was exercised

over the Simon Commission which was touring India as part of its
remit to recommend the next instalment of constitutional reforms.
The British Government did not appoint on the Commission a
single member who belonged to the nation whose future constitution was being discussed. India protested with an unanimity that,
sadly, was rare.

Some of Lahore's most distinguished public figures met on the
same platform at a meeting outside Mochi Gate before marching
in the fateful procession, Dr. Muhammad Alam presiding. Among
those who spoke were Pandit Madan Mohan Malaviya and Lala
Lajpat Rai who led the procession along with Dr. Alam, Maulana
Zafar Ali Khan, Maulana Abdul Qadir, Raizada Hans Raj, Sardul
Singh Caveeshar, Gopi Chand Bhargava, K. Santhanam, Satyapal
and Maulana Daud Ghaznavi.[2] This meeting was to coincide with
the Simon Commission's arrival in Lahore that day and was only
the last of a series of meetings. A particularly large one was held
outside Lahore's Delhi Gate on October 27 at which Maulana
Abdul Qadir of Qasur presided. Malaviya addressed it. So did
Syed Ataullah Shah Bukhari, whose oratorical prowess made him
a legend in his own life time.

The demonstration on October 30 was amongst the most orderly that Lahore had witnessed. The marchers stopped near a
barbed-wire barricade near the railway station confident that their
protests would be loud enough for Sir John Simon and his colleagues to hear as they got into the cars parked outside the station.
Bukhari kept the crowd spell-bound as they waited for the unwel-
come visitors.[3]

Scott was in a foul mood. He challenged the genuineness of the
press pass held by the Senior Assistant Editor of *The Tribune*,
Pearey Mohan Dattatreya, and manhandled him as he sought to
enter the enclosure for the press. Dattatreya sued for damages and
won. In a courageous judgement after months of trial, G.D.
Khosla awarded damages, albeit on a moderate scale.[4] The precedent cries for emulation today.

Scott next turned on the demonstrators without any provocation and led the police assault. Lajpat Rai was his special target.
He received injuries on the chest and elsewhere. The marks of

injuries were apparent when he attended a meeting of the All-India Congress Committee in Delhi a few days later. On November 17 the 'Punjab Kesri' breathed his last. The country was stunned as news of the death spread.

The insulting replies given in the House of Commons three days later, by the Under-Secretary of State for India, Lord Winterton, to questions put by Labour MPs added fuel to the fire. Basanti Devi, widow of C.R. Das, cried in anguish: "I quake with shame and disgrace . . . Does the youth and manhood of the country still exist? Does it feel the burning shame and disgrace of it? A woman of the land demands clear answer to it."[5]

One man was ready with the answer. Bhagat Singh was one of the prime organisers of the procession but could not participate in it since warrants had been out for his arrest. He decided to avenge the Lala's death by killing Scott. Only hours after the deed did he realise that it was not Scott but his junior whom he and his colleague Rajguru had killed. The posters were corrected to substitute Saunders' name for Scott's. "Saunders is dead, Lalaji is avenged."

As Nehru recalled, "Bhagat Singh did not become popular because of his act of terrorism, but because he seemed to vindicate, for the moment, the honour of Lala Lajpat Rai, and through him of the nation. He became a symbol; the act was forgotten, the symbol remained, and within a few months each town and village of the Punjab, and to a lesser extent in the rest of northern India, resounded with his name. Innumerable songs grew up about him, and the popularity that the man achieved was something amazing."

He did not rest on his oars, either. From the gun, he moved to the bomb. On April 8, 1929, Bhagat Singh and Batukeshwar Dutt each threw a bomb in the chamber of the Central Legislative, while it was in session, and scattered leaflets, besides. The intention was not to kill and none was. Six members of the Assembly were injured. The intention was to deliver a message which is why Bhagat Singh fired two unaimed shots from the pistol. They disdained escape and readily gave themselves up.

By the standards of modern terrorists, both operations were

conducted with amazing ineptitude. The posters pasted on the walls in Lahore after the murder were in Bhagat Singh's own handwriting, for instance. It is more than probable that but for the daring venture in the Assembly, Bhagat Singh might have successfully eluded the police. But the pistol seized from him in the Assembly was afterwards proved to have been used in the Saunders' murder. Bhagat Singh and Dutt were both sentenced to transportation for life on June 12, 1929. A month later, the trial for the Saunders' murder began in Lahore.

But if those men, and their likes in those days, were less skilled than the wielders of the gun today, they were far more idealistic and practised in their own lives a far sterner code of personal morality. To no small extent was what Nehru called "the phenomenon of Bhagat Singh" due to the man's spotlessly clean life, his lofty vision, and a selflessness that defies belief.

Later research confirmed the impression which he had left on contemporaries. Bhagat Singh was of a scholarly bent of mind and was a thinker who gave every promise of creativity. The pages of the amazing Diary he wrote in prison testify to this. There was a certain irony in his resolve to avenge Lajpat Rai's death. He had not only drifted apart from the leader but denounced him publicly; not for any personal reasons, but because Lajpat Rai's politics became markedly communal in the mid-twenties. The historian, Dr. Bipan Chandra, records: "He printed as a pamphlet Robert Browning's famous poem, 'The Lost Leader', in which Browning criticises Wordsworth for turning against the French Revolution and the spirit of liberty. The opening line of the poem was 'Just for a handful of silver he left us', a few other lines were 'We shall march prospering—not thro' his presence; songs may inspire us—from his lyre'; and 'Blot out his name, record one lost soul'—in fact, his name appeared nowhere in it—only the front cover carried Lajpat Rai's photograph."[6]

In an informative essay on "Bhagat Singh and his Comrades", Dr. Bipan Chandra wrote: "He did not hesitate to sharply criticize Lala Lajpat Rai when he took a turn towards communalism. In 1928 he successfully argued that young men belonging to a religious-communal organization like the Akali Dal should not be permitted to become members of the Naujawan Bharat Sabha. Religion, said Bhagat Singh, was the private concern of a person, but it had to be fought as an enemy when it intruded into politics and took the form of communalism. Two of the six rules of the Naujawan Bharat Sabha were: 'To have nothing to do with communal bodies or other parties which disseminate communal ideas' and to 'create the spirit of general toleration among the pubic, considering religion as a matter of personal belief of man and to act upon it fully'."[7]

Bhagat Singh keenly realised the force of ideas. "The sword of revolution is sharpened at the whetstone of thought", he told the judges trying him. It is unlikely that those innocent souls understood him. His associate Shiv Verma, could not "remember a single occasion when he was not carrying books".[8] He was a pamphleteer in the great tradition. An article he wrote in 1927 entitled "Communal Riots and their Cure" has a contemporary relevance: "The martyrs of 1914-1915 had separated religion from politics and were convinced that religion was the private affair of an individual, hence none should be permitted to interfere with it. And likewise religion should also be debarred from encroaching in politics because once it is mixed up, it can't work in unison in the same arena . . . .

"It was because of this that a movement like the Ghadar Party remained integrated and united, in which Sikhs topped the list of those attaining martyrdom, but Hindus and Muslims also did not lag far behind . . . . At the moment some of our Indian leaders have emerged on the scene who are advocating separation of religion from politics, which is the real remedy to eradicate the communal malady. We support this position. If religion is separated from politics we can come together in political matters while remaining aloof from the religious point of view . . . . Wellwishers of India would think over the remedy I am suggesting and should come forward to save India from the disastrously suicidal course it is being pushed in."[9]

The months between the death sentence, pronounced by the Tribunal on October 7, 1930, and its execution, on March 23, 1931, were spent in study and reflection. All evidence that has come to light of his thinking in the last few years of his life and particularly of the last few months suggests that deep commitment and strong emotions spurred, rather than retarded, his intellectual growth and the process showed no signs of slowing.

A letter of February 2, 1931 "To, The Young Political Workers" smuggled out of jail that day counselled: "Compromise is not so ignoble and deplorable a thing as we generally think. It is rather an indispensable factor in the political strategy .... Compromise is an essential weapon which has to be wielded every now and then as the struggle develops. But the thing that we must keep always before us is the idea of the movement. We must always maintain a clear notion of the objective for the attainment of which we are fighting."

He wrote, also, "Apparently, I have acted like a terrorist. But I am not a terrorist .... Let me announce with all the strength at my command that I am not a terrorist and I never was, except perhaps in the beginning of my revolutionary career. *And I am convinced that we cannot gain anything through those methods.*"[10] (Italics mine, throughout)

Violence was not renounced but terrorism was: "Our party should have a military wing. Let me make myself clear. It is said that I am a terrorist, but in reality, I have been all along a revolutionary with definite ideals and ideology. I may be blamed as they blame Ramprasad Bismil that the condemned cell wrought a change in his ideology, but this is not true. I am the same man as I used to be, and have the same ideas. *It is my considered opinion that bombs cannot serve our purpose. This is proved by the history of Hindustan Socialist Republican Association. Throwing bombs is not only useless, but is often harmful as well. They are to be used on certain occasions only. Our chief aim should be to mobilise the toiling masses. The military wing should collect material for war for use on special occasions.*"[11]

One of Bhagat Singh's more famous writings is an article he wrote under the title *Why I am an Atheist* in which he bared his soul in this moving passage:

I was afraid that some day I also might not be convinced of the futility of our own programme. That was a turning point in my revolutionary career. 'Study' was the cry that reverberated in corridors of my mind. Study to enable yourself to face the arguments advanced by opposition. Study to arm yourself with arguments in favour of your cult. I began to study. My previous faith and convictions underwent a remarkable modification. The Romance of the violent methods alone which was so prominent amongst our predecessors, was replaced by serious ideas. No more mysticism, no more blind faith. Realism became our cult. Use of force justifiable when resorted to as a matter of terrible necessity: non-violence as policy indispensable for all mass movements. So much about methods. The most important thing was the clear conception of the ideal for which we were to fight. As there were no important activities in the field of action I got ample opportunity to study various ideals of the world revolution. I studied Bakunin, the Anarchist leader, something of Marx the father of communism and much of Lenin, Trotsky and others the men who had successfully carried out a revolution in their country.[12]

That Bhagat Singh drank deep at the fount of Marxism is universally acknowledged. Ajoy Kumar Ghosh, General Secretary of the Communist Party of India for over a decade from 1951, knew Bhagat Singh well. They were co-accused in the Lahore Conspiracy Case.

Writing of his colleague in 1945, Ajoy Ghosh was quite categorical: "It would be an exaggeration to say that he became a Marxist, but more and more as a result of his studies of discussions, which we held frequently, and under the impact of events outside, he began to stress the need for armed action only in coordination with and as an integral part of the mass movement, subordinated to its needs and requirements."[13]

The Intelligence Bureau made an astute assessment of the ideology of Bhagat Singh's group and their relationship with the Communists. They studied Marxism keenly and greatly admired the Soviet Union. But, the IB's Director, J.M. Ewart, cautioned in his study *Terrorism in India, 1917-1936*: "It must not be understood that terrorists have embraced the Communist doctrine as a whole, for the very creed is aimed at the elimination of their own particular class, the bhadralok. They do, however, see in Communist principles, and especially in those principles which relate to action, a great resemblance to their own, and they are unduly engaged by the hope that through Communism they will approach nearer to a mass rising than they ever did by their old terrorist methods. On the other hand there is no reason to believe that the Communist Party accepts or will ever accept the bhadralok terrorist at his face value, but there exists in Communism the obvious basis for the fusion of both schools or revolutionary idealism."[14]

One can only speculate the route this highly educable man would have finally chosen to reach his goals had he not died as young as he did. What all his comrades testify is that he left a deep impression on them in the brief months of their acquaintance; as much for the qualities of the mind as for those of character.

NOTES

1. Jawahar Lal Nehru, *An Autobiography*; New Delhi, Nehru Memorial Museum and Library, Oxford University Press, 1982, pp. 174-176.

2. Kamlesh Mohan, *Militant Nationalism in the Punjab*, Manohar, 1985, p. 146.

3. Feroz Chand, *Lajpat Rai*, Publications Division, New Delhi, 1978, p. 538.

4. Prakash Nanda, *A History of the Tribune*, The Tribune Trust, Chandigarh, p. 81.

5. Kamlesh Mohan, p. 345, f.n. 67.

6. *The Telegraph*, March 21, 1991; Article entitled "Bhagat Singh, Communalism and Religion".

7. Ravi Dayal (Ed.), Oxford University Press, 1994, p. 151.

8. *Ibid.*, p. 148.

9. Nazirul Hasan Ansari, "Bhagat Singh for Today", *Mainstream*, March 27, 1993, pp. 34-35.

10. Shiv Varma (Ed.), *Selected Writings of Bhagat Singh*, National Book Trust, New Delhi, pp. 129-131.

11. Manmathnath Gupta, *Bhagat Singh and His Times*, Lipi Prakashan, Delhi, 1977, p. 191.

12. Quoted in Bhagwan Josh, *Communist Movement in Punjab*, Anupama Publications, 1979, p. 88.

13. Ajoy Ghosh, *Bhagat Singh and His Comrades*, People's Publishing House, Bombay, 1945, p. 12.

14. J.M. Ewart, *Terrorism in India, 1917-1936*, Government of India Press, Simla, 1937, p. 65.

2

The Family and Politics

B HAGAT Singh was born to Vidyawati in the village Banga in Lyallpur, on September 27, 1907, in a family of revolutionaries and in a clime in which the spirit of revolt gripped a large number of people in the Punjab. His father Kishan Singh was in the Lahore Central Jail that day for launching an agitation against legislation modifying Canal Colony tenures and raising canal rates in the Bari Doab. An uncle, Ajit Singh, who was in prison in Mandalay then, was, by all accounts, a remarkable figure.[1]

He established the Indian Patriots' Association, along with Syed Haidar Raza to organize the peasants against the Bill as well as a secret society, the Bharat Mata Society. Kishan Singh and another brother, Swaran Singh, were also its members. On release from prison, Ajit Singh opted for exile in Iran, Germany, Brazil and several other countries. He died in India on August 15, 1947, the day the country became free.[2]

The mood of the people in the Punjab alarmed the Lieut-Governor, Denzil Ibbetson, who recorded it in a Report dated April 30, 1907 which became a mini-classic of its kind: "Everywhere people are sensible of a change of a 'new air' (nayi hawa), which is blowing through men's minds, and are waiting to see what will come of it . . . . In the towns of Rawalpindi, Sialkot and Lyallpur, an active anti-English propaganda is being openly and sedulously preached. In Lahore, the capital of the Province, the propaganda is virulent and has resulted in a more or less general state of serious unrest."[3]

The *nayi hawa* did not peter out. It gathered strength over a decade later, on December 10, 1917, the Governor General set up a Committee to investigate and report on "the nature and extent of the criminal conspiracies connected with the revolutionary movement in India" and to advise as to the legislation "necessary to enable Government to deal effectively with them". Its President was justice S.A.T. Rowlatt of the High Court of England. Its members were: Sir Basil Scott, Chief Justice of Bombay, Justice C.V. Kumaraswami Sastri of the Madras High Court, P.C. Mitter, a Calcutta lawyer and a British civil servant, Verney Lovett. They quoted copiously from Ibbetson's Report, not omitting his indignant reference to the fact that "on two recent occasions Europeans had been insulted as such". It was regarded as an injury grave enough for the Viceroy to denounce, in his Legislative Council, those "gratuitous insults to Europeans".[4]

The Rowlatt Report recalled that nine batches of conspirators were tried by Special Tribunals set up under the Defence of India Act, enacted on the outbreak of the First World War. The First Tribunal observed in its judgement that "a wave of sedition had been ebbing and flowing in the Punjab since 1907". Together, these were known as the Lahore Conspiracy cases.

Bhagat Singh grew up on stories of exploits of his uncle and his father. The Ghadar movement left a deep imprint on his mind. Kartar Singh Sarabha, hanged when he was only nineteen after conviction in the first Lahore Conspiracy case, became his hero. The massacre at Jallianwalla Bagh on April 13, 1919 drove him to Amritsar where he kissed the earth sanctified by the martyrs' blood and brought back home a little of the soaked soil.[5]

Lala Lajpat Rai, Bhai Parmanand and Sufi Amba Parshad formed the National College in Lahore on the lines of national schools and colleges and universities established in response to Gandhi's call to shun Government-aided institutions and establish, instead, national educational institutions.[6] Bhagat Singh left the D.A.V. School in Lahore in 1921 and joined the National College where he met colleagues of future years like Sukh Dev,

Bhagwati Charan Vohra, and Yashpal. Prof. Jai Chandra Vidya-lankar, who taught history, was close to this pupil and introduced him to revolutionaries in the United Provinces, now Uttar Pradesh.

How self-consciously dedicated he had become is apparent in Bhagat Singh's famous correspondence with his father when he was pressed to marry.[7]

Respected Father,
    This is not the time for marriage. The country is calling me. I have taken oath to serve the country physically, mentally and monetarily (*tan, man* and *dhan*). Moreover it is not a new thing for us. Our whole family is full of patriotism. After two or three years of my birth in 1910, uncle Swarn Singh died in jail. Uncle Ajit Singh is living a life of exile in foreign countries. You have also suffered a lot in jails. I am only following your footprints and thus dare to do this. You will kindly not tie me down in matrimony but give me your blessings so that I may succeed in my mission.

Kishan Singh's protest, "We have already settled your marriage . . . you should not create any difficulty" brought a firm refusal.

Respected Father,
    I am astonished to read the contents of your letter. When you, who are a staunch patriot and brave personality, can be influenced by such trifles, then what will happen to ordinary men?
    You are caring for Dadi (my grandmother), but in how much trouble is our Mother of 33 crores, the Bharat Mata. We still have to sacrifice everything for her sake.

While leaving the home he left this note:

Revered Father,
    Namaste. I dedicate my life to the lofty goal of service to the Motherland. Hence there is no attraction in me for home and

fulfilment of worldly desires.

I hope you remember that on the occasion of my sacred thread ceremony Bapuji had declared that I was being donated to the service of the country. I am just fulfilling that pledge. I hope you would forgive me.

This, when he was still in his teens and just a few years before that fateful act in Lahore on December 17, 1928 which was to cost him his life. Bhagat Singh went to Kanpur where Ganesh Shankar Vidyarathi gave him a job at his press. Attempts to induce him to return proved of no avail. Intercession by Maulana Hasrat Mohani, one of the great Urdu poets of the century and himself a revolutionary, succeeded. Kishan Singh's prodigal son returned home but with added fervour for the causes to which he had dedicated his life.

For, in the six months he had spent in Kanpur, he had learnt a lot. Vidyarathi was a member of the AICC and knew Kishan Singh. His home was a rendezvous of political activists. It is here that he met Batukeshwar Dutt, who taught him Bengali, Chandrashekhar Azad, Jogesh Chandra Chatterjee and Bejoy Kumar Sinha. Bhagat Singh formally joined the Hindustan Republican Association formed by the UP revolutionaries. Its moving spirit was Sachindra Nath Sanyal, who was involved in the Banaras Conspiracy Case along with M.N. Roy and Rash Behari Bose.

The HRA was formed in 1923. The object clause of its Rules and Regulations declared: "The object of the Association shall be to establish a Federated Republic of the United States of India by an organized and armed revolution."[8] Funds were raised by, among other things, committing dacoities. Three went unnoticed. The fourth was near the Kakori railway station near Lucknow on August 9, 1925. A train going to Lucknow was stopped and a safe containing cash belonging to the Government was broken. The booty was not large, just Rs. 4,679, but the Kakori Conspiracy Case became a legend. Four of the accused were hanged, Ashfaqullah and Ram Prasad 'Bismil' to whom the famous poem "Sarfaroshi ki tamanna ab hamaare dil mein hai" is attributed;

wrongly, according to the scholar-poet Ali Sardar Jafri.[9] Five, including Jogesh Chandra Chatterji and Sachindra Nath Sanyal were sentenced to transportation for life while eleven received sentences for various terms of imprisonment. These savage sentences weakened the HRA but did not kill it.[10]

Bhagat Singh continued to remain in touch with his comrades in U.P. after his return to Lahore and made more contacts nearer home. In March 1926, he formed the Naujawan Bharat Sabha along with Sukh Dev, Bhagwati Charan Vohra and Ram Krishan. Kamlesh Mohan tersely sums up the function of this militant youth organization. It "took up the unfulfilled mission of the Hindustan Republican Association". As well as the young, its members included men of eminence like Saifuddin Kitchlew, Satyapal, Mir Abdul Majid, Sardul Singh Caveeshar and the poet Lal Chand *Falak*.[11] Ram Krishan was its President; Bhagat Singh, its Secretary.

The Sabha's progress was impressive by any standards. Similar bodies were formed in other provinces. Branches proliferated in the Punjab. An All-India Naujawan Bharat Sabha was established in Delhi. Soon links were forged with the Hindustan Republican Association and the Kirti Kisan Party, founded by Sohan Singh Josh. Already, on his return to Lahore, Bhagat Singh had established contacts with the Kirti Kisan Party. This Party owed its existence to the united efforts of the emissaries of the Ghadar Party (Bhag Singh 'Canadian') and of the Communist Party of Great Britain (Philip Spratt) and of Sohan Singh Josh, Mir Abdul Majid and Kedar Nath Sehgal. Intended to be a Workers and Peasants Party, it was named the Punjab Kirti-Kisan Party.[12] Its organ *Kirti* was published in Punjabi and Urdu so that it could be read by the masses. Manmathnath Gupta recalls: "In the Punjab, Punjabi was spoken and understood, but in schools only Urdu was taught . . . That is why an Urdu edition of *Kirti* began to be published with additional pages."[13] Bhagat Singh worked for some time, assisting Sohan Singh Josh, in the Urdu edition.

This was the penultimate phase. The last phase is characterised as "the conspiracy" in the Judgment of the Tribunal which sent Bhagat Singh to the gallows. It presents a total contrast to later works by scholars. Their researches and insights provide the reader with good glimpses of the mainsprings of the actions by the participants in the drama, their motivations and their distinctive styles. The Judgement records conclusions from evidence adduced by the prosecution alone. The defence did not seriously contest the case and led no evidence. The Judgement, as in all such cases, reeks of tedious, albeit relevant, details of houses rented and abandoned and such. It is concerned essentially with culpability, individual and collective. Scholars and Bhagat Singh's colleagues have since brought to light some significant facts not to be found in the Judgement. Both are relevant.

Where all agree is that the defining moment was when the revolutionaries met at Feroze Shah Kotla in Delhi on September 8-9, 1928 and decided to launch a new body in order to unite the provincial groups on one platform.

There was the Bihar group which included Phonindra Nath Ghosh, Man Mohan Bannerjee and Kanwal Nath Tewari, the U.P. group of Shiv Varma and Bejoy Kumar Sinha and the Lahore group comprising Bhagat Singh, Sukh Dev, Jai Gopal and Hans Raj Vohra. There was, of course, considerable interaction among them; particularly between the U.P. group and each of the other two. Phonindra Nath Ghosh, for instance, was well connected with the U.P. group. So were Ajoy Ghosh, Gaya Prasad, Sachindra Nath Sanyal and, possibly, Lalit Kumar Mukerjee.

The "conspiracy" was unravelled before the Tribunal by the participants who became approvers. They were none other than the leading lights like Phonindra Nath Ghosh and Man Mohan Bannerjee of the Bihar group, Jai Gopal and Hans Raj Vohra of the Punjab and Lalit Kumar Mukerjee of the UP group. Of these, Phonindra Nath Ghosh's case was the most pathetic. He had joined the revolutionary Bengal Anushilan Party way back in 1916 and organized groups in Bihar in 1926.

The prosecution case had, not September, but August 1928 as the commencement of the conspiracy by the renting of houses for use as secret meeting places for the party to be formed in the next month. It was Bejoy Kumar Sinha who invited Phonindra Nath Ghosh to join the new party, towards the end of August, and proposed a secret meeting in Delhi on September 8 and 9. Phonindra checked Bejoy Kumar's credentials from Sachindra Nath Sanyal when they met in Allahabad *en route* to Delhi.

The meeting was held on September 8, 1928. Phonindra Nath Ghosh and Man Mohan Bannerjee sat under a tree in Feroze Shah Kotla Fort in Delhi where Kundan Lal also joined them on Sinha's introduction. At a short distance from them another meeting went on at which Bhagat Singh, Sukh Dev, Jai Dev, Shiv Varma, Bejoy Kumar Sinha and, another who was to turn approver, Brahm Dutt. Phonindra Nath Ghosh did not know Bhagat Singh but was introduced to him and to Sukh Dev the following day.

On that day, September 9, the participants assembled at 8 a.m. in the Fort and took important decisions. A Central Committee of the new party was appointed consisting of seven members, namely, Bhagat Singh, Sukh Dev, Bejoy Kumar Sinha, Phonindra Nath Ghosh, Kundan Lal and, most important of all, one who was absent—Chandra Shekhar Azad, already famous for escaping from the police dragnet in the Kakori Case. Of those present, Jai Dev and Man Mohan Bannerjee did not make it to the CC. There was another absentee, the Bengal revolutionary party. Various explanations are offered for that from its opposition to terrorism to the young revolutionaries' rejection of the leadership of the old.

Beats were assigned to members—Sukh Dev, Shiv Varma and Phonindra Nath Ghosh were, respectively, assigned the Punjab, U.P. and Bihar. Chandra Shekhar Azad was appointed head of the Military Department. Kundan Lal was put in charge of the Central office at Jhansi. Bhagat Singh and Bejoy Kumar Sinha were appointed to act as links between the various provinces. The Hindustan Republican Association was revived with a new and highly significant name—the Hindustan Socialist Republican Association. The only change, "Socialist", was on Bhagat Singh's insistence. There was otherwise no change in the Rules and Regulations of the HRA. Other decisions taken at the conference were: To take active part in the boycott of the Simon Commission and to throw a bomb on the train carrying it, open bomb factories at Calcutta, Saharanpur, Agra and Lahore; arrange a good instructor for giving training to its members in making bombs; murder the informers in the Kakori Dacoity Case and to free Jogesh Chandra Chatterjee from jail; and intensify the commission of dacoities for raising funds but, as far as possible, to loot Government treasures rather than individuals.[14]

The proceedings were interrupted by a watchman employed at the Fort, Bara Singh. Sukh Dev and Bhagat Singh told him that they were students preparing for their examinations. Little did they suspect that he would, one day, testify against them along with some of their trusted colleagues.

The Tribunal's Judgement said that the name of the new party was "Hindustan Socialist Republican *Army*" and the IB's Director J.M. Ewart repeated the assertion in the text of his compilation, *Terrorism in India, 1917-1936* (p. 73). The texts of two Manifestoes he appended to it belie that. It was an "Association," and an "Army" only when it acted. It had a unique credo which one of the manifestoes proudly proclaimed: "The food on which the tender plant of liberty thrives is the blood of the martyr."

NOTES

1. Vide Gurudev Singh Deol, *Shaheed Bhagat Singh*, Publications Bureau, Punjabi University, Patiala; 1985 and K.K. Khullar, *Shaheed Bhagat Singh*, Hem Publishers Pvt Ltd., New Delhi, 1981. The author is indebted to these works for their accounts of events covered in this chapter.

2. Bejoy Kumar Sinha, *Bhagat Singh and His Times* in *India's Freedom Struggle*, edited by J. Sarkar, A.B. Bardhan, and N.E. Balaram, People's Publishing House, New Delhi, 1986, pp. 51-52.

3. For the text see Khullar, pp. 98-110.

4. Superintendent Government Printing Press, Calcutta. Report of the Sedition Committee, 1918, pp. 127-28 and p. 157.

5. B.K. Sinha, p. 53.

6. Vide the writer's account of the formation of one such institution, the Jamia Millia Islamia in *President Zakir Hussain*, Popular Prakashan, Bombay, 1967.

7. Deol, pp. 18-19; Khullar, pp. 34-35; and Manmathnath Gupta, p. 85.

8. Vide Ewart, pp. 195-99 for the text of the Rules and Regulations of the Association.

9. Interview with the author on September 17, 1995. The poem was written by a poet in Bihar. He was Bismil Azimabadi.

10. B.B. Mishra, *The Indian Political Parties*, Oxford University Press, p. 273.

11. Kamlesh Mohan, pp. 79-81.
12. *Ibid.*, p. 106.
13. Manmathnath Gupta, p. 99.
14. Kamlesh Mohan, p. 324; and Deol, p. 30.

3

Saunders Murder

SOON after the Feroze Shah Kotla conference was over, Bhagat Singh returned home. There was a lot of work to do. The new organization had to make its presence felt. For a start, a suitable reception had to be arranged for the Simon Commission when it arrived in Lahore. Around the middle of September 1928 Bhagat Singh cut his hair and beard at Ferozpur. That had been decided at the Fort.

A lot of movements and exchanges were carried out. Phonindra Nath Ghosh visited the Punjab, for the first time ever, and stayed in Amritsar at the party's house in Moghul Bazar. Sukh Dev came to meet him and brought along a bomb shell and two books on *Manufacture and Uses of Explosives* and *Small-Arms Training.* Bhagat Singh also visited Ghosh in Amritsar and later went to Bettiah to discuss a proposal for dacoity. *En route* he apprised Lalit Kumar Mukerjee of the decisions taken in Delhi. Bettiah had another visitor whose presence in the councils was a rare event, Chandra Shekhar Azad. He had an appropriate alias, Panditji. Food was provided by Man Mohan Bannerji. Phonindra Nath Ghosh supplied some revolvers to Bhagat Singh, for use in Agra in the rescue of Jogesh Chandra Chatterjee. A revolver was given to Sukh Dev.

It would seem from the record of the proceedings that, apparently, no one stayed at the same place at a stretch for long. Everyone was on the move. One activity undertaken discreetly but energetically was to acquire premises for work and residence. The most important of them was the Arain Building at Mozang in Lahore which Mahabir Singh acquired on rent under the name of Pratap Singh on November 9. Another was arranging for clothes, literature on arms. Azad brought a mauser pistol and four revolvers to Lahore. Lala Lajpat Rai died on November 17. That night, at the Mozang House, Mahabir Singh was host to Kundan Lal, Shivram Rajguru alias 'M' who had arrived from the U.P., Bhagat Singh, Sukh Dev, Chandra Shekhar Azad and Kishori Lal. Besides them, there were present in Lahore other members of new party, the HSRA—Jai Gopal, Hans Raj Vohra and Kali Charan—who were frequent visitors to the Mozang House. With the arrival in Lahore of Bejoy Kumar Sinha, on December 7, as many as four of the seven members of the party's Central Committee were present in town. The only absentees were Shiv Varma, Kundan Lal and Phonindra Nath Ghosh.

By now accommodation was no problem. In the middle of November, Kishori Lal had taken on rent a house in Sohel Singh Street, Gowal Mandi in Lahore and Sukh Dev obtained another at Kripa Ram Street, under the name of Devi Dass. A house in Prem Gali, rented by Agya Ram, was also used by some members.

What was in short supply was money. A resource crunch was felt acutely. It could be overcome only by a bank raid. The Punjab National Bank in Lahore seemed a good target to Bhagat Singh.[1] But the plan fizzled out. Bhagat Singh and Mahabir Singh were to reach the bank at 3 p.m. on December 4 in a hired car which Mahabir Singh was to drive away after the raid. The two drove to the Shalimar Gardens and back in a taxi but Mahabir Singh's attempt to drive it on the way back from the Gardens failed. They stopped in the Lawrence Gardens from where Mahabir Singh proceeded to the Bank in a tonga to inform Azad of the fiasco. The group, which included Sukh Dev, H.R. Vohra and Jai Gopal, returned to the Mozang House with their arms.

Six days later party members met there to discuss another venture—to murder the Superintendent of Police, J. A. Scott. The Judgement was imprecise on this point as on some others "on the 9th *or* 10th December there was a meeting at the Mozang House to discuss the murder . . . ."[2] Scholars have been able to pinpoint the event precisely—the night of December 10.[3] Those present were—Azad (Panditji), Sukh Dev, Bhagat Singh, Kishori Lal, Shiv Ram, Rajguru, Mahabir Singh and Jai Gopal.

Jai Gopal was deputed to keep a watch on Scott's movements at the precincts of police office from December 11 to 15 when he reported to Azad. It was the "Panditji" who fixed December 17 for the murder. Bhagat Singh prepared posters in pink bearing the heading "Hindustan Socialist Republican Army" and underneath it the announcement "Scott is dead" followed by an explanation for the action. These, he showed to both Jai Gopal and H.R. Vohra on December 15, as they testified on turning approvers.

Even on the appointed day, December 17, Bhagat Singh was seen by Vohra writing out the posters at the Mozang House. Vohra copied three or four of them to assist him. Kishori Lal was present. An hour and a half later, Vohra returned to the house and was imparted several of the details of the plot. He was not assigned any role, though.

The plot was finally settled at 2 p.m. when arms were distributed. Jai Gopal had visited the Police Office, as before, and seen a British police officer in uniform ride to the office on a red motorcycle and surmised that Scott had used a motorcycle, instead of a car, that day. The only role assigned to him was to remain in the vicinity of the office and give a signal once Scott came out. Azad (alias Panditji) took the mauser pistol. Bhagat Singh received an automatic pistol while Shivram Rajguru was given a revolver. Mahabir Singh was to stay put in the Mozang House. Sukh Dev, though privy to the plot, was not assigned any part in it.

Details of the incident are drawn from the Tribunal's Judgement. Jai Gopal and Bhagat Singh went to the police office on bicycles. Jai Gopal put his bicycle near the Boarding House latrine of the D.A.V. College compound opposite the police office. Panditji and Bhagat Singh brought their two bicycles to that compound. Jai Gopal then took one of these bicycles from the compound back to the latrine leaving it with the bicycle already placed by him there. Returning to the College Compound opposite the police office, he took the third bicycle and stationed himself with it on the road near the corner at which Court Street branched off. Jai Gopal retained this bicycle with him in order that if the first shot at the victim should miss, Bhagat Singh might be able to chase the victim on that bicycle. Panditji took up his station inside the College Compound adjoining the road and opposite the police office, while Bhagat Singh and Shivram Rajguru walked about on the road, near the police office.

About 4 p.m. Saunders, Assistant Superintendent of Police, who was the officer whom Jai Gopal had seen riding to the office at 10 a.m. on a red motorcycle and whom he had then mistaken for Scott, came out of the police office followed by Head Constable Chanan Singh. Saunders started his motorcycle and began to ride slowly down the road after coming out of the police office gate. Jai Gopal then made a signal upon which Rajguru took out his revolver and moving in the direction of Saunders, fired at him as soon as the motorcycle was near. Saunders being hit lifted up his hands and fell with his motorcycle on the road with one leg under the motorcycle. Bhagat Singh then ran up and discharged several shots from his automatic pistol into Saunders as he lay. That pistol became an exhibit (Ex. P. 480) in the trial. Saunders was a mere probationer.

Bhagat Singh, Rajguru and Jai Gopal then ran down Court Street, chased by Head Constable Chanan Singh and W.J.G. Fearn, Traffic Inspector. While the firing was going on, a motor car driven by one Abdullah had come up and stopped near the Court Street turning. While Fearn was chasing Bhagat Singh and Rajguru down Court Street, one of those two, "probably Bhagat Singh", the Judgment said with remarkable lack of judicial circumspection, fired at Fearn, who ducked and fell. Bhagat Singh and Rajguru then turned out of Court Street into the D.A.V. College Compound through the small gate, still pursued by Chanan Singh, while Jai Gopal continued his way down Court Street, pushing his bicycle. After entering the College Compound, Chanan Singh was shot in the right groin "probably by Panditji" with the mauser pistol. He died about an hour later at the Mayo Hospital.

Bhagat Singh, Panditji and Rajguru, passing behind the D.A.V. College and across the volleyball ground and to the west of the

Botanical Garden, entered the.E block of the buildings pertaining to the College Boarding House. Passing alongside that block, they came out from the upper storey of Block B near the place where Des Raj, later an accused in the trial, had a room, No. 28. Jai Gopal had, in the meanwhile, reached the same point by another route. Of the two bicycles which Jai Gopal had previously left near the latrines not far from the spot, one had been in the meanwhile removed altogether by Des Raj and the other had been placed by him or by "a scullion" named Milkhi, under the instructions of Des Raj, near the kitchen in that vicinity.

Panditji then took Jai Gopal's bicycle, Shivram Rajguru riding with him, while Bhagat Singh took the bicycle which had been placed near the kitchen. Bhagat Singh changed the cap that he was wearing with the *lungi* that Jai Gopal was wearing, but as he did not manage to tie it round the head he left it at that spot where it was subsequently found by Head Constable Taleh Mand that same afternoon. Panditji (Azad), Rajguru and Bhagat Singh then rode off through the small gate of the D.A.V. College Compound to the Dev Samaj Road. Here, they met three students, one of whom was Ajmer Singh from whom they tried to take the bicycle which he was wheeling, but, abandoning the attempt on resistance being shown, they proceeded towards the cycle shop of Ata Muhammad. From this shop "either Panditji or Shivram Rajguru, who was on foot at the time, took a bicycle, while Bhagat Singh, alighting from his own bicycle, halted nearby." The Judgement is studded with imprecision and speculation. Ata Muhammad, taking another bicycle, then chased the culprits who, abandoning his bicycle to him near the Swimming Bath, passed through wire fence and proceeded towards the Secretariat. The three thus got away and eventually arrived at the Mozang House.

In the meanwhile, Jai Gopal had climbed a wall into the grounds of the Veterinary College and, making a circuit, came to the neighbourhood of the Swimming Bath. There he met Morris, Deputy Superintendent of Police, with a party searching for the culprits. They questioned him, but he denied that he had seen any persons passing that way on bicycles and pretended to be a student reading a book. He then went to the Mozang House, where he reached about 5.30 p.m. and found Mahabir Singh as well as his three colleagues—Panditji, Bhagat Singh and Rajguru—there. He was then informed by Bhagat Singh that the murdered man was not Scott but Saunders.

Sukh Dev was not there having, in the meanwhile, taken the arms away into another house. After the murder, the body of Saunders was taken to the Hospital in the motor car driven by Abdullah which had arrived at the scene of murder while the firing was going on. At 6 p.m. that evening Jai Gopal met Sukh Dev who was accompanied by Bejoy Kumar Sinha and Bhagwan Dass. These persons already knew the details of murder. While Jai Gopal and Mahabir Singh remained that night at the Mozang House, Panditji, Bhagat Singh and Rajguru, accompanied by Sukh Dev, left the house about 9 p.m. "and probably went into the house in Kirpa Ram Street". The Tribunal revelled in dwelling on probabilities.

Hans Raj Vohra was arrested on suspicion of his connection with the murder in the evening of December 17 and remained in custody until he was bailed out on January 3, 1929, "without having made any statement concerning his knowledge of the affair". After the Saunders murder, several pink posters were found affixed to various public places in Lahore. They bore the legend "Saunders is dead, Lalaji is avenged". Several were "in the handwriting of Bhagat Singh." He had changed the victim's name.

The Judgment mentioned an interesting fact. "On the 30th *or* 31st December, Jai Gopal went to Lahore and on the following day he, Sukh Dev and Kishori Lal were at the Canal Bridge across the Ferozepur Road" when Scott's car passed and was seen by them. Although Sukh Dev had a revolver with him, he refrained from firing upon Scott remarking that as he had escaped once, it was pointless to fire at him again.

The poster in pink found pasted on the walls carried the following inscription:

"Notice:

By Hindustan Socialist Republic Army.

'Bureaucracy Beware'

With the death of J.P. Saunders, the assassination of Lala Lajpat Rai has been avenged.

It is a matter of great regret that a respected leader of 30 crores of people was attacked by an ordinary police officer like J.P. Saunders and met with his death at his mean hands. This national insult was a challenge to young men.

Today the world has seen that the people of India are not lifeless; their blood has not become cold. They can lay down their lives for the country's honour. The proof of this has been given by the youth who are ridiculed and insulted by the leaders of their own country.

'Tyrant Government Beware.'

Do not hurt the feelings of the oppressed and suffering people of this country. Stop your devilish ways. Despite all your laws preventing us from keeping arms and despite all your watchfulness, people of this country would continue to get pistols and revolvers. Even if these arms are not adequate in numbers for an armed revolution, they would be sufficient for avenging the insult to the country's honour. Even if our own people condemn us and ridicule us and even if the foreign government subjects us to any amount of repression, we shall ever be ready to teach a lesson to the foreign tyrants who insult our national honour. Despite all opposition and repression, we shall carry forward the call for revolution and even when we go to the scaffold for being hanged, we shall continue to shout.

" Long Live Revolution!"

We are sorry to have killed a man. But this man was a part of a cruel, despicable and unjust system and killing him was a necessity. This man has been killed as an employee of the British Government. This government is the most oppressive government in the world.

"We are sorry for shedding human blood but it becomes necessary to bathe the altar of revolution with blood. Our aim is to bring about a revolution which would end all exploitation of man by man.

"Long Live Revolution!"

Sd/- BALRAJ

18th December, 1928.   Commander-in-Chief, HSRA"[4]

On December 20, Bhagat Singh left for Calcutta along with Rajguru and Bhagwati Charan Vohra's wife Durga "Bhabi" to his young comrades. She had proposed that a person be selected for the task and even offered her own services but Azad declined. Her help would be invaluable in the escape as, indeed, it was. Bhagat Singh was the first to volunteer for the job followed by Rajguru, Sukh Dev and Jai Gopal.[5]

It is more than probable that had Bhagat Singh and Batukeshwar Dutt not thrown the bombs in the Central Assembly Chamber on April 8, 1929, the police would not have been able to unravel the plot to kill Scott and bring to book those who had killed Saunders and Chanan Singh. For in those nearly four months the investigations had made little progress.

Soon after the murder sixteen persons were arrested on suspicion of complicity. Five of them were members of the Lahore Students' Union. Hans Raj Vohra, as we have noted, was one of them. The rest were members of Naujawan Bharat Sabha, namely Ahmeduddin, K. N. Sehgal, M. A. Majid, Santram, Mir Mohammed Abdul, Labhuram, Santram Pondha, Amolak Ram, Hari Kishan Sethi, Keshav Bandhu and Raj Kishore Singh.[6] The *Civil and Military Gazette* of December 22 reported: "The police have made thorough search of the country on the banks of the Ravi with the hope of finding some clue which may lead to the identity of the murderer of Mr. Saunders, but that search has disclosed nothing."[7]

S.R. Bakshi's research in the archives yielded three documents which reveal sheer despair in the Viceroy's House. On December 29, 1928, Lord Irwin wrote: "I think we ought to inform the Secretary of State that the investigation in the Saunders murder case is not making much progress. We might at the same time take the opportunity of informing him of the policy of prosecuting seditious speakers." The Secretary of State, when so informed replied: "It is very disappointing to hear the progress of investigations is not so satisfactory." On January 12, 1929, the Viceroy wrote to the Secretary of State: "Release on bail of all persons arrested had ended first phase of investigation . . . *There are several eye witnesses who profess ability to identify one or more of murderers* . . . It is also thought that fired cartridge cases bear sufficiently distinctive marks to lead to identification of firearms used *if they are recovered."*[8]

This is a document of crucial importance in judging the fairness of the trial that took place, especially the worth of the testimony of the "several eye witnesses who profess ability to identify one or more of murderers". Two points may be noted. First, none of these witnesses could identify the perpetrators *by name.* They were unacquainted with them. That included also the Traffic Inspector of Police W.J.G. Fearn who might have seen them earlier, as well. He dismally failed to identify the accused before the Tribunal, as we shall see. Identification by others was challenged. On this, more later.

Secondly, none of these witnesses was sure even about the number of persons who committed the murders; hence the Viceroy's reference to "one or more of murderers". His hope rested only on identification of firearms used "if they are recovered".

Bhagat Singh and Batukeshwar Dutt's act, on April 8, 1929, to which the entire party was privy, fulfilled the Viceroy's hope.

NOTES

1. Kamlesh Mohan, p. 162 citing Dr. M.K. Nigam (alias Gaya Prasad); *Balidan*, p. 27; an instance of a detail discovered by scholars and unknown to the Tribunal.

2. *Lahore Conspiracy Case Judgement* (LCCJ), National Archives of India, p. 53 (typed number).

3. Deol, p. 35; Vide also Hansraj Rahbar; *Bhagat Singh and His Thought*, Manak Publications, Delhi, 1990, p. 141.

4. For the text *vide* Rahbar, pp. 142-43.

5. Deol, p. 36.

6. Khullar, p. 44.

7. Quoted in Kamlesh Mohan, p. 156.

8. S.R. Bakshi, *Bhagat Singh*, Anmol Publications. New Delhi, 1990, pp. 47-48.

4

Bombs in the Central Assembly

HAVING wielded the gun to great effect, the group decided to take to the bomb. Its manufacture and use was mandated by the resolutions of the Feroze Shah Kotla conclave. In Calcutta, Bhagat Singh sought the assistance, in this endeavour, of Phonindra Nath Ghosh and Jatindra Nath Dass.

Agra was selected as the Centre for that purpose. Jatindra Nath Dass and Lalit Kumar Mukerjee, a science student at Allahabad, performed the prime roles as educators in the craft. Ghosh and Kanwal Nath Tiwari bought chemicals and apparatus from shops in Calcutta, on requisitions by Jatindra Nath Dass and with money provided by Bhagat Singh. In Agra, two houses, in Hing ki Mandi and Nai ki Mandi, served as the rendezvous. "Bomb-making began to take place at the Hing ki Mandi house on the afternoon of the 14th February" according to the Judgement and a bomb was made by Jatindra Nath Dass the next day. The process was "gathered" from him, it said, by Bhagat Singh, Azad, Ghosh, Sukh Dev, B.K. Sinha, Shiv Varma, Sadashiv and Lalit Kumar Mukerjee.

Bhagat Singh returned from Lahore bringing five bomb shells given by Sukh Dev. They were filled in by Bhagat Singh, Shiv Varma, Azad, Ghosh, B.K. Sinha, Batukeshwar Dutt, Rajguru and Gaya Prasad. The bombs were tested in the forests in Jhansi in March by Azad and Bhagat Singh. That month the party centre was moved from Agra to Saharanpur. Dr. Nand Kishore Nigam under his alias Gaya Prasad opened a dispensary in Saharanpur as he had earlier in August 1928 in Ferozepur. They helped to get money besides providing sanctuaries for party members and safe storage houses for explosives, arms and apparatus.

Plans were made for the rescue from prison of Jogesh Chandra Chatterjee by using the newly-manufactured weapon but circumstances foiled them. Around the same time, a meeting of the HSRA's Central Committee was held at the Hing ki Mandi house in Agra at which the Delhi decision to throw bombs on the members of the Simon Commission was rescinded "as it would have involved considerable cost in travailing". Men like these, unlike the terrorists of today, were not flush in funds. They lived frugal lives. "It was decided, instead, that Bhagat Singh and Batukeshwar Dutt should throw a bomb in the Legislative Assembly Hall at Delhi and that, after doing so, they should be rescued by Panditji (Azad), Jai Dev and Sadashiv," the Tribunal's judgement recorded.[1]

The whole truth emerged from research conducted years later. The Committee's preference was for Batukeshwar Dutt and Shiv Varma to undertake the task, according to one account[2] while another mentions B.K. Sinha, instead of Shiv Varma.[3] Where all agree is that, despite Bhagat Singh's insistence, his participation was initially ruled out; not least, because of his participation in the Saunders murder. Azad, in particular, was set against any such role for his colleague and wisely so. Sukh Dev was not present at the meeting and was livid when he learnt of its decision. It was his bitter reproach and biting taunts that drove Bhagat Singh to insist on his participation with consequences that proved tragic for all, Sukh Dev included. According to Manmathnath Gupta, a revolutionary who was convicted in the Kakori case, Sukh Dev went so far as to call Bhagat Singh "a coward".[4] The reason was not personal. Sukh Dev felt that Bhagat Singh alone could accomplish the result. The objective was not to murder but to deliver a warning, the bombs were so designed as not to kill.

Sukh Dev was to regret his action. Though he was not a participant either in the Saunders murder or in throwing of bombs in the Assembly, he was sentenced to death and was hanged. With his headquarters in Lahore, he had begun to enlist recruits for a revolutionary party in 1926. The approvers, Jai Gopal and H.R. Vohra, were his finds. In 1927, Sukh Dev began to organize a Students' Union. His energetic contribution is apparent throughout the drama, whether on or behind the stage. The party took another decision, no less fateful. The bomb throwers should *not* try to escape. They should surrender themselves, Ghosh testified in the Tribunal.

The historian of the Indian National Congress, Dr. Pattabhi Sitaramayya, recalls that the situation in India early in 1929 was of "a trying character".[5] The repressive Public Safety Bill was moved in the Central Legislative Assembly on September 10, 1928 and referred to a Select Committee by 62 votes to 59, five days later. On September 24, Sir James Crerar, the Home Member, moved that the Bill, as reported by the Select Committee, be taken into consideration. This motion was defeated—62 to 61— thanks to the President Vithalbhai Patel's casting vote. Its reintroduction in January 1929 created a furore.

On April 2 the President made a statement in which he said that he had found that "the fundamental basis of the Public Safety Bill is virtually identical" with that of the case against the 31 accused in the Meerut Conspiracy Case. Real debate on the Bill was, therefore, not possible without violating the *sub judice* rule that forbids debate on pending court proceedings. "I have decided, instead of giving any ruling, to advise the Government" to consider his observations and either postpone the Bill pending the Meerut trial or withdraw the case "and then proceed with the Bill". He promised to give his ruling on April 8.[6] Resentment was no less intense over the Trades Disputes Bill. It was passed in dramatic circumstances on April 8, 1929. The Official Report of the Assembly's proceedings records:

"The Assembly divided. The motion was adopted by 56 to 38.

Mr. President: As the Trades Dispute Bill is now out of the way, I propose to give my ruling . . .

At this stage two bombs were thrown from the Visitors' Gallery, and burst among the Benches occupied by the Official

Members, causing injury to certain Members. Confusion prevailed and Mr. President retired. After a few minutes, Mr. President resumed the Chair.)

Mr. President: In view of the most shocking and deplorable incident, I propose to adjourn the house till Thursday morning 11 o' clock.

The House then adjourned till Thursday 11th April 1929."[7]

The action had been well prepared. Two days earlier, Bhagat Singh and Batukeshwar Dutt had been to the Assembly "to make a preliminary reconnaissance" as a police report put it. Their presence had been noticed.[8] On April 8, President Vithalbhai Patel's ruling and the Viceroy Lord Irwin's response were expected. It is strange how even careful accounts of that day's events aver either that the Viceroy's "Proclamation" enacting the two Bills was announced or was to be announced.

In truth the Trades Disputes Bill was *passed* by the Assembly and the bombs were thrown *before* the President could deliver his promised ruling on the Public Safety Bill.

Both visitors were dressed in Khaki shirts and shorts. Bhagat Singh wore a bluish coat, Dutt a light blue one. Two bombs were thrown in quick succession to land behind the Home Member. James Crerar. Pandemonium broke loose on the Official Benches. "Bhagat Singh also fired two unaimed shots from a pistol" as the IB's Director recorded. While in Court both were charged with throwing a bomb each, Dutt's counsel, Asaf Ali, revealed two decades later in an article that Bhagat Singh had flung *both* the bombs.[9] Indian leaders like Motilal Nehru, Jinnah and Malaviya— who gave evidence as a defence witness—kept their cool and remained seated.[10] Bhagat Singh and Dutt began shouting slogans "Inquilab Zindabad" and "Down with British Imperialism" and threw copies of a leaflet into the Assembly Chamber. It bore the caption "The Hindustan Socialist Republican Army—Notice" and read thus:

"It takes a loud voice to make the deaf hear, with these immortal words uttered on a similar occasion by Valliant, a French anarchist martyr, do we strongly justify this action of ours.

"Without repeating the humiliating history of the past ten years of the working of the Reforms (Montague-Chelmsford Reforms) and without mentioning the insults hurled at the Indian nation through this House—the so-called Indian Parliament—we want to point out that, while the people are expecting some more crumbs of reforms from the Simon Commission, and are ever quarrelling over the distribution of the expected bones, the Government is thrusting upon us new repressive measures like the Public Safety and the Trade Disputes Bill, while reserving the Press Sedition Bill for the next session. The indiscriminate arrests of labour leaders working in the open field clearly indicate whither the wind blows.

"In these extremely provocative circumstances, the Hindustan Socialist Republican Association, in all seriousness, realizing their full responsibility, had decided and ordered its army to do this particular action, so that a stop be put to this humiliating farce and to let the alien bureaucratic exploiters do what they wish, but they must be made to come before the public eye in their naked form.

"Let the representatives of the people return to their constituencies and prepare the masses for the coming revolution, and let the Government know that while protesting against the Public Safety and Trade Disputes Bills and the callous murder of Lala Lajpat Rai, on behalf of the helpless Indian masses, we want to emphasize the lesson often repeated by history, that it is easy to kill individuals but you cannot kill the ideas. Great empires crumbled while the ideas survived. Bourbons and Czars fell.

"We are sorry to admit that we who attach so great a sanctity to human life, we who dream of a glorious future, when man will be enjoying perfect peace and full liberty, have been forced to shed human blood. But the sacrifice of individuals at the altar of the 'Great Revolution' that will bring freedom to all, rendering the exploitation of man by man impossible, is inevitable.

"Long Live the Revolution."

Sd/-
BALRAJ
Commander-in-Chief[11]

Neither of them made the slightest move to escape or resist
arrest. They surrendered readily to Sergeant H.D. Terry as he
walked up to them followed later by Traffic Inspector C. Johnson.
Ironically, Sir John Simon was a witness to the scene. He was in
the galleries and so were Vallabhbhai Patel, Devdas Gandhi and
Mahadev Desai. Asaf Ali was in the Chamber itself, while his
wife, Aruna, was in the Ladies' Gallery above. Sir Sobha Singh
had only just arrived and taken a seat in the Visitors' Gallery. He
had arranged to lunch with friends whom he was to meet in the
House and his first anxiety was to discover their whereabouts. He
found them sitting near the other end of the Gallery in front of the
place occupied by Bhagat Singh and Dutt. Hence at the critical
moment his gaze was directed towards these two. He sent two
policemen towards them from the opposite end of the Gallery and
started to follow them. He met the policemen after they had
arrested the bomb throwers. Sir Sobha Singh gave evidence for
the prosecution in the court (P.W.7).

Sir Bomanji Dalal was wounded in the thigh and had to be sent
to hospital. Sir George Schuster and four others were slightly
injured. In a report to London a week later, Irwin admitted that
"the bombs, I should think, were not very high class of their kind
and may, indeed, have been tightly loaded *in order to restrict the
damage to* the Government side".[12] This proves that the Viceroy
knew that Bhagat Singh and Batukeshwar Dutt did not *intend* to
kill anyone on the Government Benches. This was the only issue
in the trial. For, as the Sessions Court's judgement noted, "The
accused have admitted throwing bombs." They insisted, however,
that it was done, not to kill, but to deliver a message.

The trial began a month later in the District Jail on May 7, 1929
before the Additional District Magistrate, F.B. Pool. Asaf Ali
appeared for the defence, while Rai Bahadur Suraj Narain appeared for the prosecution. Present in court were Bhagat Singh's
parents, his uncle Ajit Singh's wife and Aruna Asaf Ali. As they
were brought to court, Bhagat Singh and Batukeshwar Dutt adopted
a defiant stance to which they adhered throughout. They lustily
shouted the slogans which rang through the court room "*Inquilab
Zindabad*" and "Down with Imperialism". The magistrate ordered

that they be hand-cuffed and, thus, set a bad precedent.

Bhagat Singh had informed his father of the date of the hearing in a letter he wrote, on April 26, from the Delhi Central Jail. He wrote in Urdu to members of his family and in English to some of his friends like Jai Dev Gupta. He was at pains to assure the family that all was well. There was no need to engage a lawyer. "But I want to take legal opinion on certain matters, but they are not so important . . . If possible, please bring the biography of Napoleon and bring some good English novels from some friend. You may get good novels from people in the Dwarka Das Library."[13]

The magistrate found that a prima facie case existed. Accordingly, he framed charges against both the accused under S. 307 of the Indian Penal Code (attempt to murder) and S. 3 of the Explosive Substances Act, 1908 and committed them to trial by the Sessions Court.

Curiously among the formal questions the Magistrate asked Bhagat Singh was "When you arrived yesterday and today in the court, you shouted 'Long Live Revolution'. What do you mean by it?" Asaf Ali objected and the objection was upheld. *The Hindustan Times* reported the exchange on May 10, 1929.

Regular trial began before the Sessions Judge, Leonard Middleton, in the first week of the next month. On June 6, Bhagat Singh and Batukeshwar Dutt made a joint statement which was read out by Asaf Ali.[14] In an article entitled *Bhagat Singh—An Obsolescent* published in a journal *Common Weal* published from Poona. On March 23, 1949, Asaf Ali claimed that while substantially the draft was Bhagat Singh's, he had polished the language. It read thus:

"We stand charged with certain serious offences, and at this stage, it is but right that we must explain our conduct.

In this connection, the following questions arise:

1. Were the bombs thrown into Chamber, anu, if so, why?

2. Is the charge, as framed by the Lower Court, correct or otherwise?

To the first half of first question, our reply is in the affirmative, but since some of the so-called 'eye witnesses' have perjured themselves and since we are not denying our liability to that extent, let our statement about them be judged for what it is worth. By way of an illustration, we may point out that the evidence of Sergcant Terry regarding the seizure of the pistol from one of us is a deliberate falsehood, *for neither of us had the pistol at the time we gave ourselves up.* Other witnesses, too, who have deposed to having seen bombs being thrown by us have not scrupled to tell lies. This fact had its own moral for those who aim at judicial purity and fairplay.

At the same time, we acknowledge the fairness of the Public Prosecutor and the judicial attitude of the Court so far.

In our reply to the next half of the first question, we are constrained to go into some detail to offer a full and frank explanation of our motive and the circumstances leading up to what has now become a historic event.

When we are told by some of the police officers, who visited us in jail that Lord Irwin in his address to the joint session of the two houses described the event as an attack directed against no individual but against an institution itself, we readily recognized that the true significance of the incident had been correctly appreciated.

We are next to none in our love for humanity. Far from having any malice against any individual, we hold human life sacred beyond words.

We are neither perpetrators of dastardly outrages, and, therefore, a disgrace to the country, as the pseudo-socialist Dewan Chaman Lal is reported to have described us, nor are we 'Lunatics' as *The Tribune* of Lahore and some others would have it believed.

We humbly claim to be no more than serious students of the history and conditions of our country and her aspirations. We despise hypocrisy. Our practical protest was against the institution, which, since its birth, has eminently helped to display not only its worthlessness but its far-reaching power for mischief. The more we have pondered, the more deeply we have been convinced that it exists only to demonstrate to world India's humiliation and helplessness, and it symbolizes the overriding domination of an irresponsible and autocratic rule. Time and again the national demand has been pressed by the people's representatives only to find the waste paper basket as its final destination.

Solemn resolutions passed by the House have been contemptuously trampled under foot on the floor of the so called Indian Parliament. Resolution regarding the repeal of the repressive and arbitrary measures have been treated with sublime contempt, and the government measures and proposals, rejected as unacceptable by the elected members of the legislatures, have been restored by a mere stroke of the pen. In short, we have utterly failed to find any justification for the existence of an institution which, despite all its pomp and splendour, organized with the hard earned money of the sweating millions of India, is only a hollow show and a mischievous make-believe. Alike, have we failed to comprehend the mentality of the pubic leaders which help the Government to squander public time and money on such a manifestly stage-managed exhibition of India's helpless subjection.

We have been ruminating upon all these matters, as also upon the wholesale arrests of the leaders of the labour movement. When the introduction of the Trade Disputes Bill brought us into the Assembly to watch its progress, the course of the debate only served to confirm our conviction that the labouring millions of India had nothing to expect from an institution that stood as a menacing monument to the strangling of the exploiters and the serfdom of the helpless labourers.

Finally, the insult of what we consider, an inhuman and barbarous measure was hurled on the devoted heads of the representatives of the entire country, and the starving and struggling millions were deprived of their primary right and the sole means of improving their economic welfare. None who has felt like us for the dumb driven drudges of labourers could possibly witness this spectacle with equanimity. None whose heart bleeds for them, who have given their life-blood in silence to the building up of the economic structure could repress the cry which this ruthless blow had wrung out of our hearts.

Consequently, bearing in mind the words of the late Mr. S.R. Das, once Law Member of the Governor-General's Executive

Council, which appeared in the famous letter he had addressed to his son, to the effect that the 'Bomb was necessary to awaken England from her dreams', we dropped the bomb on the floor of the Assembly Chamber to register our protest on behalf of those who had no other means left to give expression to their heart-rending agony. Our sole purpose was "to make the deaf hear" and to give the heedless a timely warning. Others have as keenly felt as we have done, and from under the seeming stillness of the sea of Indian humanity, a veritable storm is about to break out. We have only hoisted the "danger-signal" to warn those who are speeding along without heeding the grave danger ahead. We have only marked the end of an era of Utopian non-violence, of whose futility the rising generation has been convinced beyond the shadow of doubt.

We have used the expression Utopian non-violence, in the foregoing paragraph which requires some explanation. Force when aggressively applied is "violence" and is, therefore, morally un-justifiable, but when it is used in the furtherance of a legitimate cause, it has its moral justification. The elimination of force at all costs is Utopian, and the new movement which has arisen in the country, and of that dawn we have given a warning, is inspired by the ideals which guided Guru Gobind Singh and Shivaji, Kamal Pasha and Riza Khan, Washington and Garibaldi, Lafayette and Lenin.

As both the alien Government and the Indian public leaders appeared to have shut their eyes to the existence of this movement we felt it as our duty to sound a warning where it could not go unheard.

We have so far dealt with the motive behind the incident in question, and now we must define the extent of our intention.

We bore no personal grudge or malice against anyone of those who received slight injuries or against any other person in the Assembly. On the contrary, we repeat that we hold human life sacred beyond words, and would sooner lay down our own lives in the service of humanity than injure anyone else. Unlike the mercenary soldiers of the imperialist armies who are disciplined to kill without compunction, we respect, and, in so far as it lies in our power, we attempt to save human life. And still we admit having deliberately thrown the bombs into the Assembly Chamber. Facts, however, speak for themselves and our intention would be judged from the result of the action without bringing in Utopian hypothetical circumstances and presumptions.

Despite the evidence of Government Expert, the bombs that were thrown in the Assembly Chamber resulted in slight damage to an empty bench and some slight abrasions in less than half a dozen cases, while Government scientists and experts have ascribed this result to a miracle, we see nothing but a precisely scientific process in all this incident. Firstly, the two bombs exploded in vacant spaces within the wooden barriers of the desks and benches, secondly, even those who were within 2 feet of the explosion, for instance, Mr. P. Rau, Mr. Shankar Rao and Sir George Schuster were either not hurt or only slightly scratched. Bombs of the capacity deposed to by the Government Expert (though his estimate, being imaginary is exaggerated), loaded with an effective charge of potassium chlorate and sensitive (explosive) picrate would have smashed the barriers and laid many low within some yards of the explosion.

Again, had they been loaded with some other high explosive, with a charge of destructive pellets or darts, they would have sufficed to wipe out a majority of the Members of the Legislative Assembly. Still again we could have flung them into the official box which was occupied by some notable persons. And finally we could have ambushed Sir John Simon whose luckless Commission was loathed by all responsible people and who was sitting in the President's gallery at the time. All these things, however, were beyond our intention and bombs did no more than they were designed to do, and the miracle consisted in no more than the deliberate aim which landed them in safe places.

We then deliberately offered ourselves to bear the penalty for what we had done and to let the imperialist exploiters know that by crushing individuals, they cannot kill ideas. By crushing two insignificant units, a nation cannot be crushed. We wanted to emphasize the historical lesson that *lettres de cachets* and Bastilles could not crush the revolutionary movement in France. Gallows and the Siberian mines could not extinguish the Russian Revolution. Bloody Sunday, and Black and Tans failed to strangle the movement of Irish freedom.

Can ordinances and Safety Bills snuff out the flames of freedom in India? Conspiracy cases, trumped up or discovered and the incarceration of all young men who cherish the vision of a great ideal, cannot check the march of revolution. But a timely warning, if not unheeded, can help to prevent loss of life and general sufferings.

We took it upon ourselves to provide this warning and our duty is done.

I, Bhagat Singh, was asked in the lower court as to what we meant by the word "Revolution". In answer to the question, I would say "Revolution" does not necessarily involve sanguinary strife nor is there any place in it for individual vendetta. It is not the cult of the bomb and the pistol. By "Revolution" we mean that the present order of things, which is based on manifest injustice, must change. Producers or labourers in spite of being the most necessary element of society, are robbed by their exploiters of the fruits of their labour and deprived of their elementary rights. The peasant who grows corn for all, starves with his family, the weaver who supplies the world market with textile fabrics, has not enough to cover his own and his children's bodies, masons, smiths and carpenters who raise magnificent palaces, live like pariahs in the slums. The capitalists and exploiters, the parasites of society, squander millions on their whims. These terrible inequalities and forced disparity of chances are bound to lead to chaos. This state of affairs cannot last long, and it is obvious, that the present order of society in merry-making is on the brink of a volcano.

The whole edifice of this civilization, if not saved in time, shall crumble. A radical change, therefore, is necessary and it is the duty of those who realize it to reorganize society on the socialistic basis. Unless this thing is done and the exploitation of man by man and of nations by nations is brought to an end, sufferings and carnage with which humanity is threatened today cannot be prevented. All talk of ending war and ushering in an era of universal peace is undisguised hypocrisy.

By "Revolution", we mean the ultimate establishment of an order of society which may not be threatened by such breakdown, and in which the sovereignty of the proletariat should be recognized and a world federation should redeem humanity from the bondage of capitalism and misery of imperial wars.

This is our ideal, and with this ideology as our inspiration, we have given a fair and loud enough warning.

If, however, it goes unheeded and the present system of Government continues to be an impediment in the way of the natural forces that are swelling up, a grim struggle will ensue involving the overthrow of all obstacles, and the establishment of the dictatorship of the proletariat to pave the way for the consummation of the ideal of revolution. Revolution is an inalienable right of mankind. Freedom is an imperishable birth right of all. Labour is the real sustainer of society. The sovereignty of the people is the ultimate destiny of the workers.

For these ideals, and for this faith, we shall welcome any suffering to which we may be condemned. At the altar of this revolution we have brought our youth as an incense, for no sacrifice is too great for so magnificent a cause. We are content to await the advent of revolution. Long Live Revolution."

On June 9, 1929 "certain portions" of this statement were, however, expunged from the record as being "irrelevant".

Since the accused had admitted to the throwing of the bombs, the evidence was of a formal nature and the only issues in the case were their intention and, accordingly, the quantum of punishment. The Judgement delivered on June 12, was anything but fair as these extracts bear out.

"The two persons most seriously injured were Sir Bomanji Dalal and Sir George Schuster, *neither of these has appeared as witness and there is no direct evidence as to which of the two explosions caused their injuries.*"

The Judge recorded the opinions of the assessors: "Very diverse opinions have been recorded by the Assessors. One Assessor considers that both the accused were guilty of an attempt to murder and that both were guilty under Section 3 of the Explosive Substances Act; he considers that all the persons injured were injured by the first bomb *and not by the second.* He therefore considers that Bhagat Singh caused hurt in an attempt to murder whilst Dutt did not.

"Another assessor is of opinion that Bhagat Singh may have thrown *both* bombs and that *possibly Dutt did not throw either of them.* He considers Bhagat Singh guilty of an attempt to murder in which he caused hurt, and also considers him to be guilty under Section 3 of the Explosive Substances Act. He is of opinion that Dutt is not guilty of either of the offences with which he has been charged." The man was stumbling on the truth which Asaf Ali revealed twenty years later. Batukeshwar Dutt did not throw a bomb. His conviction of the offence testifies to the quality of the evidence and the Judge's approach.

"A third assessor considers that both accused are guilty under Section 3 of the Explosive Substances Act, and that *neither are guilty of an attempt to murder.* His opinion is that *there was no intention of causing death or other intention or knowledge necessary to the offence of attempted murder.*

"The fourth assessor considers that the bombs were of such a nature that they *could not* cause death, and that neither of the accused *had any intention beyond that of creating a panic.* He considers that they both committed very rash acts." Two of the four assessors thus found them not guilty of attempt to murder. The Judge said, "It is submitted that *the direct evidence against the two accused leaves room for such elements of doubt as to their identity with the person or persons who threw the bombs that were it not for the admission by the accused that they did throw the bombs, they would be entitled to acquittal for any offence connected with bomb throwing . . .*"

"Arguing on these lines, learned Counsel for the defence has suggested that the most serious offence for which a conviction is maintainable is that punishable under Section 286 I.P.C. (negligent conduct with regard to explosive substance) or at the very most, that punishable under Section 324 of I.P.C. (voluntarily causing hurt by dangerous weapon or means).

"In this case the avowed motive of the accused was to provide a warning and this is allied with an allegation that their act was directed against an institution rather than an individual . . . the general attitude of the accused, their practice of shouting out particular phrases on appearing before the court (phrases which have certainly not been directed against the court or against the judicial proceedings, for apart from the use of those phrases, the accused have adopted an exemplary attitude in court and have followed the proceedings with intelligent interest and without obstruction) afford an indication of their motive . . .

"It is possible to argue that the accused took an action less violent than they could have taken; but it is an inversion of reasoning to argue that that act, which is inimical in its very nature, is thereby rendered a friendly act. And to carry such argument further and to urge that because it was a friendly act, the accused must be credited with every intention of rendering it as innocuous as possible, is ingenious but untenable . . .

"The alleged object of the accused is totally inconsistent with the means they adopted in carrying it out. The alleged intention of the accused is based upon this alleged objective or motive. Their allegation as to object is falsified by the means they employed, and hence the basis on which the alleged intention rest is no basis at all.

"When a man throws a live bomb, capable of exploding with sufficient force to cause the damage which was in fact caused, into an occupied building the natural inference is that he intends to take life or to cause such hurt as he knows to be likely to cause death . . .

"In both cases I find that the bombs were thrown *with an intention of causing death* or of causing bodily injury known to the thrower to be likely to result in death.

"I find it proved that Bhagat Singh threw the first bomb with the intention of causing death or with the intention of causing bodily injury which he knew to be likely to cause death. I find that by doing so he did cause hurt to Sir George Schuster, Mr. P.R. Rao and Mr. Shankar Rao. These facts constitute an offence punishable under Section 307 I.P.C. with transportation for life or with lesser punishment.

"The same acts include the causing of an explosion of a nature likely to endanger life, unlawfully and maliciously which constitutes an offence punishable under Section 3 of the Explosive Substances Act of 1908.

"I find it proved that Dutt threw the second bomb with similar intention and that by doing so he caused hurt to Mr. S.N. Roy and Rai Bahadur A.P. Dube. He too has committed both the offence punishable with transportation for life under Section 307 I.P.C. and the offence similarly punishable under Section 3 of the Explosive Substances Act.

"I find both the accused guilty of both the offences with which they are charged and convict them accordingly."

The Judge decided to award not only deterrent but a *retributive* punishment: "From the retributive point of view (it) merits a severe punishment."

He remarked: "The accused are young men but their acts were deliberate and they had preparation for those acts of a complicated nature. In these circumstances, these youth must not be allowed to lead to the infliction of an inadequate punishment.

"I sentence Bhagat Singh and Batukeshwar Dutt to transportation for life."

The enormity of the wrong will be apparent to anyone who goes through the proceedings which, one hopes, will be published in book form by the National Archives of India or the Publications Division of the Government of India. Asaf Ali's cross-examination was brilliant. On June 6, for instance, he got an expert witness, Dr. Robson, to make admissions damaging to the prosecution case. Replying to Asaf Ali, he admitted that *he was not shown the place of occurrence* and it was possible that if he had seen the surroundings and the damage done, he might have changed his opinion as to the nature of bombs. Witness agreed that the wooden protection afforded by the benches saved them from the damage caused by the explosion. He considered the bombs were of such nature as could only explode after striking against something solid. They would not explode in the air but would explode in whatever position they fell on the ground. He had examined a large number and variety of the bombs in India and they usually contained stones, nails, etc. But amongst the fragments of the present bombs, he came across no projectile of any sort.

Dr. Robson agreed that certain chemicals were forbidden by the Government as they give a large volume of carbon monoxide but there was no trace of such chemicals in the fragments.[15]

The accused appealed to the Lahore High Court. But Justices Sir Cecil Forde, K.C. and James Addison, I.C.S. upheld the judgement of the Sessions Court and dismissed the appeal on January 13, 1930. Asaf Ali appeared for the appellants. The High Court's judgement is reported in the law reports (*Bhagat Singh and another* vs. *Emperor*, A.I.R. 1930 Lahore 266).

As for the proceedings in the Assembly, interrupted on April 8 and adjourned to April 11, the President made a statement that day and moved a resolution which was passed unanimously:

"Mr. President: We meet today under the shadow of a great tragedy which, but for the merciful intervention of Providence, would have resulted in consequences the seriousness of which it is not difficult to imagine. But the fact that the dastardly outrage did not result in more serious injuries does not make it any the less deplorable or condemnable. I am sure it is the unanimous wish of the House that we should place on record our emphatic condemnation of the outrage, and I, therefore, place the following motion before you, namely:

'This House places on record its sense of horror and indignation at the dastardly outrage that was committed in the house on the morning of the 8th instant, offers its deep sympathy to Sardar Sir Bomanji Dalal and others who received injuries, and expresses its profound relief that, thanks to a merciful Providence, the results were not more serious. The House condemns unreservedly this outrage and assures the authorities of its full support in such reasonable steps as may be necessary to prevent a recurrence of such crimes.' "

Immediately thereafter, the President gave his long-awaited ruling on Crerar's motion on the Public Safety Bill. He ruled it out of order. That very day, however, he received a message from the Viceroy which he read out to the House. It required the members' attendance in the Chamber the next day, April 12. Irwin addressed both Houses, the Assembly and the Council of State, in a joint session. He had two purposes. One was to condemn "the outrage" on April 8. The other, while criticising Vithalbhai Patel's interpretation of the rules of procedure and his claim to "inherent power" to prevent abuse of "the forms and procedure of this House" was to announce that he would be issuing an ordinance in order to give himself the powers he had sought in the Bill. S. 72 of the Government of India Act, 1919 conferred the power.[16] Vithalbhai wrote, in protest to the Viceroy on May 8. The correspondence that followed was conducted in excellent taste on both sides. It was read out to the Assembly in President's statement on September 2, 1929.[17]

Meanwhile, that episode and the proceedings in the Assembly Bomb Case[18] were both eclipsed by somethings that happened immediately after the bombs were thrown on April 8. They triggered off a chain of events that were to send Bhagat Singh to the gallows. Irwin, the Viceroy, wrote to the famous editor of *The Times*, Geoffrey Dawson, on April 29: "The bomb business in the Assembly may turn out to be a blessing in disguise by enabling us to get on the track of the good many miscreants when we want."[19] Bhagat Singh was a suspect in the Saunders' murder investigations. The pistol he used, "unaimed" as the IB's Director admitted and for no real reasons, gave him away. The posters were also identified in his handwriting.

The first prize catch was made on April 15, exactly a week later, in the Kashmir Building on McLeod Road, Lahore. Rented by Bhagwati Charan in March 1929, the rooms were used as a bomb-factory under Sukh Dev's care. They came under police surveillance by sheer chance. The police party's raid caught the inmates unprepared. Sukh Dev, who had a loaded revolver in his possession, was arrested along with Kishori Lal and Jai Gopal. A live bomb, eight bomb-shells and a large quantity of chemicals were recovered together with notebooks containing formulae and books and documents.[20]

On April 19, four days after the raid, Irwin informed the Secretary of State: "Investigation of Assembly outrage, so far as it has proceeded, seems to have considerably improved prospects of a solution of the Saunders' murder. The leaflets thrown down in Assembly by persons arrested were typed on pink paper with printed heading which is identical in all respects with that used in threatening manuscript notices pasted up in Lahore after murder. Moreover, for some time past suspicion has been hardening that Bhagat Singh, arrested in Assembly, was party to Saunders' murder and preliminary microscopic examination of automatic pistol found with him favours view that it was one of weapons used in actual shooting of Saunders. On this point proper scientific proof is being sought."[21]

The Hing ki Mandi House in Agra was raided on May 2 and evidence of bomb making was unearthed. The Saharanpur headquarters in Mohalla Chob Faroshan were raided on May 13, when Shiv Varma and Jai Dev were arrested. Six bombs, three shells, three loaded revolvers, ammunition and books including one on *'Manufacture and Use of Explosives'* and a large quantity of chemicals and some apparatus were seized. Two days later, Gaya Prasad, unaware of the raid, returned to the Saharanpur house and was arrested. Shivram Rajguru was arrested in a garage in Poona on September 30, 1929; he was found in possession of a revolver and ammunition. Once again, Chandra Shekhar Azad escaped. So did Kali Charan, Bhagwati Charan and Yashpal.

First Jai Gopal and, next, Hans Raj Vohra confessed. The result was more arrests of active workers in three Provinces—the Punjab, U.P. and Bihar. Ajoy Ghosh was arrested just as he was preparing to go underground. The mood in that hour was well captured in his pamphlet written years later: "It all seemed over, our dreams and our hopes. More depressing than anything else was the shocking fact that, unable to stand police torture, no less than seven—two of them members of our Central Committee—had turned approvers.[22]

NOTES

1. *LCCJ*, p. 71.
2. Rahbar, p. 153.
3. Kamlesh Mohan, p. 71, 354.
4. Manmathnath Gupta, p. 153.
5. Pattabhi Sitaramayya, *The History of the Indian National Congress*, Volume I (1885-1935); Padma Publications, Bombay, 1946, pp. 339-40.
6. Gordhanbhai Patel, *Vithalbhai Patel*, R. A. Moramkar, Bombay, 1930, Book Two, p. 869.
7. *Legislative Assembly Debates*, Vol. III, 1929, p. 2985.
8. Deol, p. 43.
9. Deol p. 45, f. n. 10.
10. Khullar, p. 50.
11. Deol, p. 46; Khullar p. 50.
12. Kamlesh Mohan, p. 173.
13. Deol, p. 140.
14. *The Tribune*, June 8, 1929, p. 2.
15. *The Tribune*, June 8, 1929.
16. *LAD*, March-April 1929. Vol. III, p. 2995.
17. Gordhanbhai Patel, pp. 896-903.
18. National Archives of India, Delhi Court Papers: Trial No. 9 of 1929, Vols. 1-17 and Sessions Judgement (both in original).
19. Quoted in Kamlesh Mohan, p. 174.
20. Ewart, p. 76.
21. Quoted in Bakshi, pp. 49-50.
22. Ajoy Ghosh, p. 7.

5

Hour of Trial

I T was a dark hour for Bhagat Singh and his comrades. They had been betrayed by some of their most trusted associates; men who were privy to all their plans and whose integrity they never questioned. Their alienation from the mainstream of nationalist opinion was greater than any time before. Saunders' murder, in vengeance, was disapproved by many leaders, but it struck a chord in some people's emotions in the wake of Lala Lajpat Rai's death. Throwing the bombs in the Chamber of the Central Assembly was a different matter altogether. It was denounced by many a staunch nationalist, including its President, Vithalbhai Patel. A rare exception was Pandit Madan Mohan Malaviya.

Apparently, none of the revolutionaries had quite reckoned with the consequences that followed. They had nearly got away with the Saunders' murder. Their reckless act in the Assembly led inexorably to the unravelling of the mystery of the murder. In a very short time the police succeeded in building up a formidable case for prosecution, albeit, not without recourse to unworthy methods.

In but a few weeks, however, there was a sea change in the situation. On April 10, 1929 *The Tribune* of Lahore, a committed nationalist daily in contrast to its British-owned contemporary *Civil and Military Gazette*, reported on the front page the "Bomb Explosion in Legislative Assembly" under this sub-heading: "Two young men, one a Punjabi and the other a Bengali, entered the

Legislative Assembly dropped Red-leaflets, threw bombs and fired pistols." Another sub-heading read: "A Punjabi arrested."

A little over two months later, Bhagat Singh and Batukeshwar Dutt became household names; national heroes who compelled admiration and affection. Alienation from the nationalist mainstream was gone. Jawaharlal Nehru came to see them and their associates in prison. So did Motilal Nehru, Subhas Chandra Bose, K.F. Nariman, Rafi Ahmed Kidwai, Mohanlal Saxena, one of the counsel in the Kakori case, Baba Gurdit Singh, the Raja of Kalakankar and many others, besides. Mohandas Karamchand Gandhi, conspicuously, did not; an omission for which Bhagat Singh's devoted biographers and contemporaries like Manmathnath Gupta criticise him; unjustly, in the writer's opinion.[1]

Committed as he was to non-violence, Gandhi felt that, in all conscience, he simply could not, by word or deed, express any sympathy for the men involved, lest it be misconstrued as approval of their deeds. He had, in February 1922, called off the non-cooperation movement, over the criticism of his colleagues, because in Chauri Chaura, in U.P., a mob had set fire to the police station whereby a police inspector and 21 police constables were burned to death. Gandhi was appalled. "Non-violence is spreading like the scent of the otto (*sic*) of roses throughout the length and breadth of the land, but the foetid smell of violence is still powerful, and it would be unwise to ignore or underrate it", he explained to Jawaharlal on February 22.[2]

Revolutionaries saw it differently. Chauri Chaura widened the chasm that lay between them and Gandhi. Doctrinal differences were accentuated by disagreement on tactics. Thirty-five years later, V.P. Menon, who was in the know, wrote: "Had the non-cooperation movement not been ended by Gandhiji at a time when it was causing the utmost anxiety to the Government, the latter might possibly have been induced to take some action to appease Indian sentiment."[3] The chasm was to have tragic consequences.

Ironically, the weapon which Bhagat Singh and associates used and which was to win them acclaim was distinctly Gandhian. It was the hunger-strike. The Sessions Court handed down the sentences in the Assembly Bomb case on June 12, 1929. Three

days later Bhagat Singh went on a hunger-strike. Dutt followed
suit soon thereafter. Others on trial with them, in what became
known as the Lahore Conspiracy Case with the Saunders' murder
as the main overt act of the conspiracy, emulated their example.
This prompted the Government, first, to try to amend the Criminal
Procedure Code in order to provide for trial in the absence of the
accused and, next, to set up a Special Tribunal, ousting the regular
Sessions Court, to try the case by invoking the Governor-General's
emergency powers. It is, therefore, important to appreciate correctly the reasons why Bhagat Singh and his fellow-accused took
the extreme step that they did. *It was not a devious stratagem to
obstruct the proceedings. It was a conscious effort to assert their
rights as political prisoners.* Nor was it a novel move. As the
historian, Kamlesh Mohan, reminds us, the Babbar Akalis had
blazed the trail by their hunger-strike on April 26, 1925. It lasted
for a month and a half.[4]

Bhagat Singh's letter, dated June 17, 1929, to the Inspector-
General, Punjab Jails, Lahore from the Mianwali District jail set
out the reasons and the demands. Neither was unreasonable as the
text reveals:

> "I have been sentenced to life imprisonment in connection
> with the Assembly Bomb Case, Delhi and an obviously a
> political prisoner. We got special diet in Delhi Jail, but since
> my arrival here, I am being treated as an ordinary criminal.
> Therefore I have gone on hunger-strike since the morning of
> 15th June 1929. My weight has decreased by lbs. 6 than my
> weight at Delhi Jail in these two or three days.
>
> "I wish to bring to your kind attention that I must get special
> treatment as a political prisoner.
>
> "My demands being
> 1. Special diet (including milk and ghee, rice and curd etc.)
> 2. No forcible labour
> 3. Toilet (soap, oil, shaving etc.)
> 4. Literature of all kinds (History, Economics, Political
> Science, Science, poetry, drama or fiction, newspapers.)
> I hope you will very kindly consider what I have said and

decide favourably."

Sukh Dev's letter to the Superintendent, Central Jail, Lahore
dated July 30 read:

"I want to let you know and the higher authorities that I
demand the following things on the ground of being a 'Political
Prisoner'.

"After the bomb incident in Assembly, Lord Irwin in his last
speech said that, 'These bombs were not directed towards any
individual but towards the institution.' Again, Mr. Middleton
in his judgement mentioned that 'These persons (Dutta and
Bhagat Singh) used to enter the court with the cries of 'Long
Live Revolution', 'Long Live Proletariat', etc. which shows
clearly what sort of political ideas they cherish. In order to put
a check on propagating these ideas I transport them for life.'

"Again I must mention that when an European breaks an
ordinary law in order to fulfil his selfish motive, he gets all
kinds of privileges in the jail. He will get well-ventilated room
with electric fittings, best food (such as milk, butter, toast, meat
etc.) and good clothing while we politicals are deprived of such
things.

"The comments of Lord Irwin and Mr. Middleton are sufficient to prove that we are politicals, and on this ground I
demand that Dutta and Bhagat Singh should be treated as
politicals. I must get better food as it is necessary to keep a
man's health. At the same time, I must get all kinds of literature
and the newspapers in order to discuss the different politics.
People call us rash, misjudged and impatient youths. So we
must be given a fair chance of studying the various books in
order to see that whether we are really impatient, misguided
youths or not, whether our life work is wrong or right.

"My demands are as follows:

1. Better food, including loaf and milk in the morning, rice,
dal and *ghee*, one vegetable and sugar in the noon; and bread,
meat and *chattni* at night.

2. No labour.

3. All kinds of literature and newspapers.
4. Toilet, including soap, oil and barber etc.
5. Better accommodation.
6. Civil dress.

"I used to get all these things in Delhi Jail, before and after my conviction from the Jail expenses. But here I am deprived of all those things; that is why I have begun hunger-strike since 14th June 1929. My comrade Bhagat Singh in Mianwali Jail is also on hunger-strike for these very reasons and I will not give up my hunger-strike till the Government accedes to our (I and Bhagat Singh) demands.

"Expect an early reply and will gladly discuss over this matter with any Government officer whoever comes to me."[5]

These letters were read out to the Central Assembly by Malaviya on September 14, 1929. Bhagat Singh was soon thereafter trans-ferred to the Central Jail in Lahore, where Dutt was lodged as a convicted prisoner. Their associates were in the Borstal Jail as those under trial—Sukh Dev, Jatinder Nath Das, Rajguru, Shiv Varma, Ajoy Ghosh, Gaya Parshad and B.K. Sinha. They lost no time in going on hunger-strike. Political leaders in Lahore like Saifuddin Kitchlew, Gopi Chand Bhargava and Mohammad Alam publicised their grievances and the plight they were in. It soon became a national affair. June 30 was observed as Bhagat Singh Day all over India.[6]

Jawaharlal Nehru could restrain himself no longer. On July 5, he issued a statement to the press which was all the more notewor-thy for the fact that he was then General Secretary of the Congress. "I have learnt with deep grief of the hunger-strike of Bhagat Singh and Dutt. For 20 days or more they have refrained from all food and I am told that forcible feeding is being resorted to. The two young men may have done wrong, but no Indian can refrain from admiring their great courage and our hearts must go out to them now in their great and voluntary suffering. They are fasting not for any selfish ends but to improve the lot of all political prisoners. As days go by, we shall watch with deep anxiety this hard trial and shall earnestly hope that the two gallant brothers of ours may triumph in the ordeal."[7]

It is in this setting that proceedings in the Lahore Conspiracy Case began on July 10, 1929 in the Court of the Special Magistrate, Rai Saheb Pandit Sri Kishen. The trial was held in the Central Jail, Lahore. The law gave him a narrow remit. He was *not* required to ascertain whether the accused were guilty or not, but whether the evidence disclosed that a prima facie case existed of the kind grave enough to be tried exclusively by a Court of Session. If it did, he had to commit the accused to stand trial in a Sessions Court.

The charges covered a conspiracy and overt acts in pursuance of it; namely the murder of Saunders and Chanan Singh, throwing of the bombs in the Assembly Chamber, establishment of factories in Lahore, Agra and Saharanpur to manufacture bombs, the attempt to rob the Bank, etc. The prosecution proposed to produce 600 witnesses to prove the charges against the accused.

There were twenty-five of them of whom nine were declared absconders—Chandra Shekhar Azad alias Panditji; Bhagwati Charan Vohra; Kailashpati alias Kali Charan; Yashpal; Sat Gurdyal; Kailash; Bejoy Kumar Sinha; Shivram Rajguru; and Kundan Lal.

The sixteen who were put on trial before the Rai Saheb were, in the order as officially listed, Sukh Dev, Kishori Lal, Agya Ram, Des Raj, Prem Dutt, Surindra Nath Pandey, Jai Dev Kapur; Shiv Varma, Gaya Parshad alias Dr. B.S. Nigam, Jatindra Nath Das, Mahabir Singh, Bhagat Singh, Batukeshwar Dutt, Ajoy Kumar Ghosh, Jatinder Nath Sanyal and Kanwal Nath Trivedi alias Tiwari. Before long three of the absconders B.K. Sinha, Shivram Rajguru and Kundan Lal were put on trial with the sixteen.

As in the Assembly Bomb Case, Bhagat Singh declined to be represented in Court by a lawyer but wished to have the services of a legal adviser. As he wrote to his father over a year later after the trial had ended: "I had only one idea before me throughout the trial, i.e., to show complete indifference towards the trial in spite of the serious nature of the charges against us. I have always been of opinion that all political workers should be indifferent and should never bother about the legal fight in the law courts and should boldly bear the heaviest possible sentences inflicted upon them. They may defend them. elves but always from purely political considerations and never rrom a personal point of view."

Indifference to the proceedings in Court is hardly compatible with defence for political reasons. Not for the first time, Bhagat Singh's idealism got the better of his sense of the practical. It was a political trial in which, as Prof. Otto Kirchheimer put it in his classic *Political Justice: The Use of Legal Procedure for Political Ends*, the regime staged a trial in an attempt "to incriminate its foe's public behaviour with a view to *evicting* him from the political scene." But the accused is not altogether helpless. He can use the trial to propagate his views—as Maulana Azad did—or to turn the tables on the State by exposing the flaws in its case, as Aurobindo Ghose did.

The case against the accused was strong but not a hopeless one. Skilful cross-examination might have helped to expose, if not break down, the approvers. Two of them were abandoned as unreliable by the prosecution. A lot turned on the identification of Bhagat Singh and Rajguru by those who claimed to have seen them firing the fatal shots at Saunders.

Why Asaf Ali, a brilliant cross-examiner who had appeared in the Assembly bomb case, was not retained in this is a mystery. He defended Harikishan who, along with three others, was charged with attempt to murder the Punjab Governor, Geffrey de Montmorency on the convocation of the Punjab University at Lahore on December 23, 1930. The Governor received two minor wounds. Harikishan was none too keen on securing an acquittal from the Court. In such cases defence is gravely hampered.

Bhagat Singh chose as his legal adviser Lala Duni Chand, one of the political leaders who had participated in the protest movement against the Simon Commission. He also formed a small group consisting of Sukh Dev, Bejoy Kumar Sinha and himself to chalk out their strategy.[8] *The Tribune* of August 1, 1929 reported a statement by Feroz Chand, Secretary, Lahore Conspiracy Case Committee, which sought to provide "wider publicity to the existing defence arrangements". He said that "an influential Defence Committee was formed considerably before the commencement of the trial in the Central Jail Court room and that Committee is in charge of the entire defence arrangements. All subscriptions are received by Pandit K. Santhanam, as the treasurer of the Committee." Among its fourteen members, including the two office-bearers, were Gopi Chand Bhargava, Lala Duni Chand, Saifuddin Kitchlew and Bhagat Singh's father, Kishen Singh.

The proceedings began on July 10 before the Special Magistrate Rai Saheb Pandit Sri Kishen in the Central Jail, Lahore. The accused, now reunited as comrades, marched into the court room shouting the slogans "Inquilab Zindabad" (Long Live the Revolution) and "Down with Imperialism". The Crown was represented by C.H. Carden Noad, the Government Advocate, with Khan Saheb Kalandar Ali Khan, the Public Prosecutor, and Gopal Lal. Kalandar Ali Khan acted as advocate, interpreter and Court clerk rolled into one. Loud as he was, this major-domo was an appropriate figure in proceedings that varied from the farcical to the violent. No official transcript can provide a flavour of the happenings in the court-room in the jail as *The Tribune*'s detailed reportage did, day after day.

Lala Duni Chand, Malik Barkat Ali, Mehta Amin Chand, Lala Bishan Nath, Amolak Ram Kapur, Dewan Chand Khanna, W. Chandra Dutt and Mehta Puran Chand appeared for some of the accused. They were joined later by Lala Amar Das, Bashir Ahmed and Baljit Singh. Not all Counsel were present all the time. Some were more constant in attendance than others. A majority of the accused, however, chose not to be represented.

Armed police guarded approaches to the venue of the trial. The District Magistrate, the Legal Remembrancer, the Deputy Inspector-General of Police (D.I.G.), the Senior Superintendent of Police (SP), Khan Bahadur Abdul Aziz. and other senior officers were present in strength. It was not a trial in open court. The general public was not admitted to the court-room in the Central Jail. Relations of the accused were given permits for admission only after considerable difficulty. Defence Counsel were stopped at the door and were allowed to enter only after some delay.

The first thing the Rai Saheb, the Special Magistrate, did was to record an Order prohibiting the raising of slogans in his court. Lala Duni Chand, who was sitting nearest to him, objected and said, in the hearing of all, that the wording of the order had been dictated in court by the Public Prosecutor, Khan Saheb Kalandar Ali Khan. The Khan Saheb denied having done so. Lala Duni Chand said, however, that he would advise the accused not to raise slogans in court.

Next, he objected to the trial being held in prison and in the ambience in which it was as "a small gaol". Admission should not be restricted arbitrarily by permits. The Court remarked, unfeelingly: "Should the whole city come here?" Counsel replied: "Everybody who wants to come should be admitted provided there is room." The upshot of it all was that the court issued some more permits for some of the relations of the accused waiting outside.

A defence counsel, Mehta Amin Chand, complained of discriminatory curbs on the parking of cars by defence counsel outside the Central Jail. He was not permitted to enter the gate since he had no permit until an European police officer came over and patronisingly said "I give you permission to enter". Malik Barkat Ali and W.C. Dutt said that they had similar experience. The Government Advocate joined the fray with a complaint of his own. He had seen some of the persons present in court giving flowers to the accused.

These preliminaries over, the proceedings proper began with the Government Advocate, Carden Noad, filing the Government's sanction to the prosecution, through the SP, Lahore, Hamilton Harding. 25 persons were cited as accused, the absconders included. They were charged with various offences under the Penal Code—waging war against the British Crown since 1924, forming a conspiracy for the purpose, collecting arms with this intention, concealing the existence of "a design" to wage war (Sections 121, 121A, 122 and 123, respectively)—and under the Explosive Substances Act (vide Appendix I for the text of the complaint).

As soon as Carden Noad asked for leave of the Court to make an opening speech for the prosecution, Malik Barkat Ali, Lala Duni Chand, Mehta Amin Chand and other defence counsel objected strenuously. The accused did not desire any elucidation of the prosecution case beyond what the complaint stated, they said, "We know our interests better." The objection was overruled.

The Government Advocate said that 32 persons were involved in the case of whom 7 were approvers, 9 were absconding and 16 were placed on trial in court. "I desire to emphasise the fact that this is an ordinary trial under ordinary law (although of singular importance) and that these individuals alone are upon their trial. No political section or system is in any way involved; no social, religious or educational body, or institution is or can be affected by the outcome of this prosecution . . ." He would do his best to assist the Court "in giving the accused a fair, patient and impartial enquiry".

After mentioning the murders of Saunders and Chanan Singh, he began to trace the conspiracy from the meeting in Feroze Shah Kotla in Delhi in August 1928. Overt acts in pursuance of the conspiracy were the two murders; the bombs in the Assembly; the attempt, though abandoned, a dacoity at the Punjab National Bank in Lahore; dacoity at Maulina in Bihar and Orissa; attack on the DSP, Bannerjee; embezzlement of Rs. 3,199 from the post office by Kali Charan, an absconder, who was a postal employee; and manufacture of bombs. Two plans were not carried out; namely, blowing up the train carrying members of the Simon Commission and the escape from prison of Jogesh Chander Chatterjee. He proceeded to describe how the conspiracy was unravelled by the police (vide Appendix II for the text of the speech).

The next day, July 11, began with the shouting of slogans *de rigueur*; the Magistrate objecting likewise. Bhagat Singh stood up to make certain requests on behalf of the accused: (1) That they be given newspapers to read; (2) be provided with better food in gaol at Government expense; (3) the accused, other than Dutt and himself, should be kept together in gaol so that they might consult each other about the case; (4) they should be permitted freely to interview their counsel and relations; and (5) their relations should be allowed permits to attend the court. Not one of these requests could be called unreasonable. The Magistrate promised to pass orders on them the next day.

As on the first day, many of the friends and relations of the accused were not allowed to enter the court room. Seating arrangements were irregular.

Press representatives were consigned to a far corner from where they could follow the proceedings only with great difficulty. Nor could the accused any better. They complained that the proceedings were not audible to them. Kalandar Ali functioned as interpreter for the benefit of the accused. *The Tribune*'s correspondent reported: "For the most part, there continued to be noise and confusion in the court room throughout the proceedings." A European police officer saw Kiron Chandra Das talking to his brother Jatindra Nath, caught him by the neck and pushed him away.

The first to step in the witness box was Khan Bahadur Abdul Aziz, Superintendent of Police, to depose to the investigations. He revealed that in January 1929 he came to know that a member of the Naujawan Sabha, Babu Singh, who used to visit the Boarding House of the Oriental College at Roshnai Gate, offered to provide a clue to the Saunders murder if he were given a reward of Rs. 1,000. From the information he supplied, it appeared that Bhagat Singh was one of the murderers. After singing like a canary for some time, he shut up and did not give further information. The sum of Rs. 1,000 promised to Babu Singh was withdrawn from the treasury but lay in deposit with the Khan Bahadur who reported to the Inspector-General of Police. Back came his order to Abdul Aziz to take in hand investigation of the Saunders murder in addition to the Dussehra bomb explosions of 1926 and 1928 which he had been investigating. He soon ordered the arrest of Bhagat Singh.

The SP's evidence was fascinating. Two things stood confirmed from what he said. One was that a warrant for Bhagat Singh's arrest was out even as his party was deliberating as to who should throw the bombs in the Assembly Chamber. The other was that he had, nonetheless, succeeded in eluding the police.

The SP deposed that it was ascertained that the suspect was not in the Punjab but was to be found in Bengal or the United Provinces, where he was working with the revolutionaries. Attempts were made to arrest him in those provinces, but he could not be traced, until he was arrested on April 8 in the Assembly.

On April 9, witness was informed that some hollow oblong

parts of machine were cast in the shop of Ghulam Rasool Mistri, a blacksmith, on the Brandreth Road. An Assistant Sub-Inspector, Ghulam Sarwar gave that information to witness, who was going to Parachinar the same night on some other business. He, however, got inquiries made from Ghulam Rasul. The information was verified and witness was told that two youngmen had got those iron instruments moulded by the blacksmith and they had been saying that they were parts of a gas machine. He could not, however, give information as to the identity or residence of the two youngmen. The SP had orders issued that the blacksmith should shadow the two youngmen when he saw them next and discover their residence. On April 12, on his return from Parachinar, the SP was informed by Ghulam Rasul that he had followed one of the youngmen on a bicycle to a room in the Kashmir Buildings. He got the register of the proprietor of the buildings examined and discovered that Bhagwati Charan was the tenant of the house. As Bhagwati Charan had a house in Milkhi Ram Street, witness suspected that the house in the Kashmir Buildings was a bomb factory. Thereupon he deputed a private individual to keep watch on the house. He informed witness that the house remained closed during the day and was only opened at night and that the water-shoot (*Parnala*) of the house and the drains near it had thick deposits of sulphur.

On the night of April 13, Stead, Inspector-General of the Police, returned to Lahore after observing the site of the Assembly bomb explosion. The SP communicated his information to the IGP, who informed him, in turn, that the bombs thrown in the Assembly were oblong and were of the same shape as the hollow iron pieces moulded by Ghulam Rasul Mistri. Thus Abdul Aziz, the witness's suspicions that the building was used as a bomb factory were confirmed. On April 15, in the morning at about 7, he received information on the phone from his private agency that the house was open and some persons were present within because water was coming out of the *parnala*.

Mehta Amin Chand objected to certain questions being put to the witness on the ground that he had no personal knowledge of the matters in question. The Court said those questions merely supplied the links in the chain of evidence and noted the objection. Counsel insisted that the court should give its ruling at once. Amolak Ram Kapur quoted authorities to show that the admissibility or otherwise of a question should be decided as soon as objection was taken. Kalandar Ali Khan, who was examining the witness, did not dispute the contention of the defence that decision of the question should not be deferred. The court made a note on the subject and promised to pass an order later.

Witness decided at once to raid the house, and sent for his Deputy SP Niaz Mohammad and two Sub-Inspectors. After leaving a few persons around the building, witness went up to the building with DSP Niaz Mohammad and Sub-Inspectors Shah Mohammad and Kundan Lal. Simultaneously witness sent Sub-Inspector Nanak Chand to arrest Bhagwati Charan and search his house. Abdul Aziz saw three youngmen in the first floor in the room next to the one in which the staircase opened. He had an Honorary Magistrate, the proprietor of the house and some other witnesses with him. Witness inquired the name of one of the three men. He gave his name as Sukh Dev.

To a further question, he told witness that he was the tenant of the house. Witness told him that Bhagwati Charan was the tenant. Sukh Dev replied that he did not know Bhagwati Charan. The SP wondered whether he had gone to the wrong house. The other two youngmen gave their names as Jai Gopal and Kishori Lal. All three refused to give the names of their fathers, residence and other particulars, but said they were Indians. That removed the doubts. The SP was convinced that he was in the right house. Witness ordered that Sukh Dev's person be searched. Sukh Dev rushed towards the door and was arrested by S.I. Kundan Lal under orders of the SP. Sukh Dev pretended to have fainted, and witness ordered Kundan Lal not to leave him. After that Sukh Dev asked for water; witness had some water given to Sukh Dev. Then Sukh Dev turned his back towards witness and pretended to vomit. Kundan Lal did not lose his grip on Sukh Dev. Sukh Dev was then taken to the inner door, where he suddenly put his hand into his inner pocket and brought out a revolver, which was caught hold of by Inspector Saeed Ahmad Shah or Kundan Lal. The revolver was fully loaded. Sukh Dev then pointed to a tin box in a shelf on a window and said it contained a live bomb. He also said that the room contained acids, chemicals and literature for manufacture of bombs, and that they should be handled with care to avoid explosion.

The SP had an inventory prepared of the articles found there. As one of the bombs was a live one, witness called Thomas, Chemical Examiner, to the spot. He put the bomb in a bucket of water and took it away. There were also 21 cartridges, a practice air pistol, four note books containing recipes of bomb-making as well as other literature on bomb-making. The following books were also recovered—1. *Martyrs of Kakori*, 2. *What do We Want?*, 3. *Revolutionary Work* by Needham, 4. *Administration of Ireland*, 5. *Constitution of Federated Republic of India*, 6. *The Revolutionary, an Organ of the Revolutionary Party of India*, 6 copies, 7. *Infantry Training*, 8. *Small Arms Training*, 9. *Sepoy Officers Manual*, and 10. A Red English Notebook, containing formulae for making bombs.

Continuing his evidence, Abdul Aziz, the SP, stated that the chemicals and eight bomb-shells were recovered from an almirah which was locked, and the key was produced by Jai Dev. A handful of the deposit in the drain was taken away by Thomas for chemical analysis. A photograph of Batukeshwar Dutt was also discovered. Abdul Aziz arrested Sukh Dev, Kishori Lal and Jai Gopal on the spot. Dr. Nigam alias Gaya Prashad (accused) gave information about Pratap alias Mahabir Singh (accused). That information was given in the presence of Stead, the Inspector-General. In consequence of that information, Mahabir Singh was arrested at the address given by Gaya Prashad.

Cross-examined by Amar Das, the witness said the search lasted until about 2 p.m. The important articles, such as bombs, were first collected and kept apart; but in the list everything was included as it came on. Nearly all the articles produced in court were found in the room which was occupied by the accused. The list was prepared by Inspector Said Ahmed and Sub-Inspector Shah Mohammed. The SP did not remember how they prepared it. All such articles as could be signed were signed by the witnesses to the search as well as the witness. No serial number was put on the list. Witness signed only the last page, which alone was attested by witnesses. He could not say how the articles were removed as he had left after the list was ready while all other officers remained. The SP did not visit the house subsequently that day. He took no interest in describing or running the articles when the list was being prepared. He did not know what articles would be recovered from the building. He had reasonable grounds for believing that it was being used as a bomb factory.

"*Q*. Did you under Section 165, Cr.P.C. prepare a record of the grounds on which you suspected the house to be a bomb factory?

A. Yes. I submitted a report to the Inspector General of Police before the search, in which I gave the grounds of my suspicion. That report fulfils the requirements of Section 165."

Further questioned the witness could not say that Section 165 was in his mind when the record was made, though its provisions were complied with. Copy of the report was not sent to any Magistrate under Section 165(5). The SP was not the investigating officer, it was the DSP. No other officer, to the witness' knowledge, did so. Inspector Said Ahmad Shah was the investigating officer at the search. The SP refused to put in court the record which he prepared and which he thought was covered by Section 165 because it was confidential. Babu Singh did not make any statement to the witness. He was not a prosecution witness.

When proceedings were resumed on the third day of the trial, July 12, it was not the Rai Saheb Pandit Sri Kishen, the Specia' Magistrate, who announced his promised decision on the request which Bhagat Singh had made on behalf of the accused, but Khan Saheb Kalandar Ali Khan, one of the prosecution lawyers, who did so. The Magistrate, he declared, had decided that he had no jurisdiction to suggest to the jail authorities to keep the prisoners together with a view to their consulting each other about the various points arising in the case. Nor was the court prepared to make any suggestion to the jail authorities as to their request for better food. The accused were, however, permitted to have paper, pencils and *authorised* newspapers. The court passed no order on the prisoners' request that the witnesses should be placed in such a position as to enable the prisoners to hear their evidence.

As on the previous days, the accused constantly complained that they could not hear what the witnesses deposed. Kalandar Ali Khan examined the witnesses in Urdu and went on translating the replies given by witnesses in English for the benefit of the Court stenographer, the accused, the press reporters and defence counsel.

After four witnesses had been examined that day, the Khan Saheb "announced in a loud voice that the Court was rising for the day and Counsel and relations of the accused persons could interview them". He was running the show and enjoyed it. So, evidently, did *The Tribune*'s correspondent in reporting the prosecutor's quaint performance.

There was a mild affray in court before the proceedings began. With the permission of the Government Advocate and in his presence, a press representative handed over copies of the *Civil and Military Gazette*, *The Tribune*, the *Bandemataram*, the *Pratap*, the *Milap* and certain others local newspapers to the accused to enable them to read the previous day's proceedings of the case. A police constable took exception to this and roughly handled the press representative who, in turn, gave a rattling blow under the lower jaw of the constable. This created a commotion in Court. Later, when the representative of *The Tribune* arrived in court, he learnt that all the other newspapers including *The Tribune* had been taken away from the accused and they were allowed to retain only a copy of the *Civil and Military Gazette*. As soon as the Special Magistrate took his seat, *The Tribune*'s representative brought this fact to his notice and inquired the reason for banning the paper and other newspapers and permitting the undertrial prisoners to read only the *C. and M. Gazette*. The exchanges that followed revealed a lot.

Magistrate: The *C&M Gazette* contained the Government Advocate's opening speech and the accused were allowed to keep it for their benefit.

The Tribune's Representative: *The Tribune* also contained that speech. Besides, I fail to see how the accused persons are interested only in the Government Advocate's speech and in the statements of witnesses, recorded yesterday. Do I understand that *The Tribune* is banned by the court or only by the police?

Magistrate: I shall ask the jail authorities. I shall recommend to them that the accused may be permitted to read all newspapers which are not proscribed. It depends, you know, on what the Jail Rules prescribe.

Representative: Thank you, Sir. I think so long as the accused are present in Court the Jail Authorities have nothing to do with them and the matter rests entirely within the discretion of the court. All I have to submit is that there is no justification to place my paper under a ban, as was done today under the instructions of K.B. Abdul Aziz (the SP), so far as I have been able to ascertain. I protest against this action.

Magistrate: I shall look into the matter.

Representative: I am much obliged to you, Sir.

A new enclosure had been put up for press representatives where they and the relations of the accused were huddled together. The press representatives could not clearly follow the proceedings. It is also worthy of note that while the relations and friends of the accused and, members of the Defence Committee could not, in all cases, get permits, a very much larger number of policemen and C.I.D. agents, in plain clothes or uniform, were present in the court and were always listening to every word that anybody uttered. "The court, in fact, had all the appearance of a police office and the press representatives and relations or friends of the accused were put to the utmost inconvenience and not unoften gratuitously insulted", *The Tribune*'s correspondent complained. In addition to the heat, due to there being no fan over the small press table, the inaudibility of the proceedings and lack of chairs, there was constant noise, which made it impossible for them properly to do their work. The seats allowed to press reporters were so few that some of them had to sit on the table.

The SP's evidence on the raid was followed by that of persons called by the police to witness it. The first of them was one Khwaja Bashir Baksh. Not the one to conceal his views, *The Tribune*'s reporter described him as "a beardless lad who was seen having a long chat with the police outside the court." He was the proprietor of the Kashmir Buildings and had leased out House No. 69 on March 16, 1929 to Bhagwati Charan on Rs. 13 a month. The police asked him to witness search of the persons of Sukh Dev, Jai Gopal and Kishori Lal. He acknowledged that the SP, Abdul Aziz, was his father's friend. He found none else in the room besides the three accused and police officials. He was cross-examined closely by Lala Amar Das.

The next witness Syed Buddhe Shah was a *"rais"* (wealthy man) and honorary magistrate of Amritsar. On Kalandar Ali Khan's suggestion, he was allowed to give his evidence sitting on a chair placed in the witness box. While on a visit to Lahore, he "accidentally" met the SP who asked him to witness a search. He was present when one of the three arrested men himself handed over a revolver to the police. One of them also said, "Whatever had to happen has happened: there is a live bomb in that tin box. Handle it carefully."

The correspondent noted: "Witness was asked to identify the box in court, but he failed to do so in spite of the fact that a police officer did his best to attract the witness's attention towards one of the boxes by closing with a bang the lid of the box which was open."

Cross-examined by Amar Das, witness stated that he did not remember who was Superintendent of Police or Inspector of Police at Amritsar when he was appointed. He did not recollect having obtained certificates from police officers for services rendered by him.

Kalandar Ali Khan objected to the question as irrelevant.

Amar Das said the witness was being examined on a very important question in a case which might result in some men being hanged. The defence was entitled to show the connection of the witness with the police and the Crown.

Witness, in reply to other questions, said he considered it his duty to render every possible help to the authorities in the maintenance of law and order. He did not recollect if any police officer had recommended him for honorary magistracy. He was going to the railway station to leave for Amritsar, when he was stopped on the way by Abaul Aziz. He did not remember if he went to the station in a tonga or a car nor whether he took food that day or not.

Q. Were you made an honorary magistrate after you had given evidence against Ratan Chand and Bugga during martial law?

Carden Noad objected to the question and said defence counsel should not get their instructions from the gutter.

Witness: I gave no evidence in any martial law case

Q. Were you made an honorary magistrate before or after the martial law regime of 1919?

A. I do not exactly remember. I am a truthful witness, do not compel me to tell lies by putting such questions to me.

Buddhe Shah got excited and in an angry tone avowed that he was a truthful witness (*loud laughter*) and a great well-wisher of the public.

Chaudhri Din Mohammed was another such "chance witness" to the search. He was going in his car to see a friend and was asked by police officers, standing outside the Kashmir Buildings to stop. He was taken upstairs to witness the search. He embroidered the story claiming that "Sukh Dev said that they would have defended themselves and shot down at least the Khan Bahadur, the SP, if they had not been taken unawares and if the revolver had not been taken away."

The last witness of the day was Munshi Ahmad Din, a servant of Mohammed Baksh of Australia. He deposed to the lease of House No. 69 in the Kashmir Buildings.

To anyone observing the trial it was obvious that the hunger-strike was exacting its toll on Bhagat Singh and Batukeshwar Dutt. *The Tribune*'s Special Representative noted: "Both these prisoners looked very weak. It is understood that yesterday evening eight Pathans were employed in each case to forcibly feed them. They were forcibly laid on the ground, their neck, legs, hands and chest being violently pressed to the floor by the Pathans while a rubber tube was inserted into the nose and throat for the passage of milk. Both the prisoners suffered considerably as the result of their struggle with the Pathans, and Bhagat Singh bore marks of violence on his body." Such was his state on July 12. He had been on hunger-strike for four weeks. The charge of forcible feeding was no concoction. In memoirs published sixteen years later, Ajoy

Ghosh testified to the revolting methods used by the police and the manner in which he and his associates foiled those attempts:

"For ten days nothing big happened. Hunger grew and with it physical weakness. Some had to take to bed after a week and as the trial continued, it was a real strain for them to sit in the Court Room. But our first terror had gone. Hunger-strike did not seem such a hard job after all. But we did not know that the real fight was yet to come.

"After ten days forcible feeding was started. We were all in separate cells at that time. Accompanied by a number of tough and strong *Nambardars* (convict overseers), the doctors came to each cell; the hunger-striker was thrown on a mattress, a rubber tube was forcibly pushed into his nostril and the milk poured into it. Violent resistance was offered by everyone but with little effect at first. It almost seemed as if they had already beaten us . . . the strike became grim and determined . . . Soon the hospital was full. Court proceedings were now adjourned . . . Many were the methods we devised to defeat the doctors. Kishori swallowed red pepper and boiling water to cause sore-throat so that the passage of the tube led to such coughing that it had to be taken out lest he might die of suffocation. I swallowed flies immediately after forced feeding to induce vomiting. These devices came to be known to the doctors and guards were kept on us.

"Determined to break us the jail officials removed all water from our cells and placed milk, instead, in the pitchers. This was the worst ordeal imaginable. After a day thirst grew unbearably. I would drag myself towards the pitcher, hoping every time to find water but drew back at the sight of milk . . . . Fury took possession of me. I snatched the pitcher and hurled it against the door, breaking it to pieces, spilling the milk on the guard. He recoiled back in horror. He thought I had gone mad. He was not far from right.

"The same torture was being undergone by Kishori and others who were then in cells. And everyone, as I learnt later, had done the same thing—break their pitchers before their guards.

"The jailor gave away. Water was brought to our cells. I drank and drank. Then I fell sick and vomited out every drop."[9]

Mass meetings and demonstrations were held all over the country. Communist leaders and associates who were on trial in the Meerut Conspiracy Case and political prisoners in many a jail went on hunger-strike in sympathy. It created a stir in England.

Repeated adjournment of the Court's proceedings was the least of the consequences of the truly historic hunger-strike. It had a political impact, drove the Government to knock at the doors of the High Court and, when it lost there, tried to amend the law.

Evidently, Gandhi did not share the enthusiasm which the strikes had generated and even disapproved of the publication in the *Congress Bulletin* on July 1 of the joint statement by Bhagat Singh and Dutt. He wrote to the Congress General Secretary, Jawaharlal Nehru, that very day, on July 1, pin-pointing his objections with a lawyer's skill and in the lucid, elegant prose that has come to be associated with his name.[10] First, it was "out of place" in a publication which was meant to record the Congress activities. "On merits too I understand that it was prepared by counsel", Nehru's close friend, Asaf Ali. "It is not the outpourings of earnest souls as you and I thought it was." He did not stop there but came closer to the recent events. "Nor did I like your advocacy and approval of the fast they are undergoing. In my opinion, it is an irrelevant performance and in so far as it may be relevant it is like using Nasmyth-hammer to crush a fly. However, this is for you to ponder over."

Nehru replied on July 13 in apologetic confusion: "I am sorry you disapproved of my giving Bhagat Singh and Dutt's statement in the *Congress Bulletin*. I was myself a little doubtful as to whether I should give it but when I found that there was very general appreciation of it among Congress circles I decided to give extracts. It was difficult, however, to pick and choose and gradually most of it went in. But I agree with you that it was somewhat out of place. I think you are mistaken in thinking that the statement was the work of their counsel. My information is that counsel had nothing, or practically nothing, to do with it. He might have touched up the punctuation. I think the statement was undoubtedly a genuine thing.

"Have I been advocating the fast? I had not intended doing so and I do not know to what statement of mine you are referring to. In Delhi I had stated that we could not help sympathising with Bhagat Singh and Dutt during their long fast. As a matter of fact I am not in favour of hunger-strikes. I told this to many young men who came to see me on this subject but I did not think it worth-while to condemn the fast publicly."[11]

Nehru visited the prisoners and issued a forthright statement in Lahore on August 9: "I visited the Central Jail and the Borstal Jail yesterday and saw Sardar Bhagat Singh, Mr. Batukeshwar Dutt, Mr. Jatindranath Das and all the other accused in the Lahore Conspiracy Case, who are on hunger-strike. Attempts have been made for many days past to feed forcibly all these hunger-strikers. In the case of some of them, the results of this forcible method were so injurious that, all forcible feeding had to be given up in the face of a greater danger . . .

"The condition of Mr. Jatindranath Das is specially critical. He is very weak and cannot easily move. He speaks in whispers. He is in considerable pain and looks for release in death . . .

"It was very painful for me to meet these extraordinarily brave young men and to see their manifest suffering. I gathered from them that they would adhere to their resolve, whatever the consequences to their individual selves might be. Indeed, they did not care very much for their own selves. They could not undergo such tremendous suffering for a little personal comfort in future. They feel strongly, however, that the lot of political prisoners in India is bad and must be improved.

"The position, as explained to me by Sardar Bhagat Singh, was that all political prisoners, with one exception if necessary, should be given special treatment. This exception was the case of an actual perpetrator of murder.

"I can only hope that the great sacrifice which these young men are making will bear fruit."[12]

Earlier, to R. Bridgeman, Nehru had pointed out another abuse on July 23: "In the Lahore Conspiracy Case the accused are kept even in court handcuffed with a policeman on either side and the policemen have actually thrashed them in court while the magistrate is trying to look the other way. When an application was made for a transfer of the case from this magistrate's court it was thrown out as being frivolous. It was ordered, however, that handcuffs need not be kept on inside the court room . . . Meanwhile the hunger-strike of Bhagat Singh and Dutt is in its sixth week."[13]

Meanwhile, on July 15 Carden Noad had made the Government's first move to break the hunger-strike. Batukeshwar Dutt simply could not be brought to court as he was running high temperature. Bhagat Singh was visibly weak. None of the accused regarded the paltry concessions, which the Government had announced, as satisfactory. The Government Advocate boldly asked the Magistrate to dispense with Dutt's attendance, under sub-section (1) of S. 540-A of the Criminal Procedure Code, on the ground that he was "incapable of remaining before the Court". This, however, applied only when the accused was represented by counsel, not when he appeared in person.

Amar Das promptly objected and pointed out that Dutt himself had made no such application. Moreover, "I shall require his express authority for doing so." Bhagat Singh, who always followed the proceedings closely, got up and supported the objection saying that Dutt's lot could well be theirs in the future.

Amar Das told the court that he would not represent Dutt in his absence without his express authority. On the Court's suggestion he went to interview Dutt but returned to convey to the Court that Dutt objected to the court proceeding with case in his absence and did not agree to his being represented by counsel in his absence, either.

The case was adjourned to the next day when, once again, Dutt was unable to attend. The Magistrate now did the incredible. Disregarding the clear limitations of the provision (S.540A-(1)), he acceded to the prosecution's request and appointed an advocate to represent Dutt.

The proceedings soon became increasingly unpleasant. The accused were being handcuffed even when they were obviously in no condition to make an escape. Hand-cuffing in such a situation could not have been for reasons of security. It was a gratuitous insult of a piece with the harsh treatment which the accused received throughout. They resented it and resisted the hand-cuffing. Bhagat Singh, who was carried on a stretcher, got up in spite of his weak state of health. As he addressed the court, his face began to glow. Denouncing the Special Magistrate, he said: "Mr. Magistrate, we take it to be an insult to be handcuffed by the policemen. You have not to blindly obey the police. You should be fair to us. You have not listened to any of our complaints. We have no confidence in you because you are completely controlled by the police in every matter. How can we take notes being handcuffed in the manner in which the police wants to handcuff us? How can we talk to each other about the case or consult each other?

"We do not expect justice from this court. Why enact this farce? Are you or is K.B. Abdul Aziz the presiding officer of the court?" The Magistrate took it as an "assaulting attitude and an act of rowdyism". He suggested to the Superintendent of the Jail in a letter that disciplinary action be taken against Bhagat Singh.

Carden Noad soon realised that he was running a high risk. If the ever obliging Magistrate's order was quashed, as it was bound to be, the entire trial would be vitiated. He asked the High Court for a ruling in the exercise of its inherent powers "to secure the ends of justice", appoint Counsel to represent any accused who were any time unrepresented before the Magistrate or "authorise and empower the Special Magistrate or some other persons so as to appoint counsel for such accused at Government expense". That is, counsel imposed on the accused, against their will, to act without their authority and confidence. This is altogether distinct from *amicus curiae* appointed by a Court to assist it on complex issues.

The Government Advocate invoked S. 561-A of the Code of Criminal Procedure, 1898 which saved "the inherent powers" of High Courts to prevent any abuse of the judicial process or to secure the ends of justice. (It figures as S. 482 in the Code of Criminal Procedure of 1973.)

The application was heard by the Chief Justice Sir Shadi Lal and Justice Alan Brice Broadway. Both were barristers and not civilian judges from the Indian Civil Service (I.C.S.) or the Provincial Civil Service (P.C.S.) who notoriously tended to be pro-executive; there were some exceptions, though.

Shadi Lal, delivering judgement for himself and Broadway,

noted that "The application is admittedly one of a novel character, and Mr. Carden Noad for the Crown frankly admits that he cannot cite a single decision in support of his contention. Indeed, S. 353, Criminal P.C., which deals with the mode of taking and recording evidence in enquiries and trials, makes it clear that, except as otherwise expressly provided, all evidence in an enquiry into a case triable by the Court of Session, or High Court shall be taken in the presence of the accused, or, when his personal attendance is dispensed with, in the presence of his pleader."

In 1923, however, the Criminal Procedure Code had been amended to insert a new provision, Section 540A. It read thus: "(1) At any stage of an inquiry of trial under this Code, where two or more accused are before the Court, if the Judge or Magistrate is satisfied for reasons to be recorded, that any one or more of such accused is or are incapable of remaining before the Court he may, if such accused is represented by a pleader, dispense with his attendance and proceed with such inquiry or trial in his absence and may, at any subsequent stage of the proceedings, direct the personal attendance of such accused.

"(2) If the accused in any such case is not represented by a pleader, or if the Judge or Magistrate considers his personal attendance necessary, he may, if he thinks fit, and for reasons to be recorded by him, either adjourn such inquiry or trial or order that the case of such accused be taken up or tried separately."

This provision, the Chief Justice pointed out, provided for a case in which there are a large number of accused persons, and one or more of them cannot remain before the Court. In such a case, the Court, instead of adjourning the enquiry or trial, has the discretion to dispense with the personal attendance of the accused and proceed with the hearing provided that such accused is represented by a pleader. But sub-S. 2 of this section laid down that, if such accused is not represented by a pleader, the Court cannot proceed with the case, and has either to adjourn it or direct that his case may be heard separately. "It is manifest that the pleader contemplated by the section must be one who represents the accused and not a person who is appointed without his consent."

He referred to an old but apposite English precedent, *Reg* vs.

Yscuado, in which the prisoner stood "mute of malice", a legal expression which signified deliberate silence and refusal to plead in order to obstruct the trial. But Justice Erle ruled that he had no authority to assign counsel to the accused without his consent lest "I might be authorising a defence which the prisoner himself would never have made, and yet for which he must be responsible."

Chief Justice Shadi Lal's concluding remarks touched the facts of the case. "The absence of an accused on medical ground may delay the disposal of the case, when the pleader, who has been appearing for him, ceases to represent him. If this course has, as suggested by the learned Counsel, been adopted in order to protract the proceedings, the conduct of the person or persons concerned cannot but be regarded as reprehensible. *The present application does not, however, disclose the exact circumstances which led the pleader to withdraw from the case in so far as Batukeshwar Dutt was concerned, nor are we concerned in this case with the conduct of the pleader.* We cannot, therefore, make any pronouncement upon the question of whether he had any justification for taking the course attributed to him."[14] On July 26, the High Court dismissed the Government's application. Undeterred, the Government moved the High Court, once again, for the same purpose and with the same result.

The record clearly showed that the hunger-strike, which commenced on June 15, four weeks before the trial began, was a bona fide strike; one undertaken openly to secure acceptance of demands which were fair and reasonable. It was not a devious stratagem for collateral ends; least of all to obstruct the trial.

The accused made no attempt to obstruct or disturb the proceedings. As prisoners they were entitled to certain privileges and amenities. These were denied to them. They decided to go on a hunger-strike. It was universally admitted that prison conditions in India were appalling, then; as, indeed, they are, now.

A spate of adjournments of the hearings followed from July 15 onwards—from July 26 to September 24; from September 25 to October 3; and, later, from February 22 to March 8, 1930. Some of the adjournments were occasioned by the accused refusing to attend court in protest against the authorities' high-handed behaviour.

On September 2 the Government relented. It appointed a Punjab Jails Enquiry Committee, 81 days after Bhagat Singh and Dutt had gone on the strike and 55 days after their comrades had followed suit. All, except Jatindra Nath Das, immediately called off the strike. It was too late to save their dying colleague. Two days later Bhagat Singh, Dutt and three others resumed the strike on the ground that Jatindra Nath was not unconditionally released and the two convict-prisoners, Bhagat Singh and Dutt, were not allowed to associate with their non-convict co-accused in the same case.[15]

The Jails Enquiry Committee consisted of eleven members with Lt. Colonel F.A. Barker as its President. Four members visited the prison, met the hunger-strikers and promised amends. But nothing happened. "Where are those members of the Jails Enquiry Committee who held out many good promises to us?" Bhagat Singh asked Kalandar Ali Khan when he accompanied Pandit Sri Kishen, the Special Magistrate, to the Jail to intimate to them adjournment of the case to September 24 owing to Jatindra Nath's illness. Defence counsel, Amar Das, D.C. Khanna, Daljit Singh were present. So were pressmen. Bhagat Singh's father Kishen Singh and Dutt's sister Pramila Devi were allowed to accompany the Magistrate inside the Jail.

Bhagat Singh was in cell No. 103, Dutt in cell No. 120. Kalandar Ali Khan asked Dutt how he was doing to which Dutt replied that he was lingering on. "Are you studying some books?" Dutt responded: "Yes, some novels." The Prosecutor inquired, "Aren't you given a chair, a table and all other facilities supplied to the other undertrial prisoners in the Borstal Jail?" Dutt's reply must have come as a surprise: "No, we are, as the Government says, 'convicts'."

When the party met Bhagat Singh, he had a long chat with Kalandar Ali Khan. He asked why Jatindra Nath was not being released, only to be told that "the Government is prepared to release him on bail".

Bhagat Singh persisted: "Could not the Government release him unconditionally in order to save his life? He could be re-arrested when he would regain his health. I dare say you know that Seth Damodar Prashad, an accused in the Kakori Case, was released unconditionally and he is still out?"

Thrown on the defensive, Kalandar Ali Khan could only say "Yes, I know that. But the Punjab Government is not prepared to go beyond the concession offered."[16]

The next day, September 13, Jatindra Nath Das breathed his last. The Court had adjourned the case, only the day before, for a fortnight because of his illness. When proceedings were resumed on September 24 Carden Noad rose to express regret. "With the permission of the court, I ask leave on behalf of my colleagues and myself to say a brief word of reference to the tragic event which has occurred since the last sitting of the court.

"I desire on behalf of all to express the sincere regret and genuine sorrow which we feel on account of the untimely death of Jatindra Nath Das. There are qualities which compel admiration of all men alike, and pre-eminent among them are the qualities of courage and constancy in the pursuit of an ideal. Although we do not share the ideals which he followed, we cannot but admire the unwavering fortitude and firmness of the purpose he displayed."[17]

By far the most touching tribute came from Mary, wife of Terence McSwiney, Lord Mayor of Cork, who had died in similar circumstances: "Family Terence McSwiney unites patriotic Indians in grief and pride on death of Jatindra Nath Das. Freedom will come."[18]

A wave of protests swept the country. Lala Duni Chand revealed at a public meeting on September 25 at the Bradlaugh Hall. organised by the Lahore Students Union, that he had made every effort to interview Jatindra Nath in jail as his legal adviser but not once was he allowed to see him by the jail authorities. On the day he died, Duni Chand tried, once more, to see him but neither he nor his friends were permitted to see the dying prisoner.

It was a mammoth meeting. Dr. Mohammed Alam, who presided, and public figures of eminence like Khan Abdul Ghaffar Khan and Dr. Gopi Chand Bhargava lauded the example Jatin Nath had set by his martyrdom.

Maulana Zafar Ali Khan, one of the finest orators in the country, said that the young patriot was neither a poet like Rabindra Nath Tagore, nor a saint like Mahatma Gandhi, nor a national leader like Tilak or Lala Lajpat Rai, but he was a man with a heart and in that heart there was burning patriotism. Someone said to him that when the wonderful funeral procession of C.R. Das was passing through the streets of Calcutta, followed by five lakhs of mourners, it reminded the imperialists that it was the funeral procession of Imperialism that was passing through India (shouts of *Inquilab Zindabad*).[19]

Jawaharlal Nehru readily agreed to serve on the All India Memorial Committee for Jatin Das and made a warm reference to his martyrdom in his Presidential Address to the Congress session at Lahore on December 29, 1929.

Gandhi "preferred to observe silence over the self immolation of Jatindra Nath Das because I feel that by writing on it I would have done more harm to the country's cause than good," he wrote on October 8. The next day, he explained to Raihana Tyabji: "I have been deliberately silent because I have not approved of the fast. But I have refrained from saying anything as my opinion would have been distorted by the officials and grossly misused."[20]

NOTES

1. Manmathnath Gupta, p. 179.
2. Judith M. Brown, *Gandhi's Rise to Power: Indian Politics*, Cambridge University Press, 1972, p. 328.
3. V.P. Menon, *The Transfer of Power in India*, Orient Longman, 1957, p. 29.
4. Kamlesh Mohan, p. 177.
5. Bakshi, pp. 80-82. Vide also *LAD*, Vol. IV, September 14, 1929; Vol. IV, p. 806; quoted by Pandit Madan Mohan Malaviya.
6. Manmathnath Gupta, p. 169.
7. S. Gopal (ed.) *Selected Works of Jawaharlal Nehru*, Orient Longman, New Delhi, Vol. 4, p. 8.
8. Kamlesh Mohan, p. 176; Manmathnath Gupta, pp. 177-78.
9. Ajoy Ghosh, pp. 8-10.
10. *The Collected Works of Mahatma Gandhi*, The Publications Division, New Delhi, 1970, Vol. 4, 41, pp. 152-53.
11. S. Gopal (ed), *ibid.*, p. 157.
12. *Ibid.*, p. 13.
13. Bakshi, p. 85.
14. *Emperor vs. Sukh Dev and others*, AIR, 1929, Lahore, 705.
15. Deol, p. 70 and Kamlesh Mohan, p. 180.
16. *The Tribune*, September 13, 1929.
17. *Ibid.*, September 26, 1929.
18. Kamlesh Mohan, p. 181; Deol, 1929, p. 73.
19. *The Tribune*, September 27, 1929.
20. *Collected Works of Mahatma Gandhi*, Vol. 41, pp. 528-34.

6

When Jinnah Defended Bhagat Singh

"THE man who goes on hunger-strike has a soul. He is moved by that soul and he believes in the justice of his cause," Mohammed Ali Jinnah declaimed in the Central Assembly on September 12, 1929. By all contemporary accounts, his was a magnificent performance. But it has been completely ignored in all Indian writings on Bhagat Singh and little noticed in Pakistan. An able compilation of his speeches in the Central Assembly, published in Pakistan, includes the speech but ignores it in the Introduction.[1] A rare exception is a collection compiled by the veteran human rights activist, I.A. Rehman, and two others with a most informative prefatory note to the speech. They rightly hold that "in his coolly logical and convincing manner he played a major role in foiling the attempt to make trial *in absentia* lawful".[2] This is what the Government sought to do by what was popularly called the Hunger-Strike Bill.

The Tribune's Special Correspondent reported from Simla, where the Assembly's session was held, "Mr. Jinnah created a profound impression by the excellent form in which he argued the case. The Government was sacrificing the fundamental principles of jurisprudence and wanted the House to change the law of the land to create a farce. As regards the Lahore accused, they were creatures of the present system. Mr. Jinnah was proceeding in this strain winning applause after applause from the spell-bound House when the President adjourned the House to Saturday to conclude the debate on the Bill."[3] (See Appendix III for the text of the speech.)

The debate was initiated by the Home Member of the Governor-General's Executive Council, Sir James Crerar, by moving the Code of Criminal Procedure (Amendment) Bill. It sought to insert in the Code a new provision, S. 540-B which said that "if any accused . . . has voluntarily rendered himself incapable of remaining before the Court, the Judge or Magistrate may, *whether such accused is represented by a pleader or not*, dispense with his attendance and proceed with the inquiry or trial in his absence".

Crerar's speech was disingenuous. "I should like at the outset to express the deep sense of regret with which Government find themselves compelled to bring this Bill before the House. I cannot affect to deny that the Bill is one which may naturally provoke a considerable amount of controversy . . . The measure which I have laid before the House has no reference whatsoever to, *and has no possible bearing whatever upon, the merits of any trial now pending* or any that may hereafter arise. It is a general proposition. It relates to a point of criminal procedure which has no possible relation to the guilt or innocence of any accused person." Having said that, he proceeded immediately to refer to the Lahore Conspiracy Case and to the High Court's rejection of the Crown's application for appointment of defence counsel by the Court, regardless of the wishes of the accused.

"That, then, may be taken as an authoritative statement of the law as it stands. In consequence of this, the trial, which is as I say a very important trial and in which 400 witnesses have already been cited and a large number more have yet to be cited, has been unable to proceed and is now unable to proceed . . . I anticipate that one of the first questions that will be asked of me is that before government proceeded to seek a remedy by an amendment of the law, 'was there no other possible solution which might have been attempted?' I can only suppose that question to mean ought not Government in these circumstances to comply with the demands of the accused, who decline to be represented by counsel, and who have rendered themselves incapable of appearing before the Court? Now, I wish to say, in the first instance, that it is my sincere and genuine belief that the local authorities have been throughout actuated by a very genuine desire to terminate a state of affairs which, whatever the grounds and whatever their consequences may be, is a state of affairs which no one can fail to deplore."

He justified the stand of the Punjab Government. It had declined not only to treat the accused as "political prisoners", generally, but rejected the specific and reasonable demands they had made. Crerar harked back to the first Lahore Conspiracy Case of 1915-1917 and the Kakori Conspiracy Case, painting a gruesome picture of both. There was a "complete deadlock" which the Bill sought to resolve. "If any accused person, declines to be represented by counsel, the Court has a discretion, in the special circumstances, to dispense with his presence."

The Bill brooked no delay, he argued. It was a matter of "urgency", adding "no solution other than that propounded at present is possible."

Crerar had, of course, anticipated strong opposition to the Bill but not quite the censures that greeted him. The law already provided, in S. 540-A, that if the "accused is or are incapable of remaining before Court", it may dispense with his attendance if he is represented by a lawyer or adjourn the trial if he is not so represented. It could also take up his case for trial separately. But the Court could not proceed with the trial *in absentia*. The Law Member, Sir Brojendra Mitter, argued that while the existing provision, S. 540-A, dealt with "a case of unavoidable absence, it does not deal with a case of avoidable absence, and that is where the lacuna comes in". Hence, the proposed new provision S. 540-B. "It is said that trial of an accused in his absence is unprecedented. I admit it, I admit that it is unprecedented and unusual." But his presence was required not by "an inflexible rule of law", but by a "rule of prudence". A palpably absurd assertion.[4]

In short, rather than concede the just demands of the hunger-strikers, the Government of India chose to get the law amended, flouting a fundamental principle of criminal law. Two amendments were moved. N.C. Kelkar's amendment was for circulation of the Bill "for eliciting public and legal opinion thereon". A nominated member, K.C. Roy, proposed its reference to a Select Committee which Crerar himself had suggested provided it was asked to report at an early date. All the names proposed for the Committee were either of Government Members or those of its known supporters. All others had declined to serve on the Committee since that would have implied their acceptance of the Bill in principle.

Debate began after the Question Hour with Vithalbhai Patel in the Chair. Crerar was supported by K.C. Roy, Sir Darcy Lindsay, leader of the European Group, a couple of others and the Home Secretary H.W. Emerson, who had served in the Punjab. Those who opposed the motion were N.C. Kelkar (Bombay), Abdul Haye, a Unionist, and Diwan Chaman Lall, a Congress member (both of Punjab), Jehangir K. Munshi (Burma) and Jamnadas Mehta (Bombay).

Diwan Chaman Lall read out to the House in full a joint statement by Bhagat Singh and Batukeshwar Dutt which was published in *The Tribune* of July 14. It read thus: "Sir, We, Bhagat Singh and Batukeshwar Dutt, were sentenced to life transportation in the Assembly bomb case, Delhi, on the 19th May, 1929. *As long as we were under-trial prisoners in the Delhi Jail we were accorded very good treatment and were given very good diet; but since our transfer from that jail to Mianwali and Lahore Central Jails respectively we are being treated as ordinary criminals.* On the very first day we wrote an application to the higher authorities asking for better diet and a few other facilities and refused to take jail diet. Our demands were follows:

(1) We, as political prisoners, should be given better diet and the standard of our dietary should at least be the same as that of European prisoners. It is not the sameness of diet that we demand but sameness in the standard of diet.

(2) We shall not be forced to do any hard or undignified labour at all.

(3) All books, other than those proscribed, along with writing materials should be allowed to us without any restriction.

(4) At least one standard daily paper should be supplied to every political prisoner.

(5) Political prisoners should have a special ward of their own in every jail, *provided with all necessities as those of the Europeans* and all the political prisoners in one jail must be kept together in that ward.

(6) Toilet necessities should be supplied to us, and

(7) Better clothing.

"We have explained above the demands that we made. They are most reasonable demands. The jail authorities told us one day that the higher authorities would comply with our demands. Apart from that they handle us very roughly while feeding us artificially, and Bhagat Singh was lying quite senseless on the 10th (*sic*) June, 1929, for about 15 minutes after forcible feeding, which we request to be stopped without further delay.

"In addition we may be permitted to refer to the recommendations of the United Provinces Jail Committee by Pandit Jagat Narain and Khan Bahadur Hafiz Hidayat Hussain. *They have recommended the political prisoners to be treated as better class prisoners."*

They added a postscript: "By 'political prisoners' we mean those people who are convicted of offences against the State, for instance, people who were convicted in the Lahore Conspiracy Case, 1915-17, the Kakori Conspiracy Case and the sedition cases in Bengal."

Referring to this letter, the Home Secretary, in a maiden speech, argued that the demands "simple, though they may appear, involve vital principles". They raised three issues—their reasonableness in the instant case, "the general treatment of political prisoners" and *"the racial question of the differentiation between European and Indian prisoners."* On the last, he said:

"There are two criteria: firstly, the nature of the offence, and, secondly, the character, status, and education of the prisoner. The excluded offences are, broadly speaking, those which involve violence or abetment of violence, or which involve offences against property, or seducing of soldiers or police from their allegiance, and offences committed on hire in pursuit of political causes, that is to say, a political offender who is paid to commit an offence."

The last part of this statement caused an uproar in the House but Emerson continued and started giving instances of comparable laws in some foreign countries.

K.C. Neogy intervened to ask as to how did Government define the word "European" in this connection.

Emerson replied: "The rules relating to Europeans in the jail manuals of most of the Provinces apply to any one, whether European or Indian, *who has adopted the European mode of life.*" He said there were only two ways to sweep aside whatever differentiation there was, either to level up or level down. The first option was out of the question, and the second was too costly. According to him, if the Indians were treated at a par with the Europeans the cost in the Punjab alone would be 40 lakhs of rupees a year.[5]

It was 4 in the afternoon when Jinnah rose to speak immediately after Emerson's brazen maiden speech.

He said: "Sir, one is placed somewhat in a difficult position when one has got to deal with a speaker like the last one. It was his maiden speech, and it is the tradition of this House, that when a Member makes his maiden speech, he is in a privileged position and is not to be attacked. Whatever reasons or grounds, therefore, he may have given me for criticising him, I will not wish to depart from that tradition which, I think, ought to be maintained in the House. But I would say this, that in his concluding portion he remarked that the Hon'ble Members may have admiration and sympathy for the accused in the Lahore case. I think I am speaking on behalf of a very large body of people when I say that, if there is sympathy and admiration for the accused, it is only to this extent, that they are the victim of the system of government. It is not that we approve or applaud their actions if they are guilty, which still remains to be proved. . .

"The last speaker, whom I am going to attack, almost gave away the case in his concluding remarks when he said that the only way to break the hunger-strike is to pass this Bill . . .

"The Hon'ble Member in reply to a question said that whether the man is a European or an Indian—and he accepted the definition of my honourable friend Mr. Neogy—if one wears a topee, then one is a European for the purpose of jail rules. Then why should you not treat Bhagat Singh and Dutt, who wear topees and European clothes, as such for the purpose of treatment in jails?

"What do they say in their statement which was read out? This is what they say?

"We, Bhagat Singh and Dutt, were sentenced to life transportation in the Assembly bomb case, Delhi, on 19th May,1929. As long as we were under-trial prisoners in Delhi Jail we were accorded very good treatment and we were given good diet. But since our transfer from the Delhi Jail to Mianwali Jail and Lahore Central jail,—

Which is represented by the Hon'ble Member, who spoke last—the Punjab seems to be a terrible place. . .

Mian Muhammad Shah Nawaz (West Central Punjab): Don't go there.

Jinnah: I won't. To continue what they say:

"We are being treated as ordinary criminals."

"So, in Delhi they received very good treatment and in the Punjab they are treated as ordinary criminals. Surely, Sir, if the Government of the Punjab was not wanting in statesmanship, if the Government of the Punjab had any brains, they would have found a solution to this question very easily and long ago. But, Sir, it is a question—the more I examine it and the more I analyse it, I find—it is a question of declaration of war. As far as the Punjab Government are concerned, the Government do not merely wish to bring these men to trial and get them convicted by a judicial tribunal, but Government go to war against these men. They seem to me in this frame of mind: "We will pursue every possible course, every possible method, but we will see that you are sent either to the gallows or transported for life, and in the meantime we will not treat you as decent men". . .

"But may I ask, with whom are you at war? What are the resources of these few young men who, according to you, have committed certain offences? You want to prosecute them, and after due trial, you want to secure their convictions. But before they are convicted, surely this is not a matter on which there should be this struggle, that you should not at once yield to their demands for bare necessities of life. After all, so far as the Lahore case prisoners are concerned, surely they are political prisoners and under trial. . .

Jinnah made no secret of his sympathies for the Lahore prisoners though their politics and his were poles apart. "Do you wish to prosecute them or persecute them?" Jinnah asked. He proceeded to discuss the Bill itself.

"This Bill has got to be looked at, as far as I can see, from three points of view. The first, from the point of view of criminal jurisprudence; second, political point of view or the policy of the Bill; and, third, treatment to the accused when they are under trial. I think it will be admitted, I think even the Hon'ble the Home Member conceded, that by the Bill which he has brought before the House, he is introducing a principle, in the criminal jurisprudence, of a very unprecedented character. I do not think, Sir, there is any system of jurisprudence in any civilised country where you will find such a principle in existence as is involved in this Bill . . .

"I will give you a picture as to what will happen under this Bill . . . the Government will apply to the Magistrate before whom the inquiry is going on and say: 'Here is a law which we have secured from the Legislature. Now the accused have voluntarily made themselves incapable of attending the Courts and, therefore, you have to dispense with their presence.' The inquiry will then proceed *ex parte* before the Magistrate. Evidence will be led, oral and documentary, which will go without being tested by cross-examination. The documentary evidence will go without being even seen by the accused, against whom it is produced, and how will you identify the accused in their absence? . . .

"Under this Bill the accused will not be there to give any explanation to the Magistrate with regard to the evidence that has been already recorded *ex parte* . . . I ask the Hon'ble the Law Member of the Government of India whether that will be a trial or a farce?

Sir Brojendra Mitter (Law Member): Not a farce. The accused can always go before the Court if he chooses to . . .

Jinnah: I am very glad that the Hon'ble the Law Member has given me a reply. Then you want by this Bill really to break the hunger-strikers. You want this House to give you a Statute laying down a principle generally in the criminal jurisprudence for this particular case, so that you may use it for breaking the hunger-strike in the Lahore case. Well, you know perfectly well that these men are determined to die. It is not a joke. *I ask the Hon'ble the Law Member to realise that it is not everybody who can go on starving himself to death. Try it for a little while and you will see.* Sir, have you heard anywhere in the world, except the American case, which my honourable friend Mr Jamnadas Mehta pointed out, of an accused person going on hunger-strike? *The man who goes on hunger-strike has a soul. He is moved by that soul and he believes in the justice of his cause; he is not an ordinary criminal who is guilty of cold-blooded, sordid, wicked crime.*

"Mind you, Sir, I do not approve of the action of Bhagat Singh, and I say this on the floor of this House. I regret that, rightly or wrongly, youth today in India is stirred up, and you cannot, when you have three hundred and odd millions of people, you cannot prevent such crimes being committed, however much you deplore them and however much you may say that they are misguided. *It is the system, this damnable system of Government, which is resented by the people.* You may be a cold-blooded logician: I am a patient cool-headed man and can calmly go on making speeches here, persuading and influencing the Treasury Bench. But, remember, there are thousands of young men outside. This is not the only country where these actions are resorted to. It has happened in other countries, not youths, but grey-bearded men have committed serious offences, moved by patriotic impulses. What happened to Mr. Cosgrave, the Prime Minister of Ireland? He was under sentence of death a fortnight before he got an invitation from His Majesty's Government to go and settle terms? Was he a youth? Was he a young man? What about Collins?"

The House was then adjourned. Jinnah continued his speech at the next sitting, after Motilal Nehru's adjournment motion had been admitted for discussion. He pointed out the anomalies that would arise:

"The trial would proceed in the absence of the accused. I ask the Home Member, is there a Judge or jury who would feel that they were administering law or justice in that case? The moment this Bill is passed, the prosecution can go before the Court and say: 'Here is a voluntary act of the accused persons; he has or they have incapacitated himself or themselves, and we ask you now to proceed *ex parte.*' "

Later events belied Jinnah's confidence in the judiciary: "*I say that no Judge who has got an iota of a judicial mind or a sense of justice can ever be a party to a trial of that character and pass sentence of death without a shudder and a pang of conscience.* This is the farce which you propose to enact under this procedure! I say this, that if ever there was a conscientious Judge and he was strong enough, if he had a judicial mind, and if he had any independence, let me tell you, that, in spite of this provision of yours, he would say, 'True, the law has to be administered; I am obliged to make the order that the trial shall proceed *ex parte*; but I realise and I feel that it will be a travesty of justice and I cannot be a party to it; and I shall, therefore, adjourn this case until further orders.'

Jinnah traced the development of the law in England over the centuries in order to refute the Government's case. "It must be admitted that this is a most revolutionary, unheard of, unprecedented change that is proposed in our criminal jurisprudence. I know the Home Member will tell me, 'Yes, the doctrine is that no man shall be condemned unless he is heard and until he is given a hearing; but here it is the voluntary act of the accused, and if he chooses not to go there and insist upon his being heard, it is his fault.' Sir, this is not a new question; it has been considered in England and there is a long history about it and behind it and you will find that in old days there was the strictest formality observed as to the recording of the plea of the prisoner. And if the prisoner was mute of malice, that is to say, if he refused deliberately to open his mouth when he was arraigned in a Court of law and when the question was put to him as to whether he pleaded guilty or not—he had to make his plea, and there are cases where he refused to speak, and the old law was—even England has advanced—in that case he was condemned and executed or must be committed to imprisonment . . .

"They resorted to torture. Torture for what? That he should make his plea, not that an *ex parte* trial should proceed. That is what you want to do here by this Bill, that *ex parte* trial should proceed. The old law was then altered, because the result of the torture was that some of them died and the form of torture was the most cruel form of torture, and I will read to you a passage from Stephen's *History of Criminal Law*:

'If he was accused of felony, he was condemned, after much exhortation to the *peine forte et dure*, that is to be stretched, naked on his back, and to have 'iron laid upon him as much as he could bear and more', and so to continue, fed upon bad bread and stagnant water on alternate days, till h= either pleaded or died.'

"But they did not proceed *ex parte*.
"The instance that I was going to refer to is this. In one case:

Mr. Pike produces some evidence to show that in the early part of Edward I's reign, people who refused to put themselves on their trial were executed . . .

"It is a curious thing that the Government of India, who have hardly given this House even seven days' notice and call upon this House to endorse a vital, cardinal principle of a novel or unheard of character, do not possess in their library even an edition of the *Law of Criminal Procedure* by Stephen of a later date than 1883. . . . You do not possess in your library an edition of a textbook which is the standard book except of the year 1883! And it is a tall order to ask the House to pass the Bill now and here."

Jinnah was never slow to pour scorn on the Government Benches. Having discussed the law he reverted to the Lahore prisoners and put the trial in the political context.

"Sir, can you imagine a more horrible form of torture than

hunger-strike? If, rightly or wrongly, these men are inflicting this punishment upon themselves and thereby you are inconvenienced, is that any reason why you should ask us to abandon one of the cardinal principles of criminal jurisprudence? If these young men pursue this course, and I am sorry to hear that one of them has died, what will happen? Is this a matter which can continue indefinitely? Certainly not. As I say, I am not satisfied with the version that you have placed before this House. I understand that some of the prisoners are not on strike. If you are solicitous and anxious that their trial should proceed and should not be delayed, then split up the trial. Proceed against them and bring home the guilt to them if you can. . .

"Can you imagine that 600 witnesses are necessary to prove the case against each one of the accused? And, Sir, I ask, is it not an amazing fact that, in order to prove this case, 600 persons should have been cited as witnesses? Well, Sir, it may seem a joke and it may seem that I am making fun of the statement made to this effect, but the first impression that one gets is that, when a case cannot be proved without the testimony of 600 witnesses, that case is a very bad case. Therefore, I say that it is open to Government to split up the case . . .

"Sir, I cannot understand the anxiety of the Government to proceed with this trial when these men are inflicting the greatest possible punishment upon themselves by prolonged fasting . . . I appeal to you with all the emphasis I can command, do not be vindictive. Show that you are fair, generous, that you are 'willing to treat these men decently. At any rate, before they are released or sentenced, give them proper treatment. What treatment do they want? What is it that bothers them? Do they want spring mattresses? Do they want dressing tables? Do they want a set of toilet requisites? No, Sir, they ask for nothing but bare necessities and a little better treatment. I ask you in all decency, why cannot you concede this small thing?

"Does it not come to this, that you want to carry this Bill, you want to have this Bill placed on the Statute-book, and then you want to give notice to the prisoners that, unless they cease their hunger-strike within a certain period, you are going to proceed *ex parte*? Under that threat you think these prisoners will cease their hunger-strike?"

The prediction came true as we shall see. The law *was* changed but the prisoners were not cowed down. Jinnah turned to the political situation in the country. "But there is a political aspect of this Bill and the policy underlying this measure. I think the Hon'ble the Home Member must admit that this is not a measure which is only brought here for the purpose of putting the law in order. Sir, it reminds me of a story, an old Persian story. A man got stomach-ache because he had eaten some very rotten bread. So he went to the doctor and told him that he had stomach-ache. The doctor said, yes, and he promptly started treating his eyes. Then he said, 'What have my eyes got to do with my complaint?' Then the doctor said, 'Well, if you had eyes, you would never have got stomach-ache because you would not have eaten rotten bread.' Similarly I would say to the Hon'ble the Home Member, 'Have you got eyes? Well, if you had, you would never have got this stomach-ache'. Now, will you open your eyes? Will you have a little more imagination? Have you got any statesmanship left? Have you got any political wisdom? This is not the way you are going to solve the root cause of the trouble. You may temporarily, provisionally, get over this particular trial. But now let us see what is the real cause of the trouble."

It was government by prosecution. Jinnah asked, "Is there today in any part of the globe a civilised government that is engaged, day in and day out, week in and week out, month in and month out, in prosecuting their people? You have read the daily papers for the last six, eight months. You will find prosecutions in Bengal, prosecutions in Madras, prosecutions in the Punjab, prosecutions all over the country. In fact I am afraid you will soon have to open a new department and to have an additional Member to manage these prosecutions if you go on at this rate and in this way. Do you think that any man wants to go to jail? Is it an easy thing? Do you think any man wants to exceed the bounds of law for the purpose of making a speech which your law characterises as a seditious speech, knowing full well the consequences, that he may have to go to jail for six months or a year? Do you think that this springs out of a mere joke or fun or amusement? *Do you not realise yourself, if you open your eyes, that there is resentment, universal resentment, against your policy, against your programme?*

"Then, Sir, what has happened so far as this House is concerned? What have you done since 1924 with regard to the protests that we have made session after session? What is the answer in regard to the Indianisation of the Army? You appointed a Committee to go into that very important question; I attach more importance to it than to any other question. What have you done with the unanimous Report of the Skeen Committee which was endorsed by this House, without a division, the responsible House as you call it today and to which you appeal today in the name of "responsibility"? This House endorsed that Report without a division. What have you done with it? The attitude of Government has been an amazing one. The Army Secretary stood there on the floor of this House last session and said: 'We cannot get even 20 suitable candidates'. Sir, the apparent untruth of that statement is enough to condemn the Government. You cannot get 20 young men out of 300 odd millions of people, who are suitable candidates for the King's Commission? . . .

"Don't you think that, instead of trying to proceed with an iron hand and pursuing a policy of repression against your own subjects, it would be better if you realised the root causes of the resentment and of the struggle that the people are carrying on?" .

But Jinnah kept reverting to the Lahore case, again and again. It was not, obviously, a mere episode which illustrated his argument but something he felt deeply about. He pleaded with the Government. "Give these men decent treatment, and I think you will get over your difficulty. At least I hope so. If you do not, you will, at any rate, be exonerated in the eyes of the public and at the Bar of public opinion. Behave as a humane and decent Government, and that is enough for you. I am not going to urge upon the Government to withdraw prosecution cases against men if they have evidence enough to bring home to them their guilt. So try that better treatment first. Secondly, if you do not succeed, split up the trials. Try those with whose trial you can proceed, and leave the rest. After you have made it clear to them that you stand for a decent treatment being given to them and they still wish to torture themselves and follow that course, then you cannot help it; and I venture to say that it will not last very long or indefinitely.

"And the last words I wish to address the Government are, try and concentrate your mind on the root cause and the more you concentrate on the root cause the less difficulties and inconveniences there will be for you to face, and thank Heaven that the money of the taxpayer will not be wasted in *prosecuting men, nay citizens, who are fighting and struggling for the freedom of their country.*" There was no mistaking Jinnah's high esteem for Bhagat Singh and his comrades.[6]

Jinnah had, obviously, toiled hard over his speech, as the references he cited show. So, indeed, had the others; in particular, Motilal Nehru and M.R. Jayakar. True to form, Motilal Nehru tore through the cant: "It is this case which has brought the Government before this House and if anything does not apply to this case, we can reserve it for future consideration. (*laughter*) . . . When you say there can be a trial without the accused, you go against all notions of criminal law. Under the pretence of removing a lacuna in the law, you sap the very foundation of criminal justice. You may ask us for any special executive powers that you may need, but do not slander the principles of criminal jurisprudence."

From the legal he turned to the political aspect. "The Government comes before the House and says: 'We have blundered; we have not done our duty; we have blundered in our treatment of these accused people. The matter has gone so far and we are in such a mess now that we come to this House to help to extricate us from that mess by some sort of a special procedure which, whether known to the law or unknown to the law, will save us.' That is the position."

He recalled the earlier, separate letters to the authorities by Bhagat Singh and Dutt, which the authorities had ignored. As well as the joint letter read out by Diwan Chaman Lall, there was one they had addressed to the Chairman of the Punjab Jails Enquiry Committee and the Members of the Hunger-Strike Sub-Committee, dated September 6. It was sent through the Jail Superintendent. Motilal Nehru read it out, in full, to the Assembly: "Dear Sirs, We beg to bring the following to your kind notice: (1) That we did not abandon hunger-strike, but merely suspended it pending the decision of the Government. We think we made this point clear to you, and further repeatedly requested you to make it clear to the public and the Government alike. We are surprised to note that this point has not been even mentioned in the Press statement given by the members of the Hunger-Strike Sub-Committee as published in the *Civil and Military Gazette*, dated the 4th September, 1929. However, we hope you will do so at the earliest opportunity.

"(2) We suspended the hunger-strike but only on the assurance that you and the remaining members of the Inquiry Committee will make unanimous recommendations practically meeting all our demands to our satisfaction. One of us pointed out to you that Government in most of the cases in the past did not accept such recommendations of the Inquiry Committees as it did not serve their purpose, and as an instance cited the glaring instance of the Skeen Committee. We feared that the recommendations of your Committee as well might be treated in the same manner."

"In reply you said that you had consulted the Local Government before coming down to us, and that you were therefore in a position to assure us that Government would not do so in this case. It was on this clear and most important assurance that we agreed after full nine hours discussion to suspend the hunger-strike.

"Besides you gave us further assurance that in compliance with our strong desire comrade Jatindra Nath Das would be released immediately and unconditionally, in view of his critical state of health. Secondly that our demands as under-trials, the most important of which was to keep all of us together (including Comrades Bhagat Singh and Dutt) in a general association barrack, would be accepted by the Government within a day or two.

"But our fears came true when, despite the strong and unanimous recommendations of all the members of the sub-committee, the Government did neither agree to release Comrade Das nor to keep Comrades Bhagat Singh and Dutt with us. Thus we have been furnished with immediate proofs of the fact that the Government does not care for your recommendations, and we hope you will excuse us when we say we believe that *all Government wanted was to exploit your individual positions as public men in getting hunger-strike broken.* We may further mention that before we suspended our hunger-strike we carefully considered how far we could rely on the promise of the Inquiry Committee. On that, Comrades Bhagat Singh and Dutt suggested that the present occasion would serve as a test case. Now that we find that the Government has not paid any heed to even two of the most ordinary recommendations of yours, we have been forced to resume hunger-strike immediately.

"The condition of Comrade Das is now absolutely hopeless, and if the Government thinks that after his death we will shirk our duty it is a fatal mistake. Let us all state that we are all prepared to share his fate. For the sake of convenience, however, and keeping the idea of continued fight in view, we are dividing ourselves into two groups, the first of which is resuming hunger-strike at once. It is resolved that, as soon as a member of the first group meets his death, one member from the second group will come forward to fill the gap. We have arrived at this decision in full realisation of its gravity. There is no other proper and honourable course left to us now but to follow in the footsteps of our Comrade Das. We regard our cause as just and honourable, *which any fair Government would have conceded without forcing the necessity of such a serious step.* We repeat that we are going into this fight with a firm conviction that nothing can be more glorious and honourable than to fight till death for a just and noble cause. In conclusion, we feel that we fail in our duty if we do not express our heart-felt thanks for the sincere interest and great trouble that you have taken to uphold our cause before the Government."

Motilal Nehru recalled the first instance of a hunger-strike in Ireland, by Thomas Ashe in 1916. "After five days of fasting, he was reduced to the very last stage of weakness. Forcible feeding was resorted to and on the sixth or the seventh day he actually died in the hands of the prison doctor. There were others also who were on hunger-strike and why? Exactly upon the same grounds and for the same cause as these people at Lahore are now on hunger-strike." He quoted copiously from *The Life of Michael Collins*, the Irish leader who signed the Anglo-Irish Treaty of 1921 and paid for it with his life. "But although these men were guilty of the gravest crimes according to the English laws in force in Ireland, they were, according to themselves, only doing what any people would have done situated as they were. They were taken, more often than not, before the military courts. But never was a trial of these men—even by a court martial—conducted without the presence of these men."

The prisoners in Lahore "merely wanted the same treatment as was extended to European prisoners: These not being granted they went on hunger-strike. . . You say that you apply the same rules to persons who are not Europeans if they come up to the same standard. Sir, I have no respect for the man or for his mode of living or for his colour or for his station in life if he has been convicted of theft or embezzlement or some such disgraceful crime. On the other hand, I have every respect for the man who—it may be he is misguided, it may be he has acted as I would not have acted—has acted under the best of impulses and in the fullest belief that he was acting for, and in the cause of, his country."

Jayakar made important points. The Bill was not confined to some persons who revealed an *intention* to defeat and obstruct justice. It was a catch-all measure. Even in the case of absconders (covered by S. 512), it was the High Court alone which could order the trial to proceed in grave cases.

Like Jinnah, Jayakar was restrained in his comments on Emerson but Emerson's bad manners earned him sharp criticism. "He does not know what courtesy means", B. Das remarked. The U.P. Jail Enquiry Committee had opined that "No self-respecting Indian can agree to any differential or special treatment being meted out to any one in Indian Jails on the ground of his race, creed or colour, and if he finds that such treatment is sanctioned by the Government, then it is his duty to raise his voice in protest, even if his cry may be a cry in the wilderness and nothing may come out of it."

Jayakar was scathing about Emerson's defence of racialism.

"The Honourable Member from the Punjab said yesterday that a
European is defined as a man who has adopted European manners.
May I tell him—possibly he does not know—that in many places
in this country the word European is interpreted so as to give the
benefit of these humane jail rules to Chinese silk hawkers who
wear a topee, and to white complexioned loafers? Is that the
definition of a European? It has now come to this practically, and
I will say so frankly for the benefit of the Honourable Member
from the Punjab—the sole test is in practice the presence or
absence of a certain quantity of pigment in the skin of the individual.

"Let him accept this definition of the term European and I shall
thank him for his frankness. May I further point out to him what
this Committee says, that these humane provisions are common to
European and Eurasian prisoners. My Honourable friend Colonel
Gidney (who represented the Anglo-Indians) will forgive my
referring to the Eurasian community. May I know what is the
principle under which Europeans and Eurasians are classed together in the same category? What is it except the absence of
pigment in the skin, in other words, the white complexion? That
is the plain truth. It is a pure apotheosis of the white complexion."

He made a detailed comparison of the menu of the Sunday and
week day diet of European prisoners, their clothing and the furniture they were provided with what the Indian prisoner was allowed in his own country.

It was an extremely able performance. "Honourable Members
are all aware—and I do not wish to go into details—that their
main grievances are such that every Indian Member on this side of
the House will sympathise with them, whatever shade of political
opinion he may belong to. An attempt was made in this House to
show that these young men, some of whom are very bright spirits,
are fighting for a selfish purpose. May I here say—though some of
us may not agree with their political views—that if India today
were a self-governing country these intrepid and brave men would
have been the material out of which were created captains of ships
and commanders of armies."

Shortly after Jayakar had ended, Motilal Nehru rose to move

his motion for adjournment to which the House had already granted leave soon after it met that day, September 14, to resume the debate on the Bill. Jatindra Nath Das's death the previous day, the 63rd day of his strike, cast a pall on the proceedings. Jayakar described the end movingly:

He died slowly, inch by inch; one hand gone paralysed for want of sustenance, another hand gone atrophied for want of nourishment, one foot gone, another foot gone, and the last of nature's precious gifts, eyesight, gone; the fire of those orbs slowly quenched, inch by inch, not by the sudden and merciful death of the guillotine, but with the slowness with which nature builds or destroys. Oh, the anguish of this slow torture.

Many Indian members refrained from speaking lest the motion got talked out with the closing hour. Motilal declined to reply to the debate. On the question being put, the adjournment motion, which was in effect a censure motion, was carried by 55 votes against 47. Jinnah voted for the motion along with Jayakar, A. Rangaswami Iyengar, Rafi Ahmed Kidwai and Thakur Das Bhargava. Among those who voted for it, sadly, was a highly respected jurist and a man of great integrity, Dinsha F. Mulla. As a member of the Judicial Committee of the Privy Council, he was to hear Bhagat Singh's appeal against the death sentence only seventeen months later.

When the Assembly resumed debate on the Bill, on September 16, Crerar, sensing the mood of the House, agreed to its circulation. Even by the high standards of parliamentary debate that prevailed in those times, never had its leading members risen to the challenge as nobly as they did on September 12 and 14, 1929.

Jinnah's speech on those two days won him high admiration, but caused no surprise. It was of a piece with his speech on February 15, 1929 when the Assembly debated the circumstances of the death of Lala Lajpat Rai, with whom, as his biographer Feroz Chand notes, Jinnah had cordial relations, and his stand on civil liberties, generally. He pleaded for the release of Sikh leaders gaoled in connection with the Sikh Gurdwara Act (September

1925), protested against the detention without trial of Satyendra Chandra Mitra (1927), of Vallabhbhai Patel (1930) and of Sarat Chandra Bose (1935) as vehemently as he did against the internment of the Ali Brothers (1914), of Annie Besant (1917) and the detention of Maulana Hasrat Mohani (1924).

It is a matter for serious reflection in *both* countries, India and Pakistan, that some of the pro-British members of the Assembly, like Ghazanfar Ali Khan and Abdullah Haroon, who opposed the adjournment motion which Jinnah supported, became his staunch supporters a decade later when Indian politics took a fateful and tragic turn.

NOTES

1. M. Rafique Afzal (ed.), *Qaide-i-Azam M.A. Jinnah*; speeches in the Legislative Assembly of India, 1924-1930, Research Society of Pakistan, University of Punjab, Lahore, 1976.

2. Mohammed Jafar, I.A. Rehman and Ghani Jafar, *Jinnah as a Parliamentarian*, Azfar Associates, Islamabad, 1977. It contains an excellent resume of the entire historic debate.

3. *The Tribune*, September 14, 1929.

4. *L.A.D.*, 1929, Vol. IV, Part I, pp. 711-16.

5. Mohammed Jafar, I.A. Rehman and Ghani Jafar, pp. 212-13.

6. *L.A.D.*, 1929, pp. 752-55 and 757-65. See Appendix III for the text.

7

The Magisterial Farce

NEITHER the death of Jatindra Nath Das nor the ignominious defeat over the Hunger-Strike Bill produced any change in the attitude of the Government of India, from whom the Provincial Government of the Punjab took its cue, or in the behaviour of the Special Magistrate, the prosecutors and the police. The prisoners' grievances remained unredressed. They and their friends and relations were treated shabbily in court more than once.

Des Raj, who seemed to be the most enterprising of all in moving the courts, applied for bail. The application was heard on September 25. His counsel Amolak Ram Kapur said that Des Raj had been ill ever since his admission to the jail. He was suffering from some abdominal disease and piles and his temperature was throughout sub-normal in the mornings and above the normal in the evenings. He had been kept on milk diet by the jail authorities and given injections. His weight had gone down by 26 pounds. It was a fit case for the court to release the accused on bail in view of his ill-health.

Carden Noad, the Government Advocate, opposing the application, argued that the statements about the alleged ill-health of the accused were not supported by any affidavit.

Kapur wanted to reply to the arguments, but the Court ruled that he had no right of reply. He was, however, eventually permitted to do so. The accused, he submitted, was in custody and the

Court could call for a report from the jail authorities, if it desired
to satisfy itself as to the present condition of the health of the
accused. The accused wanted to be examined by a private doctor,
but he was not permitted to have that done. The Court reserved
orders on the bail application.

Recording of evidence was resumed. Pandit Sarvanand, instructor, Bharat Training College, was examined. He deposed that
Partab Singh was admitted to his College and received training for
about two months.

At this stage, Bejoy Kumar Sinha drew the attention of the
court to the fact that the accused had been shown to prosecution
witnesses by the police.

Cross-examined by Kapur, witness stated that he could not
name any other student receiving training at the college. He had
been attending court for 3 or 4 days. He was present the day before
when the accused got into the lorry on leaving the court. He saw
one or two of them.

Lala Mohan Lal was the next prosecution witness. When he
entered the witness-box; Sinha submitted to the court that the
accused were shown to that witness also, on the previous day. He
deposed that he was proprietor of the Khalsa Hindu Hotel. He also
received training at the Bharat Motor Training College when
Partab Singh was also a student there. When he fell ill, witness
used to see him, and found another young man nursing him. He
could identify both of them. He identified Mahabir Singh accused
as Partab Singh.

Cross-examined, he said he got training in driving as a hobby
for about six months. He was now part proprietor of a hotel. He
had been going every day to the Servants of the People Society
Library, located in the bungalow of Lala Lajpat Rai, for about a
month and stayed there 5 or 6 hours daily. Once, he was lying on
a charpoy in Lala Lajpat Rai's bungalow when he was asked to go
to the Reading Room or leave the place. He had come to court 3
or 4 times to give evidence and was made to sit in a room behind
the court-room.

Jai Gopal, one of the approvers, then stepped into the witness-
box escorted by a number of policemen, who stood in a line

behind him. K.S. Niaz Ahmad, Deputy Superintendent of Police, S.H. Gopal Singh, S. Pratap Singh, Chaudhri Shahab Din and other police officers, who had taken part in the investigation of the case were present in the court-room in addition to other police officers.

Defence counsel objected to the approver being examined in that atmosphere and submitted that his statement could not but be influenced by the presence of the investigating police officers in the court-room. However, the Magistrate permitted all the police officers to remain in the court room.

Bejoy Kumar Sinha and Bhagat Singh informed the Court that they were undefended and their request made the day before to be permitted to interview Feroz Chand, Secretary of the Defence Committee, with a view to making arrangements for their defence, had not been granted. They requested the Court to postpone recording the statement of the approver for a day or two, so that they might be able to arrange for their defence. They also requested the court to appoint counsel to defend them at Government expense.

The Magistrate held that he had no power to postpone proceedings in the midst of the examination of a witness. With regard to the request for the appointment of counsel to defend the accused at Government expense, he promised to refer the matter to the higher authorities because he himself had not the power to do so. In the meantime, the court ordered that the statement of Jai Gopal should be recorded. Amolak Ram Kapur protested that the Court had passed orders rejecting his application objecting to the presence in court of investigating police officers during the examination of the approver, even before the written application was submitted. He submitted that having given him time to write the application, the Court should have waited for it before passing orders.

Bejoy Kumar Sinha at this stage addressing the Court said: "You do not want to give us an opportunity to have Counsel to cross-examine the approver. Nor have you agreed to exclude the police officers who took part in the investigation of the case from the court during the examination of the approver. You have passed an order even before the written application for exclusion of the police officers was put in. You force us to the conclusion that we should not expect justice from this Court."[1]

Noad pointed out that it was not the fault of the prosecution if an accused who was defended before was now undefended. The proceedings in the case could not be held up on this account.

Sinha said they did not want to delay the proceedings. The statements of other witnesses could be recorded. They wanted only the approver to be examined after they had arranged for their defence. He requested the Court to adjourn the proceedings in order to enable him to move the High Court for transfer of the case to some other court. Some of the other accused also joined in that request. The case was accordingly adjourned until October 3.

On the same day, September 25, the Defence Committee issued an appeal for funds. It reveals, at once, the handicaps under which the defence functioned and the lack of material support from quarters who had the capacity to help. No staggering amounts were required.

"Now that the Lahore conspiracy case is once again being proceeded with from day to day, it seems necessary to call urgent public atention to the defence fund. During the last two months mass collections have been made in most of the important towns of the Province, but the total amount collected so far is too inadequate to make fullest arrangements for defence. The Defence Committee was very fortunate in securing the services of Lala Amar Das, advocate of Sialkot, at a remuneration which involved a great monetary sacrifice for him. Knowing the slender resources of the Defence Committee, Lala Amar Das accepted no fees for the past two months or so. He has also kindly promised to render occasional aid from time to time whenever necessary, even though he is no longer in charge of the defence.

"Considering the nature of the case and the large number of the accused, it can easily be seen that it is very difficult for one defence counsel to conduct the case; and, yet, it is not possible to strengthen the defence arrangements further till there is a better response from the public in the shape of money for the defence fund."[2]

On October 4, when proceedings were resumed, the accused not only raised the usual slogans "Inquilab Zindabad" and "Down with Imperialism", but sang a song on the theme *Bharat na reh sakega hargiz Ghulam Khana* (India will never remain a house of slaves). Evidence of a formal nature was recorded. A milk vendor, a couple of proprietors of hotels, a domestic servant and such.

Lala Feroze Chand, editor of the *Bandemataram* and Secretary of the Defence Committee, was summoned to give evidence for the prosecution. He said he knew Sukh Dev, accused, who, about a year and a half ago, worked for a few months as a clerk in the Manager's Department. The photographs of Bhagat Singh and Batukeshwar Dutt shown to him in court were published in the *Bandemataram* a few days after the Assembly bomb outrage. A few days after the Assembly incident a man went to witness and asked him if he was interested in publishing the photographs of Bhagat Singh and Dutt. He did not know the name of that person. His impression was that he had been sent to him on behalf of Sardar Kishan Singh, father of Bhagat Singh. Witness expressed his inclination, as a newspaper man, to publish those photographs in his paper. Two or three days later, he found two photographs at his residence. He could not say who had left them there. Nor did he find any chit along with the photographs. From those two photographs blocks were prepared which were published in the paper. He could not say if the photographs of Bhagat Singh and Dutt had appeared in any other paper before their publication in the *Bandemataram*.

Further questioned, the witness stated that he got a traced picture of Bhagat Singh on the very day of the Assembly outrage. That was taken from a group photograph of College students. He could not say whether that group photograph was delivered at his office by someone or the reporter of the paper had secured it. Cross-examined, he stated that the traced picture of Bhagat Singh was published in the *Bandemataram* on the day following the Assembly incident.

The Magistrate rejected defence counsel's application that the approvers should be removed from the police custody to that of the court. He remarked that "the proposition suggested is obviously preposterous". He also rejected a request by the accused for copies of confessional statements by the approvers.[3]

On October 2 Amolak Ram Kapur filed an application in the High Court for transfer of the case from the Special Magistrate's Court. It was to no avail.

By now the Punjab Jails Enquiry Committee had submitted its Report. On October 4, Bhagat Singh and his colleagues suspended their hunger-strike "till the final decision by the Government as regards the question of treatment of political prisoners in Indian Jails."[4] This was "in obedience to the resolution of the All-India Congress Committee and the wishes expressed in Sardar Sardul Singh's message." They did not stop there, but added: "We are very anxious that all those who hunger-struck (*sic*) in sympathy with us should also discontinue it forthwith. We here wish to point out that as special care was taken by the jail authorities about our health we have not suffered much from its evil effects like some of our other friends whose nursing was generally neglected. Under the circumstances, if for no other reason at least for the sake of such of our sympathisers whose suffering was much more acute than ours, we find it is, indeed, very embarrassing for us to continue the hunger-strike further."

A message sent by Bhagat Singh and Batukeshwar Dutt was read out to the second All-Punjab Students Conference when it met at the Bradlaugh Hall in Lahore on October 19, by its President, Subhas Chandra Bose. He said it had been received by "wireless". It said: "We cannot advise youngmen to take up bombs and pistols. The students have greater work to do. The Congress is going to declare a grim fight for the country's liberation in the coming Lahore session. At that critical moment of national history, a tremendous responsibility would rest on the shoulders of the young community.

"All over the world, students have fought till death in the front ranks of the battle for freedom. Will the Indian youths in this hour of trial hesitate to display the same grim determination? The youth have to convey the message of revolution to the farthest corner of the country, to the sweating millions in factories, slums and village huts, a revolution that will bring freedom and would render exploitation of man by man impossible. The Punjab is considered rather politically backward. (Here, Subhas Bose, as President, interjected that he questioned this and did not agree with Bhagat Singh and Dutt.) For that, the responsibility of youth is still greater. Let them prove the contrary by their unswerving fortitude and firmness in the ensuing struggle following the glorious example of our great martyr Jatindra Nath Das."[5]

Subhas Chandra Bose watched the proceedings in the case for about three hours that day, October 19, along with Baba Gurdit Singh of the Komagata Maru fame. He was, however, not allowed to meet the accused in the court-room. They had been detained for nearly an hour at the jail gate though they had been granted permits to enter the premises without search. When Amolak Ram Kapur informed the Magistrate about it, the Rai Bahadur asked whether they had come to witness the *tamasha* (farce).[6]

As soon as Bose and others entered the court-room, the accused stood up in the dock and greeted them with loud shouts of "Long Live Revolution", "Long Live Proletariat" and "Down, down with Imperialism". Bose acknowledged the greetings with folded hands. The party were given seats in the press enclosure.

The proceedings then commenced and the prosecution began to examine Mathra Dutt Joshi, D.S.P., Saharanpur.

While the examination of the witness was proceeding, Sanyal, accused, addressing the Magistrate, said:

Sanyal: Sir, I understand that Mr. Kiron Chandra Das, brother of Mr. Jatindra Das, is waiting outside. We want he should be allowed to come in.

Magistrate: I have issued the necessary pass.

Sanyal: It is an insult to our national self-respect that he should not be allowed to come in without being searched.

Bhagat Singh: There are persons who are allowed into the court without search . . . May I know what are the grounds for the search of Kiron?

Magistrate: He may be allowed but not without search.

Ajoy Kumar Ghosh: The pass was originally issued without search. But at the instance of C.I.D., it was changed.

He was informed that it was for one Karam Chand and not for

Kiron.

Ajay Kumar Ghosh: Why should Karam Chand be not searched and Kiron be?

Bhagat Singh: Why is Kiron asked to be searched, your honour?

Magistrate: Because he happens to be the brother of Jatindra Nath Das. (*laughter*)

Bhagat Singh: Then prosecute him. We don't understand your logic. It is not only an insult to him but to every Indian. You have paid homage to the memory of JatindraNath Das. Now you give a practical proof of that homage by not allowing his brother to come in.

Magistrate: You wish all persons should have been searched.

Bhagat Singh: We wish you had passed that order.

Magistrate: But he can come in.

Bejoy Kumar Sinha: You want to take vindictive steps. It is a farce of a public trial. It is unnecessary harassment.

Sanyal: If you feel helpless against the tactics of the C.I.D., you should resign. That is the most honourable course for you (*laughter*).

Magistrate: That is a good suggestion (*laughter*).

Bhagat Singh: In the morning your honour assured us about the change of attitude. But within two hours everything has changed.

Sanyal: Will the British Empire fall to pieces if Kiron is allowed in? In the Kakori case Bhai Parmanand was allowed to sit along with the accused.

Bhagat Singh: This is the impression that Mr. Bose will carry of the Punjab to Bengal!

The accused then submitted the following application to the court:

"As we are made to understand at this stage by your honour that your honour has got absolutely no control over the regulation for the admission of visitors in the Court and that the matter rests entirely in the hands of the police authorities, we request you to kindly inform us as to whom we should apply for the admission of our friends and relatives in court. Kindly be pleased to furnish us with this information immediately and enable us thereby to get permission for Mr. K.C. Das's admission.

"Further we pray that your honour be pleased to stay the proceedings till the time we are able to get the desired permission for the admission of our friends and relatives whose presence is indispensable in connection with our defence."

The accused requested the court to pass orders on the application immediately.

The Government Advocate said there was no wrong about search. Why should this be made a grievance? This was not a matter concerning him or the Magistrate. It rested with the police.

Bhagat Singh: The Magistrate is not expected to be a puppet in the hands of the police. The police is under his authority.

Ajoy Kumar Ghosh: It would be better if a police officer sits in the chair and not the Magistrate.

Bhagat Singh: We are making the Punjab's position ridiculous. In spite of so many sacrifices made by the Punjabis, the weakness, as shown by the Magistrate, is responsible for the backwardness of the Punjab.

Court: The coming from outside is regulated by the police.

Bhagat Singh: Sir, Kiron is coming to the Court and not to a police station. The order of the Magistrate is to be obeyed by the police and not that of the police by the Magistrate. It means that in future we should apply to Khan Bahadur Abdul Aziz and not to your honour.

Amar Das, Defence Counsel, said the Court might make its position clear.

Kapur said, "Let us know where we stand."

Magistrate: Searches are being made under the orders of the Executive. I have no hand in the matter.

The Court passed the following order on the application of the accused: "Searches are controlled by the police outside."

The accused said the Court should also state in its order whether it had control over the police or not. Amar Das then said the question is whether you have or have not control over the police. If you have, write it down.

Bhagat Singh: Your honour, this question should be decided first.

Magistrate: You may understand in any manner you like. I will go on with the evidence.

Bejoy Kumar Sinha: Then note down our objection.

The Court said the objection should be made in writing.

The accused, thereupon, submitted a petition. The Magistrate, however, proceeded with the recording of evidence.

The accused's application stated:

"The question that has just cropped up for decision is whether the admission and searches of the visitors is conducted under orders of the court or the police. The court was requested to decide the matter so that there may be no misunderstanding. The court has, after considerable hesitation, passed the following order: "Searches are controlled by the police outside." So far the court has been issuing passes directing searches of persons in some cases and not in the others. But now the learned Magistrate says he has nothing to do with the question of search. The points on which we pray your honour to make definite orders are:

"(1) Is it at the discretion of the court or the police to search and admit a person coming to court?

(2) If the searches and admission are at the discretion of the police authorities, is it without control of the court?

Orders on the application were not passed and the case was proceeded with.

The accused also asked the court to allow them an interview with Subhas Bose. "The matter was not decided immediately; and it appears that the Government Advocate consulted the higher authorities—on the phone, and communicated the orders to the court."

The Magistrate informed the accused that the order of the Executive was that interviews could only be allowed by the Jail Superintendent and so the application should be made to him.

Bejoy Kumar Sinha: May I understand that it is the local Government who control interviews? Are you helpless in the matter?

Magistrate: My orders were and are I can't grant interviews in court.

Bejoy Kumar Sinha: A great principle is involved in the matter.

Magistrate: Interviews are regulated according to the Jail Manual.

Bejoy Kumar Sinha: In this court also.

Bhagat Singh: This is court and not jail. It is your court-room. We will be in the jurisdiction of the jail authorities in the evening.

As the interview with the accused was not allowed, Mr. Bose and Dr. and Mrs. Dharamvir left the court at about 2 p.m. Baba Gurdit Singh followed a few minutes later.

The accused raised their usual slogans when Bose and others left the place.

Towards the close of the proceedings, the court passed the following order: "All applications for interviews with the accused during the interval are to be submitted to court before the proceedings start. As to the food it should be handed over half an hour before lunch." The time of lunch was fixed from 1.30 to 2 p.m.

The accused asked that orders should be passed on the second application, submitted by them, regarding the admission to the court-room.

The Magistrate said: "Entries to the court-room are regulated by the executive. I can't discuss the question. So far as I know never has any person been refused admission. It is not for the accused to question the propriety of my orders."

All the remaining witnesses whose evidence related to the alleged recovery of bombs, etc., at Saharanpur, were examined by the prosecution.

Pandit Mathra Dutt Joshi, D.S.P., gave an account of the raid on the mysterious house wherefrom, according to him, bombs, shells, chemicals, some objectionable books etc. were recovered.

Cross-examined by Mr. Amar Das who also appeared for the accused, witness said before proceeding to the house from where the bombs etc. were recovered, he had entered in the Police *roznamcha*: "Received secret information. I am going to the spot lest the accused should abscond." Before starting the search of the house, he did not record the reasons why he was going to search.

Witness admitted that the Criminal Procedure Code provided that reasons should be recorded prior to the search. But when the bombs were recovered there was, he said, no need of recording reasons. The recovery of one article led to the search of other articles.

The book "Bande Jiwan", which witness saw in that house, was not read by him. He had seen it while in the C.I.D. He had not read the book after it was recovered from that house.

Q. When you had not read the book, how did you say to the accused, when you found that book in their house, that its study would turn their head? You knew it because you had come from the Intelligence Branch.

A. I said this, because it dealt with revolutionary literature. My impression was that it has been proscribed.

Q. What was the source of your information that the book dealt with revolutionary literature? Was your knowledge derived from some man or document?

The question was objected to by the prosecution, but was allowed by court.

A. I had read in the C.I.D. books that this book is revolutionary. I had also talked about it with some officials.

The Magistrate's replies could not have inspired confidence in his independence. The accused, on their part, made no effort to conceal their distrust of him. Matters came to a head two days later, on October 21. One of the accused, Prem Dutt Verma, threw a slipper at the approver, Jai Gopal, who was in the witness-box. He was sentenced to three months' solitary confinement by the Jail Superintendent.[7]

Although the other accused expressed regret, the Magistrate ordered, the next day, that all the accused should be brought to court with hand-cuffs on both hands. The practice hitherto was to bring them from the Borstal Jail in hand-cuffs on only one hand, which were removed as soon as they entered the dock. Bhagat Singh and Dutt, who were lodged in the Central Jail, used to come to the court-room without any hand-cuffs. On October 22, however, the police tried to hand-cuff the two at the gate of the Central Jail which faced the court-room. They refused to go to Court. The Borstal prisoners also refused to submit to the new order. But they were brought to the porch of the Borstal Institute and forcibly handcuffed. Only six of the accused—Pandha, Agya Ram, Ajoy Ghosh, Gaya Parsad, Shiv Varma and Kamal Nath Tewari could be thrown into the lorry forcibly. When it reached the Central Jail, they refused to come out and were taken back.

But while they were at the gate of the Central Jail, Tewari managed to tell all who were present there, the press included, what had happened. They had been caned and abused. Some had received injuries. All had been roughly handled. The case was adjourned for the day; but the stage had been set for an ugly confrontation. It happened the very next afternoon.

After the lunch interval, the accused returned to the court-room with hand-cuffs on both their hands. They had been forcibly hand-cuffed and virtually dragged and thrown into the dock. Shiv Varma and Ajoy Ghosh, already enfeebled, became unconscious. Bhagat Singh and Dutt were gasping as they were brought to court in clothes besmeared with dust.[8] When they were brought in that condition to the dock, the atmosphere in the court-room, which was relaxed upto this time, became tense. The other accused received them with shouts of "Long Live Revolution", "Long Live the Proletariat" and "Down with Imperialism".

Immediately afterwards, Bhagat Singh angrily addressed the Magistrate and said: "Have you ordered the police to kick us? Can't you control the police? (Some of the accused cried out "shame, shame".) We were doing passive resistance and they were kicking us.

Magistrate: Who kicked you?

Bhagat Singh: These police officers. Several persons were sitting on us and kicking on all parts of our body.

Batukeshwar Dutt, who spoke in court today for the first time, also complained of having been very badly handled by the police. He said, "I have received severe blows on my chest." At this stage most of the accused said that they had been roughly handled by the police the day before.

Prem Dutt: Yesterday fingers were thrown in our rectum and kicks were given on our testicles. Is it civilization? You call it civilization? The time will come when we will turn revolutionaries.

Carden Noad, the Government Advocate, asked the court to note down the last sentence. The Court agreed.

Bejoy Kumar Sinha: I want to make a statement.

Magistrate: The time for a statement has not come. You may give it in writing.

Bhagat Singh: We were treated in that way by the police, acting under your orders.

Bejoy Kumar Sinha: I have got 102 fever. I cannot write.

Batukeshwar Dutt: I have got ample pain in my chest. I can't sit here.

Bhagat Singh: You are here, but you refuse to record our statement.

Magistrate: This is not the time.

Bhagat Singh: When will it be? You have passed orders without recording our statement. Is this how you are acting in accordance with the High Court's ruling to keep at an arm's length from the police and the prosecution? He added that as both their hands were handcuffed, it was not possible for them to make a written statement.

Bhagat Singh: Why have we been handcuffed? Is it under your orders?

Magistrate: Yes.

Bhagat Singh: Why?

Magistrate: Because there was danger to everybody here.

Bhagat Singh: How many have died?

Magistrate: Don't discuss the matter with me. I won't argue with you.

Bhagat Singh: A few days ago you paid a tribute to our reasonable attitude. You appreciated it. Why should we have been made to suffer for the mistake of one?

Sanyal: We dissociated ourselves from that act and expressed regret. It is unjust to order us to be handcuffed in that way.

Bhagat Singh: Your attitude, Mr. Magistrate, is most absurd. You refused to record our statement. I want to move the High Court. Will you note that we are going to the High Court?

Government Advocate: That is noted.

Bhagat Singh: I want to give a written statement. Will you please order that one of my handcuffs be removed?

Magistrate: I can't at this time.

Sinha asked the Magistrate to permit him to make a statement on behalf of the unrepresented accused, but did not fare better.

The Magistrate asked the prosecuting counsel, Gopal Lal, to proceed with the examination of witnesses.

October 23 was fixed by mutual arrangement for the cross-examination of Dr. Robson, Inspector of Explosives in India, Calcutta. But as his examination-in-chief took place before the accused Raghunath alias 'M' was brought in, the prosecution decided to examine him again.

Handcuffs on one of the hands of the accused were removed in the court-room and they were taken for lunch to a *shamiana*, pitched outside in the court compound for the purpose.

After lunch, the situation took a critical turn. The accused were prepared to come back to the court with handcuffs on only one hand. But the police wanted to handcuff both of their hands. They refused to submit to that.

Great excitement prevailed in the court-room, especially when the police constables were summoned to the court compound.

Bejoy Kumar Sinha returned to the dock and, addressing the Magistrate, said that the accused had come to the court without offering any resistance with the object of explaining their position. In the morning they were given an assurance that if they came to the court without resistance, their handcuffs would be removed.

The Government Advocate said that no assurance was given. Sinha then said that they refused to be handcuffed. They were not going to be handcuffed for the fault of one. The Magistrate should have made enquiries before passing any order. But he had not done so.

When the accused definitely refused to come to court with handcuffs on both hands, the police authorities decided to handcuff them forcibly. Several accused were seen in the court compound, lying prostrate on the ground, and overpowered by a number of policemen, who were handcuffing them. They were then bodily removed to the dock. Some of them were lifted up, while others were virtually dragged. In not a few cases, they were thrown into the dock from over the benches, without caring whether they would get hurt or not. Some of them were hurt and were gasping. As the number of accused was sufficiently large, it took a considerable time to bring all of them in. Those brought later were thrown, in some cases, one over the other, at the entrance of the dock. They continued lying there for some time. Shiv Varma and Ajoy Kumar Ghosh became unconscious. Several accused remained in a semi-conscious condition for a time. While this scene was being enacted in the court-room, an accused addressing the Magistrate, said: "Thank you very much. This is happening in your presence."

Magistrate: They themselves are responsible for it.

Bhagat Singh: I want to congratulate you for this. You don't listen to us, and this trouble is due to that. This thing is going on under your very nose.

Moments later, Bhagat Singh added: "Shiv Varma is lying unconscious. If he dies, you will be responsible for it."

At this stage, the Senior Superintendent of Police asked the press representatives to "clear out" and they were made to leave the court-room. The visitors were also asked to go. Counsel came out a few minutes later. While the press representatives were standing in the court compound, the police officers asked them to go out, as the case had been adjourned. They could not, therefore, watch the later developments.

About 15 minutes later, shouts of "Long Live the Revolution", "Long Live the Proletariat" and "Down with Imperialism", raised by the accused while leaving the dock were heard outside.

Fortunately, an amicable settlement was arrived at on the following day, October 24. It was agreed that both sets of accused, the two in Central Jail and the rest in the Borstal, would be brought to court with handcuffs on only one hand. The prosecution had its own reason for relenting. Its explosives expert, Dr. Robson, was due to leave for London. In view of the High Court's ruling and the collapse of the Hunger-Strike Bill, he could not be examined in the absence of the accused.[9]

Bhagat Singh rose to make a statement describing in detail how the confrontation arose and what he and his colleagues had undergone. It bears quotation at some length for it brings out sharply the behaviour of the minions of the Raj: "I understand you want us to express regret. There appears to be no necessity for it. After submitting our written application, dissociating ourselves from the act of an individual and expressing regret for it, we thought it would not be necessary in order to calm down the atmosphere, we are prepared to repeat the expression of regret. But it should not imply that we are in any way responsible for that incident."

The Magistrate said he (Bhagat Singh) had, the day before, cried out "shame, shame". It was necessary that they should give an assurance that no untoward event would happen in future.

Bhagat Singh, in reply, said that he had uttered "shame, shame" at the time when his whole body was awfully aching as the result of beating. Both, he and Dutt, were given a severe beating near the jail gate. They were thrown in the dock like baggage. After lunch they were again given a severe beating. A European Police officer, probably Roberts was his name, standing near him, was saying "This is the man, give him more beating." The result of all this beating was that he could not sleep last night. Dutt spent the whole night sitting. It was necessary to explain the position and therefore he had asked that his statement should be recorded. They, the accused, also required that an assurance should be given to them that such a thing would not happen again and that they would not be treated in the manner in which they were actually treated by the police. "Apart from the question of handcuffing", he concluded, "the police had definite orders to beat us. Whom should we complain? I request this fact may also go on the record."[10]

Bejoy Kumar Sinha said that as he was suffering from fever, it was not possible for him to submit his statement in writing. He, therefore, requested the Court to record his statement.

He said: "Extraordinary events have taken place during the last few days and before this case proceeds, it is essential, in the interests of the accused as well as the court, to get the matters settled so that the case may henceforth proceed in an atmosphere of trust and right and clear understanding.

"At the outset, I will begin by relating the incident that happened on Monday last. Jai Gopal, approver was brought in and he began his statement. Just after 2 or 3 minutes he, in a provoking (*sic*) manner, uttered: 'I personally feel, at the instance of the prosecution, the words *Janab ye ap ke kiye huye hain, aur sachchi hain.* (These acts have been committed by you and are true.) This utterance was very provoking (*sic*) and one of us, Prem Dutt—the youngest of all—got excited and in the heat of the moment threw a slipper at the approver. Thereafter the learned prosecuting counsel pointed out that there was danger to the lives of those present in court and that the court should adjourn the proceedings. Before the learned Magistrate passed the order for adjournment, I, Bhagat Singh and others wanted to make a statement regarding the regrettable incident as there was much scope for misunderstanding. The learned Magistrate did not give us an opportunity to get our statement recorded. We, therefore, hastened to file a written statement—the only course left for us—making it clear that all of us dissociated ourselves from the act committed by one individual. After that petition was made, I think, there was no reason why we should be made to suffer for the act of one."[11]

The next day, proceeded Sinha, the accused in the Borstal Jail were surprised to learn that an order had been issued that they should be taken to the court with handcuffs on both hands. They refused to come to the court in that manner. At first they were allowed to return to their cells. But after some time they were again summoned to the Jail portico. There were present a strong party of policemen and jail warders, about 300 in number, most of them were armed. The accused, once again, refused to come to the court with handcuffs on both hands.

"Thereupon", Bejoy Kumar Sinha said, "Mr. Hardinge ordered the policemen, and Inspectors to get us handcuffed by any means. The constables and Inspectors pounced upon us, and began assaulting us. Each of us was assaulted by at least 20 to 25 policemen. The method of assault was most inhuman and unheard of."

Fingers, continued Sinha, were put in their rectum and kicks were given on their testicles. They were also kicked systematically. "All the time we were strictly non-violent because we realised the unequal forces that were at work. We knew all the while that all we could do was to gain a moral victory and in the position in which we stood—15 against 300 armed police—we could not do otherwise. The struggle continued for more than an hour, and the police were able to bring only six of us in the lorry to this court.

"As the result of the severe injuries, received that day, five of us—myself, Des Raj, Mahabir Singh, Gaya Prasad and Kishori Lal—got fever. All the others had acute pain in different parts of their body. Mahabir Singh and Rajguru had fallen senseless on the spot. During assaults, canes were also freely used. Marks can still be seen on the bodies of some of us—especially Rajguru. I pray the court may examine him just now."

Bhagat Singh also wanted to make a statement but the court asked him to do so later and continued with the recording of evidence of Dr. Robson, the explosives expert.

The proceedings went on smoothly. Handcuffs of the accused were later removed. Robson gave his evidence and was cross-examined by Amar Das.

At long last, four months after the trial began, the first substantive witness, the approver Jai Gopal gave substantive evidence in court. He gave an account of different meetings of the members of the revolutionary society and identified a pistol and revolver, exhibited in court, which, he said, were used by Bhagat Singh and Rajguru *alias* "M" respectively in assassinating Saunders. The approver also described the plan which, he said, the members of the Society had made to commit dacoity at the Punjab National Bank in the beginning of December 1928, which had to be abandoned.

Since he repeated at the trial the evidence he gave in these committal proceedings it is unnecessary to record it in any detail here. Suffice it to say that he described in detail how Saunders was murdered and the preparations that preceded the act.

He mentioned an interesting aftermath. Three or four days after the murder, the witness proceeded to Ferozepur and remained there till the 30th or 31st December, 1928. He returned to Lahore again and met Sukh Dev on the 1st January, 1929. Sukh Dev, Kishori Lal and the witness went to the canal bridge on the Ferozepur Road. At that time the motor car No. 6728, carrying Scott, his wife, a driver and an orderly, passed that way. He suggested to Sukh Dev that Scott could now be fired at. Sukh Dev replied that it was no use shooting him, as luck had saved him once.

This has passed muster even with scholars of repute. Sukh Dev denied it in a marginal note to the proceedings, as we shall see.

Vigilant as ever, Bhagat Singh complained to the Magistrate on October 28 about misstatements in the record of the proceedings of October 23. The accused had not said that "the Magistrate should remember that the days of revolution are not gone and that the revolutionaries would take revenge, etc." They did not object to the first part, on principle. But what was actually said was "By such brutalities, inhuman treatment and barbarous torture, you cannot kill our spirit. The Government will soon learn that they are dealing with revolutionaries, etc." Also, there was no reference in the record to the beating given the other day.

On November 5 Kanwal Nath Tiwari made a formal application recording the happenings on October 22 and 23. Bejoy Kumar Sinha, while associating himself with it, sarcastically asked the Magistrate as to whom they were to send their applications: It would be better, he said, if the Magistrate informed them as to who were those executive officers to whom the accused's applications were forwarded, so that they might not give any trouble whatever to this court.

Magistrate: I send these petitions to the District Magistrate.

Sinha: Will your honour kindly introduce me to the District Magistrate (*laughter*).

Sinha enquired as to what had happened to their application which was already given.

Magistrate: I forwarded it to the District Magistrate. There is no reply received yet. I am helpless.

Sinha had another complaint to make on November 7: "We are told that several college students are waiting outside the prison gate, and their applications have been torn off by the police. We also understand that in several cases, students have been refused admission on the ground that there is no proof of the Principals of their colleges having permitted them to attend this court. This is scandalous. The proceedings are supposed to be public." The Magistrate, as ever, promised to look into the matter. Admission to the court-room remained severely restricted, throughout.[12]

It was an important hearing. Two Magistrates, Chaudhri Roshan Lal and Ram Lal Anand, deposed to the parades held for the identification of the accused.

Chaudhri Roshan Lal, Magistrate, Lahore, deposed that on May 27 last he held an identification parade for the identification of Agya Ram and Sukh Dev, who were mixed up with fourteen other persons of approximately the same age and size. The accused were asked whether they had any objection against any of their associates, who had been mixed up with them, but they said they had none. The accused were also given the option of changing clothes with anyone. Agya Ram changed his *dhoti* and shirt with Ram Parshad. Sukh Dev had a growth of hair on his chin, and a barber was sent for to shave him. The identifying persons reached the District Police Lines after the witness and were seated at a distance of about 300 yards from the accused. There was no chance of the accused of being shown to them. Ram Sahai identified Sukh Dev. Manga Mal failed to identify anyone. Hira Lal identified Sukh Dev as a man who had been visiting his hotel. Khushi Ram identified wrong persons and failed to identify either of the accused. Kapura Ram and Dina Nath failed to identify either of the accused.

There were altogether 18 witnesses at the parade. The result of the proceedings was embodied in a memorandum which the Magistrate produced in court. On the same day, another parade was held at the Railway Police Line for the identification of Kishori Lal. Of the eleven witnesses, six failed to identify him, while the other five did, correctly.

Q. Was the accused made to change his position after each identification?

A. It is not stated in the memorandum. I think the accused must have been given that option. I do not remember whether the accused did avail himself of that option.

Another identification parade was held on June 7, 1929, at the Lahore Fort, for the identification of Shiv Varma. Jai Gopal identified him and stated that he had seen him at Ferozepore. Jai Gopal wept copiously and embraced the accused. Hans Raj Vohra failed to identify the accused. On the same day another identification parade was held at the District Police Lines, at which Jai Gopal and Hans Raj Vohra failed to identify Jai Deva Kapur.

After describing other identification parades, the Magistrate deposed that on June 24, he accompanied Mahabir Singh to various places in Lahore which the latter wished to point out. Mahabir Singh had already made a statement before R.S. Lala Nathu Ram, City Magistrate, Lahore under Section 164, Cr.P.C. The witness warned the accused that he was not bound to point out the places, and that any statement made by him might be used against him. The accused, however, said he was acting voluntarily.

Further questioned, the witness enumerated the various hotels and other places to which the accused Mahabir Singh took him to show where the several accused persons stayed or took their meals. The accused, amongst other places, showed the room in the Arain Building and pointed to bullet marks on a wall. He produced the memorandum which he had prepared on the occasion. The memorandum was signed by Mahabir Singh who also pointed to the Punjab National Bank and stated that they would have raided it but they could not drive the car hired for the purpose.

Ram Lal Anand, Magistrate, described the identification parade held at Lahore Cantonment on May 26 under his supervision for the identification of Bhagat Singh. Atta Mohammed identified Bhagat Singh as the man who had removed the bicycle with another man. Aftab Ahmad identified the accused, saying he had seen Bhagat Singh in the D.A.V. College Volleyball Ground on the day of the Saunders' murder. Kamal Din and Abdullah identified him as the person seen by them in front of the District Police Office on the day of the murder. Chaudhari Habibullah identified the accused and said he had seen him assault Saunders. Ganda Singh and Wahid-ud-Din identified the accused and said they had seen him in the chowk opposite the Police Office. Chet Singh, Gosain Kanshi Ram, Hari Nath, Pat Ram, Sardari Lal, Gurkirpal Singh, Mohammed Nadir, Amolak Ram, Ghota Mal, Hari Lal Mukhi, Sundar Das, Gajju Ram, Mohammed Din, Ajmer Singh and Dina Nath did not identify the accused. Out of the 32 witnesses only 15 were able to identify him. On May 30, witness held another parade at the same place. Out of seven witnesses only one witness, constable Ibrahim, identified Bhagat Singh and said he had seen him running away with another person after Saunders' murder followed by Chanan Singh. The other six, namely, Champat Rai, Ganga Bushan, Gurbachan Singh, Amritsarya, Gyanchand and Fearne failed to identify the accused.

After Jai Gopal, it was Hans Raj Vohra's turn to spill the beans which he did on November 26. He had been tendered pardon by the District Magistrate and made his confessional statement to the City Magistrate from May 21 to 23. Admission was even more strictly restricted. So much so that the visitors' gallery was almost empty. The accused had earlier objected to the position of the witness-box. It was placed immediately behind the seats of the prosecution counsel and witnesses could read their statements which the Crown Counsel held in his hand while examining them as well as hear the remarks which the prosecuting counsel made amongst themselves during the examination or cross-examination of witnesses.

This fact had been brought to the notice of the court several times. On every occasion Crown Counsel had protested that they did not desire to tamper with witnesses. There can, however, be little doubt that any witness whose powers of sight and hearing were normal could read the papers which counsel held in his hands, while conducting the examination in chief, as well as hear the remarks made by Crown Counsel on the replies given by the witness to questions put to him during cross-examination.

Bhagat Singh asked the Magistrate what orders had been passed on the application of Bejoy Kumar Sinha regarding the admission of visitors to the court-room.

Court: Admission of students?

Bhagat Singh: No. Visitors in general.

Bejoy Kumar Sinha: On the 24th October, when our handcuffs were removed, you gave us a promise that all facilities would be given to us. Now, in spite of your assurance, we understand that we are to be prosecuted for disobeying the order to come to the court that day.

Bhagat Singh: Sir, the assurance was given by you to Mr. Amolak Ram Kapur, Advocate.

Court: The order on the application filed on Saturday, was: 'The general order of this court regarding non-admission of students to the court room does not in any way concern the accused or the conduct of prosecution. Copies of any such orders cannot be granted, not being a part of judicial proceedings.'

Bhagat Singh: If accused, some of whom are students, are allowed in the dock, why should not the students be allowed in the visitors' gallery? Section 352, Criminal Procedure Code, says that the place where any criminal court is held "shall be deemed an open court to which the public generally may have access so far as the same can conveniently contain them." Under that Section you cannot stop any particular class of the public from having access to the court-room. Your order is, therefore, illegal. Moreover, some of the accused are students, and their student friends who take interest in the case should be allowed admission. I will, therefore, request you, Sir, to reconsider your order.

The court did not accept the request.

Vohra's evidence was on expected lines. He had been recruited by Sukh Dev who functioned as his handler, as it were. Like Jai Gopal, he also repeated his deposition at the trial.

Those were troubled times. The defence cause was not exactly helped when it was learnt that two of the absconders in the case, Bhagwati Charan and Yashpal, had tried to wreck the Viceroy's train. A "flex" wire was laid under a sleeper, buried three inches in the ground and connected to a battery and switch hidden near the Purana Qila in Delhi. Yashpal exploded the mine on December 23, 1929, while the conspiracy case trial was in progress. The Viceroy who was on the train, however, escaped unhurt. There was no loss of life.[13]

The next approver to be examined was Manmohan Bannerjee followed by Phonindra Ghosh.

On January 24, 1930 the accused entered the court with "red" scarves around their necks raising slogans appropriate for the occasion. "Long Live Lenin" was one of them. It was Lenin Day. Tongue firmly in cheek, Bhagat Singh handed over the Magistrate a telegram to be forwarded to the President of the Third International, Moscow. It read: "On the occasion of the Lenin Day, we express our hearty congratulations on the triumphant and onward march of Comrade Lenin's success for the great experiment carried on in the Soviet Russia. We wish to associate ourselves with the world revolution movement. Victory to the workers' regime. Woe to capitalism. Down with Imperialism."

The Magistrate said he would forward the telgram to the executive authorities for necessary action. Bhagat Singh requested the court to get an immediate reply whether the authorities were willing to despatch the telegram or not. He informed the court that the accused were prepared to pay full charges for the transmission. He hoped that it should not meet the same fate as the telegram addressed to the President of the Political Sufferers' Conference on the Kakori Day.[14]

The accused learnt from some witnesses how their secrets were unravelled. One of them was a cast-iron moulder at Bandreth Road in Lahore, Mistri Jalaluddin, who gave evidence that day. About a year ago, in the month of Ramadhan, a tall young man came to the witness's shop with five articles and asked him to prepare plugs for them and screw threads for their inside.

After 5 or 6 days, the same person came again and brought five more parts and they were also made ready. The next day, when he came to take them, the witness's son inquired of him as to what machine these parts related. The young man replied that a new gas machine was being invented and that they were parts of that new machine.

After about a week he came again along with another young man who was squint-eyed. He brought ten parts of the same size for which identical work was to be done. He asked the witness to hand over the parts to his companion when ready.

The day following, when the witness's son was at work, Haji Mohammed Hussain arrived and enquired of him as to what he was doing. His son replied that he was preparing parts of a new gas machine. He asked the witness's son to make further inquiries as to what the parts related and instructed him not to take up such work. Those parts were handed over to the squint-eyed young man later on.

A few days later, Nur Shah, a C.I.D. constable, arrived and began to smoke *hukka*. To the witness's query as to where he was working, he replied that he was posted in the special C.I.D. staff investigating the Ramlila Bomb case. The witness pointed out to him that certain young men were getting strange parts of a machinery made at his shop. Nur Shah arrived the day after and told the witness that his son was wanted by the Superintendent of Police. On his return, the witness's son said that the Superintendent of Police wanted him to follow the young man who got those parts prepared by them and find out his house.

After a few days the young man came again and the witness prepared for him an iron stand with bars. The witness's son followed him quietly and on return informed him that the house was situated in Kashmiri Buildings. Next day, when Nur Shah arrived, the witness's son showed him the house.

About a week later they heard that a bomb factory had been discovered by the Police. He said that it was in the same house which was pointed out by his son to the C.I.D. constable, Nur Shah. He was shown some bomb-shells in the court. He identified the plugs and screws prepared by him and said that he had prepared 20 such parts in all.

The witness was asked to go to the dock and identify the accused. He replied that since a year had passed he would not hazard that task. He was exposed to ridicule in the cross-examination by Amar Dass as an ignoramus. But the details he gave went on record. One comment is in order. Even if the bombs had not been thrown, Mistri Jalaluddin's disclosures might well have exposed the plot. But the bombs in the Assembly assisted the police enormously.

The issue of political prisoners' privileges was revived when Bhagat Singh sent telegrams to the Home Member on January 20 and 28, 1930. The latter read "Suspended hunger-strike on assurance given by the Jail Committee that the question of the treatment of political prisoners was going to be finally settled to our satisfaction within a very short period. Copies AICC Resolutions regarding hunger-strike withheld by jail authorities. Authorities refused Congress deputation to meet the prisoners. The conspiracy-case under-trials were assaulted brutally on 23rd and 24th October, 1929, by the orders of the high police officials.

Sd/-
Bhagat Singh, Dutt and others."[15]

The Committee's Report was none too satisfactory. As a note of dissent by one of the members, Chaudhri Afzal Haq, noted: "The Committee have created a class distinction which is equally, if not more, harmful than the racial distinction. The new principle that the criminals may be treated inside the jail, not according to their motive or character of their offence, but in accordance with their mode of life and social status, education or character propounds a novel theory and is absolutely against the accepted principle of jail administration all over the world."[16]

Meanwhile, there had occurred yet another ugly incident in court. Lala Duni Chand, a barrister and a senior member of the High Court Bar, was legal adviser to Bhagat Singh. On January 29, he was allowed to take his seat neither among defence counsel, nor as a member of the Bar elsewhere, nor even in the press gallery. He walked out of the court in protest at what was clearly a calculated insult to him and a provocation to the accused. Thereupon, all of them who were represented by counsel withdrew their authority and refused to take part in the proceedings.

The exchanges, reported fully in *The Tribune* of January 31, 1930, show to what a pass a petty-minded prosecutor and a spineless judge could bring judicial proceedings. Duni Chand, legal adviser of Bhagat Singh, had a short conversation with Bhagat Singh before the commencement of the proceedings. Noad, Government Advocate, enquired from the court for whom Duni Chand was appearing. Duni Chand informed the court that he was the legal adviser of accused Bhagat Singh. Noad said that Duni Chand had no 'locus standi' as legal adviser, though, he said, he could sit as counsel representing the accused.

Duni Chand said that he also represented all the accused who were represented by Amar Dass. He, therefore, not only acted as legal adviser of Bhagat Singh but also represented the accused. The Government Advocate again repeated his objection and said that Duni Chand could sit there only if he represented the accused.

As legal adviser, he said, could not be allowed. He could see the accused in Jail.

Amar Dass: Let us know whether we are in prison or in court. We are not in prison, then why are we punished for our offences in court by the Jail authorities?

Bhagat Singh: I want a definite ruling whether Duni Chand could remain in this court and watch the proceedings.

The Magistrate passed an order to the effect that there was nothing as legal adviser in law. Therefore, Duni Chand could not sit with counsel in that capacity.

Lala Duni Chand then enquired from the court whether as a member of the High Court Bar, he could sit there when the sign plate "For members of the Bar only" had been fixed on the pillar behind.

The Magistrate said that the sign plate was meant only for Lala Amar Dass and Baljit Singh, defence counsel and it did not empower any other member of the Bar to sit there.

Duni Chand enquired whether he could sit behind the Press reporters' table. The Magistrate replied that he could not. He could only sit in the visitors' gallery as a visitor.

Lala Duni Chand said that he was a member of the Bar and as such he claimed his right to sit there.

Magistrate: No! You can not sit there.

Duni Chand: In no part of the world the members of the Bar have been treated in the manner in which they are treated in this court. I strongly protest against this treatment and I walk out of the court.

Lala Duni Chand then walked out of the court.

Jatin Sanyal (accused): This is an insult to the High Court Bar. Had it been Calcutta, things would have been different and the members of the Bar would not have tolerated this insult.

Bhagat Singh: The proceedings are entirely highhanded and the prosecution and the Government and court are not giving us opportunity for defence. This is negation of justice. This highhandedness does not mean anything else, except that we should be hanged. If that is the desire of the Government we are prepared for it. If the country has any spirit, it will see to it. If we are going to be deprived of all facilities for defence and if we are to be treated in this manner, we don't want to produce any defence. Whatever is happening in this court is nothing but a farce. Let the British Government be proud of this justice. We have nothing to do with this case. I declare on behalf of the accused in court that they withdraw their representation. Let the civilised world know what this Government is doing. We are prepared to be hanged.

After this all accused who were represented by L. Amar Dass announced in court that they withdrew representation and that they refused to be defended by L. Amar Dass any further.

L. Amar Dass enquired from the court whether under changed conditions he could sit there any longer. He said that he had been appointed by the Defence Committee and wanted to watch the case on behalf of the committee. The Government Advocate said as far as he was concerned he had no objection in Amar Dass's sitting there on behalf of the Defence Committee.

Bhagat Singh: Lala Amar Dass cannot sit here when my legal adviser is not allowed. The Defence Committee is a third party.

Jatin Sanyal: Let us see how far is the court consistent.

Magistrate (to L. Amar Dass): Have you withdrawn representation?

Amar Dass: No Sir! Accused have withdrawn their representation. I want you to allow me to sit here and watch the proceedings.

Magistrate: I allow you to sit.

Jatin Sanyal: Sir! What was your order about Duni Chand? How can you allow L. Amar Dass to sit here?

Bhagat Singh: If Duni Chand cannot be allowed, how can L. Amar Dass be allowed? Please don't reduce all proceedings to a farce.

Magistrate: Then Lala Amar Dass can also go away.

Bhagat Singh: Let your order be read out.

Magistrate: Sit down. You cannot fight with me.

Prem Dutt (accused): Here we are under the jurisdiction of jail. You have no authority over us (*laughter*).

Bhagat Singh: Let the court supply us with both its orders and let the High Court know of the absurd attitude of this court. This is justice . . .

The accused then held consultations amongst them for a few minutes. After consultations Bhagat Singh addressed the court on behalf of all the accused and said: "I am instructed by all my comrades to request you to send us back to jail and proceedings may be carried on in our absence. Let us sit in peace in jail and let the proceedings also go on here in peace."

Amar Dass: We are spectators and are watching the proceedings.

Bhagat Singh: Then what is the order?

Magistrate: But, what you request is unreasonable.

Bhagat Singh: If it is not reasonable then we inform you that we shall refuse to come to court from tomorrow.

Bejoy Kumar Sinha: I also associate with the request made by S. Bhagat Singh. The proceedings in this court have been most unfair to us. We have been deprived of all facilities for defence which had been given to similar cases. Everything had been unprecedented in this court. If the court is bent upon not giving us any facilities, then we have no other course left than refuse to take any further part in the proceedings of the case. These facilities are our right and we demand our right. We are helpless for today but from tomorrow we will not come to the court.

At this stage Bhagat Singh enquired from the Magistrate if he would go on with the examination of the approver, who had been waiting in the witness-box for a long time. The court replied in affirmative. But before the witness could be proceeded with Bhagat Singh said: "We do not want to waste our time in watching such farcical shows. We have got to think of more serious things."

At this the Magistrate asked the Assistant Jailor to take away the accused to Jail and the proceedings were adjourned.

Only a few days earlier, the accused had given notice to the Government of their decision to go on hunger-strike in a letter which set out the record on the subject (see Appendix IV for the text). On February 4, 1930, the hunger-strike was resumed. Five days later, Bhagat Singh and Dutt wrote a letter to the Magistrate explaining their refusal to attend court:

"The majority of the accused belong to distant provinces and all are middle class people. In these circumstances, it is very difficult, nay altogether impossible, for their relatives to come here every now and then to help them in their defence. They wanted to hold interviews with some of their friends whom they could entrust with all the responsibilities of their defence. But repeated requests made to that effect to the court have one and all gone unheard.

"Mr. B.K. Dutt belongs to Bengal and Mr. Kanwal Nath Tiwari to Bihar. Both of them wanted to interview their friends, Shrimati Kumari Lajyawati and Shrimati Parbati Devi respectively. But the court forwarded all the applications to the jail authorities, who, in their turn, rejected them on the plea that interviews could be allowed to relatives and counsel only. Even after they had appointed those friends as their attorneys and the power of attorney had been attested by the court, no interview was allowed to them. The accused could not even move the higher courts. But the trial was being proceeded with.

"The unrepresented accused could not afford to engage a wholetime counsel to represent them throughout the lengthy trial. They wanted legal advice on certain points. And at a certain stage they wanted their legal adviser to watch the proceedings personally to be in a better position to form his own opinion. But he was refused even a seat in the body of the court. Counsel are permitted to attend the courts to watch the interests of their clients—who are not present nor even represented by them. What are the 'special circumstances of this case' that led the Magistrate to adopt such an attitude towards a barrister, thus discouraging any counsel who might be invited to attend the court to assist the accused? The accused desire to discuss with our legal adviser the question of interviews with attorneys and to interact with him to move the High Court on this point. But they could not get the opportunity to discuss it with him at all and nothing could be done. In these circumstances they all thought that either they should have a fair chance of defending themselves or they should be prepared to bear the sentences passed against them after a trial held in their absence."

The third main grievance, they said, was about the supply of newspapers. Undertrials should never be treated as convicts and only such restrictions can justifiably be imposed upon them as may be necessary for their safe custody. Nothing beyond that can be justified. The accused, who cannot be released on bail, should not be subjected to such hardships as may amount to punishment. Hence, every literate undertrial is entitled to get at least one standard daily newspaper. "The Executive" agreed on certain principles to give the accused one daily English newspaper in the court. But things done by half are worse than not done at all. Their repeated requests for a vernacular paper for non-English reading accused proved to be futile. They had been returning *The Tribune* daily as a protest against the order refusing them a vernacular paper.

"Anyhow, these were the three main grounds," they concluded, "on which we announced on the 29th January our refusal to come to the court. As soon as our grievances will be removed, we will ourselves quite willingly attend the court."[17]

At long last, on February 19, 1930, the Government of India issued a press communique on the classification of convicted prisoners and undertrials.[18] Ever ready to respond to any concilia-tory gesture, the accused gave up the hunger-strike the very next day. But, as Ajoy Ghosh recalled in his memoirs, the Government soon went back on its assurances. All the accused "were placed in 'C' class and treated with vindictive brutality".

The case was adjourned from February 8 to March 8 as a result of the hunger-strike. (See Appendix V for the text).

From March 8 onwards the proceedings went on relatively smoothly till May 3, the last day of the proceedings before the Magistrate. Two days earlier, an Ordinance was promulgated to set up a Tribunal to try the case. That Noad paid tributes to Rai Saheb Pandit Sri Kishen's impartiality was understandable. But, despite the treatment he had meted out to them, Bhagat Singh spoke without rancour. His words revealed the man.

Thanking the Magistrate on behalf of his comrades and him-self, Bhagat Singh said that he wanted to tell the Magistrate that although on many occasions they had to defy the bureaucracy whose representative the Magistrate was, they had nothing to say against him personally. He remarked that the Magistrate was polite and too lenient and the prosecution had taken advantage of his leniency many a time while the accused did not try to do so. Bhagat Singh was as free from hate as he was from fear.

NOTES

1. *The Tribune*, September 26, 1929, p. 3.
2. *Ibid.*
3. *The Tribune*, October 6, 1929, p. 1.
4. *The Tribune*, October 6, 1929, p. 1. Vide also C.S. Venu, *Sardar Bhagat Singh*, p. 123.
5. *The Tribune*, October 22, 1929, p. 2.
6. *Ibid.*, pp. 9-10.
7. *Ibid.*, October 23, 1929, p. 3.
8. *Ibid.*, October 25, 1929, pp. 1 and 7.
9. *Ibid.*, October 26, 1929, pp. 1-2.
10. *Ibid.*
11. *Ibid.*, November 7, 1929, p. 9.
12. *Ibid.*, November 9, 1929, pp. 1-2.
13. B.B. Misra, p. 276.
14. *The Tribune*, January 26, 1930, p. 2.
15. Deol, p. 75.
16. Kamleśh Mohan, p. 363.
17. *The Tribune*, February 12, 1930.
18. *Ibid.*, February 21, 1930, for the full text see Appendix II.

8

Trial by Tribunal

THERE was something else, besides, which Bhagat Singh said to the Special Magistrate on May 3, 1930, the last day of the hearings before him. It concerned the Viceroy's edict two days earlier. By a stroke of his pen, as it were, Lord Irwin not only interrupted the committal proceedings then pending in the Special Magistrate's Court—an essential preliminary safeguard which the law provides to the accused in all grave cases before they are tried by the Sessions Court—but aborted them as well as a trial before the Sessions Court with a right of appeal to the High Court.

Instead, a Tribunal of three High Court judges was set up to try the case without any right of appeal. The right to trial by jury available to common criminals in Sessions Courts was taken away in cases of conspiracy. Trial by jury was abolished in India in the mid-fifties. The British Raj could not take such liberties in the Alipore Bomb Case two decades earlier, in which Aurobindo Ghose, his brother Barindra Kumar, and thirty-five others were charged with waging war against the King and other grave offences.

Bhagat Singh told the Magistrate that the appointment of the Tribunal was a victory for the accused because from the very beginning they wanted to expose the Government and bring home to the public that there was no law. By appointing the Tribunal the Government had shown themselves in their true colours. So, indeed, it had.

A Tribunal specifically to try the Lahore Conspiracy case was set up by an Ordinance made by the Governor-General, Lord Irwin, on May 1, 1930. It was not subject to re-enactment and, thus, ratification by the Central Legislative Assembly and the Council of State as an Act of the Indian Legislature as Ordinances promulgated by the President and Governors are. It was a legislative power conferred on the executive without any control by the legislature; a legislative power to be exercised by the executive parallel to and *independent* of those exercised by the legislature. The Assembly, as we have noted, could censure the Government as it did on Jatin Das's death. The Viceroy was not assured of a majority there.

There were only two checks on his power. One was that the Governor-General's Ordinance could not operate beyond a maximum term of six months. The other was that it could be made only "in cases of emergency".

India's constitution then was embodied in a law made by the British Parliament, the Government of India Act, 1919. Section 72 of the Act said: "The Governor-General of India may, *in cases of emergency*, make and promulgate ordinances for the peace and good government of British India or any part thereof, and any ordinances so made shall, *for the space of not more than six months* from its promulgation, have the like force of law as an Act passed by the Indian legislature . . . ."

It was open to the British Government to "disallow" such an Ordinance in the same way that it could set at naught a law passed by the Indian legislature and assented to by the Governor-General. The last word always belonged to London (S. 69).

What was the "emergency" which warranted this drastic step? The word had been used advisedly in S. 72. Significantly, it did not exist in S. 71 which conferred on "the local Government of any part of British India" (i.e., that of a province) the power to propose to the Centre "the draft of any regulation for the peace and good government of the part". It became law if the Governor-General assented to it, whether an emergency existed or not.

Along with the Ordinance, Irwin issued from Simla, where the

Government of India moved to avoid the summer heat of what then was truly New Delhi, a Statement which set out the reasons for promulgating it. (See Appendix VI for the texts of the Ordinance and the Statement.) The offences, it said, were of an "unusually serious character". They arose from "revolutionary activities" spread over many different places and with events occurring over a considerable period of time. "It would be necessary to produce about 600 witnesses."

Irwin referred to the "hunger-strike before the commencement of the inquiry" by the Magistrates and the adjournments it entailed, from July 26 to September 24. He added: "It was then resumed, but there were numerous interruptions owing to defiant and disorderly conduct by some of the accused or demonstrations by members of the public"; a charge totally belied by the record.

He conceded that by then 230 witnesses had been examined. But the conduct of the accused rendered it impossible "to count upon obtaining a conclusion by the normal methods of procedure within any calculable period". The proceedings should not be allowed "to drag out to a length which cannot at present be foreseen". The charges should be "finally adjudicated upon with the least possible delay".

Of course, none of those statements brooked scrutiny. As *The Tribune* recalled in an editorial on May 6, "It would, indeed, be the negation of justice to any that if there is a demonstration by members of the public in connection with a criminal trial, that trial should not be conducted according to the ordinary forms of law . . . . It has not been alleged that during the last two months there was any interruption in the proceedings or that during the whole of that period the conduct of the accused was not unexceptionable. *It is, however, an open secret that the extraordinarily slow progress of the case during this period was entirely due to the apparent anxiety of the prosecution to produce as few witnesses as possible, because they knew that the Ordinance was coming.* During this period, the court seldom sat for the full working hours, and the witnesses were produced and examined in a somewhat leisurely manner. It is no exaggeration to say that the evidence which was spread over two months could have been recorded within a fortnight, if the prosecution were at all anxious to expedite the proceedings."

Bhagat Singh refuted the charges in a letter to the Viceroy:

"The entire text of the ordinance for the early disposal of our trial has been read over (to us), whereby a tribunal has been constituted under the jurisdiction of the Punjab High Court. If no reference had been made to the attitude adopted in this case and if we had not been held responsible for that, we would have probably kept our mouths closed. But in the present situation, we consider it necessary to issue our statement.

We have known from the beginning that Government has been deliberately creating misunderstanding about us. After all, it is a war and we very well know that in order to face its enemy, the Government would spin a web of misunderstanding as its first stratagem. We have no means of preventing this mean act. But there are certain things in view of which we are forced to say something.

In the ordinance promulgated about the Lahore Conspiracy Case, you have made a mention of our hunger-strike and said that two of us had started our hunger strike weeks before the trial investigations started in the Court of the Special Magistrate Pandit Shri Krishna. Anyone with common sense can understand that the hunger-strike had nothing to do with this trial. There were special reasons for starting the hunger-strike. When Government agreed to solve the problem and appointed the jail enquiry committee, we called off the hunger-strike. We had been given the assurance that the problem would be solved by November. But it was delayed till December. The month of January also passed, but there was no indication whether the Government would really do anything in the matter or not. It appeared to us that the matter had been shelved. Under these circumstances, we again started our hunger-strike on 4th February, 1930, after giving a full week's notice. It was only after this that the Government took some steps to finally settle the matter.

When the Government issued a communique to the Press in

this regard, we called off the hunger-strike. We even did not wait to see whether the Government implemented its latest decision or not. Only today, we have realised that the Government does not feel shy of taking recourse to deception even in trivial matters. In any case, it is not the proper occasion to enter into an argument on this issue, but we want to emphasise that the hunger-strike was not a step against the trial. We did not suffer all the oppression for such a trivial matter. Jatindra Nath Das did not sacrifice his life for this trivial matter, nor did Rajguru and Sukh Dev endanger their lives for this reason."[1]

The contrast with another "unusual" case is glaring. The Meerut Conspiracy Case began *in camera* on March 15, 1929 when the District Magistrate of Meerut issued warrants of arrest against the accused. The Special Prosecutor, Langford James, opened the case before the Magistrate on June 12. He committed the accused to trial by the Sessions Court on January 13, 1930. The trial began in that Court before a judge *and five assessors*, applications for trial by jury having been rejected by the Chief Justice of the Allahabad High Court, on January 31, 1930. Not till January 17, 1933 was judgment delivered. The High Court delivered judgment on appeal only on August 13, 1933.

The charge in that case also was "conspiracy to deprive the King-Emperor of his sovereignty of British India". There were 320 prosecution witnesses in the Magistrate's court, 281 in the Sessions Court and a mass of documents, inevitably. For, the charge was that the accused had entered into a conspiracy to further the objectives of the Communist International in Moscow. The accused were some top leaders of the Communist movement and of trade unions in the country—S.A. Dange, Muzaffar Ahmad, S.V. Ghate, S.S. Mirajkar, Sohan Singh Josh, M.A. Majid, P.C. Joshi and others, besides well-known figures like Philip Spratt, Benjamin Bradley and Lester Hutchinson.

There was a big difference, however. A Meerut Prisoners' Defence Committee was formed, to no small degree due to Jawaharlal Nehru's efforts, with his father, Motilal Nehru as Chairman. *There was little help from counsel of national emi-*

nence in the Lahore conspiracy case, generally; and, particularly, on the outrageous Ordinance. The Lahore High Court Bar protested promptly and most ably, as we shall see. The accused themselves were rather disdainful of legal procedures. Their popularity rankled in the mind of officialdom. Their relative isolation from the political mainstream encouraged it.

If there were 600 witnesses in the Lahore case, whatever gave the Viceroy the assurance that the case would be finished by the Tribunal within six months even if the accused enthusiastically cooperated with it?

The Ordinance could not last a day longer than that. Its expiry by efflux of time spelt the demise of its creature, the Tribunal. The Viceroy sought to ensure despatch by investing the Tribunal with "powers to deal with wilful obstruction". Thus, the Judges appointed to serve on it were told from the start that the accused were obstructionists and they were advisedly endowed with power to bring them to heel. Uniquely, this was a criminal court on the heads of whose judges dangled a Damocles' sword requiring them to speed up things or else exit from the scene in ignominy.

Not even on its worst construction could the behaviour of the accused be said to create a situation of "emergency" so as to warrant invocation of the executive's power to legislate without any recourse to the legislature; a power which was abandoned in England centuries ago.

But, why was Irwin so determined to get this case out of the way? Was it because he had a political agenda? In May 1929 a Labour Government, headed by Ramsay MacDonald, had come to power in Britain. On October 31, Irwin declared on his return from London after consultations: "I am authorised on behalf of His Majesty's Government to state clearly that in their judgment it is implicit in the British Government's declaration of 1917 (which promised "responsible Government in India") that the natural issue of India's constitutional progress, as there contemplated, is the attainment of Dominion Status" (on par with Dominions like Canada and Australia).

Gandhi was convinced of Irwin's sincerity, and rightly so. Jawaharlal was not but was not prepared for a break with Gandhi.

Subhas Bose set his face against compromise and said, "Jawaharlal
has now given up Independence at the instance of the Mahatma."[2]
The Viceroy was well aware of the problems the Congress Left
would create once he began to implement his programme of
conciliation on the basis of Dominion Status, as distinct from
complete independence. The problems which those even more to
the Left could create were not to be underestimated.

It would be wrong to suggest that, for this very reason alone,
the Meerut conspiracy case was launched in order to put the
Communists out of action. Still less would that be true of the
Lahore case, where overt criminal acts were charged along with a
conspiracy. It would, however, be fair to suggest that the Ordinance was made in order to enact the Hunger-Strike Bill by this
devious stratagem, since the Assembly was unlikely ever to accept
it, and that the growing popularity of Bhagat Singh and his
comrades and fears of their infectious example had steeled the
Government in its resolve speedily to secure their conviction and
with it deterrent death sentences for their leaders; Bhagat Singh, in
particular.

The Lahore Conspiracy Case Ordinance, 1930, as it was formally called, was tailored to suit these objectives. It dealt with that
case alone. The Chief Justice of the Lahore High Court was
enjoined to constitute a Tribunal consisting of three High Court
Judges for the trial of "all cases pending in the Court of Rai Saheb
Pandit Sri Kishan" against the accused mentioned in the Schedule
to the Ordinance. Its judgment would be "final and conclusive".
There would be no appeal from any order or sentence of the
Tribunal. The High Court's jurisdiction was completely excluded.
That included the jurisdiction to issue a writ of habeas corpus.

Under the ordinary law of the land, a death sentence pronounced by a Sessions Judge was subject to confirmation by the
High Court. Not so, in this case.

The proceedings already taken before the Special Magistrate
were deemed by the Ordinance to be committal proceedings
whereunder the accused were committed to the Tribunal for trial,
instead of the Sessions Court.

"The Tribunal shall be deemed to be a Court of Session" to

whom they had been committed. But, with brazen inconsistency, it was provided that the Tribunal would *not* follow the procedure for trial by a Sessions Court, laid down in the Criminal Procedure Code, but the procedure which the Code prescribes for the trial of warrant cases by Magistrates.

Despatch is one thing. Departure from established procedure is another. By April 1930 evidence of four out of seven approvers and witness who provided significant corroboration had been recorded. It was enough to warrant committal. No such application was made. Nor one to have the case tried by the High Court itself under S. 526(1)(e)(iii) and (iv). As we shall see later, the Prosecutor abruptly closed his case before the Tribunal on August 26 after 457 witnesses had been examined in order to conclude the case before the Ordinance expired on October 31, 1930.

A key provision of the Ordinance was a re-enactment of the Hunger-Strike Bill in a more stringent form. It was Section 9 which read thus:

"(1) The Tribunal shall have powers to take such measures as it may think necessary to secure the orderly conduct of the trial; and where any accused by his voluntary act has rendered himself incapable of appearing before the Tribunal, or resists his production before it, or behaves before it in a persistently disorderly manner, or in any other way wilfully conducts himself to the serious prejudice of the trial, the Tribunal may, at any stage of the trial, dispense with the attendance of such accused for such period as it may think fit and proceed with the trial in his absence.

(2) Where a plea is required in answer to a charge from an accused whose attendance has been dispensed with under sub-section (1), such accused shall be deemed not to plead guilty.

(3) An order under sub-section (1) dispensing with the attendance of an accused shall not affect his right of being represented by a pleader at any stage of the trial."

Three Judges of the Lahore High Court were appointed to the Tribunal. Two of them were English members of the I.C.S., John Coldstream and G.C. Hilton. The third was an Indian barrister, Sayad Agha Haider. Coldstream was appointed President. Any doubt as to the Government's mala fides intent in promulgating the Ordinance was removed when, exactly seven months later, it sponsored legislation in order to confer on the accused in a subsequent Lahore Conspiracy Case the right of appeal to the High Court. Charges in both cases were equally grave. Bhagat Singh's popularity and fears of his infectious example dictated reckless despatch and a short cut to the gallows. The story of the second case is told briefly in the Epilogue. The last appendix contains the Punjab Statute setting up a Commission to try the later case and the Central Act which supplemented it in order to provide a right of appeal which a Provincial law could not.

The battle was hereafter to be waged on two fronts. One was the Tribunal set up as it was with special powers and hostile intent. The other was the High Court before which one of the accused, Des Raj, challenged the constitutional validity of the Ordinance with the enthusiastic support of the Lahore Bar.

The one before the Tribunal was doomed to failure as everyone could guess from the context of its appointment. It is truly amazing that the Indian Bar generally and counsel of national eminence did not protest as strenuously as they ought to have at the palpable legal monstrosity of a court of law which lacked security of existence as an institution and whose members lacked security of tenure. The Tribunal would cease to exist in six months' time and its members were removable at will—as, indeed, two of them were less than two months later. To think that this was a Tribunal empowered to award a sentence of death and against whose judgment there was no appeal whether on law or on facts.

The historic significance of the legal proceedings against Bhagat Singh and his colleagues, both, at the committal stage before the Special Magistrate and in the trial proper by the Special Tribunal, does not lie so much in the content of the evidence, important though it is, but in the manner in which it was produced and accepted. A full record of the trial is available in the National Archives of India in the collection in the private papers section of Dianat Rai Handa, one of the accused in the *Punjab Conspiracy Case* (1930-33) as well among the unpublished Government Records in the *Proceedings of Lahore Conspiracy Case before the Special Tribunal 1930* (Phase III A/8/2) and *Lahore Conspiracy*

Case Judgment, October 7, 1930 (Phase III A/9/3). Also available are the *Delhi Court Papers: Assembly Bomb Case,* Trial No. 9 of 1929; Vols. I-VII and the *Assembly Bomb Case Sessions Judgment,* dated June 12, 1929.

The reader will not find in them the kind of lively exchanges or feats of cross-examination in the great State Trials like the Alipore Bomb Case in which C.R. Das defended Aurobindo Ghose and the prosecution was led by an equally formidable counsel Eardley Norton, a member of the Congress in its early years who sympathised with Indian aspirations, or the Karachi trial in which the Ali Brothers and the Shankaracharya of Sharadha Peeth were jointly charged with sedition. Large parts of the evidence in Bhagat Singh's case were of a formal nature. What holds one's interest is the story of betrayal which only an approver in such a case can tell. As many as five of them did that monotonously. The quality of the evidence as to identification was questionable. All this is interesting; but not of great significance.

What is of truly historic and enduring significance in this case is the conscious use of the court of law as a political weapon by the regime of the day in order to crush the rebels against the system. Bhagat Singh was foremost among them.

The Tribunal commenced its proceedings on May 5, 1930 in the Poonch House at Lahore. All the eighteen accused were present in person. They entered the court-room in the usual manner. The Tribunal was not amused. "They shouted revolutionary slogans for a short time and then for a period of eight minutes altogether they chanted a revolutionary hymn." Predictably, the legality of the constitution of the Tribunal was challenged but the Tribunal declined to decide the issue itself or to adjourn the proceedings for a fortnight in order to enable the accused to prepare their case on this point.

Imposition of a six-months' deadline by the Ordinance was destructive of confidence all round. The Tribunal was determined to hustle through; the accused acquired a vested interest in delay. An application by five of the accused for a fortnight's adjournment to arrange for their defence was rejected.

Rajguru, speaking in Marathi, complained that he did not

understand the language of the court He was provided an interpreter. Jatindranath Sanyal, Mahabir Singh, Batukeshwar Dutt,
Gaya Parshad and Kundan Lal, in a prepared statement read out by
Sanyal, attacked the Raj and challenged the Tribunal: "We decline
to be a party to the farcical show and henceforth we shall not take
any part in the proceedings of this case." Each of the accused was
asked whether he wished to be represented at State expense. Four
consented. They were Ajoy Ghosh, Kishori Lal, Des Raj and Prem
Dutt. Amar Dass was engaged for the first three and Baljit Singh
for the fourth. The rest either declined to answer or flatly rejected
the offer.

The proceedings record that "Bhagat Singh, accused, then put
in an application stating that he wanted a legal adviser to watch the
proceedings of the Tribunal and to give him advice on lines of
cross-examination. He also stated that the said legal adviser will
not cross-examine the witnesses, nor address the Court, and that
for the present he wanted Mr. Duni Chand. Mr. Noad, Public
Prosecutor, stated that he had no objection to this arrangement
provided seating accommodation was available. The Tribunal
sanctioned the arrangement proposed."[3]

Witnesses who deposed before the Magistrate in committal
proceedings are recalled to give evidence in the Sessions Court; in
this instance before the Tribunal. As in the Magistrate's Court,
C.H. Carden Noad, Government Advocate, led Khan Saheb
Kalandar Ali Khan, Government Pleader and Public Prosecutor,
and L. Gopal Lal, for the prosecution. None of the accused was
represented by Counsel. Carden Noad opened the case for the
prosecution, describing the charges brought against the accused
and stating by what evidence he proposed to prove their guilt.

The first prosecution witness was a formal one. G.T. Hamilton
Harding, Senior Superintendent of Police, only put forward the
complaint, dated July 10, 1929, which he had filed in the Court of
the Special Magistrate. "I do not know the facts of the case nor did
I make the statements made in the complaint. I am acting only as
a formal complainant under the instructions of the Government."

The very next prosecution witness (P.W. 2) was the approver
Jai Gopal, followed in succession by the other approvers—

Phonindra Nath Ghosh (P.W. 3), Man Mohan Bannerji (P.W. 4), Hans Raj Vohra (P.W. 5), and Lalit Kumar Mukerji (P.W. 6). Phonindra Nath Ghosh and Man Mohan Bannerji dealt with the Bihar and Calcutta phases of the Conspiracy, but Ghosh's evidence also included important facts regarding activities in the U.P., Delhi and to some extent the Punjab. The evidence of Lalit Kumar Mukerji was almost exclusively concerned with Allahabad and Agra. The evidence of the two remaining approvers, Jai Gopal and Hans Raj Vohra, was almost entirely concerned with activities in the Punjab. While there was a close connection between Phonindra Nath Ghosh and Man Mohan Bannerjee in their work regarding which they deposed, the Tribunal noted that "the connection between the two Punjab approvers, Jai Gopal and Hans Raj Vohra, is slight. Their personal contact with each other was spasmodic and their characters, as revealed by their evidence and demeanour in the witness-box, are by no means similar."

Jai Gopal was in the tenth class at the National School in Lahore in 1926 when he became acquainted with Sukh Dev through a Hindi teacher, Yashpal.

"Sukh Dev asked me whether being student of the National School, I had ever thought of serving the country. I said that I would wear Khaddar clothes and do Congress work. Sukh Dev gave me a lecture urging me to become a member of the secret society the object of which was to overthrow the present Government . . . After that Sukh Dev met me in November 1926 and told me that I should become a member of the secret society which he had organised. I agreed.

"Sukh Dev used to meet me off and on. In January 1927, Sukh Dev again came to my house and asked me to meet him the next day outside the Bhati Gate. The next day I met Sukh Dev. He came with me to Pari Mahal along with a zinc handbag which he had. He asked me to keep this handbag with me. He showed me two keys, saying that I should deliver the handbag to the person who showed the said keys . . . .

"Twenty or 25 days after that one Pandit Jai Chand, ex-professor of the National College, came to me and enquired from me whether Sukh Dev had left any box with me. I said I did not know

Sukh Dev. Thereupon he exhibited the two keys which Sukh Dev
had shown to me and I handed over the handbag to him. Jai
Chand, after having asked me to wait outside, opened the box and
after locking it again he made it over to me and took away the
keys. I heard the noise of the handbag being opened. A few days
after that, Sukh Dev came again to take back the box . . . and took
it away. Sukh Dev told me that as I used to learn photography
work with the Head Master of the National School, I had the keys
of the school. Sukh Dev said that as I had all the keys with me, I
should procure all kinds of helpful things such as mercury, ther-
mometers, batteries and some books of science. I said I would
supply whatever I could."

He had become a good recruit. Jai Gopal met Bhagat Singh in
1927, though he knew him well before that as a student in the
National College. So, he went on; describing in detail the chores
.ie was assigned by his mentor Sukh Dev. His first major role was
in the aborted dacoity at the Punjab National Bank. Besides, he
was present at the meeting at Mozang House at which Chandra
Shekhar Azad alias Panditji proposed the murder of Scott. Other
participants were Bhagat Singh, Sukh Dev, Partap Singh, Rajguru,
Kali Charan, Ram Chandar and Hans Raj Vohra.

Jai Gopal told it all—how he kept watch on Scott's movements, as he was detailed to, and stood outside the police office on
the appointed day to give a signal as soon as Scott came out of the
office. "The sahib who I believed to be Mr. Scott came out of the
office. A tall Sikh constable in uniform followed him . . . The
Sahib had started the motorcycle and taken his seat on it. He
moved off slowly. At this time "M" (Rajguru) and I were quite
near and I made a sign to say that sahib was coming. On this he
took out his pistol and moved towards the sahib. I stood at the
turning of the road Bhagat Singh at that time was close to Pandit
Ji but outside the gate in the road. "M" fired at the officer as soon
as the motor bike reached near him. "M" had a revolver with him.
The officer who was hit lifted up his hands from the cycle and fell
on one side of the cycle.

"The cycle engine went on turning. One of the officer's legs fell
under the cycle. Bhagat Singh ran towards the officer and fired

several shots at him. Bhagat Singh fired a Brownie automatic pistol (Ex. P/480). Bhagat Singh may have fired 5 or 6 times. Some sort of sound came out of the officer's mouth as he fell. Afterwards he did not speak. We three then ran down the Court Street. As we ran off a sahib came out of the office followed by the same tall Sikh constable who had come to put something into the hand of the first sahib. These two ran after us. That sahib was Mr. Fearn, Traffic Inspector. I identified him later.

"In the meantime, a motor car came from the direction of the District Courts. That motor car stood near me. This was while the firing was going on. I do not know how many men were in that motor car. The tahsil building is close to the Police Office. I cannot say if anybody was there. Mr. Fearn and the tall Sikh constable were running after Bhagat Singh and "M" down the street. Bhagat Singh fired at Mr. Fearn who had just passed Bhagat Singh. Mr. Fearn ducked and fell. Bhagat Singh and "M" then entered the D.A.V. College compound through the smaller gate. I went on down Court Street with my bicycle. The Sikh constable turned into the compound after Bhagat Singh."

Jai Gopal proceeded, in the same strain, to describe the aftermath till the arrests in Kashmir Buildings on April 15: "I was dressing myself when the Police arrived at about 8 o'clock in the morning. Khan Sahib Niaz Ahmad Khan and Sayyed Ahmad Shah came to our room. The Deputy Superintendent of Police, Khan Bahadur Abdul Aziz, and several other persons were outside the room. I came to know of these names later on. On the arrival of these persons we were searched and arrested. Sukh Dev pretended to be feeling sick and went out of the room in order to drink water. He was brought in and was being searched when he took out a revolver from his pocket which was snatched away from him by Sayyed Ahmad Shah, Deputy Superintendent, Police. The revolver in question is Exh. P/122.

"The Police enquired from Sukh Dev whether the revolver was loaded and he said yes. The Deputy Superintendent, Police, handed over this revolver to Deputy Niaz Ahmad Khan. After the searches we were handcuffed. Sukh Dev then pointed to a box lying above a window saying that it contained a live bomb. The box was opened by the Police and the bomb wrapped up in papers was recovered. Exh. P/2 is that box.

"The Police then opened an almirah, the key of which was given by Kishori Lal. Bomb-shells, acids, chemicals and glasses, etc., were recovered. Somebody was writing down the recovery list. Exh. P/O is the recovery list in question. It bears my signature.

"The list of articles recovered from my person also bears my signature. It is Exh. P/E/4. Sukh Dev and Kishori Lal both signed the recovery list, Exh. P/C, in my presence. I identify their signatures. At the time of the search I enquired from Sukh Dev why he had not used this revolver. He said that he had a mind to fire at the topiwala, i.e., Khan Bahadur, and take me and Kishori Lal along with him; but that he had no opportunity to do so.

I identify the following articles which were discovered from the Kashmir Buildings at the time of the search:

"Eight bomb-shells, Exhs. P/4 to P/11.
18 cartridges recovered from Sukh Dev, Exh. P/13.
A revolver recovered from Sukh Dev, Exh. P/122.
Five books, Exh. P/27, P/28, P/29, P/159 and P/160 . . ."

There are some important marginal comments in the record of the Proceedings in the National Archives. They suggest Sukh Dev's authorship. Next to a para in which Jai Gopal deposed that Sukh Dev had told him that "the Central Body had decided to murder Tassaduq Hussain, Bannerji . . ." occurs this denial: "Wrong, I never told him such." If this, indeed, was Sukh Dev's version, it is unfortunate that Jai Gopal was not cross-examined at all. None of the other witnesses was. There is also another important comment: "I myself handed over the revolver to the police before I was searched." Sukh Dev had no possible motive for making false statements on the margin of the official record of the proceedings. Jai Gopal had every motive to lie. Arrested on April 15, "I accepted the tender of pardon on the 30th of April 1929."

Sukh Dev's marginal comments raise a problem for any serious student of the trial. They merit detailed study. The intrinsic evidence clearly suggests his authorship. A different version from what a witness deposed could have been inscribed by any reader of the record. Not so bitter laments: "I believed him too much. Many times I disclosed before him what I should have not. It was (indistinct; careless?) on my part to take him (Jai Gopal, the approver) to Jora Mori house. I committed the same mistake when I took him to Kashmir Buildings."

If the comments are, indeed, Sukh Dev's, his denials of accepted versions of certain episodes ring true. For, to repeat, he had no reason to lie. This holds good for his denial of Jai Gopal's version that they saw Scott and his wife the day after the Saunders murder but Sukh Dev refused to shoot at him though he had his revolver with him. His comment reads: "Nonsense. As a member of a body I could not do so."

But even more important is Sukh Dev's version of Bhagat Singh's role in the Saunders' murder and the fateful mistake as to the victim's identity: "Bhagat Singh was to fire, first, M. (Rajguru) was sent only to guard Bhagat Singh. Pandit (*sic*) was to guard these both, while escaping. B.S. marked (*sic*) that the Sahib is not Scott so he turned towards p. ji to tell him so. Meanwhile 'M' fired which he should not. He never recognised Scott. Then B.S. was duty bound to fire the wrong victim. Thus happened the murder of Mr. Saunders."

These poignant comments are scribbled on the margin of the deposition by the approver Jai Gopal—the man who was to give the signal when Scott left the police office.

A week after the Tribunal commenced its proceedings, a most unfortunate incident occurred with consequences none of those involved had then foreseen. It arose over the raising of slogans in court. The Lahore case accused were not the only ones to do so. It had become a feature of most political trials. Those arraigned in the Kakori case and, even more so, the Communist leaders in the Meerut Conspiracy case were no less enthusiastic in this respect. Judges dealt with this, undoubtedly irregular, innovation in procedure tactfully. They would either ignore it or enter the court-room after the accused had delivered themselves of their sentiments. Only, no visitors were admitted until the effusion was over.

Judges on the Tribunal adopted the same course. On May 12, however, they entered the court-room while the police were yet removing the handcuffs on the accused. They began singing the usual song. Wherepon the President, Justice Coldstream, ordered that they be handcuffed. The accused resented this punishment.

Bhagat Singh got up and submitted that there was no occasion to handcuff them. As a matter of fact on the first day it was after they had sung their usual song that the Judges ordered that their handcuffs should be removed. Anyhow under the Ordinance the Tribunal had power to proceed with the case in their absence and so the best thing would be to send them back to the jail and proceed with the case in their absence and avoid any unpleasantness, for they were not prepared to be handcuffed and humiliated like that.

The President, however, ordered that they should be handcuffed and removed from the court-room back to the jails. More than 16 constables sprang on each accused and handcuffed them one by one. by force. During the struggle, the accused continued raising their cries. Three of them, Prem Dutt, Ajoy Ghosh and Kundan Lal became unconscious. Most received injuries.

Bhagat Singh, addressing the Tribunal said: "You are cowards and mercenaries." The accused vehemently protested against what they called high-handedness of the police to the Judges and called upon the Indian Judge to resign. The hearing was adjourned till the next day.

When proceedings were then resumed, Justice Agha Haidar made a statement at the very outset. Although read out on May 13, it was in fact made the previous day and deserves to be reproduced in full from page 38 of the *proceedings*:

ORDER

I was not a party to the Order of the removal of the accused from the Court to the Jail and I was not responsible for it in any way. I dissociate myself from all that took place today in consequence of that order.

AGHA HAIDAR

12th May 1930.

In protest, all the accused, bar one, decided not to attend court on the next day, May 13. Only four were represented by Counsel. Amar Dass sought permission to interview the accused which was granted. Baljit Singh told the Tribunal that the accused apprehended that the authorities might take action against them. Justice Agha Haidar observed: "Personally, I think officials would do nothing against the accused." The proceedings were adjourned for two hours. When the Tribunal re-assembled, Amar Dass said that he was instructed to say that "the situation of yesterday was brought about intentionally to proceed with the case in the absence of the accused. Without going through this the trial could not be finished within six months." His clients refused to be represented and "I beg to withdraw". Baljit Singh made a similar statement.

The President Justice Coldstream said, "We will take such legal measures as are open to us, including the removal of the accused, as may be considered necessary for the proper conduct of the proceedings." He did not pass orders for dispensing with the presence of the accused. There was no question of dispensing with the presence of defence counsel.

On May 14 matters came to a head when the accused (unrepresented by counsel) not only persisted in their refusal to come but those represented by Amar Dass instructed him not to defend them. For the first time, the Tribunal had recourse to the extraordinary powers conferred on it by the Ordinance. It made an Order, under S. 9(1), dispensing with the presence of the accused. Counsel were released.

There existed now a deep rift not only between the Tribunal and the accused but also between Justice Agha Haidar and the two European Judges, Coldstream and Hilton. Unlike the European Judges, Agha Haidar questioned·the witnesses closely. Both rifts were public knowledge.

After Jai Gopal came Phonindra Nath Ghosh. He described how "we began bomb-making", the plans to rescue Jogesh Chander Chatterji and abandonment of the ones to attack members of the Simon Commission. His deposition went on from May 16 for nearly a week followed ! y that of Man Mohan Bannerji. It was for the clever Hans Raj Vohra that Justice Agha Haidar reserved the

most pointed grilling, to the obvious disapproval of his colleagues. Vohra retired in the sixties as *The Times of India*'s
correspondent in Washington, D.C. Like Jai Gopal, he was also a
Sukh Dev recruit. Even as recorded in court jargon his deposition
on his recruitment and its aftermath makes fascinating reading. He
was only 21 and still a student when he gave evidence:

"I can express myself better in English than in *Urdu* and, if
allowed by the Court, will give my evidence in Court in English.

(The evidence of this witness will be given in English and will
be recorded in English at the dictation of the Court. An authenti-
cated translation of that evidence in *Urdu* will be placed on the
record. A memorandum of the substance of the evidence of the
witness is also being made by the President of the Tribunal (see
section 356 of the Criminal Procedure Code).

"I passed my matriculation examination from the Central Model
School, Lahore. While in school, I took special interest in History.
During 1921-1922 the headmaster caned some students who took
part in picketing school gates. He was an European. That created
a deep impression on my mind. I began to think about the reason
why those students were caned for their nationalistic tendency.

"After passing my matriculation examination I joined the Forman
Christian College, Lahore, in the year 1925. At that college I took
special interest in politics and began to study the books of *Mahatma* Gandhi and *Lala* Lajpat Rai such as Lajpat Rai's "England's
Debt to India" and *Mahatma* Gandhi's "Home Rule".

"Sukh Dev, an accused in this case, was the brother of my
uncle's wife, and I knew him owing to this relationship apart from
any connection with the party concerned in this case."

(Prosecutor asks for the production of Sukh Dev in Court for
identification by this witness. The matter is under consideration.
Examination-in-chief to proceed.)

"He used to visit our house but later on was disallowed by my
father because of his political tendencies. We used not to talk
politics at my house. I was once sitting on the tennis lawn of the
Central Training College preparing for my Faculty of Science
medical examination when Sukh Dev came to me and enquired
about my mission in life. I told him that I wanted to serve my

country through journalism. Later on he promised to give me some literature and help me in my study of politics. This first meeting was in August 1926.

"Sukh Dev again saw me at the same place after a few days and gave me a book entitled "Collections from *Bande Matram*" written, most probably, by Arbindo Ghosh.

"In our subsequent meetings we began to discuss about the futility of the Congress programme and the necessity under special circumstances and the justification, both moral and political, of the creation of revolutionary parties. He told me that, inasmuch as India had no constitutional means by which to determine her progress, we must necessarily resort to unconstitutional means. In these meetings he also gave me some other books, e.g., *Cry for Justice* by Upton Sinclair, Sedition Committee's Report, *Life of Barrister Savarkar*, *Life of Mazzini*, etc. By "unconstitutional means" we meant "pressure brought on the Government from outside the constitutional chambers". By "constitutional chambers" I mean the "Legislative Assembly and the Legislative Councils". We talked about the need of terrorising the Government following the example of Ireland.

"My father is both Professor and Superintendent of the Central Training College Boarding House and I was, therefore, entitled to sit in the grounds of that establishment. The Central Training College and its hostel are quite close to each other. They are opposite the District Courts. My father was living in quarters near the boarding house provided for him as Superintendent of that boarding house.

"After those meetings I have described we began to meet in other places such as the Gol Bagh, the University grounds and the canal bank.

"At the end of November or the beginning of December 1926 Sukh Dev summoned me to the Lawrence Gardens where he showed me a yellow leaflet which was a printed copy of the constitution of the Hindustan Republican Association. It related to the aims and objects of the association which was a secret association, and to the duties of its members and its officers. According to it the revolutionaries wanted to create a sort of Government within a Government. There were to be provincial heads under whom there were to be district organisers and local organisers. These provincial heads were to form a central body who were to guide the activities of the association. Sukh Dev asked me to read that leaflet and, and after I had read it, I was told by him that I had been enlisted as a member of that association and that I would be required to abide by its rules."

(Prosecutor states that he proposes to produce a copy of the said leaflet in due course. He cannot produce one at the present moment as the available copy has been exhibited in another case.)

"I identified Sukh Dev in the Court of the Special Magistrate. He used to sit in the dock of the accused in that Court amongst the other accused.

"After I had been enlisted a member of the Hindustan Republican Association, the same evening Sukh Dev told me that he would be going away, and that, in his absence, I should propagate revolutionary ideas by circulating revolutionary literature amongst students. He told me he would be away from Lahore for about two months. I did not again meet him for about that period. He gave me for distribution amongst students copies of those books which I myself had read and which had converted me to revolutionary ideas. According to his instructions, I did distribute literature to some of my friends during his absence.

"After his return, perhaps in March 1927, I introduced Durga Das, *Khanna*, one of my class-fellows, to Sukh Dev, so that he might convert him to his creed and enlist him a member.

"In April 1927 I appeared in the Faculty of Science medical examination and then proceeded to Simla for about two months. After my return from Simla at the end of August I read a number of articles, mostly in the *Tribune*, on the necessity of forming a Students' Union at Lahore. I was myself anxious for the formation of such a union at Lahore and I consulted Sukh Dev about it. He gave his consent and then I, with the help of some of my friends, for instance, Mr. A.C. Bali, Mr. Durga Das, *Khanna*, and Mr. Sampuran Singh, M.A., organised the union. It was named 'The Lahore Students' Union.' The object of the students' union was to preach the creed of nationalism But my association with it was due to the fact that I wanted to create public sympathy amongst students for the revolutionary acts that might be committed by the revolutionary party later on and also to get a ready stock of men for that party.

"I was elected the first secretary of the students' union and I succeeded in making about 400 or 500 members of the union. I carried on the propaganda of the union up to the middle of December 1927. After that one day I was told by Sukh Dev that, as I was not of very great help to the revolutionary party at Lahore because of the conflict of views with my parents, it was necessary to send me to some outside station. At that time he did not specify any outside station. I consented to go and I was told by Sukh Dev that I would be sent away on the 3rd January 1928. The same evening I was taken by Sukh Dev to a house situated in Gowalmandi in a street probably named Lachhman Gali. *The house was locked and one key of it was given to me and the duplicate kept by Sukh Dev. The key was given to me in order to enable me to enter the house in the absence of Sukh Dev.* I first visited the house, probably, and so far as I remember, on the 17th of December 1927. I began to frequent that house and I usually saw that the same house was being frequented by two of the members of the revolutionary party, namely, Bhagat Singh and Jai Gopal. It was Sukh Dev who told me that Bhagat Singh was a prominent member of that party. Sukh Dev also told me about Jai Gopal's connection with the party. Bhagat Singh is one of the accused in this case, and I identified him in the Court of the Special Magistrate. Jai Gopal is an approver in this case.

(Prosecutor asks for the production in Court of Bhagat Singh for identification by this witness. *The matter is under consideration*. Examination-in-chief to proceed.)

The official record is misleading. The matter was not "under consideration" in the sense in which the expression is used. It was foreclosed. After the incident on May 12 the accused refused to attend Court until amends were made for it.

When he said he entered his own and his father's name "incorrectly" in the visitors' register at the Rawalpindi office of the Arya Samaj, Justice Agha Haidar asked: "Did you feel any compunction in putting these deliberate lies in the register?" Vohra replied: "Inasmuch as I was speaking a lie for a higher purpose, I did not feel any compunction."

When he testified to Bhagat Singh's hand-writing on the posters Justice Haidar questioned him and elicited the details. There, followed an interesting exchange which serves to explain why this Judge was removed from the Tribunal a few days later.

Questioned by *Justice Agha Haidar*: "I am certain in my mind that these are in the hand-writing of Bhagat Singh. The only occasion I saw Bhagat Singh writing was on the 17th December when he was copying the posters. At that time I did not scrutinise his hand writing. He and I were sitting quite close to each other at that time.

Q. After joining the party were you frank with the members of the party in matters relating to the affairs of the party?

A. As a general rule the leaders of the party did not give any information to the subordinate members unless that information directly concerned them, while the subordinate members were expected to give every information and not to keep any secret from the leaders.

Q. Did you act up to this principle?

A. As far as it was possible for me I acted up to this principle. The members were not expected to exchange their information with each other except with the leaders. I could speak frankly about any matter with Bhagat Singh or Sukh Dev but not with Jai Gopal or Kishori Lal or Rajguru who were ordinary members. I was frank with the leaders and kept nothing from them. I told them that, after my return from Rawalpindi, I was shadowed by the police. In spite of that they decided to take me to the bank raid.

Q. Was the plot for the assassination of Mr. Scott communicated to you?

A. It was not fully communicated to me. Only some of it was given because it was expected that I would be arrested.

Q. In spite of your being shadowed by the police did they divulge to you a part of the plot?

A. They did so for the very reason because I was being shadowed by the police and because my arrest was expected. The object of divulging a part of the plot was that I might remain firm and realise my responsibility as a member.

By Justice Hilton: I was particularly being shadowed at the time of the visit of the Simon Commission to Lahore, but afterwards surveillance slackened. That was in the month of December. I am quite certain that no police officer followed me to the Punjab National Bank.

By Justice Agha Haidar: It was the plain clothes police officers who shadowed me. Surveillance never remained secret for very long. I do not think it ever remained secret from me except at the beginning till I became accustomed to it. I always knew when I was being followed and when not. I used to be followed by different C.I.D. men.

By the Prosecutor: Whenever I had to go to the Mozang House or to visit any member of the party I took precautions to avoid being followed by the C.I.D. official. On other occasions I never took any precautions. I took such precautions as the use of back doors.

At this stage Justice Agha Haidar expressed the following opinion:

In my judgment the answers given to my question by the witness were perfectly clear and did not require any further elucidation. The questions which I put to the witness were in the interests of justice and in order to get at the truth as far as possible. I do not think it is necessary at all in the interests of justice and having regard to the provisions of section 165 of the Indian Evidence Act to grant permission to the Public Prosecutor to put any cross-questions arising out of the answers given to the questions put by me to the witness. It shall be open to the learned President and my brother Hilton to put such questions as they might consider desirable.

Justice Hilton: As the questions were actually put and the answers recorded after a statement made by the Prosecutor that he intended to put such questions, I think the answers already given and recorded should remain on the record and the permission, if necessary, to put those questions should be taken as having been granted.

The President, Justice Coldstream: I agree with Mr. Justice Hilton."

The next approver, Lalit Kumar Mukerji, was "of little importance" relatively, as the marginal comment on the record put it. He stepped in the witness-box on May 29 which was brisk progress in the 24 days since the Tribunal held its first sitting.

On May 30, another approver, Ram Saran Das, blew the lid off. He retracted his statement and said it had been made at the instance of the police. He had made a statement before the Magistrate on June 11, 1929, but it was later altered and he was made to affix his signature on the altered statement.

He told the Tribunal: "*I wish to put in a document which shows how approvers are tutored. I hand in the document. I do not wish to remain in the custody of the police. This document was given to me by a Police Officer who told me to learn it by heart. This was shown to me off and on by the officer who was with me. It passed on from officer to officer as they changed. I hand in the document.*"

Order: "Let this witness be sent to the judicial lock up and not kept in the custody of the police. He should be produced in court at 11 a.m. tomorrow. He should not be allowed to converse with the accused persons in the case."

Coldstream
[Page 202 (printed) of the Record]

In view of the repeated demands by the accused that the approvers should not be kept in police custody, Ram Saran Das's exposure should have prompted a similar order in respect of *all* the approvers, besides *an inquiry into police conduct*. Neither was done. What is worse, despite the damning exposure *based on documentary evidence*, the evidence of the *other* approvers was not discounted on this ground. The Tribunal's judgment was not a bit affected by proof of a gross irregularity that vitiated their evidence.

Examined by Gopal Lal, Public Prosecutor, Ram Saran Das said that after meeting Sukh Dev at Jullunder he did not go with him to Agra. "He had been several times to Delhi but never in the company of Sukh Dev, accused. He had never been to Agra and had never met Bhagat Singh and Sukh Dev there. From Kapurthala he came to Lahore and then went to Calcutta.

Q. What was your object in going to Calcutta?

Justice Agha Haidar objected that the questions were in the nature of cross-examination and in his judgment the prosecution should have taken permission of the Court before it commenced putting such cross question. The Chairman did not see any ground to hold that the questions put were in the nature of cross examinations. Prosecution counsel was allowed to proceed.

The approver said that he was arrested at Kapurthala and was brought to Lahore on June 6, 1929. On June 13 he made a statement before the Additional District Magistrate. The witness identified his signature on the document bearing the statement but said that the statement he made on June 13 was altered and his signature was taken on it later. The police asked the Additional District Magistrate E.S. Lewis to alter the statement. Although he had put the date as June 13, in fact he put this signature three or four days later. On June 13 also he put signature to a document but the present document was not the same as was exhibited in Court. He did not know where that document was. But the document in Court was the very document he signed a few days after June 13.

Inspector Atta Ullah Shah told the witness at the time when he took his signature on these documents that this was an altered version of his statement which he had given on June 13. He said that the alteration included the statement that other witnesses met Shiv Varma at Amritsar house, his visits to Delhi and Agra and details of the conversation he was said to have had with Bhagat Singh.

When Inspector Atta Ullah brought this document to him before he signed it, he did not read it. He read it once before becoming an approver. On June 25, 1929 he was produced before the Additional District Magistrate, Lahore. He did not make any representation to him that the document on which the police got his signature was not his true statement, nor did he ask him whether his statement was that which the Additional District Magistrate had made him to sign. The document contained many matters which the witness never stated before the Court. He put down his signature and put the date as June 13 at the instance of the Police Inspector Atta Ullah Shah. The witness made no protest as approvers were not in a position to protest. He was made to sign it in the Court. On June 25 he was taken to the Additional District Magistrate and pardon was tendered to him.

At this stage Mr. Gopal Lal, counsel for the Crown, submitted that he be allowed to cross-examine the witness because he had turned hostile and had denied certain facts previously stated by him before the Magistrate. Permission to cross-examine was granted.

Cross-examined by Gopal Lal the witness said that when he met Bhagat Singh and Sukh Dev, he did not learn that they had started a secret society nor did he know that there were branches of the secret society in U.P. and other provinces.

Q. Did you state before the Magistrate that you learnt that they had formed a secret society and that their object was the same as that of the Ghadar Party of the Lahore conspiracy case of 1915?

A. Yes, I made this false statement at the request of the police.

Q. Did you also state as follows before the Magistrate. "The object of this party was to uproot the British Government by all possible means and to spread seditious views amongst the public and especially to propagate them amongst students.

A. Yes, but this is also a false statement.

Justice Agha Haidar: What do you mean by false statement?

A. That I made this statement at the instance of the police.

Justice Hilton: Who were those police officers at whose instance you made these statements?

A. Inspector Atta Ullah Shah and the Superintendent of Police, Kapurthala, who is a Sikh gentleman, and whose name I don't remember.

Further questioned, the witness said that while it was true that Sukh Dev met him in the Jallianwala Bagh at Amritsar, it was false that he was led to a house when he saw the two U.P. young men.

Q. Did you identify one of those two young men during the investigation?

A. Yes, I picked up a U.P. man at an identification parade *but he was previously shown to me by the police.*

Q. Did you state before the Magistrate that you told **Bhagat** Singh that you were about to go to Calcutta and upon this he said,¯ you should try to obtain bombs etc. from your friends at **Calcutta?**

A. I stated so but it was false.

Questioned by Justice Hilton the witness said that he had made all these statements at the instance of the police. The prosecution announced that since the witness had turned hostile they did not want to proceed with his statement.

The approver requested the Court to grant him permission to state why he made this false statement. But the Court said that this was not allowed by law.

The prosecution withdrew their request for the production of Bhagat Singh and Sukh Dev in Court to be identified by the approver.[5]

Besides some formal witnesses, Sergeant H.G. Terry deposed to the throwing of the bombs in the Assembly since that act was part of the main charge of conspiracy.

June 20, 1930 was the last day on which the Tribunal sat; that is, as originally constituted. *The Tribune* of Sunday June 22 carried on the front page a news item, under a Lahore June 20 dateline, which read thus: "It is understood that the Special Tribunal for the trial of the Lahore Conspiracy case has been reconstituted and that with effect from Saturday it will be presided over by Mr. Justice Hilton and the other two members of the Tribunal will be Mr. Justice Tapp and Justice Sir Abdul Qadir."

No explanation for this "reconstitution" was given. Scholars differ on the reasons for this development. Kamlesh Mohan opines that it was "to resolve the deadlock" created as a result of the demand by the accused for an apology from Justice Coldstream and for his removal from the Tribunal. He was sent "on long leave". But Justice Agha Haidar was also dropped because he "had declined to submit to the dictates of his colleague".[6]

There was no official announcement of any resignation by these Judges. Section 5(1) of the Ordinance read thus: "If, for any reason, any member of the Tribunal is unable to discharge his duties, the Chief Justice shall appoint another Judge, Additional

Judge, or officiating Judge of the High Court to be member of the Tribunal."

There was no official announcement, that either Judge was "unable to discharge his duties". It was a clear case of removal of an inconvenient Judge from the Tribunal. For, while Coldstream did go on long leave as the law reports suggest, Agha Haidar was perfectly able "to discharge his duties" as Judge of the Lahore High Court immediately thereafter (Vide *Fateh Khan* vs. *Emperor* A.I.R. 1930 Lahore 950. He delivered judgment on July 12, 1930).

Justice J.K.M. Tapp belonged originally to the Provincial Civil Service. Sir Abdul Qadir was a barrister and a man of letters. He served as Minister for Education in the Punjab Government in 1925-26. In 1927 he was appointed a member of the Governor's Executive Council. He served as High Court Judge from 1930 to 1934 when he retired. He was a member of the Council of the Secretary of State for India from 1934 to 1937. In 1939 he was briefly a Member of the Governor-General's Executive Council. The judicial office was an interlude in a career in Government. It did not diminish his distinction as a man of letters. It could not inspire confidence in his independence, either.

If Judges appointed on the Tribunal at its inception could be removed by the Government, there could be no assurance of security of tenure for their successors, either. More to the point, what could be the outlook, judicial and other, of Judges who agreed to serve on the Tribunal *in such circumstances*? Besides, such a "reconstituted" Tribunal cannot possibly inspire confidence in the minds of those arraigned before it nor of the public at large.

Justice Agha Haidar was *removed* from the Tribunal. This is attributed by scholars to his order in dissociation on May 12, 1930. The record shows a *sustained* dissent from colleagues who were openly pro-prosecution.

As for Des Raj's petition, challenging the legality of the Ordinance setting up the Tribunal, he was petitioner only in name. It was in truth the Lahore High Court Bar Association's challenge. It set up a Committee to consider and report on "the validity and propriety" of the Ordinance consisting of Dr. Sir Moti Sagar; Lala Jagan Nath Aggarwal; Dr. Gokal Chand Narang MLC; Malik Barkat Ali; Lala Nanak Chand and the great poet Sir Muhammad Iqbal who then practised actively in the High Court. The first two did not participate in the Committee's deliberations. The Report was signed by Narang, Barkat Ali, Nanak Chand and Iqbal. (See Appendix VII for the full text.)

Tracing the course of the proceedings in the conspiracy case, the Report concluded that the facts did not disclose the existence of an "emergency" which alone could have warranted promulgation of the Ordinance. Proceedings had begun as far back as on July 11, 1929. The Hunger-Strike Bill had been abandoned in September. Since March 8, 1930, "the case went on in the Magistrate's court without any interruption or undesirable incident". The Ordinance was not only invalid, it opined, but "most ill-advised". The Report was particularly critical of the denial of the right of appeal to the High Court.

On July 2, 1930 a habeas corpus petition was filed in the High Court on behalf of Des Raj challenging the validity of the Ordinance. The petition was signed by six lawyers—G.C. Narang, M. Sleem; J.N. Aggarwal; Mehar Chand Mahajan; M. Barkat Ali, and Moti Sagar, all of whom appeared in the High Court. It was heard by a Bench consisting of Justices Alan Broadway and M.V. Bhide. The Crown's case was argued by the Advocate-General of Bengal, N.N. Sarkar, while J.N. Aggarwal argued for the petitioner. He and his colleagues were lawyers of great ability. It is no disrespect to them to say that appearance of counsel of national eminence would have been appropriate in such a case. It is equally fair to admit that it would not have affected the result. Des Raj's petition was dismissed but Justice Bhide dissented from Justice Broadway's view that the Governor-General's opinion as to the existence of the emergency was "final and not liable to consideration by the courts."

Justice Bhide disagreed: "The existence of an 'emergency' is a condition precedent to the exercise of the power of promulgating Ordinances conferred upon the Governor-General. Similarly, the section requires the power to be exercised only for the peace and good government of British India or any part thereof. It follows, therefore, that unless these conditions are fulfilled, no Ordinance promulgated under Section 72 will be valid. If, then a Court of law has power to enquire into the validity of an Ordinance, it must necessarily have power to see whether these conditions are fulfilled. If, for instance, it is found that an ordinance was promulgated in the absence of an emergency whatever or for a purpose wholly unconnected with the peace or good government of the country (a contingency which is, of course, not very likely to arise in practice, but is not inconceivable) can it be maintained that a court of law has no power to declare the Ordinance to be invalid?"

However, he went on to add that a court of law must not interfere with the Governor-General's discretion "unless it is clear that there were no circumstances which could reasonably be considered to constitute an 'emergency' . . ."[7]

Interestingly in a similar case decided around the same time by the Bombay High Court, Chief Justice Beaumont and Justice Madgavkar took the same view as Broadway did. But Justice Blackwell differed from them. He said, "There has been a difference of judicial opinion upon this question in the Lahore High Court (see *Des Raj* v. *Emperor*). I incline strongly to the view that the Court is entitled to enquire into the matter. Assuming that it is, the Court is not, in my opinion, entitled to enquire into the question whether the facts placed before the Governor-General were accurate or inaccurate. The Governor-General must obviously act promptly, and may sometimes have to make up his mind on information which may afterwards be found to be erroneous. In considering whether there was a case of emergency within the meaning of S. 72, the Court, in my opinion, is only entitled to require to be satisfied that facts were placed before the Governor-General which, if true, might reasonably lead him to conclude that an emergency existed."[8]

It is fascinating to delve into the archives to find how officialdom reacted to its victories and defeats in courts of law. The National Archives of India do not provide a feast to students of history alone. A lawyer who enters the portals of its impressive building on 1, Janpath in New Delhi in earnest quest will not be disappointed. File No. 250—Political of 1930 reveals that Justice Bhide's judgment caused panic among the officials of the Punjab Government. It asked the Central Government on July 29 to have the "defect" in the law removed by amendment of Section 72.

To the Home Secretary, H.W. Emerson, who had incurred no small odium in the debate on the Hunger-Strike Bill in the Central Assembly, Justice Bhide's view "that the courts can go into the existence of an emergency, reveals a joint in one armour of which we were previously not aware and which may be the cause of very serious embarrassment."

His minute of August 6 suggested amendment of the law. "In the meantime it would appear advisable to 'sit tight' until the danger is more serious than at present." The matter was referred to the Legislative Department of the Law Ministry.

There Sir George Hemming Spence, as he later became, provided sober counsel. A member of the ICS since 1912, he served in the Punjab till 1919 before moving to the Centre and was Secretary in the Legislative Department from 1935 till independence. He was in the Reforms Department while the partition plan was being carried out (June to August 1947) and became Legal Adviser to the Nizam of Hyderabad in 1949-50.

Spence's minute of August 13 must have startled Emerson: "I find it very difficult to refute Mr. Justice Bhide's view that as the law now stands, the courts have jurisdiction in a proceeding challenging the validity of an Ordinance to enquire, to the very limited extent indicated by him, into the existence of the emergency which must exist before an Ordinance is made. It was conceded by Mr. Justice Broadway, and is fully established by the previous case law, that the Courts have jurisdiction to examine an Ordinance in order to decide whether it was lawfully made and promulgated. It is plainly necessary to the lawful making and promulgation of an Ordinance that there should be an emergency, and prima facie the only possible conclusion is that the courts have jurisdiction to satisfy themselves that an emergency existed. With great respect. I find Mr. Justice Broadway's reasoning in refutation of this conclusion far from convincing."

This officer of the British Raj expressed on August 13, 1930 a view which some eminent Judges of the Supreme Court of independent India hesitated to accept, half a century later, in 1980.[9] Spence said "the existence of an emergency is a necessary condition to the valid exercise of the legislative power conferred thereby and consequently that the admitted jurisdiction of the courts to examine an Ordinance in order to decide whether it was lawfully made necessarily carries with it jurisdiction to enquire into the existence or otherwise of an emergency." There was no case for legislation to override the Bhide ruling.

The file went to Sir David George Mitchell, as he became after he was knighted. In 1929 he was Joint Secretary in the Legislative Department. He fully agreed with Spence. The Law Member, Sir Brojendra Lal Mitter, was against any "immediate steps" according to his own note of August 18. But Emerson recorded a week later that he had spoken to Mitter and found that he favoured amendment of the law "when the Act next comes up for revision" so as to make the Governor-General's view final. Mitter was Advocate-General of India from 1935 to 1945 and Dewan of Baroda from 1945 till independence.

Why not ask the Reforms office which dealt with amendments to the Constitution i.e., the Government of India Act, 1919, to look into the matter, asked the Home Member, Crerar?

The Reforms Office had an interesting figure in W.H. Lewis (Sir William Hawthorne Lewis, eventually). He was born in Kasauli, in the now Himachal Pradesh, in 1888 and was in the ICS when he was 24. The man was, obviously, a smart Alec as his minute of August 27 revealed. It suggested a sleight of hand: "The view taken in this Office is that mention in the Reforms Despatch of the need to amend Section 72 might attract undue, and perhaps undesirable, attention to a point of detail. It is suggested that the wishes of the Honourable Home Member may best be met by passing through the amendment simply as a drafting point, when the present Act is revised." On this Emerson, Crerar and an Indian official, S.N. Roy, jointly minuted: "We may perhaps agree."

That was not the end of the matter. The fundamental question was the finality of the Government's own satisfaction, to the exclusion effectively of judicial review, in cases where the law conferred on it power to be exercised only if the government "is satisfied" that certain conditions exist. A few months later this doctrine of subjective satisfaction was to spell the doom for Bhagat Singh's appeal to the Privy Council against his death sentence despite all the valiant efforts of D.N. Pritt, K.C.

In 1930 the Government of India had no cause for disquiet. Its Ordinance had passed muster and it could play as it wished with the composition of the Tribunal it had established. The file could rest, for the moment. In Curzon's words "Round and round, like the diurnal revolution of the earth, went the file, stately, solemn, sure and slow; and now, in due season, it has completed its orbit . . ." That was written in a minute dated May 24, 1902. Nearly a century later, the file has yet to pick up speed in any Government office.

NOTES

1. Rahbar, pp. 176-7.
2. S. Gopal, *Jawaharlal Nehru: A Biography*, Volume One, 1889-1947, Oxford University Press, 1976, p. 128.
3. Proceedings of the Lahore Conspiracy Case (PLCC), p. 14.
4. *The Tribune*, May 14, 1930.
5. *The Tribune*, June 3, 1930, p. 7.
6. Deol, p. 76, f.n. 4 (1978 edition) and Kamlesh Mohan, p. 368, f.n. 100.
7. Des Raj *vs.* Emperor, All India Reporter 1930, Lahore, 781.
8. Emperor *vs.* Chanappa Shantirappa (1930) 32 Bombay Law Reporter, 1613 at p. 1646.
9. Vide the writer's comment on the Minerva Mills *vs.* Union of India (1980), 2 S.C.C. 591 in *Public Law in India* edited by him; Vikas, New Delhi, 1982, p. 300.

9

A Hand-picked Tribunal

THE reconstituted Tribunal, comprising Justices G.C. Hilton, now Chairman, J.K.M. Tapp and Abdul Qadir, met for the first time on June 23, 1930. All the accused voluntarily came to Court, after a whole six weeks' absence. Agya Ram alone refused to attend. Bhagat Singh and B.K. Dutt had held consultations with their colleagues in the Borstal Jail for three hours. It was a collective decision. The seventeen accused marched into the court-room raising slogans, as before, and singing the usual song once they had taken their seats. The Judges entered the court-room thereafter.

Bejoy Kumar Sinha asked for the removal of their handcuffs. Justice Hilton asked the Police Officer in charge if he had any objection. He had none. The handcuffs were then ordered to be removed.

Bakshi Lal Chand, Assistant Jailor of the Borstal Jail, informed the Tribunal that Agya Ram had refused to come to Court. Shiv Varma asked the Tribunal if he could ask one question from the witness. Justice Hilton replied that Agya Ram or his Counsel alone could examine the witness. Bhagat Singh intervened to say that Agya Ram was their co-accused who had refued to come along with them *and his grounds for the decision were quite different*, he emphasised. They must be permitted to put only one question. At this, the question was allowed.

Bhagat Singh asked: "What is the reason for Master Agya

Ram's refusal to come to court?"

The Assistant Jailor replied: "He says that he does not recognise this Tribunal as a Court."

The others could well have taken an identical stand and kept away. They had every provocation for doing so. The Ordinance, depriving them of a right of appeal to the High Court, was bad enough. They were now being tried by a Tribunal from which the one Judge who showed any concern for their rights had been summarily removed without any explanation to the public; as if it was a private affair between the Viceroy and the Judges.

Their attendance proved that they were not out to obstruct the proceedings or hold the Tribunal to ridicule. Sinha tried to make a statement on behalf of the unrepresented accused on their position in regard to attendance in court.

Justice Hilton would have none of it. "You can put it at the time of defence" he said, obtusely. But the accused wished to explain their position on the immediate situation, not on the charges against them. Sinha tried to explain: "It has nothing to do with our defence."

Justice Hilton testily replied: "If it has nothing to do with your defence, it has nothing to do with the trial."

Bejoy Sinha: But we want to clear our position.

Justice Hilton: You give it in writing.

Sinha: Alright, my lord.

He handed over a written statement to the Tribunal. The Tribunal ruled that it could not go on record at that stage. The accused could hand it over while giving their statements when the time for it came. That, of course, meant at the end of the trial.

Ajoy Ghosh expressed a desire to be represented by Lala Amar Dass; Kishori Lal, by Amolak Ram Kapur and Ram Dutt by Baljit Singh. Des Raj said that he was not in a position to state at that time who should represent him.[1]

All this must have been discussed during the consultations in jail when the seventeen decided to attend court. The desire for legal representation by some of the accused removed all doubt—they were going to participate in the proceedings, if only amends were made for their ill-treatment on May 12.

In the last days of the former Tribunal they had suffered a terrible blow; Bhagat Singh, in particular. It was the death of their colleague of old, Bhagwati Charan Vohra. The Central Committee of their party, the Hindustan Socialist Republican Association, had decided to try to free Bhagat Singh and the task was entrusted to Bhagwati Charan. A bomb was to be thrown near the main gate of the Central Jail on the police party at a time when he was to be brought to court. Bombs were manufactured. On May 28 the group went to the banks of the Ravi to test a bomb. It exploded near Bhagwati Charan, killing him instantly. His wife Durga—Bhabi to the comrades—had run grave risks for all. Bhagat Singh fled from Lahore to Calcutta, after the Saunders murder, in her company along with her child. Rajguru posed as the family's servant.[2]

When the Tribunal resumed the proceedings the next day, June 24, a couple of unimportant witnesses gave evidence. The approver Jai Gopal was next called. Carden Noad said that since he had been examined in chief in the Magistrate's court in the presence of the accused, he was now being tendered for cross-examination. In law, the witness had to be examined afresh by the prosecution. Nothing in the Ordinance altered that rule laid down in the Code of Criminal Procedure, 1898. Carden Noad was battling against time, and tried to short-circuit the regular procedure even by flouting the law. Amolak Ram Kapur and Baljit Singh asked for copies of the record of the case and time to study it. The case was adjourned for the day.[3]

Bhagat Singh handed over a statement to the Tribunal recalling the incident of May 12 and their demands. "Since that day we have not been attending the court. Our condition, on which we were prepared to attend the court, was laid before the Tribunal the next day, namely, that either the President should apologise or should be replaced, by which we never meant that a judge who was a party to that order should take the place of the President. Justice Hilton was a party to this maltreatment as is evident from page 38(A) of the court proceedings.

"According to the present constitution of the Tribunal, both the President and the other judge who had dissociated himself from

Pages from the Diary in which Bhagat Singh reproduced passages from the books he read in prison. The Diary is in the Archives of the Nehru Memorial Museum and Library, New Delhi.

Rabindra Nath's address to an
assembly of Japanese Students :—

"You have your own industry
in Japan; how scrupulously honest
and true it was, you can see by
its products — by their grace and
strength, their conscientiousness in
details, where they can hardly be observed.
But the tidal wave of falsehood has
swept over your land, from that part of
the world where business is business, and
honesty is followed merely as the best policy.
Have you never felt shame when you see
the trade advertisements, not only
plastering the whole town with lies and
exaggerations, but invading the green fields,
where the peasants do their honest labour,
and the hilltops, which greet the first
pure light of the morning? .... This
commercialism with its barbarity of ugly
decorations is a terrible menace to all
humanity, because it is setting up the
ideal of power over the perfection. It is making
the cult of self-seeking exult in its
naked shamelessness .... Its movements
are violent, its noise is discordantly
loud. It is carrying its own damnation
because it is trembling into distortion

It was not against Louis XVI, but against despotic principles of government, that the nation revolted. The principles had not their origin in him, but in the original establishment, many centuries back; and they were become too deeply rooted to be removed; and the Augean stable of parasites and plunderers too abominably filthy to be cleansed, by anything short of a complete revolution. When it became necessary to do a thing, the whole heart and soul should go into the measure, or not attempt it ..... The Monarch and the Monarchy were distinct and seperate things; and it was against the person or principles of the former, that the revolt commenced and the Revolution has been carried.   PP. 19.

————— : o ` —————

Natural &
Civil
rights   Man did not enter enter into society to become worse than he was before, but to have those rights better secured. His natural rights are the foundation of all his civil rights.
          Natural rights are those which appertain to man in right of his existence: (intellectual - mental etc.
          Civil rights are Those that appertain to man in right of his being a member of society.
                              PP. 44

————— : o : —————

Is really self government within the Empire a practicable ideal? What would it mean? It would mean either no real self-government for us or no real overlordship for England. Would we be satisfied with the shadow of self-government? If not, would England be satisfied with the shadow of overlordship? In either case England would not be satisfied with a shadowy overlordship, and we refuse to be satisfied with a shadowy self-government. And therefore no self-government compromise is possible under such conditions between self-govt. in India and the overlordship of England. If self-govt. —— (real) is conceded to us, what would be England's position not only in India, but in British Empire itself? Self-govt. means the right of self-taxation; it means the right of self-control; it means the right of the people to impose protective and prohibitive tariffs on foreign imports. The moment we have the right of self-taxation, what shall we do? We shall not try to be engaged in this uphill work of industrial boycott. But we shall do what every nation has done. Under the circumstances in which we live now, we shall impose a heavy prohibitive protective tariff upon every inch of textile fabric from Manchester, upon every blade of knife that comes from Leeds. We shall refuse to grant admittance to a British soul into our territory. We would not allow British capital to be engaged in the development of Indian resources, as it is now engaged. We would not grant any right to the British capitalist to dig up the mineral wealth of the land and to carry it to their own isles. We shall want foreign capital, but we shall apply for foreign loans in the open markets of the whole world, guaranteeing the credit of the Indian Govt., the Indian nation, for the repayment of the loan . . . . . And England's commercial interests would not be furthered in the way these are being furthered now, under the condition of popular self-government, though it might be within the Empire. But what would it mean within the Empire? It would mean that England would have to enter into some arrangements with us for some preferential tariff. England would have to come to our markets on the condition that we would impose upon her for the purpose, if she wanted an open door in India, and after a while, when we have developed our resources a little and organized our industrial life, we would want the open door not only to England, but to every part of the British Empire. And do you think it is possible for a small country like England with a handful of population, although she might be enormously wealthy, to compete on fair and equitable terms with a mighty continent like India with immense natural resources, with her teeming populations, the soberest and most abstemious populations known to any part of the world?

   If we have really self-government within the Empire, if the 300 millions of people have real freedom of the Empire, the Empire would cease to be British. It would be the Indian Empire, . . .

                    Bepin Ch. Pal ↓
                    New Spirit 1907.

Sukh Dev's marginal notes on the Transcript of the Trial.

I did not meet Sukhdev but I met Kishori Lal who told me that Sukhdev was not in the station but that he would come the next day. I stayed the night in the Mozang house. Next day at about 4 P.M. I met Sukhdev and Kishori Lal and we three went to the 10 canal bridge which is on the Ferozepore Road. While we were there Mr. Scott's motor car, No. 6728, passed on the road. Mr. and Mrs. Scott, the motor driver and a person in white clothes were in the car. Sukhdev had a revolver and I said to him " you can shoot him here ". Sukhdev said " he has already escaped from our hands once, there is no use firing at him again ".

After Kishori Lal had left us at the canal bridge Sukhdev told me that Bhagat Singh and " M " had gone by Bombay Mail towards Delhi on 20th or 21st December and on 25th or 26th *Pandit Ji* also left for Delhi and that his (Sukhdev's) mother and sister and Kishori Lal had gone with him and that after leaving *Pandit Ji* at Delhi they had returned to Lahore.

After this Sukhdev took me to his house in Jora Mori, inside Shahalmi Gate, Lahore. There Sukhdev called someone by the name of Dev Dutt and Kishori Lal answerd the call. Kishori Lal, myself and Sukhdev spent the night in that house in Jora Mori. Next I and Kishori Lal went to the Mozang house and ght our things from there. We vacated the house Mozang. In Jora Mori we had our meals and Sukhdev cleaned and oiled the revolver which he had, Ex. P/122. Sukhdev then gave me Rs. 5 and asked me to go to Ferozepore. I went to Ferozepore and stayed at Dr. Nigham's house. This must have taken place about the 2nd of January 1929. After two or three days Sukhdev came there. He talked for a long time with 40 Partap Singh and gave him Rs. 25 or Rs. 30.

After this the *sahib* who I believed to be Mr. Scott came out of the office. A tall *Sikh* constable in uniform followed him. The constable put something into the hand of the *sahib* and turned towards the office. The *sahib* had started the motor cycle and taken his seat on it. He moved off slowly At this time "M" and I were quite near and I made a sign to say that that *sahib* was coming. On this he took out his pistol and moved towards the *sahib*. I stood at the turning of the road. Bhagat Singh at that time was close to *Pandit Ji* but outside the gate in the road. "M" fired at the officer as soon as the motor bike reached near him. "M" had a revolver with him. The officer who was hit lifted up his hands from the cycle and fell on one side of the cycle. The cycle engine went on turning. One of the officer's legs fell under the cycle. Bhagat Singh ran towards the officer and fired several shots at him. Bhagat Singh a Brownie automatic pistol (Ex. P./480). Bhagat Singh may have fired 5 or 6 times. Some sort of sound came out of the officer's mouth as he fell. Afterwards he did not speak. We three then ran down the Court street. As we ran off a *sahib* came out of the office followed by the same tall *Sikh* constable who had come to put something into the hand of the first *sahib*. These two ran after us. That *sahib* was Mr. Fearn, Traffic Inspector. I identified him later. In the meantime a motor car came from the direction of the District Courts. That motor car stood near me. This was while the firing was going on. I do not know how many men were in that motor car. The *tahsil* building is close to the Police Office. I cannot say if anybody was there Mr. Fearn and the tall *Sikh* constable were running after Bhagat Singh and "M" down the street. Bhagat Singh fired at Mr. Fearn who had just passed Bhagat Singh. Mr. Fearn ducked and fell. Bhagat Singh and "M" then entered the D. A.-V. College compound through the smaller gate. I went on down Court street with my bicycle. The Sikh constable turned into the compound after Bhagat Singh.

Letter to Mitchell from Sir Edward Chamier.

                              24th- February.

My dear Emerson,
        I enclose a copy of an air-mail letter I
have just received from Sir Edward Chamier.
Crerar will be interested.

                    Yours sincerely,

                    [signature]

Copy of an air-mail letter received by me to·
. day from Sir Edward Chamier.

                    - - - - -

My dear Mitchell,
        I was agreeably surprised to find that
Lord Dunedin presiding over the Board which
heard the petition in the Lahore Conspiracy
case - with any other President I think the
petition would have been admitted to a regular
hearing - but Dunedin took a very strong line
from the start and carried the others with him
not that Lowndes (or Saunders ?)* and Mulla
wanted any "carrying". - They evidently felt
that in the end the petition must fail and it
was useless to prolong the agony.
        I will send you with their "reasons" a
transcript of the shorthand notes - you may be in
interested to see exactly what line the board
took.

                    Yours sincerely,
* Probably Lowndes   E. Chameir.

that order of the President have been replaced by two new judges. The third judge who was a party to that order has now been appointed the President of the Tribunal.

"In these circumstances we want to emphasise one thing that we had absolutely no grudge against Mr. Justice Coldstream personally. We had protested against the order passed by the President on behalf of the majority and the subsequent maltreatment meted out to us. We have every respect for Mr. Justice Coldstream and Mr. Justice Hilton that should be expected from man to man. As our protest was against a certain order, we wanted the President to apologise which meant an apology by the President on behalf of the Tribunal. By the removal of that President the position is not changed, because Mr. Justice Hilton who was a party to that order is presiding in place of Mr. Justice Coldstream. All that we can see is that the present position has added insult to injury.

"In conclusion we wish to point out that in case Mr. Justice Hilton dissociates himself from that order referred to above and give us an assurance for future or is replaced by some other judge, we are prepared to continue coming to this court, otherwise we shall have to refuse to attend the court from tomorrow."[4]

The language was not only dignified but graceful. If the Tribunal had shown a modicum of these qualities in its response to the young men's pleas, a new chapter could have been opened in the record of the proceedings. It was not. Hilton continued as before. The next day, June 25, the dock was completely vacant. None of the accused moved from the jail. The Assistant Jailor told the Tribunal that they had given him a petition in writing stating that they would not attend the court until they received a reply to their earlier petition.[5]

That the Tribunal passed orders under the Ordinance, dispensing with the presence of the accused, was but to be expected. The defence Counsel who were present, Baljit Singh and Amolak Ram Kapur were in an awkward position. Amar Dass could not accept the terms of engagement offered by the Tribunal, as the President informed Ajoy Ghosh on June 24. Sir Abdul Qadir made a strange suggestion to the two defence counsel. He appreciated that they had no instructions from their clients but said that they could proceed with the cross-examination, regardless; interview their clients and take a decision the next day. They properly refused to take this advice and insisted on meeting their clients immediately. They returned from the Borstal jail only to inform the Tribunal that they had explicit instructions not to represent their clients in their absence and that they, therefore, withdrew from the proceedings.

Magistrate Roshan Lal was examined-in-chief on the identification parade. So was Robert Churchil, a firearms expert, who had come from London specially to give evidence in the case.

In a case in which a lot turned on identification of the accused, absence of the accused and their counsel was a boon to the prosecution. As it is, even with advantage of the absence of their adversaries, it stumbled every now and then. W.J.G. Fearn, who was fully examined in less than a day, on July 8, was Traffic Inspector of Police in Lahore. Though he was present on the scene right from the beginning, as Saunders had begun to move his motor-bike out of the gate, till Chanan Singh collapsed at the end of the chase, he could not identify either Bhagat Singh or Rajguru in any of the identification parades he had attended. There were "several" of them: "I attended several identification parades but failed to pick out the two assailants of Mr. Saunders." One of them had actually fired at Fearn himself as he ran after them. "When we had gone up Court Street a little distance, he turned and aimed at me. As he fired, I ducked so he missed me. I continued running after him."

Fearn's foot slipped in a small drain at the side of the road "and I came down very heavily. While I was on the ground, the man whom I was pursuing aimed at me again, but his shot misfired". The second shot was fired three minutes after the first. He had seen two assailants, one of slim built and about five feet five to six inches tall. The other was taller. "To the best of my knowledge this man did not fire at me." A few minutes later he said: "I was not certain which of the two men had actually fired at me."[6]

A chance witness, as such are called, came next. Fakir Syed Wahiduddin was relieving himself in the compound of the Tehsil office facing the Government College, with his back to the police office, when he heard the sound of revolver shots. He turned around to see what had happened and saw two men, revolvers in hand, stand near a police officer who had just fallen off his motor cycle. He saw also a car coming to a halt near the Government College Hostel. Three or four persons in it came out and went towards the spot where Saunders lay. He identified Bhagat Singh as the taller of the two assailants at an identification parade and Rajguru at another such parade.

Ata Muhammad, owner of a bicycle shop, gave evidence about the grabbing of a bicycle from his shop by someone on the day of the murder. He had identified Bhagat Singh in the identification parade. "I had no doubts about his identity."

On July 10 the Tribunal framed charges against 15 accused. Copies of the charges were served on them in prison with an order that their pleas would be recorded the next day. The case against Batukeshwar Dutt was withdrawn since he had already been sentenced to transportation for life in the Assembly Bomb case.

Agya Ram and Surendra Pandey were discharged. A public meeting was held outside the Delhi Gate that evening to felicitate Agya Ram and Pandey. Agya Ram had a sad piece of news to break. Kanwal Nath Tiwari had developed insanity owing to his confinement in solitary cell for a month in the extreme heat inside it.[7]

Recording of pleas by the accused in response to the charges was dispensed with on July 11 by invoking the Ordinance. The Tribunal made successive orders, as a matter of routine, to dispense with the presence of the accused after recording evidence as to their refusal or medical unfitness to attend. On July 16 came the evidence of the occupants of the car which drove up just as Saunders was being killed.

Chaudhri Habibullah was with his nephew, Kamal Din, in his car which was being driven by Abdullah. He was witness to the actual firing at Saunders and had identified Bhagat Singh and Rajguru in the identification parades. Kamal Din also gave evidence. So did, in train, a host of witnesses, unchallenged by the accused. They swore to have seen Bhagat Singh and Rajguru that day after the murder; whether they were students in the hostel of the D.A.V. College—like Som Nath, Abnash Chand and Aftab Ahmad—or others such as Ajmer Singh, whose bicycle was just about snatched away from him, or professed eye witnesses to the incident itself like Ganda Singh, Sub-Inspector of Police.

None of the accused participated in the proceedings. Those who were medically fit declined to leave the prison; others on hunger-strike could not. So, it went on till August 26 when Carden Noad suddenly closed the case for the prosecution. 457 prosecution witnesses had been examined; 256, listed in the challan, were abandoned. The Government Advocate said most of the witnesses who had been given up were included in the list for the purpose of corroborating the evidence of the approvers, while others had not to depose about material points; their statements being on very minor points which had been already stated by others. Their reproduction in court would, therefore, be nothing but duplication of evidence already tendered. Hence, in order to save time, the prosecution had given them up. Noad, however, urged that six persons, who could not be summoned by the prosecution in time and on whom the summons could not be served, should, if possible, be summoned as court witnesses. The Tribunal passed an order that those witnesses be summoned as court witnesses and that the accused be informed of their right to tender evidence in defence if they so liked.

Reasons for the rejection of Kishorilal's petition, questioning the legality of the Ordinance and the jurisdiction of the Tribunal to hold trial in this case, were given that day in a lengthy order passed by the Tribunal. It remarked that they declined to go into this question or to record any finding. If they were to record a finding that they were a properly constituted Tribunal, appointed under a valid Ordinance, the application would fail. If, cn the other hand, they were to record a finding that they were not a properly constituted Tribunal or not appointed under a valid Ordinance, their very finding on that point would "ex hypothesi" be a finding of an illegal Tribunal and, therefore, void and of no effect.

Continuing, the judges observed, "Again, if we record a finding that our proceedings are invalid, we could then pass no valid order either releasing the accused persons or remanding them to custody or in any way directing ourselves or the case or directing the accused persons to be tried by any other court. To record such finding would be infructuous. We are of opinion that a finding to the effect that the proceedings of this Tribunal are not valid and issuing of an order consequent upon such finding, regarding the stay of the proceedings and regarding the disposal of the accused persons, could only come from a court or authority other than ourselves." The application was dismissed.

Proceedings were adjourned for the day in order that the accused may be questioned "generally on the case", as the Code (S. 342) enjoined, without administering any oath. The object of such an examination is not to cross-examine the person who is accused of an offence, but to enable him "personally to explain any circumstances appearing in the evidence against him." Copies of the order were served on each of the accused in prison. They took no notice of it and declined to go to Court on August 27 for their examination.

The Tribunal made an order which read thus: "In view of their absence from Court, we are unable to comply with the provisions of Section 342, Criminal Procedure Code, by examining them generally on the case. Having regard to the provisions of section 6 of the Ordinance (III of 1930), which lays down that the procedure prescribed in Chapter XXI of the Criminal Procedure Code shall be followed by us subject to the provisions of the Ordinance and further that the provisions of the Criminal Procedure Code other than those contained in Chapter XXI shall apply to the proceedings of this Tribunal only in so far as they are not inconsistent with the Ordinance, we do not consider it necessary to take any further steps towards examining the accused persons under Section 342, Criminal Procedure Code, inasmuch as the order passed under Section 9 of the Ordinance dispensing with their attendance today precludes such examination."

The Tribunal also passed a separate order under section 256. Criminal Procedure Code, 1898 calling upon the accused to enter upon their defence and to produce their evidence. It adjourned the case to the following day for production of their evidence. A copy of the order was also served upon each of the accused persons in jail, as before.

It was a charade that was being played out. The Tribunal had only to mollify the hurt feelings and assure those arraigned before it that they would be treated fairly. A little tact would have helped. But this was not a Tribunal set up to put those men at ease. Quite the contrary. They, on their part, resisted production to court on successive days, the Tribunal passing the ritual orders dispensing with their presence.

The silence was broken on September 1—just the day before the Government Advocate was to deliver the closing speech for the prosecution—with an application by Amolak Ram Kapur on behalf of Bejoy Kumar Sinha and Ajoy Ghosh.

It read thus: "(1) That they think it was necessary to cross examine all the prosecution witnesses without which they cannot effectively place their case before the Tribunal.

"(2) That it was not possible to start cross examination forthwith without some respite enabling the accused and the counsel to go through the evidence and examine the exhibits the paper books having been applied on the evening of the 30th August, 1930. At least a week's adjournment was necessary for the purpose. The accused never anticipated that the approvers would be produced today without previous notice for cross-examination.

"(3) That the printed paper books cover about one thousand pages and more than 400 witnesses have been examined. It was, therefore, necessary that the accused must be informed of the order in which the prosecution witnesses were produced. In any case one day's notice was necessary before any witness was brought in the witness box for cross-examination.

"(4) That each of the applicant should be afforded with the help of a Counsel on Government expenses.

"(5) That in case the Tribunal did not accede to the above-mentioned prayers the accused (applicants) think that no useful purpose can be served by their taking part in the proceedings."

The President of the Tribunal, after hearing Counsel, rejected the application on the grounds that:

(1) That they had sufficient opportunity to cross-examine the prosecution witnesses but they did not avail of it.

(2) They were specifically told to furnish their list of witnesses whom they wanted to summon through the Court.

(3) Approvers were present in the Court but they were not cross-examined by the accused or their counsel.

That their application for adjournment of the case for a week would unnecessarily cause a further delay in the proceedings of the case.

Before the judges pronounced orders on the application, Kapoor withdrew from the court saying that he was simply instructed to move the application. Thereupon Carden Noad began his speech.[8] He concluded it on September 10.

Kapur's application on September 1 was an obvious and belated tactical ploy. The Tribunal was to die a legal death on October 31. He had no instructions to cross-examine witnesses, as he himself acknowledged. He met his clients in prison and returned a couple of hours later to apply for an adjournment in writing.

Bhagat Singh's father, Kishen Singh, could contain himself no longer as the day of judgment came near. On September 20 he made a petition to the Tribunal. It was obviously drafted by a lawyer. He made some good points on the infirmities in the evidence.

"There is no manner of doubt that Mr. Fearn, European gentleman and Traffic Inspector of Police, who had plenty of opportunity to see the real criminal, could not identify the culprits. This man being a Traffic Inspector had developed his sense of identifying the natives by virtue of his profession and calling in life. He could not pick out Bhagat Singh but it is curious that Ganda Singh, Head Constable, and a Naib Court Police Constable and other witnesses, who were accidentally present on the spot, could spot Bhagat Singh. It means that accused was shown to those witnesses before the identification parade."

In sheer desperation, he went to the length of pleading an alibi which was untrue: "Bhagat Singh was in Calcutta on the day of the occurrence and he actually wrote and despatched a letter to one, Ram Lal, Manager of the Khaddar Bhandar, Pari Mahal, Lahore, which was duly received by him. There are respectable gentlemen to swear that Bhagat Singh was in Calcutta on the day of the occurrence. I can produce them if I am given an opportunity . . . I still humbly pray that Bhagat Singh may be given an opportunity to produce his defence." (Vide Appendix VIII for the text).

Bhagat Singh's letter to his father, published in full by *The Tribune* on October 4 (p. 7)—three days before judgment was pronounced—reflected the depth of the wound his father had inflicted on his feelings, albeit with the best of intentions. He wrote: "I was astounded to learn that you had submitted a petition to the members of the Special Tribunal in connection with my defence. This intelligence proved to be too severe a blow to be borne with equanimity. It has upset the whole equilibrium of my mind. I have not been able to understand how you could think it proper to submit such a petition at this stage and in these circumstances. In spite of all the sentiments and feelings of a father, I don't think you were at all entitled to make such a move on my behalf without even consulting me.

"Father, I am quite perplexed, I fear I might overlook the ordinary principles of etiquette, and my language may become a little bit harsh while criticising or rather censuring this move on your part. Let me be candid. I feel as though I have been stabbed in the back. Had any other person done it, I would have considered it to be nothing short of treachery. But, in your case, let me say that it has been a weakness—a weakness of the worst type . . . I want that the public should know all the details about this complication and, therefore, I request you to publish this letter." (Vide Appendix IX for the text).

Finally, on October 7, 1930 the Special Tribunal on the Lahore Conspiracy Case delivered judgment convicting all the accused except three who were acquitted—Ajoy Kumar Ghosh, Jatindra Nath Sanyal and Des Raj. Sentence was pronounced on the other twelve. Bhagat Singh, Sukh Dev and Rajguru were sentenced to death. Kishori Lal, Mahabir Singh, Bejoy Kumar Sinha, Shiv Varma, Gaya Parshad, Jai Dev and Kamalnath Tewari were sentenced to transportation for life. Kundan Lal was sentenced to seven years' rigorous imprisonment; Prem Dutt, to five.

Jawaharlal Nehru reacted to the sentences in anger and anguish in a speech at Allahabad on October 12: "If England were invaded by Germany or Russia, would Lord Irwin go about advising the people to refrain from violence against the invader? If he is not prepared to do that, let him not raise the issue. It is for Mahatma Gandhi and others, who believe with him, to do so . . . . But let there be no mistake about it. Whether I agree with him or not, my heart is full of admiration for the courage and self-sacrifice of a man like Bhagat Singh. Courage of the Bhagat Singh type is exceedingly rare. If the Viceroy expects us to refrain from admiring this wonderful courage and the high purpose behind it, he is mistaken. Let him ask his own heart what he would have felt if Bhagat Singh had been an Englishman and acted for England."[9]

NOTES

1. *The Tribune*; June 25, 1930, p. 7.
2. Deol, pp. 79-80; Bakshi, pp. 99-100.
3. *The Tribune*, June 26, 1930, p. 7.
4. *Ibid.*, June 28, 1930, p. 7.
5. *Ibid.*, June 27, 1930, p. 7.
6. Proceedings, p. 420.
7. *The Tribune*, July 12, 1930, p. 7.
8. *Ibid.*, September 3, 1930, p. 10.
9. Gopal, Vol. IV, pp. 394-95.

10

The Judgment

FEW could have been surprised either at the convictions or the harsh sentences, least of all Bhagat Singh. He had expected both; according to some, even desired them. Neither the Special Magistrate, Rai Saheb Pandit Sri Kishen, nor the members of the Tribunal showed the slightest concern for the rights or the feelings of the accused who were young men in their early twenties. The solitary exception was Justice Agha Haidar. He was deftly removed.

The prosecution case rested on the evidence of approvers and witnesses who sought to corroborate them. Of the seven approvers, two went back on their statements, Ram Saran Dass and Brahm Dutt. Their evidence was disregarded. Ram Saran roundly accused the police, in the Magistrate's Court as well as in the Tribunal, of altering his statement. Three of the accused had made confessions which they retracted; namely Mahabir Singh, Gaya Parshad and Prem Dutt. Kishori Lal's statement was not recorded. That left the five approvers who gave evidence—Jai Gopal, Phonindra Nath Ghosh, Man Mohan Bannerjee, Hans Raj Vohra and Lalit Kumar Mukherjee. Of them, it was the evidence of Jai Gopal, Ghosh and Vohra which weighed a lot against the accused.

The Judgment was obviously written by one of the English Judges. Its provenance was given away by words like "scullion" and the like. The language was harsh. The word " murderers" was freely used instead of "the accused". The Judgment gave free rein to conjecture and suspicion. Probabilities were aired with abandon in what was supposed to be a criminal trial in which conviction required proof beyond a reasonable doubt, instead of the standard of proof in a civil suit which turns on a balance of probabilities.

The introductory portion of the Judgment was followed by a "Chronological Account of the Facts revealed by the prosecution evidence without any discussion of the proof of those facts". It was prefaced with the explanation that "there is a line to be drawn between events prior to August 1928 (when the several groups agreed to unite, by an accord which was formalised in Delhi the next month) and events subsequent to that month." The account begins with Phonindra Nath Ghose's background (at page 27) and concludes (at page 76) with the throwing of the bombs in the Central Assembly on April 8, 1929. Words like "possibly", "probably" and "presumably" occur all too often; even on incidents of consequence. "While Mr. Fearn (the Traffic Inspector) was chasing Bhagat Singh and Shivram Rajguru down Court Street, one of those two, *probably* Bhagat Singh, fired at Mr. Fearn . . . Constable Chanan Singh was shot in the right groin probably by Panditji . . ." (p. 56) (italics mine throughout).

Conjectures abound also in the portion of the Judgment reciting "What is proved regarding the connection of individual incidents as the outcome of a single conspiracy and by want of evidence" (pp. 215-33).

The law says that evidence adduced in corroboration of approvers must be independent, reliable and relevant. It must not be conjectural. The testimony of Phonindra Nath Ghosh and Man Mohan Bannerjee was regarded as "the foundation of the proof that a singly conspiracy came into being at that meeting" at the Feroze Shah Kotla in Delhi in September 1928. "The corroboration of the testimony of the approvers on this point is of several different kinds. In the first place there is the fact that the same young men who were without much money and who had no ostensible business were found associating together in many different places at the same house." But, these were all members of a political group. The point about their use of false names was well taken, though.

Even the sharing of a book was treated as corroborative evidence of a conspiracy. Perhaps, its title alarmed the Judges. "The book Ex. P. 481 *Roads to Freedom* was recovered from the possession of Prem Dutt at Gujrat and was seen by Jai Gopal in the possession of Bhagat Singh at Ferozepur. This book has notes written on it, by means of which it is identifiable, and it is noteworthy that Jai Gopal's statement, made to a Magistrate after pardon had been accepted by him, preceded the recovery of this book from Prem Dutt's possession.

Likewise, "the two air pistols, cannot be identified beyond all possible doubt but are sufficiently uncommon articles to be identifiable with a fair degree of probability. They were used by the members of the party for target practice."

This is not to dismiss the entire evidence that was produced by the prosecution as unworthy of credence or irrelevant. It is only to emphasise that in a trial in which the prosecution evidence was untested by cross-examination, a far greater duty devolved on the Judges to question the witnesses actively, as Justice Agha Haidar did, and to be more critical in their appreciation of such evidence than the members of the reconstituted Tribunal tended to be. They give, rather, the impression of a very willing suspension of disbelief, quite apart from their own political predilections; to use Laski's phrase, of their inarticulated major premises.

"One other matter which gives rise to the inference regarding the existence of a single conspiracy and also regarding the nature of that conspiracy is the recovery of literature of a revolutionary type from the possession of the various members of the party. For instance, in April 1929, there were found at the Kashmir Building Ex. P. 25 *An account of the Kabul Revolutionary Party*, Ex. P. 19 *What Do We Want* by M.N. Roy (a manuscript copy of a proscribed book); Ex. P. 21 *Revolutionary Biographies* and Ex. P. 490 *Awake Arise*, the last mentioned book having been recovered from the person of Jai Gopal when he was arrested.

"From the possession of Prem Dutt at Gujrat there were recovered Ex. P. 569 *The seven that were hanged*; Ex. P. 481 *Roads to Freedom*; Ex. P. 554 *Bande Jiwan* (a Hindi book containing an account of the modern revolutionary movements in India); Ex. P. 581 *Bharat Varsh Ka Itihas* and Ex. P. 577 a copy of the *Phansi* (execution) number of the *Chand* Magazine.

"The Mughal Bazar House, Amritsar was searched on the 11th May, 1929 by Sub-Inspector Chaudri Sahebud Din (P.W. 32) and amongst the books found there was Ex. P. 170 *Non cooperation pushed to its logical consequences.* In the raid on the house at Saharanpur on the 13th May, 1929, there were found Ex. P. 360, *The naming of Socialism* and Ex. P. 362 *Leninism.*"

In conclusion, the Judgment recorded: "Having regard to the various pieces of evidence detailed above and especially to the evidence regarding the bombs and the pink posters and that which concerns the numerous houses at different places wherein the accused persons are proved to have associated together, coupled with the testimony of the approvers regarding the proceedings of the Delhi meeting of September, 1928, there exists full proof of the existence of a single conspiracy dating from September 1928, and of the fact that subsequent activities of the various accused persons including the Saunders murder, the throwing of the bombs in the Assembly Hall at Delhi, the manufacture of explosives at Calcutta, Agra, Lahore and Saharanpur, and the Moulania dacoity were the outcome of that conspiracy."

Sukh Dev was dubbed the brain behind that conspiracy and was sentenced to death. Rajguru received the same sentence because of his complicity in Saunders' murder. But, of course, the central figure of the trial was Bhagat Singh. The evidence against him is discussed in twenty pages of the Judgment (pp. 157 - 176). "The important feature of the evidence regarding Bhagat Singh is his ubiquity . . . . He was appointed to be a link between the various provinces."

The discussion falls, broadly, into two parts; one concerns his membership of the conspiracy and the other, his culpability in Saunders' murder. His meetings with party members are recalled at length. "Regarding Bhagat Singh's presence, at the Delhi meeting of September 1928, and his appointment to the Central Committee on that occasion, there is the evidence of Phonindra Nath Ghosh and Man Mohan Bannerji, corroborated in an important manner by the testimony of the Chaukidar of the Feroz Shah Tughlak Fort, Bara Singh (P.W. 430), who spoke to Bhagat Singh at the time of the meeting and subsequently identified him in the Court of the Special Magistrate as well as at a magisterial parade. That this witness, being the Chaukidar of the Fort, should have been present on that particular occasion is a natural circumstances and there is no suspicion attaching to his evidence, which should be taken, when coupled with the evidence of two approvers, as fully proving Bhagat Singh's presence at the Delhi meeting."

This proved only his presence; surely, not what transpired there. There was no evidence in corroboration of the approvers' evidence on the proceedings nor of his complicity in plans for a dacoity in Bihar. Phonindra Nath Ghosh and Man Mohan Bannerji testified to his presence and to the plans. A servant, Raghuni, who carried the lantern on the occasion, may be said to have corroborated the evidence as to presence. He did not depose to the plans.

On the aborted raid on the Punjab National Bank in Lahore, besides the evidence of the approvers there was the retracted confession of a co-accused, Mahabir Singh "and is admissible against Bhagat Singh under section 30 of the Indian Evidence Act. General corroboration of the truth of Mahabir Singh's statement on these points is also provided by the taxi driver, Barkat Ali (P.W. 87) and the tonga driver, Feroz Din (P.W. 449) *neither of whom, however, could identify Bhagat Singh.* Further, Bhagat Singh's presence *at the Mozang House* in those days is proved by four witnesses who corroborate the approvers on this point, namely, Hussain Baksh (P.W. 64), Bura (P.W. 72), Budhu (P.W. 73) and Fakir Chand (P.W. 86), all of whom identified Bhagat Singh at magisterial parades and also in Court." These proved only his "presence at the Mozang House" and no more. Since neither the taxi driver nor the tonga driver could identify Bhagat Singh, admittedly, how could they be said to *corroborate* the approvers?

S. 30 of the Evidence Act permits the Court to "take into consideration" the confession of a co-accused. But only to lend assurance to other evidence; by itself it is worthless. Such palpably specious reasoning could come only from Judges who were out to convict and knew that there was no appeal against their decision.

Evidence on Bhagat Singh's complicity in Saunders' murder

was stronger than on his membership of the conspiracy. Evidence of the conspiracy itself was by no means unassailable. On the murder, as on other matters, the crucial question was independent corroboration of the approvers' evidence and, related to it, reliability of the evidence on his identification. That said, what could have survived the strictest tests was damning enough. For instance, the posters proved to be in his handwriting announcing "Saunders is dead".

The Judgment analysed the evidence on the murder under three heads: "There is first the evidence of various eye witnesses who claim to have identified Bhagat Singh either as one of the men who committed the murder or as one of those who were retreating from the scene of murder soon after it had been committed.

"Secondly, there is the evidence of two approvers Jai Gopal and Hans Raj Vohra and especially that of Jai Gopal, who was himself a participator in the crime and whose presence at the scene of the crime has been well proved by other evidence already referred to when dealing with the general corroboration of Jai Gopal, and certain corroboration of the evidence of Jai Gopal that Mr. Saunders was actually shot at by Bhagat Singh which is furnished by the testimony of Mr. Robert Churchill (P.W. 31) the gun expert of London, who proves that a cartridge case found near spot had issued from the automatic pistol, Ex. P. 480 which was recovered from the possession of Bhagat Singh by Sergeant Terry (P.W.18) when he arrested Bhagat Singh on the 8th April, 1929, in the Assembly Hall at Delhi.

"Thirdly, there are the posters, Exs. P.A.X., P.A.X./1, P.A.X./2, P.A.X./3, P.B.O and P.B.S. all of which are proved by the handwriting Expert Mr. Scott (P.W. 423) to be in the handwriting of Bhagat Singh and the contents of which are tantamount to a confession on the part of Bhagat Singh of complicity in the murder of Mr. Saunders in the interests of the Hindustan Socialist Republican Army. A further admission of Bhagat Singh regarding his participation in the Saunders murder is proved by the confession of Prem Dutt who mentions that in his presence, probably in January 1929, Bhagat Singh addressing Sukh Dev stated, 'Do you remember how endeavours were made by us to hit the mark accurately, but we used to miss it? When we went to kill Saunders the bullet struck his head and we thought that one of us would be arrested but none was arrested.' This is quite a reliable piece of evidence. Another confession of Bhagat Singh is proved by Phonindra Nath Ghosh. Bhagat Singh having explained to him at Calcutta at the end of December 1928, that he and his party had murdered Mr. Saunders and that Phonindra Nath Ghosh had not been asked to approve beforehand because he lived at a distance and also because Bhagat Singh had undertaken to take his consent."

There were seven witnesses who professed to have seen Saunders killed. Of them, the Traffic Inspector Fearn could not identify either of the assailants. The evidence of Sub-Inspector Ganda Singh and Wahiduddin was "disregarded owing to the fact that neither of these witnesses was prompt in giving information to the authorities about what he has professed to have seen.

"Although the evidence of Muhammad Ibrahim, Constable, Habibullah and Kamal Din is not in itself unconvincing, there are certain discrepancies in the testimony of the other witnesses which give rise to some doubt whether these three men should be believed. As a measure of precaution their evidence also is disregarded."

That knocked out six out of the seven eye witnesses leaving Abdullah alone. He was driving the car that had arrived on the scene of the murder with Kamal Din and Habibullah—whose evidence was "disregarded".

The Tribunal said "The evidence of Abdullah (P.W. 34) is, however, satisfactory and reliable. He was the motor driver whose motor arrived, while the firing was going on, at the corner of Court street near to the position which Jai Gopal had taken up. He afterwards took the body of Mr. Saunders to the Hospital in his car. He saw the attack upon Mr. Saunders and he has identified Bhagat Singh satisfactorily both at a Magisterial parade and also in Court as the taller of the two men who fired upon Mr. Saunders. This identification there is no reason to doubt."

Abdullah's testimony before the Tribunal, given on July 3, 1930, does not support the finding that it was "satisfactory and reliable". The discrepancies were far greater than those in the testimony of his companions Habibullah and Kamal Din. For once, even the Tribunal was provoked to take the witness in hand. He said, "My statement was recorded by the police four days after the occurrence. No police officer took my name and address on the day of the occurrence, nor did anyone take the name and address of Kamal Din or Habibullah in my presence." He was not sure whether Chanan Singh was in uniform or not. But, he knew Fearn's name well enough. The Tribunal's scepticism, reflected in the transcript of the proceedings, vanished in the judgment.

The other group of witnesses consisted of those who "saw the murderers (*sic*) on their way from the scene of action" passing through the DAV College grounds. These were four students— Som Nath, Abnash Chand, Aftab Ahmed, and Ajmer Singh—and the bicycle shop owner, Ata Muhammad.

How did they fare? "Of these, Som Nath saw the three murderers coming down the staircase from Block B of the D.A.V. College Hostel and noticed that one of them was armed with a pistol. He picked out satisfactorily Bhagat Singh as one of those three men at a magisterial parade, but the identification of Bhagat Singh in the Jail just before giving the evidence in this Court was not quite so *successful*. In the first instance, he picked out another man but immediately corrected himself and picked out Bhagat Singh. His evidence should be regarded as good proof against Bhagat Singh.

"Abnash Chand (P.W. 145) saw the three members near the Botanical Garden of the D.A.V. College. One of them appeared to him to be carrying a pistol. He picked out Bhagat Singh as one of those men successfully at a Magisterial parade by his back which is the only part of the man in question that he had seen on the occasion referred to, but when he went to the Jail shortly before giving the evidence he was unable again to pick out Bhagat Singh. His evidence is, not therefore, very effective against Bhagat Singh.

"Aftab Ahmed (P.W. 232) was near the Volley Ball ground of the D.A.V. College and saw two of the murderers pass by, one having a pistol. He satisfactorily picked out Bhagat Singh both at a magisterial parade and in Court as the man who was carrying the pistol. Ajmer Singh (P.W. 181) is the student from whom an attempt was made to take a bicycle. He did not succeed in identifying Bhagat Singh as one of the party who accosted him.

Ata Muhammad (P.W. 48) is the cycle merchant from whose shop a bicycle was actually taken but abandoned when the witness gave chase. He deposed that one of the three men who passed his shop stopped at a turning while other one removed the bicycle from his shop. He has satisfactorily identified Bhagat Singh at a magisterial parade and also in Court as the man who stopped at the turning and his evidence is good proof against Bhagat Singh. Thus of the witnesses named in this group Som Nath (P.W. 144) Aftab Ahmed (P.W. 322) and Ata Muhammad (P.W. 48) provide good evidence of Bhagat Singh's participation in the Saunders murder."

There was, next, the evidence of the gun expert. The pistol which Bhagat Singh had used in the Central Assembly was not exhibited at the trial of that case. His possession of the weapon was, therefore, not proved.

However, a bullet was picked up from the spot where Saunders' body lay. So were some empty cartridge cases. All these were taken to London for examination by an expert there, Robert Churchill. He made "an occular demonstration in Court to the Tribunal with the help of micro-photographs and a pair of microscopes, with one single eye piece, in which eye piece half of each of two bullets to be compared could be simultaneously compared showing whether or not they had been fired from the same weapon by relating the lines found on one bullet to those on the other.

"The comparison proved conclusively to the Expert and to this Court that the bullet, Ex.P. 864/1-I, and the empty cartridge case Ex.P. 864/1-B, had been fired from the automatic pistol, Ex. P. 480. Had the pistol been recovered from Bhagat Singh immediately after the murder, this piece of evidence would have proved by itself that he fired on Mr. Saunders. As it was recovered from Bhagat Singh nearly four months later, it cannot be said to amount to more than corroborative evidence of the statement of Jai Gopal, but as corroborative evidence it has a very high value . . . .

"Taking all the above evidence together, it is conclusively proved that Bhagat Singh took part in the murder of Mr. Saunders and actually fired at him with the pistol, Ex.P. 480."

The Judgment proceeded to trace his movements after the murder, on December 17, 1928, till April 18, 1929, when he threw the bombs in the Assembly chamber.

"To sum up, Bhagat Singh was a leader of the revolutionary party which was formed at Delhi in September 1928, and had already taken part in revolutionary activities before that party was formed. He was the active member of the Punjab Branch of which Sukh Dev was the organising member and from the time of the Delhi meeting Bhagat Singh was selected as a link between the various provinces and in this capacity was constantly travelling from place to place between the Punjab and Calcutta. As a member of the Central Committee he also took part in the important deliberations and plans of the party and was generally found participating in the active side of the movement.

"He took part in the project to raid the Punjab National Bank of Lahore, he was a protagonist in the murder of Mr. Saunders and it was he who entered into negotiations that J.N. Dass should teach bomb making to the members of the party; he actually took part in the bomb making at Agra, in the rescue party of Jagesh Chander Chatterji and in the journey to Jhansi to test a bomb and finally he was selected to throw a bomb in the Assembly Hall, Delhi, in April 1929."

That Kishen Singh denied Bhagat Singh's complicity in the murder and even pleaded an alibi which was untrue is attributable, of course, to a father's desperate attempt to save the life of a son who was in the prime of life; the life of a patriot and a life of promise. The former Secretary of State for India, Leopold S. Amery, tried frantically to save the life of a son who was a traitor to his country during the Second World War.

The Tribune's endorsement of Kishen Singh's alibi, in an excellent series of six closely reasoned editorials (October 9-17, 1930) can only be ascribed to an excess of nationalist ardour. "Nor is it easy to believe that, after successfully evading arrest for such a long time, a man of the intelligence and resourcefulness of Bhagat Singh would have got himself arrested in the Assembly Chamber with the self-same weapon which had been used in the murder of Mr. Saunders.

"Another fact which has an important bearing on this aspect of the case is the statement of S. Kishen Singh, father of Bhagat Singh, that both documentary and oral evidence was available to prove that Bhagat Singh was in Calcutta at the time when the murder was committed at Lahore."

Today, no historian contests the fact that Bhagat Singh and Rajguru did, indeed, fire the fatal shots at Saunders. Their researches have, in fact, elicited interesting details which did not emerge in the trial.

But, the issue is the fairness of the trial; the sense of fairness of those who staged it—the police, the prosecution, the Magistrate and the three judges on the Tribunal. This was the first case of its kind ever in which twelve persons were tried, convicted and sentenced to death, transportation for life and long terms of imprisonment, for the gravest offences known to law, after a trial which was conducted in their absence.

It was a trial, moreover, by a Special Tribunal set up by the Viceroy's edict in an Ordinance, without recourse to the Central Legislature. The Tribunal was set up for a brief term of six months and endowed with powers which the Central Assembly had refused to grant. The Viceroy has professed, through his Home Member James Crerar, to acquiesce in that decision—only to bring the law by the back-door through the Ordinance. Even a Tribunal such as that was not left undisturbed. Under the pretext of removing its President, Justice Coldstream, to whose presence on the Tribunal the accused had objected, the Viceroy set off the loss by removing an inconvenient judge, Justice Agha Haidar. No public explanation was provided. His substitute, Sir Abdul Qadir, a man of many qualities, was no substitute for Justice Agha Haidar.

Such games were not untypical of the sport of the times. A distinguished Chief Justice of the Bombay High Court like Sir Amberson Marten thought nothing of sending for a junior member of the bar, as M.C. Chagla then was, and advising him not to involve himself in "anti-government politics like the boycott of the Simon Commission". When the advice went unheeded, he wrote privately to the Home Member asking him not to appoint Chagla as a lecturer in the Government Law College for a further term because of his political views.

It was in a clime such as this that the authorities bestowed extra care in selecting and re-selecting—once "error" was discovered—members of the Tribunal. Chagla recalls an instance of this kind around the same time, in a case where the stakes were far lower, in his memoirs *Roses in December*: "At the time of the Simon Commission boycott, a procession of students was marching through one of the streets of Bombay and a police Sergeant named Carter assaulted two members of the procession, one of whom was the well-known young nationalist and social leader, Yusuf Meharali. These two persons had Sergeant Carter prosecuted for assault. The matter came before a Presidency Magistrate, Mr. Pandit. Mr. Pandit after hearing the evidence, convicted Sergeant Carter and passed sentence on him. Sergeant Carter came in revision before Mr. Justice Mirza and Mr. Justice Patkar. They constituted the Bench which was dealing with criminal cases during the particular term. This Bench did not issue a rule, but strangely enough asked the Magistrate's court to forward the record of the case to the High Court.

"The revisional application should have been ordinarily disposed of by Justice Mirza and Justice Patkar, but this did not happen. Sir Amberson Marten, who was then the Chief Justice, had taken what certainly was a most extra-ordinary step. He withdrew the case from this Bench, constituted a special Bench consisting of himself and Mr. Justice Kemp and acquitted Sergeant Carter. The whole incident caused a great deal of indignation at the bar. The motive behind the procedure was evident, the sole object being to acquit Sergeant Carter, and to condemn the Simon boycott agitation. Sir Amberson Marten could not trust the two Indian judges to deal with the matter, but had to have an English Bench to handle a petty case of assault . . . .

"This was a revisional application and normally the High Court does not go into the evidence, or reappreciate evidence in revision. It only interferes when a question of law is involved, or when there is a question of jurisdiction. But this Learned Bench actually went into the evidence, and came to the conclusion that the evidence had not been properly appreciated by the Presidency magistrate. In other words, the Court of Appeal acted as a Court of fact, and substituted its own appreciation of evidence for that of the Magistrate."[1]

In Bhagat Singh's case, the stakes were far greater. The Central Government's prestige was involved. It was determined to have Bhagat Singh sent to the gallows. The Bombay case shows how a Bench was fixed. It is not unlikely that the Chief Justice had received a hint from the Governor.

To revert to the Tribunal's judgment, one would have thought that the rule as to independent corroboration of evidence by approvers acquires far greater force when their evidence itself is untested by cross-examination, especially when two of them openly alleged pressures by the police and retracted their statements; as did three of the accused also. Unlike Justice Agha Haidar, none of the other four who served on the Tribunal initially or later— Justice Hilton alone serving throughout—cared to question the approvers and other prosecution witnesses closely.

A little gesture to the young prisoners would have sufficed to persuade them to go back to the court. Let alone such a gesture, never did either the Magistrate or the Tribunal take the police to task for their bestial behaviour towards the accused on October 22 and 23, 1929 and on May 12, 1930.

The police received every latitude from the Magistrates and the Tribunal. The accused were not produced in court before Magistrates for remand. Magistrates were taken to the specially selected places where they were confined, without any access to their families or legal advice. *The approvers were left throughout in police custody.* Repeated pleas by the accused for their transfer to judicial custody were brusquely rejected. This vitiated the entire trial.

The accused did not participate in proceedings before the Tribunal. But it was, surely, familiar with the record and, indeed, the fact that the approvers were in police custody. The Magistrate had rejected an application for removal of the approvers to judicial custody on October 4, 1929 in rude language: "The learned defence counsel does not hold a brief on behalf of the approvers to be in a position to plead for them quite uninvited and then the proper time for him to elicit details of the nature alluded to by him in his application would be when the approvers would come into the witness box and the accused shall have a right to cross-examine them. In short, there is no jurisdiction of the accused to dictate to the court as to how and where the approvers should be kept and to enquire as to their whereabouts at this stage and I, therefore, reject the application" (*The Tribune*, October 6, 1929).

This was part of the record. What is the worth of evidence by approvers who have been in police custody for months? Not to put too fine a point on it, how impartial could be a Magistrate who uses such language and a Tribunal which condones the lodging of approvers in police custody?

Jinnah had accurately summed up the government's policy in his speech in the Central Assembly a year earlier: "We will pursue every possible course, every possible method, but we will see that you are sent either to the gallows or transported for life; and in the meantime we will not treat you as decent men."

Abdullah (P.W. 34) was the only professed eye witness whose testimony could pass muster in the Tribunal. The others either collapsed, by reason of failure to identify, or intrinsically lacked credibility because of the gross delay in informing the authorities. None except Fearn gave a chase to the accused. Identification parades made little sense. Bhagat Singh's photographs had already appeared in the newspapers. More than once, the accused, particularly Bejoy Kumar Sinha, caught the police red-handed identifying the accused to prospective witnesses. Abdullah's evidence was not subjected to cross examination by the accused.

It is not difficult to perceive that Justice Agha Haidar's presence would have made all the difference on precisely such crucial points. It was the fear of his dissenting judgment which clinched the issue. It would have robbed the English Judges' decision of all moral force. Bhagat Singh could not have been sent to the gallows on a 2 to 1 verdict by a Special Tribunal. For all their flaws, British standards were superior to those of Zia-ul-Haq. He had Zulfiqar Ali Bhutto executed after a 4-3 verdict by Pakistan's

Supreme Court given on the basis of uncorroborated evidence of approvers.[2] The British handled such situations with greater finesse. On each occasion, in 1929 and in 1979, a murder had been arranged by the State through the instrumentality of courts of law.

NOTES

1. M.C. Chagla, *Roses in December*, Bharatiya Vidya Bhawan, Bombay, 1973. pp. 111-12.

2. For an analysis of Z.A. Bhutto's trial and appeal to the Supreme Court vide the writer's article "A murder has been arranged" in A.G. Noorani, *India, the Super Powers and the Neighbours: Essays in Foreign Policy*, South Asian Publishers, New Delhi, pp. 222-29.

11

Ritual in the Privy Council

BHAGAT Singh had even less interest in legal proceedings after the Tribunal's verdict. But he was persuaded that a petition for special leave to appeal to the Judicial Committee of the Privy Council in London would not be unproductive of political advantage, whatever its eventual fate might be. The Defence Committee, especially its members Lala Duni Chand and Dr. Gopi Chand Bhargava, were very keen on moving the Privy Council. So was lawyer Pran Nath Mehta and a counsel of national eminence, Motilal Nehru.[1] He sent a message from his sick bed in Shimla. He was to die on February 6, 1931 just five days before the Privy Council dismissed the petition without admitting it to a regular hearing.

As in any other petition to the Privy Council, issues of fact were eschewed. The sole issue was the legality of the Ordinance. It is unlikely that Bhagat Singh's counsel, the young D.N. Pritt, K.C., was aware of his client's popularity in India or the political significance of his trial. To him, it was just another brief in the Privy Council where only issues of law are contested. He had not quite made the transition "From Right to Left", the sub-title of his *Autobiography*. Though published in 1965, it makes no reference to Bhagat Singh at all.[2] Incidentally, his colleagues were also joined as parties to the petition.

The petition was heard on February 11, 1931, four months after the Tribunal delivered judgment, by a Board consisting of Viscount Dunedin, Lord Thankerton, Lord Russel of Killowen, Sir George Lowndes, an old India hand, and Sir Dinshah Mulla.

Fortunately a full transcript of the argument is available in the National Archives of India.[3] Rather than consign it to the ghetto of an Appendix, it is reproduced here in full. The reader who is not interested in them can skip the pages. The substance of Pritt's argument is set out at the end.

D.N. Pritt, K.C., Horace Douglas, C. Sidney Smith instructed by Messrs. Douglas Grant & Dold, appeared for the petitioners.

A.M. Dunne, K.C. and W. Wallach, instructed by the Solicitor, India Office, appeared for the Respondent.

Pritt: May it please your Lordships. In this case I appear with my learned friends Mr. Horace Douglas and Mr. Sidney Smith for the Petitioners, and my learned friends Mr. Dunne and Mr. Wallach appear for the Crown. If we can make good to your Lordships the proposition which we seek to advance, I hope I may submit with some confidence that it is a case that does not meet with the usual difficulties.

Viscount Dunedin: I think you may take that. It would strike at the whole jurisdiction. What you have to make out is that Section 72 does not authorise what was done.

Pritt: Yes, my Lord. Possibly the best thing will be to go straight to Section 72 and submit my arguments to your Lordships on the effect of that section. It is a section which has been in the statute for some time; it is a section of an Imperial Act of Parliament; there is no doubt whatever of its force and validity, but I do not think anyone would deny that it creates a somewhat striking power, and is one, at any rate, which any Court will construe with care.

Viscount Dunedin: It creates an absolute power.

Pritt: Yes, when the conditions are fulfilled.

Viscount Dunedin: Yes, I do not suppose Parliament has ever done anything more absolute than in passing the old Acts of Attainder.

Pritt: No, my Lord. The power it creates is a limited power of delegated legislation: "The governor-general may, in cases of emergency, make and promulgate ordinances for the peace and good government of British India or any part thereof, and any ordinance so made shall, for the space of not more than six months from its promulgation, have the like force of law as an Act passed by the Indian Legislature; but the power of making ordinances under this section is subject to the like restrictions as the power of the Governor-General in Legislative Council to make laws". I do not think I need trouble your Lordships with the words after the last semi-colon. The substance of the matter here is, in my submission, that before any ordinance can be valid three things must happen, and at least two of those are of some importance to this Petition. In the first place, there must be a case of emergency, whatever "emergency" may mean; the second is that the ordinance must be an ordinance falling within the description that it is an ordinance for the peace and good government of British India, or some part thereof; and the third point is that it must, in addition to being for peace and good government, fall within the restrictions of the legislative powers of the Indian Legislature which I think are to be found mainly, if not wholly, in Section 65.

My Lords, these three points fall into two classes; the first is that something must happen before the power comes into force at all; and secondly, when it has come into force, that is to say when there is an emergency and the Governor -General may do something, there are two limits, so far as we are concerned, to what he may do. May I state my submission in outline, in relation to this very striking power. My submission firstly is that if the exercise of the power be challenged, it is necessary to establish affirmatively that there is a case of emergency; it is not for the Executive, if I may so describe the Governor-General, to say there is an emergency; it must be proved; like any other question of fact lying at the root of a jurisdiction, it has to be established before the Courts, in my humble submission.

Viscount Dunedin: You mean really the Court is to have the power of reviewing the view of the Governor-General that there was a case of emergency?

Pritt: I do not put it in that way; I would put it in that way if I were forced to do so. I put it in this way: the Courts in British countries are places where the facts are decided. At the root of the

Governor-General's right to make an ordinance lies in every case the question of fact: Was there an emergency? If it becomes material to know whether there was an emergency or not, that is a matter which has to be proved before the Court.

Viscount Dunedin: Is it your proposition that before the Governor-General can promulgate an ordinance he would have to bring a declaratory action in the Courts for a declaration?

Pritt: No, my Lord.

Viscount Dunedin: What do you mean by "the Courts".

Pritt: I mean this, my Lord, that anybody, however eminent, who has power to act when certain facts exist, must make up his mind whether they exist or not, and then act, and that when his power is challenged and it is suggested that those facts did not exist, the question whether those facts exist or not is a question like any other question lying at the root of any jurisdiction and must be decided by the Courts.

Viscount Dunedin: Your contention comes to this, that this Board, which is the only place to which you can come, shall have an inquiry into the facts and review the view of the Governor-General that there was a case of emergency. That is what it comes to, is it not?

Pritt: In the same sense as happens when any other executive makes up its mind that there is a riot and exercises powers which it has when there is a riot, and which it does not have when there is not a riot, and then subsequently at their leisure the Civil Courts decide whether there was a riot or not.

Viscount Dunedin: I do not know quite what you mean by that. I am not aware of any clause in an Act of Parliament like Section 72 which has to do with riots.

Pritt: Not in an Act of Parliament but it is a question that often arises in English common law when the Civil Executive applies to the Military.

Lord Thankerton: You say this is a pure question of fact. I should have doubted that. Surely the trouble about an emergency is what it may lead to, as much as, if not more than, what has already happened. Does not this assume somebody having an opinion not as a question of fact?

Pritt: It is a very difficult question of fact.

Lord Thankerton: I should have said it was a question of opinion.

Pritt: Even a question of opinion is a question of fact.

Lord Thankerton: It is so treated by the Courts, I agree; but that leads to a consideration as to who is the proper person to judge of it, on the construction of this section; it is not the ordinary question of fact.

Pritt: The state of a man's mind is as much a fact as the state of his digestion.

Lord Thankerton: This is a question of administration, is it not?

Pritt: In my humble submission, section 72 is not a matter of administration; it is a matter of substituted legislation.

Lord Russel of Killowen: What is the test to be applied in ascertaining whether an emergency exists?

Pritt: The usual test as to whether Johnson has told a lie, or drove a car negligently.

Lord Russel of Killowen: This seems to be more a question of opinion. The question is: Who is best qualified to form an opinion?

Pritt: That brings me back really to my submission. I am putting my submission in two ways: firstly, that merely construing that section, the words "in cases of emergency" meant not that the Governor-General is the sole judge as to whether there was an emergency or not, but that there had to be in fact an emergency. The second limb that I am going to put on that is this. A proper method of construing one section of a statute is to see what words it uses in other sections, and a comparison of this section with half-a-dozen other sections in this Act makes it, in my submission, overwhelmingly clear that the Imperial Parliament, when conferring this very great power by section 72 on one individual, however eminent in the Executive of British India, was deliberately refraining from entrusting to him the right to decide, either as fact or opinion, whether there was an emergency or not.

Sir George Lowndes: I should have thought there was a personal element here.

Pritt: Many personal elements have to be decided by a Court afterwards. There is a personal element in every running-down case. May I call your Lordships' attention to Section 67(b) of the Government of India Act; "Where either chamber of the Indian legislature refuses leave to introduce, or fails to pass in a form recommended by the Governor-General, any Bill, the Governor-General may certify that the passage of the Bill is essential for the safety, tranquility or interests of British India or any part thereof". Those are plainly words that leave the matter in the hands of the Governor-General alone. Then it says the Bill shall become an Act by certain means which I need not trouble your Lordships with. Then sub-section 2 says: "Every such Act"—that is the Bill turned into an Act—"shall be expressed to be made by the Governor-General, and shall, as soon as practicable after being made, be laid before both Houses of Parliament, and shall not have effect until it has received His Majesty's assent". Then lower down your Lordships see: "and upon the signification of such assent by His Majesty in Council, and the notification thereof by the Governor-General, the Act shall have the same force and effect as an Act passed by the Indian legislature and duly assented to". Then in case the matter has to be dealt with so swiftly that even this is too slow, we get the proviso: "Provided that where in the opinion of the Governor-General a state of emergency exists which justifies such action, the Governor-General may direct that any such Act shall come into operation forthwith". Perhaps I can put the matter shortly in this way: There are at least eight other passages in that Statute of varying strengths and varying kinds. I do not pretend that I have not given your Lordships the best of them, but there are others as good and others not much worse, in which it is shown overwhelmingly that the Imperial Parliament, when it wants to entrust a matter to the Governor-General, has sufficient command of the English language to be able to put it beyond the range of doubt. Section 72 has existed for a long time, and some of the other Sections in which the sort of thing is dealt with have existed for a considerable time, and my first submission to your Lordships accordingly is that the Governor-General has power here to substitute himself to a certain extent and for a short period of time for the legislature in order to move more swiftly than the legislature can in Legislative matters . . .

Viscount Dunedin: I quite understand the point, but I must bring you to this: What is the remedy according to you?

Pritt: The remedy, in my humble submission, is a remedy for the Crown.

Viscount Dunedin: Is it not a remedy for the subject?

Pritt: The remedy for the subject is that when an Ordinance is sought to be applied to him, he shall submit an argument to some of His Majesty's Courts, or if one is being established by the Ordinance, I think there is authority for the proposition that he may submit it to that tribunal or he may submit it to another tribunal and say: Here is the Crown doing something which I say it has no power to do.

Viscount Dunedin: Assuming we grant leave to appeal, what would you say to the Board when the appeal was heard?

Pritt: I should say to the Board three things. The first thing I should say to the Board is: I challenge this Ordinance; it is made under a definite limited power; I say that the conditions of the exercise of the power do not exist, and never have existed.

Viscount Dunedin: What would happen after that?

Pritt: My submission on the whole of the facts would be this: The power is limited; in order to show that it has been validly exercised and that the conditions are fulfilled, there must be some proof that there was a case of emergency. I have challenged that, once before this very tribunal and once before the High Court at Lahore, and in neither instance did the Crown adduce one tittle of evidence that there had ever been a case of emergency.

Viscount Dunedin: Then you would say that the matter must be gone into, I suppose?

Pritt: I am not sure I should not take a higher line and say: The Crown having had two opportunities to establish that they had this power because there was an emergency, and having refrained on both occasions from adducing any evidence . . . .

Viscount Dunedin: The Ordinance had been promulgated long before this?

Pritt: Long before what, my Lord?

Viscount Dunedin: Long before the matter came into Court.

Pritt: This Ordinance was promulgated six or seven months after my clients first stood their trial.

Dunne: That is not the point.

Viscount Dunedin: It was promulgated before the trial took place before the special Tribunal?

Pritt: Yes, my Lord.

Viscount Dunedin: That is all that was done, is it not?

Pritt: As soon as that was done, we challenged it by *habeas corpus* proceedings, and the Crown adduced no evidence of any description.

Viscount Dunedin: And you failed on that?

Pritt: We failed on that. I think I ought to tell your Lordships at once that when the matter came before me I took the view, on behalf of my clients, which may be right or wrong, that they really ought to present to your Lordships at some stage an appeal from that decision. That was put in train at once and leave is now being applied for to the High Court at Lahore to appeal from that Judgment, and ultimately, if your Lordships think fit to grant us leave to appeal here, then either by the High Court at Lahore granting me leave, if it thinks right, or by me asking your Lordships in a supplemental petition if the High Court does not think right to grant me leave and your Lordships thought right to grant it, then ultimately by consolidation the matter would come before your Lordships in the dual form, namely, an appeal from the Judgment in the *habeas corpus* proceedings and a direct appeal from the decision of the Tribunal.

Coming back to the substance of the matter, I should most certainly submit on behalf of my clients that the Crown, having twice had the opportunity of establishing a case of emergency and not having even attempted so to do, that the decision of the Court ought to be declared by your Lordships to be entirely void, whereupon the condition of my clients, as I understand it, would be that my clients would be people as to whom there had been a preliminary hearing before the Magistrate, if that is the right description at Lahore, which was entirely void and they would be people whose trial was entirely void; and they could, if it was thought right, be re-arrested and tried according to the ordinary process of law which was mysteriously interrupted at the beginning of last May.

The second submission I should make to your Lordships, if I was granted leave to appeal and the substantive appeal came on, would be this—I am still only dealing with the emergency and not with the other difficulties which I desire to raise—let it be granted that I am wrong in asserting that it is for the Governor-General to establish that there was a case of emergency, or at any rate, let it be granted that I am wrong in asserting that it is for the Governor-General to establish that by evidence, and let me approach it in the way which one of the Courts below approached it at one stage and say: I see a statement by the Governor-General; the Governor-General is so important a person that if he says something in his Gazette, I will take it as evidence. It was not put in that crude fashion, but that is the substance of what one of the Judges said in the *habeas corpus* proceedings. Then I should submit to your Lordships' Board that we have only to look at the Governor-General's statement to come to the conclusion that there was no emergency.

Lord Thankerton: That is to say, we are to come to the conclusion that the Governor-General was wrong?

Pritt: When he said there was a state of emergency, he may not have regarded it as a matter of opinion.

Lord Thankerton: The preamble of the Ordinance gives the reasons, does it not? You say he should not have come to the conclusion that there was an emergency?

Pritt: It is not the preamble. One must be very accurate here. The preamble does say something about an emergency. It appears in the same number of the Gazette as a statement by the Governor-General; but in my very humble submission, in spite of the eminent position of the Governor-General, the statement by him proves nothing.

Viscount Dunedin: Either you look at his statement and say: Those are his reasons and he has come to a wrong conclusion that there was an emergency; or else you say: Those are not his reasons; I do not know what his reasons were; how can I say whether there was an emergency or not in the opinion of the

Governor-General? Which do you say is the correct construction for the purpose of this argument?

Pritt: I put it alternatively. In the first place, I say there must be proof of an emergency; secondly, if it is suggested that is evidence, then I say, when it is looked at, there must be some limits to the word "emergency", and that he can only act within those limits. May I put another alternative: One or two Courts in India, for reasons which I confess I do not follow as a matter of logic, have laid down expressly that it is for the Court to make up its mind and to investigate the questions of fact whether there is an emergency or not, but the Court has sufficiently investigated that when it has come to the conclusion that there is some evidence on which the Governor-General could decide, and I should submit to your Lordships, if leave to appeal was granted, that there was no evidence. This depends upon a consideration of the facts of the case and a consideration of the meaning of the word "emergency", and the question of the meaning of the word "emergency", although important and lying at the base of the whole matter, is not the whole argument that I would desire to put before your Lordships. I rely very much upon the definition of the power, or rather the definition of the power to legislate under circumstances of this sort, that it must be for the peace and good government of British India. I do not presume to challenge the proposition that "the peace and good government of British India" is a very wide phrase, but at some stage in my submission to your Lordships I do want to put it very strongly that this particular Ordinance is a privilegium of a very terrible description; whether it could possibly conduce to peace is a matter of some difficulty; that it could conduce either to good government or to government at all, I would invite your Lordships to consider very carefully indeed. My submission is that on the true construction of Section 72 it is plainly intended to empower the Governor-General in cases of general emergency or cases of a particular emergency area, or whatever it may be, to pass what may fairly be called legislation, but this is legislation which I think in every Roman law country any jurisprudent would indignantly deny to be legislation at all.

Lord Thankerton: Why?

Pritt: Because it is a privilegium. It makes no law that any man has to obey, except the civil servants of the Crown and the members of the Tribunal. It lays down no liberty to any man to do anything; it lays down no provision by way of criminal law or anything else that any man shall not do anything.

Viscount Dunedin: What about the old Acts of attainder? What did they do?

Pritt: They were passed by the supreme Imperial Parliament.

Viscount Dunedin: Certainly.

Pritt: This is not; this is dedicated legislation, and all that the Governor-General can do is to make and promulgate Ordinances for the peace and good government of British India or any part thereof, which are to have the force of law for six months. That is a privilegium, and I submit that cannot in any view be called legislation at all for peace, order and good government.

Lord Russell: Do you say that under Section 65 of this Act the Indian Legislature could not have passed an Act in these terms?

Pritt: Section 65 is not the only Section which has to be looked at in order to discover the power and restriction of the Indian Legislature, but it is much the most important. I concede reluctantly that the Indian Legislature could have done this, but then the Legislature is allowed to legislate within clauses (a) to (f), whether it is for the peace, order and good government of British India or not. It is, in my humble submission, right to bear this in mind, that what this Statute actually does is this. It says: Here are a number of men; they are all in custody; they are not running about; they are under trial; that is to say, preliminary proceedings are being carried forward against them on specific charges. They have at the moment the right of citizens in British India to have a *prima facie* case made out against them, and before they are tried to know what that case is. They have a right to be tried before the ordinary Sessions Judge with assessors or a jury, and after the trial to appeal to the established High Court at Lahore, with which Court this Ordinance cannot interfere; that is another point to which I will come in a moment. The authorities say by this privilegium, in which there is not a word about other men, not a word about other offences, not a word about means of preserving law and order and peace and good government, we say that these particular individuals shall be deprived of the right to know the case against them, shall be deprived of the right to have a *prima facie* case made against them, shall be deprived of the right of trial before a Sessions Judge and a jury or assessors, shall be deprived of the right to go to the High Court at Lahore on appeal; and we say they shall be tried before a special tribunal without knowing what the case is against them except as and when it comes out of the mouth of approvers or independent witnesses, as the case may be. At any moment the tribunal may change its personnel, and when they come to the end of the case, it may be that these people will be sentenced to death without appeal by three gentlemen who, by reason of the changes in personnel, may none of then have seen a single one of the witnesses, and they may sentence these men to death on evidence of approvers whose demeanour they never have had the opportunity to observe. I submit to your Lordships that on any reasonable meaning of the word "legislation" this is not legislation at all.

Lord Thankerton: Why is it not legislation? You may think it is bad legislation. You have admitted that under Section 65 the Indian Legislature could have passed such an Act. Would you have said that was legislation?

Pritt: I should have said that to an Englishman brought up with the idea of Parliaments with unlimited powers and of subsidiary Parliaments with very limited powers, that that would be an administrative Act disguised in the form of legislation, but which is perfectly lawful, but when one comes to a Section which does not say the Governor-General shall be invested with all the legislative powers of Section 65, but does say that he may make and promulgate Ordinances for the peace and good government of British India, that means that the Governor-General may make legislation which provides what people ordinarily call law; which provides something which applies to more than one person or one group of persons. Legislation that it shall be unlawful to wear a particular kind of hat that is insulting to one's fellow citizens would be legislature; but an administrative Act disguised as a piece of legislation dealing *ex post facto* with the trouble which has already arisen in the case of the certain individuals who are to be tried for specific offences, in my humble submission, if legislation is used in any ordinary sense or if it is used as power to make and promulgate legislative Ordinances for the peace and good government of the country, my clients ought to be given the opportunity to put before this Board on a full appeal the argument that such an Ordinance is invalid and cannot fall within the words "Ordinances for the peace and good government of anything".

The third point is important, but less important and perhaps less clear, namely, that the restrictions imposed by this Act upon the power of the Indian Legislature to make laws must also be proved. Your Lordships will probably know that in one case that has been challenged on the broad proposition whether this type of ordinance offends against the unwritten law or constitution of the United Kingdom of Great Britain and Ireland. I do not think I can advance that argument to your Lordships; that seems to be precluded; but there is another ground here, and that arises out of the *consideration of Section 84* and a later one, I think *Section 113*. Section 65 is the main section imposing the power and placing restrictions on the power. Section 84 is in a department called "Validity of Indian Laws". The only one that matters here is: "A law made by any authority in British India and repugnant to any provision of this or any other Act of Parliament shall, to the extent of that repugnancy, but not otherwise, be void". That is partly an enabling section, because it prevents repugnancy destroying the whole thing, but in my submission the effect of that is this: If any act of the British Indian Legislature be challenged, and therefore if any ordinance under section 72 be challenged, as operating repugnantly to any provision of this Act of Parliament, it will be void. My submission is that this is repudgant to the provisions of this Act of Parliament, it will be void. My submission is that this is repugnant to the provisions of this Act of Parliament because it deprives the High Court at Lahore of jurisdiction in the matter. May I refer your Lordships to *Section 113*: "His Majesty may, if he sees fit, by letters patent, establish a high court of judicature in any territory in British India. whether, or not included within the limits of the local jurisdiction of another high court, and confer on any high court so established any such jurisdiction, powers and authority as are vested in or may be conferred on any high court existing at the commencement of this Act; and where a high court is so established in any area included within the limits of the local jurisdiction of another high court, His Majesty may, by letters patent, alter those limits and make such incidental, consequential and supplemental provisions as may appear to be necessary by reason of the alteration." My submission on that point, whether it be sound or not, can be put comparatively shortly. It is simply this: The right to confer jurisdiction on what is now the High Court at Lahore is committed by this Imperial Statute to His Majesty to be done by letters patent. If the Indian Legislature, being a subordinate Legislature, seeks by any Act of its own to deprive the High Court at Lahore, established by His Majesty's letters patent, of jurisdiction, in whole or in part, the argument is the same. It is offending against section 113, which has conferred upon someone else, and someone higher, namely, His Majesty, by the executive act of letters patent to create the High Court. This particular ordinance, in order to be valid, has to be such as not to infringe section 113. If this particular ordinance took away the whole jurisdiction of the High Court at Lahore, it would, in my humble submission, equally offend against section 113.

Sir George Lowndes: Is that provided for specifically in the Act?

Pritt: There is something about it in the letters patent; I have not found anything in the Act. Section 65 is the general section which gives the power to make laws. It is suggested to me that Sir George Lowndes may be thinking of section 106. My suggestion about it is that section 65 and section 84 have to be read together. Section 65 confers a very wide, but nevertheless not universal, power on the Indian legislature, and then section 84 says: "A law made by any authority in British India and repugnant to any provisions of this or any other Act of Parliament shall, to the extent of that repugnancy, but not otherwise, be void."

Lord Russell of Killowen: I am not sure that I follow your repugnancy yet. Where is the repugnancy?

Pritt: The repugnancy, I suggest, is this: Whereas His Majesty alone can create the High Court at Lahore, or limit, or amend, or alter, or take away from its powers, before this ordinance was passed the High Court at Lahore had jurisdiction to hear my clients on appeal, and that has been taken away by the ordinance which has said they shall not have any appeal.

Lord Russel of Killowen: The ordinance has constituted a special tribunal to try particular people.

Pritt: Yes.

Lord Russell of Killowen: Is that repugnant to section 113? I do not see it.

Pritt: In my submission, yes, because my clients, when the ordinance was passed, were people who were being prosecuted on charges that were being formulated in the ordinary course, and the High Court had jurisdiction at the moment to hear an appeal, and the ordinance has entirely destroyed that exceedingly important portion of the jurisdiction of the High Court at Lahore.

Sir George Lowndes: The section I was thinking of is section 65, sub-section 3, which limits the powers of the Indian Legislature. It cannot abolish a High Court. That clearly suggests that it has power to limit the jurisdiction of the High Court.

Pritt: My submission, in answer to that, would be that the Indian Legislature cannot abolish any High Court existing when the statute was passed, neither can it interfere with the operation of section 113, which says that His Majesty can appoint a new High Court and deal with its jurisdiction.

I ought to refer, because this matter was sufficiently in the minds of the draftsmen of the letters patent, to a very few words in the letters patent which establish the High Court at Lahore; they were made on 21st March, 1919. It is a relatively recent High Court. The following words were put in: The last paragraph, which is No. 37, says: "We do further order and declare that all the provisions of any of our letters patent" etc. (reads paragraph). So it is quite plain that the Crown, as an executive Act, has sought in the letters patent to authorise the Governor-General to do that which, in my submission, if I am right, he cannot do, and that which, if I am right, in my submission, the draftsmen of the letters patent thought there might be some difficulty about doing. My submission is that nothing in clause 37 of the letters patent can affect the position, for the reason that the *Crown by letters* patent cannot create, or alter, or modify the power of the Governor-General or the Indian Legislature under the various sections of the Government of India Act.

Sir Dinshah Mulla: Is not that the same as clause 44 of the letters patent at the Calcutta High Court of 1862?

Pritt: I imagine that it must occur in at any rate any recent letters patent. I will find out for your Lordship.

Sir Dinshah Mulla: I wanted to know whether there was any distinction between the two. One is a very old High Court and the other is a new one.

Pritt: Clause 44 in the Calcutta letters patent reads as follows: (reads same). It is textually the same. I suppose the letters patents of the Calcutta High Court have been redrawn.

Sir Dinshah Mulla: The Calcutta letters patent are of 1869, and what is done is to substitute the sections of the Government of India Act of 1915 in the case of the Lahore High Court.

Pritt: Yes; that is obviously what has been done. This clause was substituted for the original clauses by amending letters patent of 11th March 1919. I am obliged to your Lordship for guiding me in the matter.

Now may I put before your Lordships some of the authorities upon the subject of the powers of the Court to investigate the question whether there was a case of emergency. There is no very direct English authority, although there is one which I think it would be right to refer your Lordships to, but there are several in India, where the matter has been expressly discussed, and the trend of Indian decisions is that the Courts have power to investigate that question, and must investigate it. They must investigate the question and see whether there was any reason on which the Governor-General could arrive at his conclusion.

Viscount Dunedin: Were these cases which arose under Section 72?

Pritt: One of them was this very *habeas corpus* case, and another arose under the same section. The particular one that I want to draw your Lordships' attention to is as recent as the 1st

September last, and was a case in the High Court of Bombay, which dealt with section 52.

Sir George Lowndes: Is that the Sholapur case?

Pritt: Yes. This is a case where there was legislation. There were riots on a widespread scale in Sholapur.

Lord Thankerton: That does not matter for this point .

Dunne: We have prints of that judgment. (Handing same).

Pritt: I want to refer to the judgment of Chief Justice Beaumont, and I will begin where he quotes the section. A few lines after the quotation of the section, after discussing the Defence of the Realm Act and the state of siege in France, he says: "As the question in this case, in my judgment, turns upon this section, I will quote it in full." I have already read that to your Lordships. "It is to be noticed that the section applies 'in cases of emergency'. The question whether the determination as to the existence of an emergency is an administrative act to be decided by the Governor-General alone, or whether it is a question of fact which can be inquired into by the Courts has been discussed by the High Court of Lahore in the case of *Desraj* v. *Emperor*, and the learned Judges who decided that case differed upon the point. In my opinion the judgment of Mr. Justice Bhide is correct, and the question whether an emergency exists or not is one of fact which the Courts can inquire into. But inasmuch as the Governor-General is the person who must, in the first instance, decide whether or not there is an emergency upon which he ought to act, and inasmuch as he may frequently have information which, in the public interest, he may be unwilling to disclose, and which no Court can compel him to disclose, I think all that the Courts can do is to enquire whether there is evidence upon which the Governor-General may reasonably conclude that an emergency exists. If that question be answered in the affirmative, there is an end of the matter."

Lord Thankerton: That involves an inquiry into what the Governor-General does not want to disclose.

Pritt: Perhaps, May I submit several points in answer to what the learned Chief Justice says. There is in the first place the Governor-General: he may disclose to the Court what he thinks is enough.

Viscount Dunedin: The first point is whether the judgment of Mr. Justice Bhide is correct. Does he give any reasons?

Pritt: No, my Lord, I do not think he gives reasons.

Viscount Dunedin: Therefore there is no argument upon that.

Pritt: It obviously was very fully argued.

Viscount Dunedin: I am not saying there was not an argument before him, but there was no argument in his judgment except to say: "I think Mr. Justice Bhide's judgment is correct". Therefore it does not help us upon that point.

Pritt: Only to this extent, that the argument that leaps to the mind, though I may be wrong, is adopted by this learned Chief Justice.

Viscount Dunedin: It does not help us, except the fact that he says so.

Pritt: That is so.

Viscount Dunedin: I do not think you need go into this matter.

Pritt: If your Lordship pleases. Then the judgment of Mr. Justice Madgavkar contains a certain amount of argument. I confess I find it a little difficult to follow, because while he is concurring it seems to me to be rather against me than for me, and therefore it is natural, and inevitable, that I must read it. The passage I am referring to is at the top of page 6. He says: "On the third point"—that is this point—"I agree with the reasoning and the conclusions of the learned Chief Justice, and have little to add".

Lord Russel of Killowen: There are no reasons of the Chief Justice at all.

Pritt: They may have been given interlocutorily. "Unlike legislation in India, the validity of Statutes of Parliament cannot be questioned in the Courts of British India. Section 72 of the Government of India Act empowers the Governor-General to pass such ordinances in cases of emergency. It is argued for the petitioners that the omission of any such words as 'in the opinion of the Governor-General' after the word 'emergency' suffices to enable us to consider whether there was such an emergency as to justify the passing of the Ordinance and further to examine also its provisions to see how far they make 'for the peace and good government of British India'. Two learned Judges of the Lahore High Court have considered the former question in the case of *Desraj* v. *Emperor*. Their difference of opinion seems to me more apparent than real. Section 72 as a whole hardly empowers the Courts to consider whether the Governor-General was right or wrong in his conclusion that an emergency existed, much less to examine how far the provisions of the Ordinance tend to the peace and good government of the country. That responsibility the statute has laid on the Governor-General and not on the Courts. Unless the Governor-General thought that there was an emergency, and he alone under the section is the judge thereof, he would not promulgate the ordinance to meet that particular emergency. The statute does not require that the Legislative Assembly should not be sitting as a necessary precedent to the exercise of the power of passing an ordinance. Therefore the fact that in some cases the Act of Indemnity has been passed by the Central Legislature and not by way of ordinance by the Governor-General is immaterial".

Viscount Dunedin: That goes to another point, does it not?

Pritt: Perhaps it does.

Lord Thankerton: The next passage rather deals with your argument. He points out that there is no law against it.

Pritt: There is no law in England against a privilegium.

Dunne: There is another passage on page 11 dealing with the third point.

Pritt: I am obliged to my learned friend. "The third point on which our decision really rests has been dealt with in detail in the judgment of the learned Chief Justice. I have already held that the ordinance is within the power of the Governor-General, and that it is not open to us to examine its provisions and whether, it at all, they go beyond the necessities of peace and good government, within the meaning of Section 72 of the Government of India Act"; and yet he concurs, as I understand it, in the judgment which says the exact opposite. It is fair that I should read it. Then Mr. Justice Blackwell says, on page 13: "It was contended by Mr. Thakore for the applicants that no case of emergency had been established. I do not agree with this contention. The reasons which moved the Governor-General are set out at the end of the Ordinance. On the materials placed before him the Governor-General was in my opinion clearly entitled to conclude that an emergency had arisen. I therefore think it unnecessary to decide whether the Court is empowered to enquire into the question whether an emergency existed, or whether that is a matter solely for the determination of the Governor-General. There has been a difference of judicial opinion upon this question in the Lahore High Court (see *Desraj* v. *Emperor*, A.I.R. 1930 Lahore, 781). I incline strongly to the view that the Court is entitled to enquire into the matter. Assuming that it is, the Court is not in my opinion entitled to enquire into the question whether the facts placed before the Governor-General were accurate or inaccurate. The Governor-General must obviously act promptly, and may sometimes have to make up his mind on information which may afterwards be found to be erroneous. In considering whether there was a case of emergency within the meaning of section 72, the Court in my opinion is only entitled to require to be satisfied that facts were placed before the Governor-General which, if true, might reasonably lead him to conclude that an emergency existed."

Viscount Dunedin: The only way to do that would be by examining the Governor-General.

Pritt: May I draw your Lordships' attention to something that I think I mentioned when I was reading the Chief Justice's Judgment? The Governor-General is in this position. The matter is challenged and it is said that there was no emergency which justified his making the Ordinance. He cannot be compelled to come into Court; he can please himself and he may do one of three things. The first, which he would be very reluctant to do, is to say: Never mind the public interest; I am challenged; I will give you every fact. If that were his only course, there would be a difficulty. His second course would be to say: I can reconcile the general public interests and the particular interest of maintaining the Ordinance; I will show you quite enough to prove an emergency without showing you everything I know.

Viscount Dunedin: In order to do that he would have to be made a party to the case?

Pritt: If it is in the direct criminal proceedings, it would be the Crown, or if it is in the *habeas corpus* proceedings it would be the Crown again. The Crown, having access to public information, on applying to whatever Department is proper, would be supplied with such evidence and information as the Department thought proper. The Crown in England often has to do the same thing. The third course which the Governor-General could adopt is a course which is adopted by the Executive in this country whenever a difficulty arises. He can go to his Legislature and say: I had to act in an emergency which I say is an emergency; I am not going to publish my facts to the Court in the disturbed state of this country at present. Give me an Act of indemnity.

Lord Thankerton: If it is an Act of indemnity, it is either at the time of the emergency or long after.

Pritt: Long after.

Lord Thankerton: I cannot understand the opinions of two of the Judges in this Bombay case. It may be that the reasons cannot possibly be disclosed. Do you say if the Governor-General does not disclose the reasons, the Ordinance is bad? If he does disclose the reasons, it may prove another emergency. The Court must either be seized of the whole of the facts or none of them.

Pritt: I respectfully agree.

Viscount Dunedin: Have you any other authority besides this that you can show us?

Pritt: Perhaps your Lordships ought to see the decision in this very *habeas corpus* case.

Viscount Dunedin: I think we know that. One judge said there was no inquiry at all; the other judge said that an inquiry was possible, but that he thought that the people had put themselves into such a position as to show that there was an emergency.

Pritt: Yes, and I think they relied as an alternative on the Governor-General's own statement. May I say in answer to Lord Thankerton I see the difficulties of the Executive. It would be impertinence on my part to say that I sympathise with them. The answer is: I did not draft this Constitution. This Constitution has said, in my humble submission, in the plainest possible terms that the Governor-General may do this very striking thing in cases of emergency, and he may do it in cases where he is of opinion there is a state of emergency for any time. Before he does it, there must be a state of emergency. That is the kernel of the case.

I was inclined to think that some of the English cases threw some light on the matter, but I do not want to weary your Lordships with them if it is thought that they do not. Your Lordships remember the line of cases under the Defence of the Realm Act, one or two of which went to the House of Lords. This covers two points of my argument; it covers the question who is to decide a question of fact like this question of whether there is an emergency, and also the question of what is legislation in the direction of peace and good government.

Viscount Dunedin: We will listen to any case you choose to give us, but I do not myself see how any case would be much use, unless there was something equivalent to Section 72, which, so far as I know, there is not.

Pritt: I agree, and that is why, even when a number of my clients have been sentenced to death, I hesitate to read them. It is a true analogy, but the words may be still so different that it may not be of much use. I must put before your Lordships why I say it is an analogy. The analogy is complete in this sense. I submit they are both cases of subordinate legislation, and they came from the same body. In the one case, the Imperial Parliament has said certain persons may pass subordinate legislation for securing the safety of the Realm and for the better prosecution of the war—I have forgotten the exact words for the moment—in the other case, the same Imperial Parliament has said in cases of emergency certain persons may pass legislation for the peace and good government of British India. The essence of the cases on which I wanted to rely—indeed, perhaps it is sufficient to state it—is that there is an efficient body, the High Court or the Court of Appeal and, I think I may say, the House of Lords in this country, dealing with the Defence of the Realm legislation to see whether the legislation passed falls within the four corners of the Section of the Imperial Statute.

Viscount Dunedin: Obviously.

Pritt: The analogy is this: It is the duty of whatever court becomes concerned with the Lahore case to construe whether the legislation passed by the Governor-General to establish this particular Court falls within the four corners of Section 72.

Viscount Dunedin: Nobody doubts that.

Pritt: The question is: Is there a case of emergency, and is it legislation for peace and good government?

Lord Russell: The analogy would be if you were able to say that this Statute exceeded the power of the Indian Parliament?

Pritt: That is only one limb.

Viscount Dunedin: It is only the argument that you have given us over again?

Pritt: Yes; I suggest that that argument is supported by some English authority. I think I can fairly leave these cases.

Viscount Dunedin: I do not think they help us at all. One is perfectly willing to concede you the proposition that obviously it must be within the four corners of the Section.

Lord Russell: It must be *intra vires*?

Pritt: Yes, and the *vires* depends on whether there is an emergency, and whether the legislation is for peace and good government.

Viscount Dunedin: That is your argument?

Pritt: Yes.

Viscount Dunedin: We are much obliged to you.

(Counsel and parties were directed to withdraw and after a short time were again called in.)

Viscount Dunedin: Their Lordships need not trouble you, Mr. Dunne. They are unable to advise His Majesty that leave to appeal be granted in this case for reasons which will be given later.

The reasons were given on February 27 in a judgment by Dunedin.[4]

In brief, Pritt argued that before he could promulgate an Ordinance, the Governor-General had to establish affirmatively as a question of fact that an "emergency" did exist. Dunedin simply did not appreciate the point when he asked the preposterous question whether the Governor-General had to bring a civil suit in the courts for a declaration before making the Ordinance. It was a conditional power and fulfilment of the condition—existence of an emergency—had to be established if any one challenged the legality of the Ordinance. Pritt revealed that he had advised his clients to come to the Privy Council in appeal from the High Court's judgment in Des Raj's case, delivered seven months earlier in July 1930. Justice Bhide's judgment might have helped the petitioners.

But this Board would not have altered its opinion. Dunedin's brief judgment showed that the consideration that weighed with him was the finality of the Governor-General's view. He was the sole judge as to the existence of an emergency. Even in the judicial clime of 1931, it was an extreme view that Dunedin propounded. "It is more than obvious that that someone must be the Governor-General and he alone. Any other view would render utterly inept the whole provision. Emergency demands immediate action, and that action is prescribed to be taken by the Governor-General. It is he alone who can promulgate the Ordinance."

Pritt's contention that the G-G's opinion was open to judicial review was dismissed out of hand. "In fact, the contention is so completely without foundation on the fact of it that it would be idle to allow an appeal to argue about it."

Dunedin went so far as to hold that the Governor-General did not have to give any reasons in support of his action: "Their Lordships must add that, although the Governor-General thought fit to expound the reasons which induced him to promulgate this Ordinance, this was not in their Lordships' opinion in any way incumbent on him as a matter of law."

Watching the proceeding before the Privy Council in London was the Legal Adviser to the Secretary of State for India, Sir Edward Maynard Chamier. He had held the office since 1917 and knew India well. He had served as Government Advocate in the North-West Frontier Province as far back as in 1875, in Oudh as Judicial Commissioner, and as Chief Justice of the Patna High Court (1911–15). He knew the legal world in India and in London, in so far as it touched India. Hence the significance of an air-letter he dashed off to D.G. Mitchell, the Joint Secretary in the Law Ministry. Mitchell hastened to forward it to the Home Secretary, H.W. Emerson, on February 24. This suggests that Chamier wrote

as soon as the Privy Council dismissed Bhagat Singh's petition.
The letters, now resting in the National Archives tell their own
tale:

24th February

My dear Emerson,
   I enclose a copy of an air-mail letter I have just received from
Sir Edward Chamier. Crerar will be interested.

Yours sincerely,
D.G. MITCHELL

Copy of an air-mail letter received by me today from Sir
Edward Chamier.

My dear Mitchell,
   I was agreeably surprised to find that Lord Dunedin presiding
over the Board which heard the petition in the Lahore Conspiracy
case—*with any other President I think the petition would have
been admitted to a regular hearing*—but Dunedin took a very
strong line from the start and carried the others with him not that
Lowndes (or Saunders?) and Mulla wanted any "carrying". They
evidently felt that in the end the petition must fail and it was
useless to prolong the agony.
   I will send you with their "reasons" a transcript of the shorthand
notes—you may be interested to see exactly what line the board
took.

Yours sincerely,
E. CHAMIER

Obviously, Dunedin led the Board. Sadly, a great jurist, Dinshah
Mulla, sat on it when he heard this case. His integrity is above
reproach. Not so, his conduct on this occasion.
   Having voted against the adjournment motion, on the hunger-
strike by the accused in this very case, in the Central Assembly on
September 14, 1929, Mulla ought to have recused himself when
their petition came up for hearing by the Privy Council, less than
a year and a half later. He had also served as Law Member on the

Viceroy's Executive Council; briefly, in place of Sir S.R. Das. Lowndes was Law Member from 1916–1920 began practice in the Privy Council and was made member of its Judicial Committee.

One is tempted to ask what its fate would have been if the petition were heard by a Board of which Lord Atkin was a member? It is not idle to pose the question. A month later he set a flutter among the dovecotes in the newly-built Central Secretariat in New Delhi.

NOTES

1. Kamlesh Mohan, p. 192.
2. D.N. Pritt, *The Autobiography of D.N. Pritt*, Part one *From Right to Left*, Lawrence & Wishart, London, 1965.
3. File 4-20/1931, pp. 71-99.
4. *Bhagat Singh and Ors* vs. *The King Emperor*, 58 Indian Appeals 169.

12

If Lord Atkin were on the Board?

T HERE is every reason to believe that if James Richard Atkin were on the Board which heard the petition for special leave to appeal by Bhagat Singh and his associates, the result might well have been different. The Governor-General's Ordinance setting up the Tribunal might not have passed muster. A retrial before the regular Sessions, with a right of appeal to the Lahore High Court, would have yielded different and unpredictable results; unlike the predictable one the Tribunal provided.

In this, one is ignoring the sage counsel of two great men who flourished a century apart and had wholly dissimilar backgrounds. Ghalib, the poet, lamented his proneness to indulge in might have beens. The historian, Sir Lewis Namier, never ceased to warn—do not argue with history.

But Atkin is very relevant to the story. On March 24, 1931, only a month and more after Dunedin's judgment on February 11, Atkin pronounced judgment in a landmark case which differed significantly from Dunedin's on the doctrine of a judicially unreviewable opinion of the executive when it exercises power which is conferred on it by the legislature on condition that it " is satisfied" that a particular set of circumstances exist. Are the courts precluded from ascertaining whether they do in fact, merely because the Government says that it "is satisfied"? Is the condition in the law complied with by such a declaration?

Is the test a subjective or an objective one? Obviously, if the situation is such that no reasonable person can honestly say that an emergency exists and the executive asserts, with manifest dishonesty, that it does, the courts would be abdicating the judicial power altogether if they hold that they are precluded from reviewing the executive's opinion. This is what Dunedin did. To leave no room for doubt, he said that the Governor-General was not obliged to state his reasons.

Atkin disagreed and took along with him the two colleagues on the Board which heard the appeal from the Supreme Court of Nigeria, Lord Blandsburgh and Sir Lancelot Sanderson.[1] It arose out of a habeas corpus petition by a deposed Nigerian Chief who was externed from a specified area by the Governor of Nigeria in exercise of powers conferred by the Deposed Chiefs Removal Ordinance.

S. 2(2) of the Ordinance empowered the Governor to order a deposed Chief's removal from a specified area "if the Governor shall be satisfied that it is necessary for re-establishment or maintenance of peace, order and good government in such area . . .". The language was far wider than that of S. 72 of the Government of India Act, 1919 under which Irwin set up the Tribunal. In the Nigerian case it turned on the Chief's deposition. The petitioner denied that he was a chief and that he was deposed.

In a passage that ranks still as a classic, Atkin said: "Their Lordships are satisfied that the opinion which has prevailed that the Courts cannot investigate the whole of the necessary conditions is erroneous. The Governor acting under the Ordinance acts solely under executive powers, and in no sense as a Court. As the executive he can only act in pursuance of the powers given to him by law. In accordance with British jurisprudence no member of the executive can interfere with the liberty or property of a British subject except on the condition that he can support the legality of his action before a court of justice. And it is the tradition of British Justice that judges should not shrink from deciding such issues in the face of the executive.

"The analogy of the powers of the English Home Secretary to deport aliens was involved in this case. The analogy seems very close. Their Lordships entertain no doubt that under the legislation in question, if the Home Secretary deported a British subject in the belief that he was an alien, the subject would have the right to question the validity of any detention under such order by proceedings in habeas corpus, and that it would be the duty of the Courts to investigate the issue of alien or not."

Both *The Tribune* and the law journal *Calcutta Weekly Notes* went to town over it. *The Tribune* provided the instant comment in a "leaderette" as news was received of Atkin's judgment. When its text reached India, the *CWN* published it on May 25 with an informed article while *The Tribune* had a lengthy editorial on June 17. Both contrasted it with the judgment in Bhagat Singh's case. That was enough to set Curzon's stately file moving to and fro.[2]

This time the initiative was taken by the Director of the Intelligence Bureau of the Home Department, H. Williamson (Sir Horace, later). Someone should study and write on this tribe. They were men of high calibre. A Deputy Director, P.C. Bamford, wrote a 270-page *Histories of the Non-Cooperation and Khilafat Movements* in 1925, with appendices and an index, for official use, which any scholar would have been proud to own. Directors of the IB, Cecil Kaye, David Petrie and Williamson himself wrote studies entitled *Communism in India* (Williamson's was entitled *India and Communism*) each covering the period of his stewardship; together we have these accounts from 1919 to 1934.

Williamson had the intellectual capacity to appreciate the import of Atkin's judgment when, on June 19, 1931, he wrote his minute to the Home Secretary: "This ruling seems to conflict with that of the Privy Council in their recent decision regarding Bhagat Singh's case but it is unwise to make deductions from extracts of judgments. I think that the Legislative Deptt. might be asked to compare this judgment regarding the Nigerian depostee with that regarding Bhagat Singh. For the extracts quoted by *The Tribune* it would appear that a High Court can challenge all executive orders for detention under Reg. III of 1818 and other such laws or Ordinances."

Emerson sent the file to the Home Member Crerar who found himself out of his depths, obviously: "I doubt however, if the Nigerian decision whatever it be, will really affect our law. The decision in the case of Bhagat Singh was not on the point of *habeas corpus*. The decision may, however, have some bearing in the necessity of the provisions barring *habeas corpus* under the regulations and the B.C.L.A.A. which has been disputed."

The file was sent to the Law Secretary, Sir Lancelot Graham. He was more keen on finding flaws in the *CWN*'s article than in understanding Atkin's judgment. The thought obsessed him— Would Atkin not have referred to Dunedin's judgment if he wished to depart from it? "No student of law could suppose for a moment that the authors of the report in the Nigerian case would not have referred to the report in Bhagat Singh's case if it was thought that there was anything common in the subject matter of the two. A perusal of the two judgments or rather reports makes it quite plain that whereas in Bhagat Singh's case it was held that the decision as to whether an emergency had arisen was not a judiciable issue, because in the words of Lord Dunedin a state of emergency is something that does not permit of any exact definition, in the Nigerian case, on the contrary, there were three perfectly plain and obviously judiciable issues; the first, whether the party concerned was a Chief within the meaning of the Deposed Chiefs Removal Ordinance, the second whether he has been deposed or removed from this, and the third whether it was the native law and custom that if a Chief had been deposed, he should be required to leave the area in question. All these are plainly questions of fact on which the Court is capable of coming to a decision. So far as I see the case, then, we need have no grounds of apprehension as to the validity of ordinance issued by the Governor General in so far the question of emergency is disputed."

He certainly had a point there. But Atkin's had held that "the whole of the necessary conditions" were open to judicial review, that would have included the condition of the existence of an emergency.

The Law Secretary opined that exercise of the power to detain persons under the notorious Regulation III of 1818 was not "judiciable" (*sic*).

The Law Member minuted his agreement, on June 25, to the obvious relief of Emerson and Crerar. B.L. Mitter opined that the two cases "are clearly distinguishable"; a view which is certainly plausible. But it misses the sense for the sound. Atkin's approach on the executive's subjective satisfaction was *fundamentally* different.

That emerged in bolder relief a little over a decade later during the worst days of the Second World War in the famous case of *Liversidge* vs. *Anderson.*[3]

Liversidge had been detained *during the War*, under the Defence (General) Regulation 18B which conferred the detaining power "If the Secretary of State has reasonable cause to believe . . ." Was it for him alone to determine whether the cause was "reasonable" or was it open to judicial scrutiny? Liversidge was represented by D.N. Pritt, K.C. Atkin wrote the solitary judgment in dissent. He held that the reasonableness of the cause was open to judicial review.

While doing so, however, Atkin took broad swipes not only against the Attorney-General, Sir Donald Somervell, but also the other Law Lords and, as in the 1931 case, struck a powerful blow for the rule of law and judicial independence. He wrote:

"I view with apprehension the attitude of judges who on a mere question of construction when face to face with claims involving the liberty of the subject, show themselves more executive minded than the executive . . . In this country, amid the clash of arms, the laws are not silent. They may be changed, but they speak the same language in war as in peace. It has always been one of the pillars of freedom, one of the principles of liberty for which on recent authority we are now fighting, that the judges are no respecters of persons and stand between the subject and any attempted encroachments on his liberty by the executive, alert to see that any coercive action is justified in law. In this case I have listened to arguments which might have been addressed acceptably to the Court of King's Bench in the time of Charles I.

"I protest, even if I do it alone, against a strained construction put on words with the effect of giving an uncontrolled power of imprisonment to the minister. To recapitulate: The words have only one meaning. They are used with that meaning in statements of the common law and in statutes. They have never been used in the same sense now imputed to them. They are used in Defence Regulations in the natural meaning, and, when it is intended to express the meaning now imputed to them, different and apt words are used in the regulations generally and in this regulation in particular. Even if it were relevant, which it is not, there is no absurdity or no such degree of public mischief as would lead to a non-natural construction.

"I know of only one authority which might justify the suggested method of construction: 'When I use a word', Humpty Dumpty said in a rather scornful tone 'it means just what I choose it to mean, neither more nor less.' 'The question is,' said Alice, whether you can make words mean so many different things.' 'The question is,' said Humpty Dumpty, 'which is to be master—that's all.' (Through the Looking Glass, c.vi.) After all this long discussion the question is whether the words 'If a man has' can mean 'If a man thinks he has?' I am of opinion that they cannot, and that the case should be decided accordingly."[4]

Indian judges fervently admired Atkin's dissent but faithfully followed the majority ruling until it was buried beyond recall in the land of its birth. A distinguished Lord Chancellor, Lord Gardiner, opined, "I think that history has taken the view that in *Liversidge* vs. *Anderson* the majority was wrong and Lord Atkin was right."[5]

Lord Simon, then Lord Chancellor, wrote to Atkin, when he read his judgment in draft, pleading with him to drop "your very amusing citation from Lewis Carroll." Atkin refused. They do not make men like him any more.

NOTES

1. Eshugbayi Eleko and Officer Administering the Government of Nigeria and Another (1931) Appeal Cases 661.
2. National Archives of India, file 13/12/1931, Home Department, Political.
3. (1942) Appeal Cases 206.
4. Geoffrey Lewis, *Lord Atkin*, Butterworth, 1983, pp. 132-157.
5. *Ibid.*, 148, fn. 3.

13

The Execution

ONCE the Privy Council dismissed the petition for special leave to appeal on February 11, 1931, nothing but remission of sentence, if not pardon, by the Viceroy Lord Irwin could have saved the lives of Bhagat Singh and the two others sentenced to death with him, Sukh Dev and Rajguru. There was some hope of the remission; not as an act of grace but as a term of an accord between Gandhi and Irwin. Their parleys began on February 17.

Meanwhile, on the legal front the assiduous Amolak Ram Kapur filed a habeas corpus petition in the Lahore High Court for the production in court of these three prisoners, confined in the Central Jail, to be dealt with according to the law—the standard prayer in *habeas corpus* petitions. It is, in essence, a challenge to the legality of a person's confinement. The application said that following the sentences of death on October 7, 1930, "it is understood that the 26th October was fixed for the execution of the sentences. Then an application for special leave to appeal to the Privy Council having been made, the execution of the sentences was postponed."

The Tribunal vanished into thin air on October 31, with the expiry of the Ordinance which established it. The date it appointed for execution of the sentences had expired. There was now no court competent "to order the execution of the death sentences or to fix the date or time of execution; nor is there any Court or

Tribunal to which the return of warrants after the execution can be made." Any warrant for execution of the sentences would be "without any legal warrant of authority". In the circumstances, the detention of the three prisoners was also without legal authority.[1]

The petition was heard by Justice Bhide on February 25 and was dismissed the same day. Admittedly, the original warrant was issued according to law and "the Local Government" (of the Punjab) had authority to suspend its execution, as it did. "It was stated by the Government Advocate that no further action has yet been taken and that certain petitions for mercy are under consideration. The question as to what steps can be legally taken to carry out the sentence is one for the Local Government to decide. Even if the Local Government finds that there is any legal difficulty in carrying out the sentences as contended on behalf of the petitioners, it would be still open to the Local Government under Section 402 Cr. P.C. to commute the sentences into one of transportation or imprisonment. It seems to me, therefore, clear that the custody in which the prisoners are kept at present cannot in any case be considered to be illegal or improper."[2]

The Gandhi-Irwin Pact, concluded on March 5, held out no hope for Bhagat Singh and his associates. There was no other course but to knock at the doors of the courts with yet greater vigour. On March 21, Rai Bahadur Badri Das asked the High Court for leave to appeal to the Privy Council against Justice Bhide's order. On the same day, he moved another habeas corpus petition on behalf of Bhagat Singh's brother Kultar Singh on the ground that Justice Bhide had only mentioned the possibility of commutation of the sentences. But he "did not dispose of the question as to the execution of the death warrants." The petitioner apprehended that the three condemned prisoners would be executed on March 23 as the last interview allowed to their relatives was fixed at 11 a.m. on that day.[3]

Both petitions, one for leave to appeal to the Privy Council and another for habeas corpus, came up for hearing, once again, before Justice Bhide on that fateful day, March 23. He said he would not hear the habeas corpus petition as he had already expressed his opinion on a similar petition. Since Badri Das said that it was that petition that he wished to argue first, it was transferred to some other judge. The one for special leave to appeal to the Privy Council was kept pending.

The Legal Remembrancer, S.L. Sale, pointedly told the Court that he had instructions from the Government to see that the petitions were disposed of that very day.

The habeas corpus petition came up before a Division Bench comprising Justice Sir Alan Broadway and Justice Johnston.

Badri Das recalled the facts. Death sentences on October 7; date for their execution fixed for October 27, and demise of the Tribunal by whom the sentences were imposed.

Justice Broadway: Who stayed the execution?

Counsel: The Government of the Punjab.

Counsel, continuing, said that the warrant was made returnable to the High Court. But the High Court could not be deemed to be a fit authority for that purpose because the ordinance itself was silent on that point. In the present case only the Criminal Procedure Code was applicable. No other authority could now pass the order for execution.

Justice Broadway: Surely it is for the Government to decide.

Counsel: According to the constitutional law, the Crown had no right outside constituted courts to execute persons sentenced to death. Section 491, Cr. P.C., authorised a High Court to bring condemned persons before it and deal with them according to law. Neither the ordinance nor the Tribunal was in existence now. Therefore these persons should be dealt with according to the Criminal Procedure Code. The Superintendent of the Central Jail had no authority now to put to death these persons. Neither had the Government any authority now to execute them when there was no state of war in the country and properly constituted courts were functioning.

Counsel finally submitted that the authorities should be ordered not to hang the prisoners and that, their custody also being illegal they should be set at liberty.

Carden Noad, arguing on behalf of the Crown, said that section 12 (2) of the ordinance authorised the President of the Tribunal to make rules and regulate executive details. Moreover, no court itself carried out sentences in any part of the world. It was a local Government's duty to carry out sentences. In the present case there could be no appeal to the High Court. Section 381 of the Criminal Procedure Code did not apply here regarding the issue of a warrant. The petitioners' counsel did not give any authority about the exhaustion of the warrant of death. Section 860 of the Jail Manual applied where delay had occurred. Counsel further submitted that the ordinary meaning of suspension was suspension and no special meaning should be attached to it. Therefore, no further warrant was necessary.

Finally, Noad said considerable delay had already occurred in the case, properly, legally or otherwise. Therefore, he asked their lordships to pass orders in this case at once.

Diwan Badri Das, replying, submitted he was not aware under what possible law the Local Government suspended the execution of the sentence. He did not know whether it was other than section 401, Criminal Procedure Code. If a warrant was necessary the question of suspension did not arise, and if a warrant was not necessary then there was an end of the matter.

Counsel, proceeding, said the High Court had no jurisdiction in this matter. Section 12 (2) did not cover this petition at all. The President of the Tribunal did not issue orders that if the warrant was not executed its time would be enhanced *ipso facto* . . . The sole question to be decided was whether it was the judicial or the executive authority that was competent to issue the warrant. If no warrant was necessary, as argued by the Crown counsel, section 389, Cr. P.C., would become redundant. This section contemplated that a warrant from a judicial court was necessary, authorising a Superintendent of the Jail to carry out a sentence of death. It should be issued by the Special Tribunal which passed the death sentence.

The petitioners did not petition for mercy, because they considered that their case was strong.

Justice Broadway: Did the petitioners put in a petition for mercy?

Carden Noad: The petitioners did not themselves put in petitions for mercy. They, however, put in another petition saying that they should be shot dead instead of being hanged.

R.B. Badri Das: That is another kind of mercy.

Justice Broadway: Do you call that a petition for mercy?

R.B. Badri Das submitted, in conclusion, that the prisoners should be set at liberty.

Their lordships reserved judgment till this afternoon.

The Division Bench pronounced orders at 3 p.m. dismissing the petition.[4]

On the same day, Justice Bhide dismissed the other petition, for special leave to appeal to the Privy Council.[5] It was argued by Jeevan Lal Kapur, who became a Judge of the Supreme Court.

In the evening on that day, Monday, March 23, at 7.15 p.m., Bhagat Singh, Sukh Dev and Rajguru were executed. Loud and continued shouts of "Inquilab Zindabad" ("Long Live the Revolution") emerged from inside the Jail alerting the people living in the area to the fact that the expected executions were taking place.

Unfortunately, owing to the conditions imposed by the jail authorities, the relations of the prisoners could not interview them earlier in the day. Nor were their dead bodies handed over to their families. They were secretly removed from the jail and transported to the banks of the Sutlej, near Ferozepore, where they were disposed of at dead of night.[6] The ashes were thrown into the river.[7]

Carden Noad's reference in the court that day to a petition was to one addressed to the Governor of Punjab by Bhagat Singh and his colleagues. It said: "The only thing we want to point out is that according to the verdict of your Court we are said to have been waging war and are consequently war prisoners. Therefore, we claim to be treated as such, i.e., we claim to be shot dead instead of being hanged. It rests with you now to prove that you seriously meant what your Court has said and prove it through action. We very earnestly request you and hope that you will very kindly order the Military Department to send a detachment or a shooting party to perform our execution" (vide Appendix X for the text).

The Government could have been in no doubt as to the public reaction to the executions. There were massive demonstrations in Lahore on March 23 in protest against the imminent executions.

They were organised by the Naujawan Bharat Sabha. The city observed a complete *hartal* (shut-down) that day. At a largely attended meeting, the Gandhi-Irwin Pact of March 5 was sharply criticised by some speakers. A rift surfaced between Congressmen and leftists like Ganpat Rai, who was in the chair and Ram Chandra, who moved a resolution denouncing the Pact. A compromise resolution was drafted. Moved by Maulana Zafar Ali Khan, it was adopted unanimously. Sardar Sardul Singh Caveeshar, Dr. Muhammad Alam and Sardar Mangal Singh also spoke. Bhagat Singh's father, Kishen Singh, received a rousing ovation as he appeared on the platform. He appealed to Congressmen and the Naujawan Sabha's members to work in unity. An appeal for a *hartal* the next day was issued.[8]

On March 24 the entire country mourned the executions. In Lahore a condolence meeting was held at which Maulana Zafar Ali Khan offered prayers amidst solemn silence. A poet, politician, writer and orator, he composed a poem for the occasion. If his considerable talent had had judgment as companion, his contribution to the Punjab's public life in later years might have been of a different order.

On March 24, Diwan Bahadur T. Rangachariar rose in the Central Assembly to register a protest and censured the Government for carrying out the death sentences. Crerar denied that the trial was not a fair one. The Nationalists walked out.

In a carefully composed statement to the press in New Delhi, on March 24, Jawaharlal Nehru said: "I have remained absolutely silent during their last days, lest a word of mine may injure their prospect of commutation. I have remained silent, though I felt like bursting and now all is over.

"Not all of us could save him, who was so dear to us and whose magnificent courage and sacrifice have been an inspiration to the youth of India. India cannot even save her clearly loved children from gallows.

"There will be hartals and mournings, processions everywhere. There will be sorrow in the land at our utter helplessness but there will also be pride in him who is no more, and when England speaks to us and talks of settlement there will be the corpse of

Bhagat Singh between us lest we forget."

In this Nehru was wrong. It was his silence that was unhelpful; silence, particularly in the councils of the Congress. The last para reflected his anguish.

Vallabhbhai Patel, as one might expect, commented briefly and tellingly: "The boast of the English law was that upon an evidence untested by cross-examination, no one could be convicted, but yet men have been hanged and killed upon the evidence that came in long after the event and without any cross-examination. Man may be made to suffer for perversity or obstinacy but surely not hanged. The court could have engaged *amicus curiae* but nothing was done and men were done to death."[9]

On March 26, the Punjab Government issued a Press communique publishing the English translation of an unfinished letter in Hindi which, it claimed, was in Sukh Dev's hand and was found on his person, on search during his transfer from the Borstal to the Central prison on the day the sentence was pronounced. The letter justified the Saunders murder and the throwing of the bombs in the Assembly and said that escape was no part of their plans. Its genuineness was contested by his uncle, Chintaram, on the ground that Sukh Dev's only brother did not know Hindi.[10]

File 139/1931 Home Department Political in the National Archives tells a different story. On October 9, 1930 the Punjab CID wrote to the Director of the Intelligence Bureau describing recovery of the letter and enclosing its English translation. It is unlikely to have been forged by the authorities. What was dishonest on their part was the suppression in the published letter of its vital concluding para in which he criticised recent terrorist outrages in the most explicit terms: "I do not understand what was the significance of these actions. So far as I think such actions have not caused special awakening in the public. *If it was only for the purpose of terrorising, I would like you to let me know how far these actions have been successful*—In this connection I would not praise the Chittagong action" (vide Appendix XI for the text of the CID's letter to the DIB, and the opening and concluding paras of the Press Communique). Bar the last para, the rest of Sukh Dev's letter was identical.

Bhagat Singh went to the gallows a brave man and, as only the brave can, without any bravado. A large number of his writings in the days preceding March 23 testify to the unique qualities which earned him undying fame as no other figure in the movement could. He read widely; tried to learn Persian and was always solicitous about fellow prisoners. "Please get Darling's *Peasant in Prosperity and Debt* and one or two such books on agrarian subjects for Dr. Alam", he wrote to a friend.

His last interview with the family was on March 3. The sight of his younger brother Kultar in tears distressed him . He wrote:

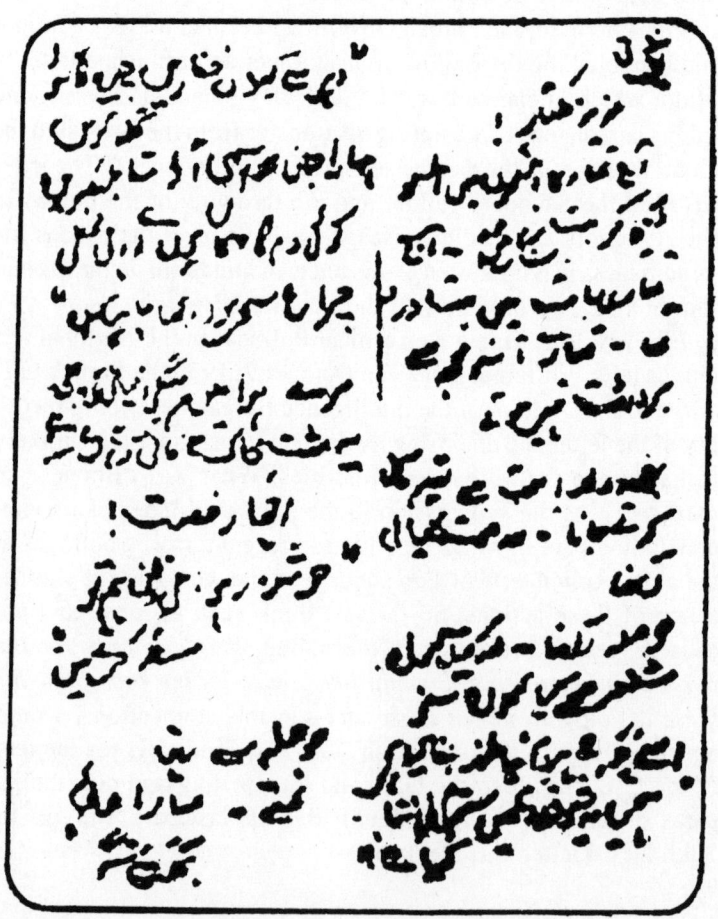

[Roman version of the original letter]
3rd March 1931

Aziz Kultar,

Aaj tumhari aankhon mein aansu dekh kar bahut ranj hua. Aaj tumhari baat mein bahut dard tha. Tumhare aansu mujh se bardasht nahin huye.

Barkhurdar, himmat se taalim hasil karte jana aur sehat ka khayal rakhna.

Hausla rakhna. Aur kya . . . . (likhun?) . . . Shaer main kya kahun suno:

Usay yeh fikr hai hardam naya tarze jafa kya hai,
Hamen yeh shauq hai dekhen sitam ki intiha kya hai.
Dair se kyun khafa rahen aur kyun gila karen,
Hamara jahan hai sahi, ao muqabla karen.
Koi dam ka mehman hoon ai ahle mehfil,
Chiraghe sahar hoon, bujha chahta hoon.
Mere hawa mein rahegi khayal ki khushboo,
Yeh mushte khaq hai, fani rahe na rahe.
Achha rukhsat.
Khush raho ahle watan hum to safar karte hain.
Hausle se rehna.
Namaste.

Tumhara Bhai
BHAGAT SINGH

[English translation of the original letter]
3rd March 1931

Dear Kultar,

It made me very sad to see tears in your eyes today. There was deep pain in your words today. I could not bear to see your tears.

My boy, pursue your studies with determination and look after your health.

Be determined. What else . . . (can I write?) . . . What couplets can I recite? Listen:

They are ever anxious to devise new forms of treachery,
We are eager to see what limits there are to oppression.
Why should we be angry with the world . . . and complain,
Ours is a just world (ideal), let us fight for it.

I am a guest only for a few moments, my companions,
I am the lamp that burns before the dawn and longs to be
extinguished.
The breeze will spread the essence of my thoughts,
This self is but a fistful of dust, whether it lives or perishes.
Well, good bye.
Be happy, countrymen, I am off to travel.
Live courageously.
Namaste.

Your's brother
BHAGAT SINGH

Not one couplet was out of place. Iqbal's was particularly apt.
So was Wajid Ali Shah's which he recited when the British
evicted him from Lucknow after deposing him from the throne. It,
however, speaks a lot for Bhagat Singh's refinement of feeling as
well as his courage that he should have studiously omitted a line
from his couplet alone. It read thus:

Dar-o-deewar pe hasrat se nazar karte hain
Khush raho ahle watan hum to safar karte hain.
[I cast my eyes longingly at the doors and the walls
Be happy, countrymen, I am off to travel.]

Bhagat Singh felt no longing for the world from which he was
about to depart. He did not care to cast his eyes back. He left the
world cheerfully fortified in the knowledge that he would live as
a symbol of integrity and courage in the hearts and minds of his
countrymen.

NOTES

1. *The Tribune,* February 4, 1931, p. 7. The text of the habeas corpus
petition.
2. *Ibid.,* February 7, 1931, p. 9.
3. *Ibid.,* March 4, 1931, p. 4. The text of both petitions are reproduced.
4. *The Tribune,* March 5, 1931, pp. 3-4.
5. *Ibid.,* p. 7.
6. *Ibid.,* p. 1.
7. Deol, p. 98.
8. *The Tribune,* March 6, 1931, p. 1. .
9. *Ibid.*
10. Venu, p. 7.

14

Gandhi's Truth

GANDHI and Jawaharlal Nehru differed on Bhagat Singh and what he symbolised throughout his travails; profoundly and openly. They agreed on his courage and patriotism as also on the futility of the methods he used to promote the ends. They disagreed on every thing else besides. They had drunk deep at different founts. Nehru accepted "the policy of non-violence because we believe in it and wish to give it the fullest trial in all honesty".[1] To Gandhi it was a creed rather than a policy. The socialist ideal, to which Bhagat Singh subscribed, commanded Nehru's allegiance as well. It did not impress Gandhi.

Bhagat Singh's admirers make scant allowance for Gandhi's commitments when they criticise him for the position he took in those days. He was determined to infuse in the people's minds the concept of non-violence and all that it implied in the Indian situation during British rule. He was equally determined to establish his own credentials to the British Government and its representative in India, the Viceroy and Governor-General Lord Irwin, as one irrevocably committed to non-violence.

The murders were gruesome. The bombs in the Assembly Chamber aroused indignation in many nationalists. Gandhi found both actions revolting. He studiously and conspicuously refrained from visiting Bhagat Singh and his associates in prison.

In this, he was not being callous even if he went to extremes that delivered a wrong message to the British. But, he was being honest and open.

Talks between Gandhi and Irwin, who was to retire in April, began in New Delhi on February 17, 1931; just six days after the Privy Council rejected Bhagat Singh's appeal. Clemency, by way of remission of the death sentence to one of transportation for life, alone stood between him and the hangman's noose. During the talks, Gandhi stayed at Dr. M.A. Ansari's house at 1, Daryaganj; an area where Old Delhi met the upstart New Delhi with ill-concealed scorn.

As Judith Brown records in her excellent account of the talks, "with him were the whole Working Committee, whom he kept constantly informed of the course of the discussion even if this meant waking them in the middle of the night for consultations".[2] The talks culminated in the famous Gandhi-Irwin Pact on March 5, 1931. Eighteen days lay between it and Bhagat Singh's execution. The Pact did not contain any provision concerning Bhagat Singh and the other two sentenced to death with him.[3] Paras 12 and 13 provided, respectively, for withdrawal of prosecutions and release of prisoners. Both were subject to two conditions. The prosecution or imprisonment related to "the civil disobedience movement" and there was no charge or conviction for violence or incitement to violence. The message was fairly clear. There was no hope for Bhagat Singh.

The next day, Gandhi held a press conference at Ansari's house. Every foreign correspondent of note in the capital and some senior Indian journalists were present—James Mill of the Associated Press of America, Peterson of *The Times*, London, William Shirer of *Chicago Tribune*, Holton James of *Boston Evening Transcript*, Ingles of *Christian Science Monitor*, J.N. Sahni of *The Hindustan Times*, and Needham of *Pioneer*, Lucknow. Needham also represented the *Civil and Military Gazette*, Lahore.

One correspondent asked:

"*Q* Would it be fair to ask, if I may do so, whether the sentences on Bhagat Singh and others will be commuted to transportation of life?

"*A*. It would be better not to ask me that question. Regarding this there is sufficient material in the newspapers to allow journalists to draw their own inferences. Beyond that I would not like to go."[3A]

On March 7, Gandhi addressed a mass meeting in Delhi at which a "red" leaflet listing a host of questions was handed to him. One of them concerned Bhagat Singh and his comrades. Gandhi responded: "May be, if you had been negotiating, you might have secured better terms from the Viceroy, but we, the Congress Working Committee, could secure no more than what we have. I may tell you that throughout the negotiations I was not acting on my own, but I was backed by the whole Congress Working Committee. We brought all the pressure we could to bear on our negotiations and satisfied ourselves with what in justice we could have under the provisional settlement. We could not as negotiators of the provisional truce forget our pledge of truth and non-violence, forget the bounds of justice.

"But it is still open to us to secure the release of all you have named and that can be done only if you will implement the settlement. Let *Young India* stand by the settlement and fulfil all its conditions, and *if God willing, Bhagat Singh and others are alive when we have arrived at the proper stage, they would not only be saved from the gallows but released.*" (Italics mine, throughout).[4]

Had Irwin given him any ground to believe that "the proper stage" would be arrived at *before* Bhagat Singh's execution? Gandhi spoke not only of his being "saved from the gallows but released". That could have been accomplished only by a wider accord with the British. For, the Pact itself did not devolve an iota of extra power or autonomy on Indian legislatures. It did no more than pave the way for talks at the Round Table Conference in London by redressing grievances of an immediate nature.

The First Round Table Conference began on November 12, 1930. The Congress was not represented at it. It concluded on January 19, 1931 with a statement embodying a proposal by the British Prime Minister, Ramsay MacDonald. It envisaged responsible Government in an Indian federation with certain powers "reserved to the Governor-General". They were: foreign affairs, defence, emergency powers and protection of minorities.

The Gandhi-Irwin Pact recorded: "In pursuance of the statement made by the Prime Minister in his announcement of the 19th
January 1931, steps will be taken for the participation of the
representatives of the Congress in the further discussions that are
to take place on the scheme of constitutional reform." Gandhi was
the sole Congress representative at the Second R.T.C. It commenced as late as on September 7, 1931, six months after the Pact.

It is true that the hope he held out was a qualified one—"and if,
God willing, Bhagat Singh and others are alive when we have
arrived at the proper stage . . ." But this implied, surely, that he
had ground enough to believe that there was reasonable probability of them remaining alive for some time longer. Had he received
any such assurance from the Viceroy? For, he added also: "I
beseech you then, if you want the release of the prisoners, to
change your methods, to accept the settlement, and then come and
ask me about the Garhwalis and Bhagat Singh. *Come to me six
months hence* after you have implemented the settlement and
gained in strength and ask me the question you are asking today
and I promise to satisfy you."[5]

The archives reveal that, so far from receiving any such assurance, Irwin had told him in the most explicit terms that the death
sentences would soon be carried out. Based on archival material a
charge has been levelled that not only did Gandhi make no effort
worth the name to save Bhagat Singh's life in his talks with the
Viceroy, but showed a lack of interest which could not have failed
to fortify Irwin in his resolve to execute the death sentences.

The first to level the charge was D.P. Das in an article in the
Independence Day 1970 issue of a weekly *Mainstream* (vide
Appendix XII for the text of the article). Das had delved into the
files of the Home Department in the National Archives of India.
He criticised Gandhi with obvious reluctance: "It will be rash to
run (*sic*) into a cynical conclusion about Gandhi." He felt that a
pact with the Viceroy was in the national interest. "He genuinely
believed that the Delhi Pact was much more important than the
lives of one revolutionary here or another there." His claims in
public of his "hard pleading", which Irwin publicly confirmed,

were untrue, he wrote. "Neither Gandhi nor Irwin had told the whole truth."

Das concluded: "There is no lack of precedents in ancient Indian history and our religion of taking resort to small lying or deception for the sake of noble objectives. There was the case of Yudhishthira of *Mahabharata* before him. Yudhisthira applied a phonetic variation in uttering a truth which amounted to worse than a most blatant lie to undo the Kuru Commander-in-Chief, Dronacharya. If this could be excused by the ancient Hindus including the modern purists, Gandhi's public statements on the Bhagat Singh case should not be taken seriously . . . So, Gandhi's deception should not make us cynical about him. Nor should the discovery of his deception for a cause considered noble by him be taken as an indication of any absence of nobility in him. He was indeed a great Indian. Let Bhagat Singh episode be just a spot in his career and a condonable spot."

But someone else consulted the same material and arrived at a different conclusion. K.K. Khullar, an eminent civil servant and writer, published his biography *Shaheed Bhagat Singh* in 1981. He devoted an entire Chapter VII to Gandhi's role, entitled "The Sun and the Star".

Some of the archival material on the topic, though not all, was published in 1971 in Volume 45 of the *Collected Works of Mahatma Gandhi* published by the Publications Division of the Government of India. (They include, of course, some documents which are not in the Government's files.)

Khullar remarked at the very outset: "The files of the Home Department now available in the National Archives, the newspapers of those turbulent days, the diaries of the freedom fighters and private correspondence of the individuals including the autobiography of the Viceroy and the writings of Gandhiji throw a flood of light on this issue. Much ink has been spilled by the critics and the historians on this issue but there is no clear cut answer. Sometimes the whole debate chokes like tea-leaves blocking the sink."[6]

Khullar's conclusion was altogether different from the one at which Das had arrived. "Das is unduly harsh on Gandhi because

from all available accounts Gandhi did his best. There can be no
doubt about Gandhi's sincerity. But one cannot say the same
about the Viceroy who proved cleverer and *duped Gandhi into
believing that Viceroy was also doing his best*. 'History', says
Manmathnath Gupta, 'is bound to say that he was fooled by the
Viceroy.' "[7]

However, Manmathnath Gupta was even more harsh on Gandhi
than D.P. Das was, as we shall see. A comment Khullar made
helps in testing the conclusions drawn by him as well as Das—
"the Viceroy who proved cleverer and *duped Gandhi into believing that Viceroy was also doing his best.*"

What, precisely, is the issue? Gandhi never for a moment
claimed that he had tried to make clemency for Bhagat Singh or
his release a condition to the Pact and failed. Subhas Chandra
Bose, who differed completely from Gandhi on the stand which
the Congress should take on Bhagat Singh, acknowledged that
Gandhi plainly refused to "go so far" as to wreck the Pact:
"Pressure was brought to bear on the Mahatma to try to save the
lives of the young men and, it must be admitted, he did try his
best. On this occasion he ventured the suggestion that he should,
if necessary, break with the Viceroy on the question, because the
execution was against the spirit, if not the letter, of the Delhi Pact.
I was reminded of a similar incident during the armistice between
the Sinn Fein Party and the British Government, when the strong
attitude adopted by the former had secured the release of an Irish
political prisoner sentenced to the gallows. But the Mahatma, who
did not want to identify himself with the revolutionary prisoners,
would not go so far, and it naturally made a great difference when
the Viceroy realised that the Mahatma would not break on that
question."[8]

The question is: What exactly transpired between Gandhi and
Irwin in the days between February 17, when the talks began, and
March 23 when Bhagat Singh was executed? *Did Gandhi try
strenuously to save Bhagat Singh's life as he publicly claimed?
That* is the issue.

The talks began in earnest only in the afternoon of February 18
when Gandhi did raise the question of commutation of the death

sentence with the Viceroy. Irwin promptly made a detailed note of the entire conversation. Its concluding para reads thus: "In conclusion and not connected with the above, he mentioned the case of Bhagat Singh. *He did not plead for commutation,* although he would, being opposed to all taking of life, take that course himself. He also thought it would have an influence for peace. But he did ask for *postponement in present circumstances.* I contended myself with saying that, whatever might be the decision as to exact dates, I could not think there was any case for commutation which might not be made with equal force in the case of any other violent crime. The Viceroy's powers of commutation were designed for use on well-known grounds of clemency, and I could not feel that they ought to be invoked on grounds that were admittedly political."[9]

Gandhi's version, available from the manuscript of Mahadev Desai's Diary, does not conflict with that of the Viceroy: "I talked about Bhagat Singh. I told him: 'This has no connection with our discussion, and it may even be inappropriate on my part to mention it. But if you want to make the present atmosphere more favourable, you should *suspend* Bhagat Singh's execution.' The Viceroy liked this very much. He said: 'I am very grateful to you that you have put this thing before me in this manner. *Commutation of sentence is a difficult thing, but suspension is certainly worth considering.'*

"I said about Bhagat Singh: 'He is undoubtedly a brave man but I would certainly say that he is not in his right mind. However, this is the evil of capital punishment, that it gives no opportunity to such a man to reform himself. I am putting this matter before you as a humanitarian issue and desire suspension of sentence *in order that there may not be unnecessary turmoil in the country.* I myself would release him, *but I cannot expect any Government to do so.* I would not take it ill even if you do not give any reply on this issue."[10]

The only point which figures in this account and is absent in the Viceroy's is Gandhi's plea that "you should suspend Bhagat Singh's execution", as distinct from commutation of the sentence. Suspension meant postponement and no more—in order to avoid "turmoil in the country". Read together, the Viceroy's minute and Gandhi's version do not exactly reveal a strong appeal by Gandhi to the Viceroy to commute the death sentences.

The matter was raised again a month later and well after the Gandhi-Irwin Pact had been concluded on March 5. It was on March 19. The Congress Session was due to be held in Karachi on March 24. Ratification of the Gandhi-Irwin Pact figured high on its agenda.

As before, Irwin recorded the conversation that very day and in fair detail for the Secretary of State for India to appreciate what was afoot. A good many topics were discussed. "The first point" Gandhi raised was the statement by the Secretary of State on the financial safeguards in the proposed Indian federation. The Viceroy's riposte was a complaint against Jawaharlal Nehru's speech. "Frankly, he appeared to have no spirit of peace". Gandhi replied that "Jawaharlal was very mercurial, but was already beginning to come down. Of this, however, I told him I saw no sign."

Gandhi anticipated no great difficulty at Karachi in ratifying the Pact. Bhagat Singh's plight was brought up at the very last, as the Viceroy recorded: "As he was leaving, he asked if he might mention the case of Bhagat Singh, saying that he had seen in the Press, the intimation of his execution for March 24th. This was an unfortunate day as it coincided with the arrival of the new President of the Congress at Karachi and there would be much popular excitement.

"I told him I had considered the case with most anxious care, but could find no grounds on which I could justify to my conscience commuting the sentence. As to the date, I had considered the possibility of postponement till after the Congress, but had deliberately rejected it on various grounds.

"(*i*) that postponement of execution, merely on political grounds, when orders had been passed, seemed to me improper;

"(*ii*) that postponement was inhuman in that it would suggest to the friends and relatives that I was considering commutation; and "(*iii*) that Congress would have been able legitimately to complain that they had been tricked by Government.

"He appeared to appreciate force of these arguments, and said no more.

(Sd) IRWIN"[11]

The tone and tenor of this conversation on March 19 are identical to those of the initial conversation on February 18. They do not support the view that the Viceroy gave any assurance of commutation of the sentences, however vaguely; reneged on it; and thus "duped" Gandhi. On the contrary, he flatly ruled out even postponement of their execution, let alone their commutation. Gandhi pleaded no more strongly on this occasion than he did on February 18. Indeed, he seemed rather to *acquiesce* in the execution which, he knew, was fixed for March 24.

The impression which Gandhi conveyed to the Viceroy on March 19 must have been confirmed by Gandhi's remarks to the Home Secretary, Herbert Emerson, that very day which the bureaucrat recorded, as the drill prescribed. They spoke for three hours that evening on the "difficulties arising out of the settlement". Gandhi mentioned the case of the Raja of Kalakankar; a case arising out of the forest satyagraha in the district of Colaba in the then Bombay Presidency; and the scope of the terms of the amnesty.

It was Emerson who raised the topic of Bhagat Singh: "I then asked him if he had seen in the papers that the Governor-General in Council had rejected the petition for mercy on behalf of Bhagat Singh. He said that he had and that he was apprehensive regarding the consequences. I did not mention the date on which the execution would be carried out, but I did explain to him that the question as to whether it should take place before or after the Karachi Congress had been very seriously considered by Government who realized the difficulties of either course, but thought it would have been unfair to the condemned persons to postpone execution and also not fair to Gandhi to allow the impression to gain ground that commutation was under consideration when this was not the case. He agreed that of the two alternatives *it is better not to wait*, but he suggested, though not seriously, that the third course of commutation of the sentence would have been better still. *He did not seem to me to be particularly concerned about the matter.* I told him that we should be lucky if we got through without disorder, and I asked him to do all that he could to prevent meetings being held in Delhi during the next few days and to restrain violent speeches. He promised to do what he could."[12]

This minute is corroborated by the letters the two exchanged the following day.[13] They reveal a certain rapport, unmistakably:

Government of India
Home Department, New Delhi.
March 20, 1931

Dear Mr. Gandhi,

I write to thank you for your letter of today enclosing translations of a circular and of notice issued by the Mamlatdar of Borsad. I will bring the matter to the notice of the local Government.

2. With reference to our conversation last night regarding the danger of excitement being worked up in connection with the execution of the sentence passed on Bhagat Singh, etc., the Chief Commissioner informs me that notice has been given in the city that Mr. Subhas Chandra Bose will address a meeting of protest tonight at 5.30. I fully realize your difficulties in the matter and I think that you realize the difficulties of Government and also their desire at the present time to avoid, if possible, preventive action, which may, however, be unavoidable if excitement grows. If a meeting is held tonight, it is almost certain to increase feeling, especially if speeches of an inflammatory character are made. Government will much appreciate any assistance you feel able to give to prevent this and to check the creation of conditions which, if uncontrolled, may have serious consequences.

Yours sincerely,
H.W. Emerson

M.K. Gandhi, Esq.
1, Daryaganj, Delhi

1, Daryaganj, Delhi,
March 20, 1931

Dear Mr. Emerson,

I thank you for your letter just received. I knew about the meeting you refer to. I have already taken every precaution possible and hope that nothing untoward will happen. I suggest that there should be no display of police force and no interference at the meeting. Irritation is undoubtedly there. It would be better to allow it to find vent through meetings, etc.

Yours sincerely,

H.W. Emerson Esq.
Chief Secretary to the Government of India
New Delhi.

By then Gandhi had clearly no ground whatever to believe that the Government was going to spare Bhagat Singh's life. He had been told repeatedly that the sentence of death would be carried out; he made no serious efforts, nonetheless, to alter that decision; led his interlocutors, the Viceroy and the Home Secretary, to believe that he was not seriously interested in commutation of the sentences; and, that he acquiesced in the Government's decision to execute them. In his conversation and correspondence with Emerson, he went a step further. He counselled the Government how best to manage the situation arising out of the imminent execution.

The historian of the Congress Dr. Pattabhi Sitaramayya, did not allege that Gandhi was "duped" by the Viceroy. Indeed, according to his recapitulation of the Gandhi-Irwin talks, Irwin was agreeable to the postponement of execution but it was Gandhi who preferred that they be carried out before the Karachi Congress met. Gandhi's version in public statements was, of course, to the contrary.

Sitaramayya wrote: "Any way Lord Irwin was unable to help in the matter, but undertook to secure a postponement of the execution till after the Karachi Congress. The Karachi session was to meet in the last days of March, but Gandhi himself definitely stated to the Viceroy that if the boys should be hanged, they had better be hanged before the Congress than after. The position of affairs in the country would be clear. There would be no false hopes lingering in the breasts of the people. The Gandhi-Irwin Pact would stand or fall on its own merits at the Congress, and on the added fact that the three boys had been executed."[14]

The Associated Press of India reported under Karachi, *March 21* dateline: "In view of Sardar Bhagat Singh's execution, which is expected to take place shortly, Mahatma Gandhi has wired to the Karachi Congress officials this morning asking them to cancel all processions and demonstrations arranged during the Congress week."[15]

Gandhi also met the press in New Delhi on that day, March 21. His answers to questions on Bhagat Singh were candid: "Do you expect to hold the National Congress to the terms of the truce with Lord Irwin?

A. Yes but if Bhagat Singh is hanged, as it now seems almost certain, it may have highly unfavourable repercussions upon the younger element in the Congress who may attempt to split the Congress.

Q. Do you entertain any hope that Bhagat Singh may be saved at the last minute?

A. Yes, but it is a very distant hope."[16]

Two days later, on the very day of Bhagat Singh's execution, Gandhi wrote a letter to Irwin which, understandably, came as a complete surprise to him in view of the discussions that preceded it, from February 18 till March 19. It was a fervent plea for commutation of the sentences: "It seems cruel to inflict this letter on you, but the interest of peace demands a final appeal. Though you were frank enough to tell me that there was little hope of your commuting the sentence of death on Bhagat Singh and two others, you said you would consider my submission of Saturday. Dr Sapru met me yesterday and said that you were troubled over the matter and taxing your brain as to the proper course to adopt. If there is any room left for re-consideration, I invite your attention to the following.

"Popular opinion rightly or wrongly demands commutation. When there is no principle at stake, it is often a duty to respect it."

Gandhi argued cogently and in his inimitably pellucid style. "Seeing that I am able to inform you that the revolutionary party has assured me that, in the event of these lives being spared, that party will stay its hands, suspension of sentence pending cessation of revolutionary murders becomes in my opinion a peremptory duty.

"Political murders have been condoned before now. It is worthwhile saving these lives, if thereby many other innocent lives are likely to be saved and may be even revolutionary crime almost stamped out."[17]

March 23, a Monday, was Gandhi's day of silence. He offered to visit the Viceroy if his presence was necessary. "Though I may not speak I may hear and write what I want to say." Irwin lost no time in rejecting Gandhi's pleas. "For the reasons I sought to explain fully to you in conversation, I cannot see my way to feel that it would be right to take the action you request."[18]

Had Gandhi taken such a stand on February 19, he might have succeeded in saving Bhagat Singh's life. Commutation of the death sentence to one of long imprisonment might have served as an acceptable via media. Bhagat Singh would have been "evicted" from the political scene to the relief of the British rulers. His life would have been spared and Indian opinion greatly assuaged. But till as late as March 19, in talks with the Viceroy and the Home Secretary, and March 20, in his correspondence with the Home Secretary, Gandhi conveyed a clear impression of disinterest in Bhagat Singh's fate. On the morning of March 23, Gandhi could have had no reason to believe that his plea for clemency at the very last minute stood any chance of acceptance by the Viceroy.

As Manmathnath Gupta wrote, "It is evident from Gandhi's own letter to Emerson that he was not at all emotionally involved in the imminent hanging of the three youths in the way in which the whole of India, including Nehru and Bose, were."[19]

In his memoirs *Fullness of Days* published nearly three decades later in 1957, Irwin, now Lord Halifax, recorded his talk with Gandhi on March 19, 1931, on the same lines as he did in his minute that day. "If the young man was hanged, said Mr. Gandhi. there was a likelihood that he would become a national martyr and the general atmosphere would be seriously prejudiced . . . Mr Gandhi said that he greatly feared, unless I could do something about it, the effect would be to destroy our pact. I said I should regret that no less than he, but it would be clear to him there were only three possible courses. The first was to do nothing and let the execution proceed, the second was to change the order and grant Bhagat Singh a reprieve, the third was to hold up any decision till after the Congress meeting was well over. I told him that I thought he would agree that it was impossible for me from my point of view to grant him his reprieve, and that merely to postpone decision and encourage people to think that there was such a chance of remission was not straightforward or honest. The first course alone, therefore, was possible in spite of all its attendant difficulties. Mr. Gandhi thought for a moment, and then said, "Would Your Excellency see any objection to my saying that I pleaded for the young man's life?"[20]

Irwin's biographer Alan Campbell-Johnson, who was to serve in New Delhi as Mountbatten's Press Secretary, had nothing more substantial to add.[21]

The content of these exchanges, between Gandhi on the one hand and Irwin and Emerson on the other, were, of course, not known to the public then; more likely than not, even Jawaharlal Nehru was unaware of them.

As news reached Delhi of the execution of Bhagat Singh, Gandhi issued a carefully drafted statement on March 24 before leaving for Karachi.

"There never has been, within living memory, so much romance round any life as has surrounded that of Bhagat Singh. Though I must have seen him as a student while at Lahore many times, I cannot recall Bhagat Singh's features. But during the past month, it was a privilege to listen to the story of Bhagat Singh's patriotism, his courage and his deep love for Indian humanity. From all accounts received by me, his daring was unequalled. That he misused his extraordinary courage, has been forgotten in the midst of his many virtues. The execution of such a youth and his comrades has given them the crown of martyrdom. Thousands feel today personally bereaved by this death. While therefore, I can associate myself with all the tributes that can be paid to the memory of these young patriots, I warn the youth of the country against copying their example. Let us by all means copy their capacity for sacrifice, their industry and their reckless courage. But let us not use these qualities as they did. The deliverance of this country must not be through murder.

"As for the Government, I cannot help feeling that they have lost a golden opportunity of winning over the Revolutionary Party. It was their clear duty in view of the settlement, at least to suspend indefinitely the execution. By their action they have put a severe strain upon the settlement and once more proved their capacity for flouting public opinion and for exhibition of the immense brute power they possess. This persistence in the exercise of their brute power is perhaps a portent showing that notwithstanding pompous and pious declarations, they do not mean to part with power. But the Nation's duty is clear. The Congress must not swerve from the path chalked out for it. In my opinion, notwithstanding the gravest provocation, the Congress should endorse the settlement. We must not put ourselves in the wrong by being angry. Let us recognise that commutation of the sentences was no part of the truce. We may accuse the Government of Goondaism, but we may not accuse them of breach of settlement. In my deliberate opinion, a grave blunder has been committed by the Government and it has increased our power for winning the freedom for which Bhagat Singh and his comrades have died. Let us not fritter away the opportunity by being betrayed into any angry action. Universal hartal is a foregone conclusion. No better mark of respect can be paid to the memory of the deceased patriots than by having absolutely silent and respectful processions. Let it even be one of self-purification and greater dedication to the service of the country."[22]

Gandhi was clearly anxious to remove any impression that the executions were a "breach of settlement". He was no less anxious that expression of the people's indignation was kept under control. On his arrival at Malir station near Karachi, Gandhi was greeted by angry demonstrators of the Naujawan Bharat Sabha wearing red shirts. He issued another press statement on March

26, in an effort to assuage public opinion. "Of course, they shouted, 'Down with Gandhism', 'Go back Gandhi'. This I consider to be a legitimate expression of their anger."

But, he warned, the cult of violence can have no meaning. "In this country of self-suppression and timidity almost bordering on cowardice we cannot have too much bravery, too much self-sacrifice. One's head bends before Bhagat Singh's bravery and sacrifice. But I want the greater bravery, If I might say so without offending my young friends, of the meek, the gentle and the non-violent, the bravery that will mount the gallows without injuring, or harbouring any thought of injury to a single soul."

He was asked a pointed question. "Does the execution of Bhagat Singh and his friends alter your position in any way with regard to the settlement?" Gandhi replied: "My own personal position remains absolutely the same, though the provocation has been of the most intense character. I must confess that the staying of these executions was no part of the truce, and so far as I am concerned, no provocation offered outside the terms will deflect me from the path I had mapped out when I agreed to the settlement."[23]

When, later in the day, he addressed the Karachi Congress, Gandhi was careful to characterise commutation of the sentences as "a distant hope" rather than a term of the accord. "By the executions the Government have given the nation grave cause for provocation. It has shocked me too in as much as my negotiations and talks had made me entertain a distant hope that Bhagat Singh, Rajguru and Sukh Dev might be saved."

He shot a sharp dart in the direction of the critics. Its meaning was fairly clear: "And now a message for the young men. If you want my service, do not disown me; come and understand everything from me. You must know that it is against my creed to punish even a murderer, a thief or a dacoit. There can be therefore no excuse for suspicion that I did not want to save Bhagat Singh. But I want you also to realize Bhagat Singh's error. If I had had an opportunity of speaking to Bhagat Singh and his comrades, I should have told them that the way they pursued was wrong and futile."

As he was winding up his speech, Gandhi was asked "What did you do to save Bhagat Singh?" He replied: "Well, I was not on my defence, and so I did not bother you with the details of what I did to save Bhagat Singh and his comrades. *I pleaded with the Viceroy as best I could. I brought all the persuasion at my command to bear on him.* On the day fixed for the final interview with Bhagat Singh's relations I wrote a personal letter to the Viceroy on the morning of 23rd. I poured my whole soul into it, but to no avail. I might have done one thing more, you say. I might have made the commutation a term of the settlement. It could not be so made. And to threaten withdrawal would be a breach of faith. The Working Committee had agreed with me in not making commutation a condition precedent to truce. I could therefore only mention it apart from the settlement. I had hoped for magnanimity. My hope was not to materialize. But that can be no ground for breaking the settlement."[24]

On March 29, the Karachi Congress adopted a resolution on Bhagat Singh and his comrades. It read thus: "This Congress, while dissociating itself from the disapproving of political violence in any shape or form, places on record its admiration of the bravery and sacrifice of the late Sardar Bhagat Singh and his comrades Syts. Sukh Dev and Rajguru, and mourns with the bereaved families the loss of these lives. The Congress is of opinion that this triple execution is an act of wanton vengeance and is a deliberate flouting of the unanimous demand of the nation for commutation. This Congress is further of opinion that Government have lost the golden opportunity of promoting goodwill between the two nations, admittedly held to be essential at this juncture, and of winning over to the method of peace the party which, being driven to despair, resorts to political violence."[25]

Nehru revealed in his speech on the resolution that it was Gandhi who had drafted it.[26] Nehru said: "We tried to get his sentence reduced to life imprisonment but we did not succeed."

Before long, Gandhi was torn by doubt as to whether he had acted rightly in drafting the resolution. "The extolling of murderers is being overdone. If we are to sing the praises of every murderer because the murder has a political motive behind it, we should proceed from praising the deed to the deed itself. The praising of Sajjan Singh as a hero raises a doubt in my mind about the wisdom of my having been the author of the Congress resolution about Bhagat Singh."[27]

To Darcy Lindsay, of the European Group in the Central Assembly, Gandhi wrote on May 8: "There is a romance around the life of Bhagat Singh. He was no coward. From all enquiries made by me I find that he was a man of spotless character and of great daring. He exercised also great influence on some young men. Somehow or other he had developed a belief that political assassination had its use. It was impossible not to notice the execution, I believe quite unwise, of Bhagat Singh and his comrades, whom the execution made martyrs. I have no doubt whatsoever that the execution has surrounded these lives with a halo which they would not otherwise have had."[28]

In *Young India* of June 11, 1931, Gandhi replied to criticism of his record on Bhagat Singh without mincing words: "I have already expressed my doubts as to the propriety of my having drafted and sponsored the Bhagat Singh resolution not because it was wrong in principle but for the misinterpretation it has lent itself to . . . I had interested myself in the movement for the commutation of the death sentence on Bhagat Singh and his comrades. *I had put my whole being into the task.* I had, therefore, to study the life of the principal actor in the tragedy. I had to come in contact with his devoted father and those who were attached to Bhagat Singh not for his deed but for his character. I was thus drawn to the resolution in the natural course."[29]

Gandhi's claim that "I had put my whole being into the task" is not borne out by the record. Except for the letter of March 23, hours before the execution, his efforts lay exclusively in an altogether different direction—the forging and implementation of a Pact with the British. There can be two opinions on the wisdom of the Pact. It was, to Gandhi, a gesture of conciliation. Certainly, it was conceived entirely in the national interest as he understood it. It is his claims on Bhagat Singh which he made in public which are relevant. "I would gladly have surrendered my life to the Viceroy to save Bhagat Singh and others," Gandhi said.[30] The record belies Gandhi's claims.

Gandhi refused to associate himself in the move to raise a memorial to Bhagat Singh and did not conceal his reasons in his letter to the Memorial Committee, dated June 20, 1931:

"A memorial erected in honour of anybody undoubtedly means that the memorialists would copy the deeds of those in whose memory they erect the memorial. It is also an invitation to posterity to copy such deeds. I am, therefore, unable to identify myself in any way with the memorial."[31]

Bhagat Singh's devoted biographer Dr. Gurdev Singh Deol criticises Gandhi on this score; unjustly, in this writer's opinion. There can be two views on his public stand on Bhagat Singh's conduct. But Gandhi cannot be criticised for lack of candour or courage. These qualities, however, were not very evident in Gandhi's discussions with the Viceroy on February 18 and March 19, 1931 nor in those with the Home Secretary on March 19; least of all in his letter to Emerson on March 20. Deol makes a far more valid point when he comments: "But a 'leader' who could go to the extent of stating to the Viceroy, that 'if the boys should be hanged, they had better be hanged before the Congress (Karachi) Session, than after it', could hardly be expected to secure the commutation of the death sentences of Bhagat Singh and his comrades."[32]

The anger surfaces in the apostrophe marks on each side of the leader. Manmathnath Gupta was embittered. Quoting Sitaramayya's remark, "It is no exaggeration to say that at that moment Bhagat Singh's name was as widely known all over India and was as popular as Gandhi's", Manmathnath Gupta proceeded to attribute to Gandhi motives which were unworthy of Gupta.[33]

Reading the record as a whole, archival and published, there is great regret on three counts.

One is that Gandhi did not know, did not try to know and to understand, Bhagat Singh's thinking when he was in prison; specifically, his renunciation of terrorism. Here was a man of enormous potentialities who would have served India far more devotedly than most. A preeminently educable young man. It was surely a life worth saving. The effort should have been made.

Secondly, there is a reference in Gandhi's letter of April 29,1931 to C. Vijayaraghavachariar to the fact that "the legality of the convictions (of Bhagat Singh and his associates) was discussed threadbare by jurists like Sir Tej Bahadur Sapru with the Viceroy."[34] It is unfortunate that the monstrous illegalities of the trial passed muster, as they did. The fundamentals of constitutional and criminal law were flouted. Sir Tej did not denounce them in public nor did any other jurist of national eminence outside Punjab.

The last regret is about Gandhi's role between February 18 and March 22. As late as on March 20 he was counselling Emerson, a bureaucrat who had exhibited his racism to the Central Assembly on September 14,1929, on damage control. It was bad enough that Gandhi spoke to the Viceroy as he did on February 18 and March 19. It was far worse that he counselled the Home Secretary thereafter on ways to contain expressions of indignation by his own people on the execution of a patriot, whose patriotism Gandhi himself admired, by the British rulers of the country.

Gandhi alone could have intervened effectively to save Bhagat Singh's life. He did not, till the very last. Later claims such as that "I brought all the persuasion at my command to bear on him" (the Viceroy) are belied by the record which came to light four decades later. In this tragic episode, Gandhi was not candid either to the nation or even to his closest colleagues about his talks with the Viceroy, Lord Irwin, on saving Bhagat Singh's life.

NOTES

1. Gopal, Vol. 4, p. 394.
2. Judith M. Brown, *Gandhi and Civil Disobedience: The Mahatma in Indian Politics*, Cambridge University Press, 1977, p. 182.
3. C.H. Philips and B.N Pandey (Eds.), *The Evolution of India and Pakistan 1858 to 1947: Select Documents*, Oxford University Press, 1962, pp. 241-242. Vide Pattabhi Sitaramayya, Vol. I, pp. 437-442 for the complete text.
3A. Pattabhi Sitaramayya, Vol. I. p. 450.
4. D.G. Tendulkar, *Mahatma*, Publications Division, 1969, Volume III, p. 62.
5. *Ibid.*, p. 63.
6. Khullar, p. 61.

7. *Ibid.*, p. 70.
8. Subhas Chandra Bose, *The Indian Struggle*, 1920–1942, p. 232.
9. National Archives of India, File No. 5-45/1931 KW2, Home Department Political Branch, Vide *CWMG*, Vol. 45, pp. 196-97.
10. *CWMG*, Vol. 45, p. 209.
11. National Archives of India, File No. 5-45/1931 KW2, Home Department Political Branch, *CWMG*, Vol. 45, pp. 315-16.
12. NAI, File No. 33-1/1931, Home Department, Political Branch, *CWMG*, Vol. 45, pp. 438-440.
13. NAI, File No. 4/21/1931, Home Department Political, pp. 31-32, *CWMG*, Vol. 45, pp. 316 and 446.
14. Pattabhi Sitaramayya, Vol. I, p. 442.
15. *The Tribune*, March 24,1931, p. 1.
16. *Ibid.*
17. *CWMG*, Vol. 45, pp. 333-34.
18. *Ibid.*, p. 334.
19. Manmathnath Gupta, p. 211.
20. *Earl of Halifax, Fullness of Days*, Collins, London, 1957, pp. 149-50.
21. Alan Campbell-Johnson, *Viscount Halifax*, Robert Hale, 1941, p. 313.
22. *The Tribune*, March 26, 1931.
23. *CWMG*, Vol. 45, pp. 344-45.
24. *Ibid.*, pp. 347-51.
25. Pattabhi Sitaramayya, Vol. I, pp. 456-57.
26. Gopal, Vol. IV, p. 505.
27. *CWMG*, Vol. 46, p. 50.
28. *Ibid.*, p. 120.
29. *Ibid.*, p. 359.
30. Venu, p. 60.
31. Deol, p. 94.
32. *Ibid.*, p. 93.
33. Manmathnath Gupta, p. 211.
34. *CWMG*, Vol. 46, pp. 51-52.

Epilogue

The Moral Abyss

IN the aftermath there was depression all around. The Lahore Conspiracy Case dealt a death blow to the Hindustan Socialist Republican Association. Almost all its leaders were either dead or in prison, except for a handful who managed to evade arrest and were in hiding. Less than a month before Bhagat Singh's execution, his comrade, Panditji, as Chandra Shekhar Azad was known, was killed in an encounter with the police.

Chandra Shekhar Azad had arranged to meet an old worker in the Alfred Park in Allahabad on February 27, 1931. Someone informed the police about it. There was a reward of Rs. 10,000 on his head. The amount meant a lot sixty-five years ago. Policemen in plain clothes surrounded him as soon as he entered the Park. He fired at them but was felled to the ground in a shower of bullets.[1]

The revolutionary movement in Northern India lingered till the mid-thirties. Even while the Lahore Conspiracy case was on, a new group was formed in June 1930 called *Aatish Chakkar* (The Circle of Fire) group. It was organised by Yashpal, one of the absconding accused in the case, and Inderpal who said that the Chakkar (the Circle) would continue the task set by Bhagat Singh.

This became known as the Second Lahore Conspiracy Case. It was also tried by a Special Tribunal; a Commission constituted by a special statute, Act IV of 1930. The Commissioners were Justice H.A.C. Blacker, as President, and Rai Bahadur Ganga Ram Soni and M. Sleem as members. But the law did not bar appeal to the

High Court. Appeals against the convictions were heard, on the facts as well as on the law, by Justices Dalip Singh and Currie of the Lahore High Court and disposed off by a judgment pronounced on December 17, 1933.[2] The contrast with the Bhagat Singh case was glaring (vide Appendix XIII for the Act which set up the Commission and related papers).

On September 25, 1930, the Chief Secretary to the Punjab Government, D.J. Boyd, wrote to Home Secretary Emerson on the need for legislation to deal with the new case. It was followed up by a letter of October 2 enclosing the draft Bill which was approved by the Centre. It agreed to initiate legislation to confer on the accused the right of appeal to the High Court. The Bill was adopted by the Legislative Council of Punjab on November 8 and became law as Act IV of 1930, two days later.

On December 2 Crerar tabled the Central Act which conferred on the accused in the second Lahore Conspiracy Case the right of appeal. Seven months earlier the Governor-General had made an Ordinance to deny this very right to the accused in the first Lahore Conspiracy Case in which Bhagat Singh was on trial. The charges were of equal gravity in both cases. Only the State's animus was overpowering in the first.

Dianat Rai Handa was one of the accused. As before, some prominent members of the party, including Inderpal, turned approver. Amolak Ram Kapur appeared in this case, as well. On February 21, 1931, while he was struggling to save Bhagat Singh's life, we find him moving the High Court in the second case for an Order that—the approvers be transferred from police custody to judicial lock-up.[3]

Depression did not spare the freedom movement as a whole, either. The Second Round Table Conference ended in failure. Differences between the Congress and the Muslim League and between Gandhi and Dr. B.R. Ambedkar widened. The Communist movement languished after the Meerut trials.

What had improved was public awakening to which all had contributed; those in the legislatures as well as the ones outside—constitutionalists, non-cooperators and revolutionaries.

A tribute to Bhagat Singh's contribution in this regard came four years after his death from a most unlikely but highly authoritative source; the Director of the Intelligence Bureau, Sir Horace Williamson. He wrote in his study *India and Communism*: "Bhagat Singh made no mistake. The prisoners' dock became a political forum and the countryside rang with his heroics. His photograph was on sale in every city and township and for a time rivalled in popularity even that of Mr. Gandhi himself."[4]

Bhagat Singh's case in the Privy Council had a sequel. The Privy Council followed its ruling later in Benoari Lal Sarma's case during the Quit India movement and the War, reversing a liberal ruling by the Federal Court of India which had come into existence in 1937. The Board was presided over by none other than Simon, now Lord Chancellor. Among other issues was involved, once again, the finality of the Governor-General's subjective satisfaction in making an Ordinance under S.72 (of the Act of 1919) now put in the Ninth Schedule to the Government of India Act, 1935. It was not invalidated, the Privy Council ruled, though the application of the Ordinance made by the Governor-General was left to the satisfaction of Provincial Governments.[5]

In an incisive analysis of the ruling, M.C. Setalvad wrote: "Colonial writers on Constitutional Law have on occasions characterized judgments of the Privy Council as having been influenced by considerations of policy. It is not surprising, therefore, that similar comments should have been made in regard to the view taken by the Privy Council in Benoari Lal Sarma's case.

"Whatever the true legal view, the stand taken by the Federal Court has proved to be a valuable aid in the preservation of the fundamental right of the Indian people to have recourse to the ordinary courts of the country."[6]

By the time he wrote, the sun was about to set on the Raj in India. Nearly half a century has rolled by since India became independent. Enough has happened since to prompt one to ask— how would free India treat *its* Bhagat Singh? That the situations are different in one fundamental respect is obvious. Bhagat Singh was a rebel against foreign rule over the country; not one who took to the arms in order to subvert democratic government according to the rule of law and instal a regime after his heart.

But such a State owes it to its citizens and to itself, no less, to abide by the established norms and to respect human rights recognised in the Constitution of India and the International Covenant on Civil and Political Rights which India ratified, belatedly, on April 10, 1949.

It is not unjust at all to say that in this crucial test every arm of the Indian State has been found to be wanting—Parliament, the Government of India and the Supreme Court. The Court's record during the Punjab crisis was none too flattering one. In June 1984 faced with a batch of *habeas corpus* petitions from Punjab, a Supreme Court Judge flew to flights of eloquence on the perils of secession quoting Abraham Lincoln, ironically, for moral support.[7] The test came in the clearest possible terms when the Supreme Court had to consider the constitutional validity of the Terrorist and Disruptive Activities (Prevention) Act, 1987, in replacement of the Act of 1985. It failed dismally. As ever, florid rhetoric—this time, in praise of patriotism and in denunciation of the menace of terrorism—prefaced illiberal rulings on the impugned provisions of TADA. Dissent by two of the five Justices on the Bench which heard the case, though valuable, was limited and muted.[8] This was as late as on March 11, 1994.

TADA was, in fact, far worse than the Rowlatt Act and, in some respects, worse than the Ordinance under which Bhagat Singh was tried inasmuch as the Ordinance did not tinker with the law of evidence as TADA did for a whole decade, till its expiry by efflux of time in mid-1995.[9]

But Bhagat Singh and his comrades have no heirs in the terrorist in independent India. The "modern" terrorist does not stand any comparison with his forebears during British rule, either morally or intellectually. As Peter Heehs points out: "During the first two decades of India's independent existence there was little organized terrorism in the country. But during the late sixties left-wing Bengali insurgents began resorting to terrorist methods to achieve their revolutionary aims. The eighties saw the rise of separatist terrorist groups in Punjab, Kashmir and Assam as well as among ethnic Indian Tamils in Sri Lanka.

"Some of these groups are distinguished by the use of brutal

methods, including indiscriminate murder, and by aims that sometimes seem more criminal than political. Writers on terrorism
often point out the immense moral gulf that separates European
terrorist groups of the nineteenth century, such as the Narodnaya
Volya, from contemporary groups like the Baader-Meinhof Gang.
A similar abyss would appear to divide the Bengali revolutionaries of the early twentieth century from their less idealistic descen-
dant in contemporary India."[10]

What distinguished Bhagat Singh from all others, besides his
courage, patriotism and commitment to moral values, was his
intellectual strength. A voracious reader, he was also willing to
rethink. He had the capacity to brood and to torment his soul over
the past. That led him to renounce terrorism and to advise the
young to follow suit; indeed, to counsel moderation and readiness
to compromise. He was only 23 when he was hanged.

On his death, Indian leaders vied with one another in lavishing
praise on him. One wonders how many of them knew then that
they had lost in him a man who, had he lived, might have had an
incalculable impact on the course of India's politics.

NOTES

1. R.C. Majumdar, *Struggle for Freedom*, Bharatiya Vidya Bhavan, 1962,
pp. 552-53.

2. *Jahangiri Lal and others* vs. *Emperor*, AIR 1935, Lahore 230. The
judgment describes the origins of the Aatish Chakkar. Vide also, Kamlesh
Mohan, pp. 244-45 and 388.

3. *The Tribune*, February 25, 1931, p. 11.

4. Horace Williamson, *India and Communism*, it was reprinted in 1976 by
Editions Indian, Calcutta, p. 275.

5. *King Emperor* vs. *Benoari Lal Sarma and others* (1945), A.C. 14.

6. M.C. Setalvad, *War and Civil Liberties*, Indian Council of World
Affairs, New Delhi and Oxford University Press, 1946, p. 67.

7. *Ram Jethmalani* vs. *Union of India* (1984) 3 SCC 696.

8. *Kartar Singh* vs. *State of Punjab* (1994) 3, Supreme Court Cases, 569.

9. Vide the writer's articles "Worse than Rowlatt", *Frontline*, April 22,
1994 and "An Oversight: The Supreme Court on TADA", *The Statesman*,
October 2-3, 1994.

10. Peter Heehs, *The Bomb in Bengal*, Oxford University Press, 1993, p.
256.

Appendix I

Text of the Complaint

The following is the text of the complaint, filed by Hamilton Harding, Senior Superintendent of Police, in the Court of R.S. Pandit Sri Krishan, Special Magistrate, against the following accused:

1. Sukh Dev alias Dayal, alias Swami alias Villager son of Ram Lal, caste Thapar Khatri of Mohalla Arya Samaj, Lyallpur.

2. Kishori Lal Rattan, alias Deo Datt Rattan, alias Mast Ram Shastri, son of Raghbar Dutt, caste Brahman of Dharampur, P.S. Hajipur, District Hoshiarpur.

3. Agya Ram alias Masterji, son of Nand Lal Brahman of Lalla P.S. Killa Sobha Singh, District Sialkot.

4. Des Raj, son of Ram Kishen, caste Khatri of Belgan P.S. Sambrial, District Sialkot.

5. Prem Dutt alias Master alias Amrit Lal, son of Ram Datt Khatri of Gujarat.

6. Surindra Nath Pandey alias Stone, son of Hira Lal Pandey, Brahman, resident of Mohalla Sabzimandi, Cawnpore.

7. Jai Dev alias Harish Chander, son of Babu Salig Ram, caste Khatri, Kapur, Sadar Bazar, Hardoi.

8. Shiv Varma alias Parbhat alias Har Narain alias Ram Narain, Kapur son of Kanhiya Lal Varma, Khatri of Hardoi.

9. Gaya Prashad alias Dr. B.S. Nigam, Ram Lal alias Ram Nath alias Desh Bhagat, caste Kurmi, resident of Khajuri Khurd, P.S. Billhaur, District Cawnpore.

10. Jatindra Nath Das, son of Banke Behari Das of 30 Dohar Road, Calcutta.

11. Mahabir Singh alias Partab of Shahpur Thela P.S. Rajaka Rampur, District Etah.

12. Bhagat Singh, son of Kishan Singh of Khatasrian, Lahore.

13. Batukeshwar Dutt alias Batta alias Mohan, son of G.D. Dutt of Bedwan, Bengal.

14. Ajoy Kumar Ghosh alias Negro-General, son of Dr. Ghosh of Cawnpore.

15. Sachindra Nath Sanyal, alias Jatin Sanyal, son of Hari Nath Sanyal, Mohalla Colonel Ganj, Allahabad.

16. Kamal Nath Trivedi, alias Kanwal Nath Tewari, student of Vidya Sagar College, Calcutta, son of Suraj Nath Tewari of Suraya P.S. Gobindpur.

17. Chandra Shekhar Azad alias Panditji, son of Baij Nath, alias Sita Ram, Brahman of Baijnath Tula, P.S. Bhilopur, Benares.

18. Bejoy Kumar Sinha alias Bachu, son of Markala Kumar Sinha of Mohalla Karachi Ganj, Cawnpore.

19. Kailash Patti alias Kali Charan, son of Hardo Narain Kayasth of Mongranwan P.S. Ghamipur, District Azamgarh, at present residing at Gorakhpur.

20. Raghunath alias 'M' alias Ram Guru of Benaras.

21. Bhagwati Charan alias B.C. Vohra, son of Rai Sahib Shiv Charan Das, Caste Brahman of Lahore.

22. Kundan Lal alias Partap alias No. 1 of Benares U.P.

23. Kalash alias Gunthala of Jhansi.

24. Yashpal, son of Hira Lal, Khatri of Nidhan P.S. Hamirpur District, Kangra, now residing at Wachowali, Lahore.

25. Satmurdyal, son of Pandit Sukhbasi Lal Avasthi, caste Brahman of Mohalla Dana Khori, Cawnpore.

The complaint is filed under Sections 121, 121A, 122 and 123 of the Indian Penal Code.

The Complainant respectfully sheweth:

I. That the accused above mentioned along with others have at Lahore and other places in British India at various times and occasions commencing from the year 1924 and continuing upto the present time of their arrest been engaged in a conspiracy to wage war against His Majesty the King Emperor and to deprive him of the sovereignty of British India and to overawe by criminal force, the Government established by law in British India and to collect men, arms and ammunitions for or otherwise to make preparation for the said object and purpose.

II. They further concealed the existence of a design to wage war against the King Emperor intending by such concealment to facilitate or knowing it to be likely that such concealment would facilitate the waging of such war.

III. With these objects as mentioned in paras I and II above these accused along with others formed a party known as the Hindustan Republican Association and Indian Republican Army and held their meetings at Lahore and other places in British India with a view to overthrow by force the Government established by law in India and to establish a Federated Republican Government in its stead.

MEANS

IV. That the means devised to be adopted to attain these objects were as follows:

1. The collection of arms, men and munitions and also money for the purchase of arms and munitions.

2. The obtaining of money for the same purpose by means of forcing and robbing banks and treasuries and by dacoity which necessarily involved murder.

3. The manufacturing of explosive bombs for the purpose of murders and to overawe the Government.

4. Murders of Police and other officials and persons interested in or the Government of British India or the persons who obstructed the carrying out of the objects of the conspiracy and persons who proved obnoxious to their party.

5. The blowing up of trains.

6. The production, possession and circulation of seditious and revolutionary literature.

7. The rescue of convicts and persons in lawful custody.

8. The seduction of educated youths with a view to enlist them in the conspiracy.

9. To obtain renewal and subscriptions among persons in foreign countries who were interested in the accomplishment of revolution in India.

V. 1. An attempt was made to murder Mr. Bannerji, Inspector C.I.D. at Benares on 13.1.1928.

2. An embezzlement of Rs. 3,199 was committed by Kailash Patti alias Kali Charan an absconder who was an employee in the sub-post office, Burhal Ganj, District Gorakhpur on 26.6.1928 to be utilised by the party in furtherance of their common object.

3. A dacoity at Punjab National Bank, Lahore was attempted on 4.12.1928.

4. Mr. Saunders, Assistant Supdt. of Police and Channan Singh, Head Constable were murdered in Lahore on December 17, 1928.

5. A bomb was thrown in the Assembly Chamber, Delhi and shots were fired therein on 8.4.1929 causing severe injuries to Sir Bomanji Dalal and others.

6. A dacoity at Maulina was committed on 7.6.1929 causing the death of Dank Mahton Koori owner of the house.

7. The accused along with others were manufacturing bombs at Lahore, Saharanpur, Calcutta and Agra, the factories at Lahore and Saharanpur having since been captured.

8. The accused visited different towns in British India to seduce youths and to induce them to join their conspiracy.

VI. That in pursuance of the said conspiracy in British India preparations for the following actions were made but did not succeed:

1. To blow up the train carrying members of the Simon Commission by means of dynamite.

2. To rescue Jagdish Chander Chatterji who was a convict in connection with the Kakori Conspiracy Case and Satindra Nath Sanyal another convict of their party.

VII. That accused Nos. 17 to 25 are absconding and are still at large.

VIII. That the order of the local Government under Sec. 196 Criminal Procedure Code, duly signed is attached herewith.

IX. That the Complainant is informed that in respect of the other offences committed in pursuance of the conspiracy separate police challans have been presented to this Court.

It is, therefore, prayed that the accused abovenamed be tried for and convicted of the offences enumerated above for any offence or offences which they may be proved to have committed.

—*The Tribune*, July 11, 1929, pp. 3-4.

Appendix II

The Government Advocate's Speech

The following is the full text of the Government Advocate Carden Noad's opening speech:

There are 32 persons involved in the case of whom 7 are approvers, 9 are absconding and are still at large and 16 are placed on their trial and are present in Court. They will be tried under the ordinary criminal law of the land for offences alleged to have been committed by them while evidence will be recorded under Section 512 of the Criminal Procedure Code against the absconding accused.

I desire to emphasize the fact that this is an ordinary trial under ordinary law (though of singular importance) and that these individuals alone are upon their trial. No political action or system is in any way involved. No social, religious or educational body or institution is or can be affected by the outcome of this prosecution except so far as it is in their interest of all citizens of a civilised community that offences against the law of the land shall, if proved according to law, be suitably punished.

I wish also to say on behalf of myself and my colleagues, Khan Sahib Kalandar Ali Khan and Mr. Gopal Lal, that we shall do our best to assist the Special Magistrate in giving the accused fair, patient and impartial enquiry and I confidently ask for the cooperation of the learned counsel appearance on behalf of the defence in attaining this object. It may not be out of place at this stage to recall the occurrence of the murder of Mr. Saunders, ASP and Channan Singh, Head Constable. Two unarmed men were shot down in broad daylight in the streets of Lahore on the 17th December, 1928 and the police were unable at that time to apprehend the culprits. Coupled with universal condemnation of this dastardly murder severe criticism was levelled against the police in Council and in the newspapers because of the delay which took place in the detection of the culprits. The Special CID with K.B. Abdul Aziz and his staff all working under the direct instructions and orders of Mr. Stead, Inspector General of Police, have now discovered the facts and are prepared to

prove that these murders were committed in pursuance of a widespread conspiracy as a part of a series of criminal acts and designs of the most serious
nature. I am confident that every member of the public will now be interested
in seeing that justice is done. I may not be misunderstood. We desire the Court
as well as the public to hold the scales evenly between the case of the Crown
and the case of the accused now before the Court.

Constitution of Revolutionary Party

I should like to give a short summary of the various intentions, designs and
acts which form part of the subject matter of the case to be placed before the
Court.

The accused above-mentioned were members of a revolutionary party
which became active throughout Northern India. At a meeting held at Delhi in
August 1928, a Central Committee was constituted representing different
provinces. In that meeting the following plans and resolutions were adopted
and passed.

1. Phonindra Nath, approver was elected officer-in-charge of Behar and
Orissa. Sukh Dev and Bhagat Singh accused were to be in charge of the
Punjab. Shiv Varma, Bijoy Kumar Sinha and Chandra Shekhar Azad, the last
two are absconding, were to be in charge of the United Provinces. Kundan Lal
alias Partab absconding was elected for Rajputana and the Central Office.
Chandra Shekhar Azad was also to be in charge of the Military Department.

2. It was decided that officers in charge should be held responsible for any
work or action to be accomplished in the Province under their orders and that
if any outside assistance were required in any provincial action the case should
be submitted to the Central Committee which would issue final orders.

3. That all matters relating to finance, income and expenditure were to be
dealt with by the central body.

4. That all arms and munitions should be placed with the central body to be
issued for use by members of any province wherever and whenever required.

Aims and Objects

The main aims and objects of this revolutionary party as will be proved by
the evidence of witnesses and of documents were as follows:

1. To establish a Republican Government by means of an organisation
known as the Hindustan Republican Association and Indian Republican Army.
For this purpose the policy of non-violence was to be discarded and armed
forces organised with a view to overthrow the present Government and to
overawe all officials and persons interested in the Administration.

2. To establish a reign of terror by the murder of officials who took a
prominent part in such cases as the Kakori Conspiracy Case and other persons
who were for various reasons obnoxious to the conspiracy. By such murders it
was hoped to obtain the approval and financial support of persons in foreign

countries interested in the propagation of revolution in India and such murders were definitely advocated as a means for obtaining funds from abroad.

3. To organise the escape of convicts undergoing sentences in the jails for complicity in the Kakori conspiracy and similar cases.

4. To raise funds by every possible means by voluntary subscription, by dacoity or by contributions from abroad. Money thus collected was to be utilised for purchasing arms, manufacturing bombs and helping the members in spreading their republican propaganda and obtaining recruits throughout India.

5. The seduction of educated youths with a view to enlist them in the Indian Republican Army.

Fictitious Names

Evidence will be led to show that in prosecution of the objects of the conspiracy secret meetings were held by the members at different places for the constitution of Committees and for the arrangement of various crimes. The accused were moving about from place to place and from province to province under fictitious names some of which were as follows:

Sukh Dev	Dayal, Swami, Villager.
Kishori Lal Rattan	Dev Dutt, Mast Ram Shastri
Agya Ram	Masterji
Prem Dutt	Master, Amrit Lal
Surindra Nath Pandey	Stone
Jai Dev	Harish Chandar
Shiv Varma	Parbhat, Har Narain, Ram Narain
Gaya Prashad	Dr B.S. Nigam, Ram Lal, Ram Nath, Desh Bhagat
Mahabir Singh	Partab
Bhagat Singh	Ranjit
Batukeshwar Dutt	Battu Mohan
Ajoy Kumar Ghosh	Negro-General
Sachindra Nath Sanyal	Sachin Sanyal

Absconders

Chandra Shekhar Azad	Panditji
Bijoy Kumar Sinha	Bachu
Kailash Patti	Kali Charan
Raghunath	'M', Ram Guru
Bhagwati Charan	B.C. Vohra
Kundan Lal	Partap, No. 1 of Benares
Kailash	Gunthala of Jhansi

Approvers

Jai Gopal	Harbans Lal, Gopal, Krishen Chand
Hansraj Vohra	Tarlok Chand
Phonindra Nath Ghosh	Dada
Brahm Dutt	Manmohan
Manmohan Bannerji	Manohar Bannerji

Overt Acts

The overt acts committed in furtherance of the conspiracy included the following:

1. *Saunders and Channan Singh Murder.* The Committee of the revolutionary party deputed Jai Gopal, approver, Bhagat Singh, Chandra Shekhar Azad, and Raghu Nath, the last two are still absconding, with arms to murder Mr. Scott. The said party of four culprits used to frequent the neighbourhood of the police office with a view to watch Mr. Scott's movements and to know the locality better. It so happened that Mr. Scott did not attend the office for a few days before the occurrence while Mr. Saunders attended the office daily. On 17th December, 1928, when Mr. Saunders came out of the office and was about to get on his motorcycle he was shot by the culprits in mistake for Mr. Scott. Hearing the report of the shots, Channan Singh, Head Constable, rushed towards the spot, ran and followed the accused when he too was fired at. Mr. Saunders died instantaneously and Channan Singh died shortly after. The culprits after shooting these men ran away.

2. *Assembly Bomb Outrage.* With a view to create terrorism Bhagat Singh and Batukeshwar Dutt were deputed to throw bombs in the Assembly Chamber, Delhi. Consequently, these two accused threw bombs and fired shots in the Assembly Chamber on 8th April, 1929 causing severe injuries to Sir Bomanji Dalal and others. Both the culprits were arrested at the spot and placed on trial with the result that both of them were sentenced to transportation for life.

3. *Dacoity at Punjab National Bank, Lahore.* When the course of activities in Lahore was a house in Mozang, a meeting was held at which several of the accused were presen:. One of the members, namely, Panditji proposed a raid on the Punjab National Bank in order to secure funds. The members who formed a party for this raid were fully equipped with arms and specific duties were assigned to each of them. Bhagat Singh and Partap had to bring a taxi there in order to take away the booty. Consequently all the members detailed for the dacoity arrived on the appointed day, i.e., 4th December, 1928 at the premises of the Punjab National Bank and waited for the arrival of Bhagat Singh and Partap. At about 4 p.m. only Partap turned up in a tonga and informed the conspirators that a taxi could not be obtained. The project was then for the time being dropped.

4. *Dacoity at Maulina in Behar and Orissa.* In order to raise funds the members of the revolutionary party resolved to commit dacoity at Maulina.

With the object in view a dacoity was conducted on 7th June, 1928 in the house of a rich man named Dank Mahton Koori, a Hindu gentleman. The owner of the house was shot and died later on and a quantity of jewellery was taken by the culprits.

5. *Attack on Mr. Bannerji, DSP, CID of UP*. Mr. Bannerji was an officer in the CID of UP who took a leading part in connection with the Kakori Conspiracy case. The revolutionary party decided to do away with him and for this purpose two of them, namely, Mani Bannerji and Tarak Nath, were deputed. Mani Bannerji happened to meet Mr. Bannerji, DSP in Benares on 13th January, 1928 who shot at him with a revolver. Mr. Bannerji got injuries but luckily survived them. Mani Bannerji was arrested, tried and convicted.

6. *An Embezzlement of Rs. 3,199*. Kailash Patti alias Kali Charan, an absconder, who was an employee in the Post Office, Burhal Ganj, District Gorakhpur, was one of the members of this revolutionary party. He embezzled Rs. 3,199 from that post office on 26th June, 1928 to be utilised by the party in furtherance of their common object.

7. *Manufacture of Bombs*. The revolutionary party learned how to manufacture bombs and during the course of their activities they were manufacturing bombs for the purpose of using them when occasion arose. Members of the conspiracy manufactured bombs at Lahore, Saharanpur, Calcutta and Agra. The factories at Lahore and Saharanpur have since been captured. On search, bombs, revolvers, ammunitions, implements for manufacturing bombs, books on bomb making and various proscribed literature were found. The Saharanpur and Agra cases have also been transferred to this province by order of the Government of India as they form an integral portion of the conspiracy under trial.

Crimes Not Carried Out

Certain crimes were discussed and planned by the conspirators but for various reasons not carried out. Among them were the following:

1. Proposal to blow up the train carrying the members of the Simon Commission by means of dynamite. For want of funds this plan could not be carried out.

2. Proposal to make arrangements for the escape of Jogesh Chandra Chatterji, a convict in connection with the Kakori Conspiracy, and Sachin Sanyal, another convict. These also could not be carried out for want of funds and also because the convicts were well guarded. The conspirators were apparently not prepared to face the personal risk involved.

Having briefly discussed the activities of the accused the next point I will deal with is how the case has been discovered.

How the Police Got Information

On the occasion of Dusehra festival in 1928 a bomb was thrown on a crowd near the Roshanai Gate in Lahore which resulted in numerous deaths and severe injuries. As a similar outrage on the occasion of the Dusehra festival in 1926 had taken place and the case had remained untraced, the Punjab Government deputed Khan Bahadur Abdul Aziz, Superintendent of Police, Montgomery to investigate this outrage. During the course of investigation of these bomb outrages, it transpired that two ex-students of the Oriental College had been frequenting the Boarding House situated on the 2nd floor of Roshanai Gate, the place where the latter bomb explosion had taken place. Enquiries further showed that these two persons belonged to the Revolutionary Party.

As a result of a statement made by one of them, the police for the first time came to know that Bhagat Singh accused was one of the murderers of Mr. Saunders and that Bhagwati Charan an absconder, a member of Naujawan Bharat Sabha, was his Chief Lieutenant in the Punjab. Bhagat Singh accused could not be found in spite of the fact that strenuous efforts for his arrests were made in the Punjab, UP and Bengal. He suddenly appeared in the Assembly as one of the perpetrators of the Assembly Bomb outrage.

Lahore Bomb Factory

Shortly before these certain persons had engaged some iron moulders of Lahore to make certain oblong implements which on enquiry they stated were intended to be parts of a gas machine. The curiosity of a local workman was aroused and he happened to mention these facts to a constable of his acquaintance. The information was passed on to the police who instructed their informant to watch the individuals who had given the orders and to follow them to their house. Sukh Dev accused happening to pass by was duly followed to No. 69, Kashmir Buildings and this house was pointed to the police. The enquiry showed that the tenant of the premises was Bhagwati Charan who has been named as the Chief Lieutenant of Bhagat Singh and of the conspiracy in the Punjab. The house appeared to be locked and empty and a strict watch was kept to ascertain when it was visited. In the meantime, information from Delhi showed that the bomb thrown in the Assembly corresponded closely with the description of the alleged oblong gas machine parts. The careful watch kept on the house eventually resulted in information which led to a raid on 15th April, 1929. Sukh Dev, Jai Gopal and Kishori Lal, accused, were captured in the house. From the facts disclosed by these accused, the whole history of the revolutionary organisation came to light. The lengthy statement of Sukh Dev cannot be referred to by me in this statement except so far as it led to discoveries which render it admissible under the Evidence Act. But it is sufficient to say that from the moment when these accused were captured, information in the possession of the police led them steadily and by regular steps to the unravelling of the whole conspiracy and to the detailed knowledge of its activities which will be placed before the Court in evidence in this case.

The Charges

The charges against the accused will include murder, abetment of murder and conspiracy to murder, conspiracy to revolution and other offences against the State and also offences under the Explosive Substance Act. With regard to offences against the State a complaint has been that in accordance with the requirements of law by the Senior Superintendent of Police, Lahore. The facts which I have very briefly mentioned will be fully proved by the evidence which will be laid before the Court.

—The Tribune, July 11, 1929, pp. 4 and 13.

Jinnah's Speech in the Central Legislative Assembly on September 12 and 14, 1929

Sir, one is placed somewhat in a difficult position when one has got to deal with a speaker like the last one. It was his maiden speech, and it is the tradition of this House, that when a Member makes his maiden speech, he is in a privileged position and is not to be attacked. Whatever reasons or grounds, therefore, he may have given me for criticising him, I will not wish to depart from that tradition which, I think, ought to be maintained in the House. But I would say this, that in his concluding portion he remarked that the Hon'ble Members may have admiration and sympathy for the accused in the Lahore case. I think I am speaking on behalf of a very large body of people when I say that, if there is sympathy and admiration for the accused, it is only to this extent, that they are the victim of the system of government. It is not that we approve or applaud their actions if they are guilty, which still remains to be proved. If they are guilty of the offences of which they are charged, then I am sure it is not that we admire them or approve of their actions, but, on the contrary, I am sure a large body of thinking people feel that these young men, whatever be the provocations, are misguided in resorting to actions for which they now stand charged.

Now, Sir, the Hon'ble Home Member asked the House that we must approach this question without prejudice, and impartially. Sir, I am sure the Hon'ble Home Member himself tried his best to follow the same principle, but has he been able to apply the same principle when he brings this before the House? Do the facts justify that? The last speaker, whom I am not going to attack, almost gave away the case in his concluding remarks when he said that the only way to break the hunger-strike is to pass this Bill.

Well, I am not concerned at present so much with the account that was given by the Hon'ble Member with regard to the treatment in jails of various classes of prisoners, but one thing is clear, and it is this. From the statement that was issued by Bhagat Singh and Dutt, what is an admitted fact now, even from the speech of the Hon'ble Member who spoke last, is that they were not given the treatment—not on racial grounds—but according to the standard and the scale which is laid down for Europeans in the matter of diet and bare necessities of life. It is not a mere question that they want to be treated as Europeans. As a matter of fact, according to the admission and the definition given by the Hon'ble Member who spoke last on behalf of the Treasury Benches, so far as I know, Bhagat Singh and Dutt wear topees, and their figures appeared in shorts. Therefore, they ought to have been treated as Europeans. The Hon'ble Member in reply to a question said that whether the man is a European or an Indian—and he accepted the definition of my honourable friend Mr. Neogy—if one wears a topee, then one is a European for the purpose of jail rules. Then why should you not treat Bhagat Singh and Dutt, who wear topees and European clothes, as such for the purpose of treatment in jails? Why do not the Punjab Government give them the treatment that they are entitled to, at once, and be done with? They wear topees and they are entitled to that treatment.

What do they say in their statement which was read out? This is what they say:

"We, Bhagat Singh and Dutt, were sentenced to life transportation in the Assembly bomb case, Delhi, on 19th May, 1929. As long as we were under-trial prisoners in Delhi jail we were accorded very good treatment and we were given good diet. But since our transfer from the Delhi Jail to Mianwali Jail and Lahore Central Jail,—

Which is represented by the Hon'ble Member, who spoke last—the Punjab seems to be a terrible place . . .

Mian Muhammad Shah Nawaz (West Central Punjab): Don't go there.

M.A. Jinnah: I won't. To continue what they say:

"We are being treated as ordinary criminals".

So, in Delhi they received very good treatment and in the Punjab they are treated as ordinary criminals. Surely, Sir, if the Government of the Punjab was not wanting in statesmanship, if the Government of the Punjab had any brains, they would have found a solution to this question very easily and long ago. But, Sir, it is a question— the more I examine it and the more I analyse it, I find—it is a question of declaration of war. As far as the Punjab Government are concerned, the Government do not merely wish to bring these men to trial and get them convicted by a judicial tribunal, but Government go to war against these men. They seem to me in this frame of mind: "We will pursue every possible course, every possible method, but we will see that you are sent either to the gallows or transported for life, and in the meantime we will not treat you as decent men."

Sir, the whole spirit behind this is that and nothing else. I do not for a moment wish to say that the Government are not bound—in fact, it is their bounden duty—to prosecute those people that commit offences. I do not wish to say that the Government should not do every thing in their power to see that their convictions are secured. But may I ask, with whom are you at war? What are the resources of these few young men who, according to you, have committed certain offences? You want to prosecute them, and after due trial, you want to secure their convictions. But before they are convicted, surely this is not a matter on which there should be this struggle, that you should not at once yield to their demands for bare necessities of life. After all, so far as the Lahore case prisoners are concerned, surely they are political prisoners and under trial. You ask me, what is a political prisoner? It is very difficult to define a political prisoner. It is very difficult to lay down any particular definition. But if you use your common sense, if you use your intelligence, surely you can come to the conclusion with regard to the particular case and say, here are these men who are political prisoners, and we do not wish to give them proper treatment. We want to give them treatment as under-trial prisoners. If you had said that, the question would have been solved long ago. Do you wish to prosecute them or persecute them?

Sir, I do not wish to base my opposition to this Bill on this issue of bad treatment, because this is only one aspect of the issue, or rather one aspect of the Bill before us. This Bill has got to be looked at, as far as I can see, from three points of view. The *first*, from the point of view of criminal jurisprudence; *second*, political point of view or the policy of the Bill; and *third*, treatment to the accused when they are under trial. I think it will be admitted, I think even the Hon'ble Home Member conceded, that by the Bill which he has brought before the House, he is introducing a principle, in the criminal jurisprudence, of a very unprecedented character. I do not think, Sir, there is any system of jurisprudence in any civilised country where you will find such a principle in existence as is involved in this Bill. Some of the Hon'ble Members who are not lawyers might not have appreciated fully the implications of this Bill. This Bill not only dispenses with the presence of the accused at the trial, but I will give you a picture as to what will happen under this Bill. Under this Bill the Government will apply to the Magistrate before whom the inquiry is going on and say: "Here is a law which we have secured from the Legislature. Now the accused have voluntarily made themselves incapable of attending the Courts and, therefore, you have to dispense with their presence". The inquiry will then proceed *ex parte* before the Magistrate. Evidence will be led, oral and documentary, which will go without being tested by cross-examination. The documentary evidence will go without being even seen by the accused, against whom it is produced, and how will you identify the accused in their absence? Then we know, and particularly those who are lawyers would know, that when the Magistrate has concluded the recording of the evidence for the prosecution, under Section 209 of the Criminal Procedure Code, he must ask the accused whether he has any explanation to offer with regard to the evidence which is recorded by him against the accused. It is after that statement is made that the Magistrate has got the power either to commit or discharge the accused. That statement of the accused under Section 209 is absolutely obligatory. It is not the choice of the Magistrate. The Privy Council has laid down that an omission in that regard would vitiate the whole trial. Under this Bill the accused will not be there to give any explanation to the Magistrate with regard to the evidence that has been already recorded *ex parte*.

Then, Sir, we come to important Sections. Under Section 287 that statement again will have to be made before the Sessions Court. There also, the accused will not be present. The evidence before the Sessions Court will be recorded *ex parte* and if it is a jury, the jury will be asked to return their verdict. If it is a case of assessors, they will be asked to express their opinion, and the Judge will pass his judgement or sentence, as the case may be. I ask the Hon'ble Home Member, and I ask the Hon'ble Law Member of the Government of India whether that will be a trial or a farce?

Sir Brojendra Mitter (Law Member): Not a farce. The accused can always go before the Court if she chooses to.

Gaya Prasad Singh: But what about the evidence that has already been recorded in his absence?

M.A. Jinnah: I am very glad that the Hon'ble Law Member has given me a reply. Then you want by this Bill really to break the hunger-strikers. You want this House to give you a Statute laying down a principle generally in the criminal jurisprudence for this particular case, so that you may use it for breaking the hunger-strike in the lahore case. Remember, you have no other case that you can cite. One swallow does not make a summer. It is the Lahore case. Well, you know perfectly well that these men are determined to die. It is not a joke. I ask the Hon'ble Law Member to realise that it is not everybody who can go on starving himself to death. Try it for a little while and you will see. Sir, have you heard anywhere in the world, except the American case, which may honourable friend Mr. Jamnadas Mehta pointed out, of an accused person going on hunger-strike? The man who goes on hunger-strike has a soul. He is moved by the soul and he believes in the justice of his cause; he is not an ordinary criminal who is guilty of cold-blooded, sordid, wicked crime.

Mind you, Sir, I do not approve of the action of Bhagat Singh, and I say this on the floor of this House. I regret that, rightly or wrongly, youth today in India is stirred up, and you cannot, when you have three hundred and odd millions of people, you cannot prevent such crimes being committed, however much you may deplore them and however much you may say that they are misguided. It is the system, this damnable system of Government, which is resented by the people. You may be a cold-blooded logician: I am a patient cool-headed man and can calmly go on making speeches here, persuading and influencing the Treasury Bench. But, remember, there are thousands of young men outside. This is not the only country where these actions are resorted to.

It has happened in other countries, not youths, but greybearded men have committed serious offences, moved by patriotic impulses. What happened to Mr. Congrave, the Prime Minister of Ireland? He was under sentence of death a fortnight before he got an invitation from His Majesty's Government to go and settle terms? Was he a youth? Was he a young man? What about Collins? So what is the good of your putting forward this argument? You have got a situation which you have got to meet, not by introducing and enacting measures which go to the root of the fundamental principles of criminal jurisprudence, and lightly, saying, "Oh! but it is common sense!" Law is common sense; it is not common sense of one individual

Mr. President: I hope the Hon'ble Member is not inconvenienced when I ask him to resume his speech at the next meeting.

Pandit Madan Mohan Malaviya: Sir, cannot we go on for another 15 minutes?

Mr. President: What is the idea of going on for another 15 minutes? I can understand the House asking me to sit till 6 o'clock, but there is no idea in sitting for another 15 minutes only.

The House was then adjourned. Mr. Jinnah concluded his speech at the next sitting, after the adjournment motion had been admitted for discussion.

Sir, when the House last adjourned I was dealing with this Bill from the point of view of criminal jurisprudence—and I brought to the notice of the House what would be the position if this Bill was passed, so far as the trial and proceedings of this particular case, or any other case under it, were concerned. It is quite clear, as I said, that the trial will be a travesty of justice. Let us consider the point further. The trial would proceed in the absence of the accused. I ask the Home Member, is there a Judge or jury who would feel that they were administering law or justice in that case? The moment this Bill is passed, the prosecution can go before the Court and say: "Here is a voluntary act of the accused persons; he has or they have incapacitated himself or themselves, and we ask you now to proceed *ex parte*". Remember, Sir, that in a particular case that procedure may be adopted from the very start. Even the plea of the accused may not be recorded, guilty or not guilty. Then the Judge will be asked to proceed to empanel a jury and the jury will be empanelled: You will have a Judge on the Bench and the jury by his side. What will they do? They hear the *ex parte* evidence, oral and documentary. I ask the Home Member, I ask this House, what would you consider of that Judge, what would you think of that Judge or jury, sitting there solemnly, seriously, proceeding with a charge of murder, going through this farce as His Majesty's Court— what conclusion do you think any jury can come to under those circumstances? That prisoner stands already condemned. What is the good of this farce? I say that no Judge who has got an iota of a judicial mind or a sense of justice can ever be a party to a trial of that character and pass sentence of death without a shudder and a pang of conscience. This is the farce which you propose to enact under this procedure! I say this, that if ever there was a conscientious Judge and he was strong enough, if he had a judicial mind, and if he had any independence, let me tell you, that, in spite of this provision of yours, he would say, "True, the law has to be administered; I am obliged to make the order that the trial shall proceed *ex parte*; but I realise and I feel that it will be a travesty of justice and I cannot be a party to it; and I shall, therefore, adjourn this case until further orders". Have you considered that? I suppose you have not. It seems to me, Sir, that the great and fundamental doctrine of British jurisprudence, which is incorporated and codified in the Penal Code and the Criminal Procedure Code, has very wisely not made such an absurd provision in the criminal law of this country and I am not satisfied that there is a lacuna in our system of criminal law.

The Home Member said that it is a well-known doctrine and a fundamental doctrine of criminal jurisprudence that the man is taken to be innocent until he is proved to be guilty. May I remind him of another doctrine which goes to the very root of the criminal jurisprudence, or for the matter of that of even civil law, that no man is to be condemned until he is given a hearing? Sir, I think there cannot be the slightest doubt that we are now engaged in considering a cardinal principle, a principle of very vital and paramount character, to be introduced into the criminal jurisprudence of this country. It must be admitted that this is a most revolutionary, unheard of, unprecedented change that is proposed in our criminal jurisprudence. I know the Home Member will tell me, "Yes, the doctrine is that no man shall be condemned unless he is heard and until he is given a hearing; but here it is the voluntary act of the accused, and if he chooses not to go there and insist upon his being heard, it is his fault." Sir, this is not a new question; it has been considered in England and there is a long history about it and behind it and you will find that in old days there was the strictest formality observed as to the recording of the plea of the prisoner. And if the prisoner was mute of malice, that is to say, if he refused deliberately to open his mouth when he was arraigned in a Court of law and when the question was put to him as to whether he pleaded guilty or not—he had to make his plea, and there are cases where he refused to speak, and the old law was—even England has advanced—in that case he was condemned and executed or must be committed to imprisonment . . .

E.L. Price (Bombay: European): Torture.

M.A. Jinnah: I am glad that you are up to date. I know that. I am only dealing with this one point, that he used to be executed or committed to prison. Further, when it was thought that it was rather a serious thing that, because a man was mute of malice, he should be condemned to death or imprisonment—then comes the point of my learned friend over there, who I understand is a member of the Bar—that they resorted to torture. Torture for what? That he should make his plea, not that an *ex parte* trial should proceed. That is what you want to do here by this Bill, that *ex parte* trial should proceed. The old law was then altered, because the result of the torture was that some of them died and the form of torture was the most cruel form of torture, and I will read to you a passage from Stephen's *History of Criminal Law*:

> "If he was accused of felony, he was condemned, after much exhortation to the *peine forte et dure,* that is to be stretched, naked on his back, and to have 'iron laid upon him as much as he could bear and more', and so to continue, fed upon bad bread and stagnant water on alternate days, till he either pleaded or died."

But they did not proceed *ex parte.* Then the old form of trial was trial by ordeal. That was done away with because the plea that a prisoner had to put forward was in a particular form. When he was asked he had to say that he wanted to be tried "By God and by my country". That was the trial by ordeal. That was done away with and in 1827 by a Statute it was enacted that in such cases a plea of not guilty should be entered. Now, Sir, before that Statute was passed there is one case which I will bring to the notice of this House and which will illustrate how much importance was attached to the form and the procedure even in olden days. Of course, my honourable friend Sir Darcy Lindsay will say that matters of this kind can be decided by the common sense of a single individual such as himself. Sir, I must remind him—for he is a man of peace, and especially when we get old we love peace, and common sense is sometimes regulated by that state of mind—, I will remind him, and I think the House will agree with me, that law is nothing but the essence of common sense, that law is the concentrated essence of experience, of knowledge, of practice of centuries and generations, and even Sir James Stephen will point out to you that, when these rules, when these forms have been laid down as the essence of common sense and experience of generations, they are not lightly to be departed from.

What do we find in this House now? Have we not got forms and are we not slavishly following them? Some of them would appear to the strangers in the gallery or any outsider to be most absurd and against common sense, at first sight. If any one passes across between you and the speaker he will be guilty of a gross breach of the forms of this House and you would call him to order at once. Why is that? Without meaning? Without reason? Without experience? What common sense is there? Why should the man not pass across? It is, therefore, no use treating these matters lightly and saying that we have got to decide everything by the common sense of an individual. The instance that I was going to refer to is this. In one case:

Mr. Pike produces some evidence to show that in the early part of Edward

I's reign, people who refused to put themselves on their trial were executed
. . .

Better, people who refuse to put themselves to trial, execute them, rather
than go through the farce of an *ex parte* trial; much better.

" . . . but this practice was opposed to the statute which provided that
'notorious felons' and which openly be of evil name and will not put
themselves in inquests of felonies that men shall charge them with before
the justices at the King's suit, shall have strong and hard imprisonment, as
they which refuse to stand to the common law of the land."

Then he cites a case which I think will interest the House. He says this:

'But this is not to be understood of such prisoners as be taken of light
suspicion.' According to Barrington this meant that the prisoner who
refused to plead was to be starved till he died, but not tortured—(so they
improved later on)—and he quotes in proof of it a pardon granted in the
reign of Edward III to a woman who *pro eo quod se tenuit mutum* was put
in *areta prisona* and there lived without eating or drinking for forty days,
which was regarded as a miracle."

Well, Sir, I know that there is a passage which is likely to be quoted in this
House in Stephen's *Digest of Criminal Procedure*. It is a curious thing that the
Government of India, who have hardly given this House even seven days'
notice and call upon this House to endorse a vital, cardinal principle of a novel
or unheard of character, do not possess in their library even an edition of the
Law of Criminal Procedure by Stephen of a later date than 1883. And they
seriously ask this House, "The Government case is that they find that a
deadlock is created. The law is paralysed, and in fact, even the Government of
India might tumble down altogether, and we, therefore, call upon the Legislature to come to our rescue—we admit it is unprecedented, we admit it is
unheard of, we admit it is unknown to any system of jurisprudence; but you as
a responsible body—would you not endorse this Bill straightaway within these
few days' notice?" You do not possess in your library an edition of a textbook
which is the standard book except of the year 1883! And it is a tall order to ask
the House to pass the Bill now and here. I will read the passage now, which is
likely to be quoted, and I want the House not to be misled by it. But before I
do so, I will request the Law Member, to consider what I am going to submit.
That is a branch of the law which comes under the category of contempt of
Court, and we know that the King's Bench in England and Superior Courts in
India, who have inherited the jurisdiction under the Charter, have got unfettered
power to deal with cases of contempt. That is the one branch of the law which

is neither codified nor restricted by any law. It is entirely left to the Supreme Court or the High Courts in India to deal with cases of contempt as they think proper. That is a branch which comes under that doctrine of law of contempt of Court and even there, while the Courts have asserted that they have the power to refuse to hear the party who is guilty of contempt of Court, the footnote says that it has never been done in a criminal case. I will read to you what it says:

"The Prisoner has a right to be present at the trial so long as he conducts himself properly, but the Court may, in its discretion, permit his absence in cases of misdemeanour, and may proceed with the trial in his absence in cases in which he has pleaded to an indictment or information in the High Court (Queen's Bench Division).

"If a prisoner so misconducts himself as to make it impossible to try him with decency, the Court, it seems, may order him to be removed and proceed in his absence."

The footnote says this:

"I have never known or heard of this being done, but Lord Cranworth (then Rolfe, B.) threatened to have Rush removed from Court, at his trial for murder at Norwich in 1849, if he persisted in a singularly indecent and outrageous course of cross-examination. I have heard from eye-witness an account of a trial before Shee, J. (then acting as Commissioner) at Dorchester, where the prisoner (a convict at Portland, tried for the murder of a warder) behaved with such desperate violence that it was necessary to fasten him down with chains and straps. He was not, however, removed from the Court, and it is obvious that in capital cases, or indeed in any trial involving severe punishment, almost any measures, short of removing the prisoner, should be resorted to."

The *raison d'etre* of this principle is very different and requires no more words to understand it. Now, Sir, I shall not weary the House with any further legal quotations. I am driven to think the object of Government in bringing in this Bill is political, but if their real object is to supply a lacuna, not for the purpose of this particular case, but in the general interest of the country and the administration of justice, if that is their object, let them remove this case from their mind, for Heaven's sake. Come to us dispassionately and without prejudice. Let them tell us that they find a lacuna, and that it is necessary to make some provision. If that is their object, then their honest and straightforward course is to come before the House and place all the facts before us. Now, I do not admit for a moment that there is a lacuna, and I do not admit that such a principle should be introduced in the criminal jurisprudence of our country, especially and admittedly when it does not exist anywhere else. I am prepared to assume that you honestly and sincerely believe that it is necessary, in the interest of the people and the administration of justice, that some such measure of the kind should be introduced. Then your honest course is to go slowly. Pause and consider. Let those outside this House who are competent to speak, express their opinion. What are you going to lose? What is the harm that will be done? Remove from your mind this Lahore conspiracy case. But if you say that this course will cause you inconvenience and that you want this instrument now and at once, then I say that I am not satisfied with your plea and I can't support it, nor am I satisfied with the version that you have placed before the House about your difficulties. I am not going to give you this power standing on the floor of this House, today, now and here.

Sir, can you imagine a more horrible form of torture than hunger-strike? If, rightly or wrongly, these men are inflicting this punishment upon themselves and thereby you are inconvenienced, is that any reason why you should ask us to abandon one of the cardinal principles of criminal jurisprudence? If these young men pursue this course, and I am sorry to hear that one of them has died, what will happen? Is this a matter which can continue indefinitely? Certainly not. As I say, I am not satisfied with the version that you have placed before this House. I understand that some of the prisoners are not on strike. If you are solicitous and anxious that their trial should proceed and should not be delayed, then split up the trial. Proceed against them and bring home the guilt to them if you can. I am told that it means expense. I am told that 400 witnesses are going to be produced and 200 more may be added. Now, I appeal to the common sense of the House and not only of Sir Darcy Lindsay. Can you imagine that 600 witnesses are necessary to prove the case against each one of the accused? And, Sir, I ask, is it not an amazing fact that, in order to prove this case, 600 persons should have been cited as witnesses? Well, Sir, it may seem a joke and it may seem that I am making fun of the statement made to this effect, but the first impression that one gets is that, when a case cannot be proved without the testimony of 600 witnesses, that case is a very bad case. Therefore, I say that it is open to Government to split up the case. You think of expense? But are we here to abandon this cardinal principle because it is going to cost some money to Government? Is that the reason? Is that a plea which can be accepted by any responsible Legislature?

Well, Sir, I was told that some of them go on a hunger-strike for a short time and then they get better for a little while and again they start, and so it goes on. Sir, I cannot understand the anxiety of the Government to proceed with this trial when these men are inflicting the greatest possible punishment upon themselves by prolonged fasting? Is it your fault? Does it mean that you are not treating them properly and, therefore you are compelling them to resort to these extreme methods? Well, then I appeal to you with all the emphasis I can command, do not be vindictive. Show that you are fair, generous, that you are willing to treat these men decently. At any rate, before they are released or sentenced, give them proper treatment. What treatment do they want? What is it that bothers them? Do they want spring mattresses? Do they want dressing tables? Do they want a set of toilet requisites? No, Sir, they ask for nothing but bare necessities and a little better treatment. I ask you in all decency, why cannot you concede this small thing? Well, Sir, if this Bill is passed, perhaps I might ask the Hon'ble Member when he goes to Court how would he base his application? Will he base his application on the point that the period of a hunger-strike which has already taken place for a short period is not to be counted? Or is it to be counted? Supposing I tried to put myself in the position of a Judge when the application is made that the presence of the accused in this case should be dispensed with, because by their own voluntary act they have rendered themselves incapable. Now, from what period shall I take the disability? From the period after this Statute is passed? Shall I disregard the disability which has already taken place before the passing of the Act? Supposing something else happens to these men on hunger-strike and they do not get well for two or three months. Will the trial not be delayed? Do you think you can avoid considerable delay even if the Bill is passed? Further, can you give a guarantee that all the prisoners will be well enough in the course of these two or three months from now to stand their trial. Even if they abandon hunger-strike? When you say that this Bill will not have retrospective effect, how is it going to work? Then will you give them notice that in view of the fact that this measure is passed, if you do not cease your hunger-strike from today and if you are not better within two or three months, as you ought to be, then we shall apply to the Court that your presence will be dispensed with and we shall proceed *ex parte*? Does it not come to this, that you want to carry this Bill, you want to have this Bill placed on the Statute-book, and then you want to give notice to the prisoners that, unless they cease their hunger-strike within a certain period, you are going to proceed *ex parte*? Under that threat you think these prisoners will cease their hunger-strike? Can you give the House that assurance, and if they do not cease their hunger-strike, what will you do? You will proceed *ex parte*? Just imagine the absurdity of the whole position.

Sir, now I have finished from the point of view of the jurisprudence. I do not wish to go into details so far as their treatment is concerned. I have, in the course of my speech, already indicated their grievances and how they can be met. But there is a political aspect of this Bill and the policy underlying this measure. I think the Hon'ble the Home Member must admit that this is not a measure which is only brought here for the purpose of putting the law in order. Sir, it reminds me of a story, an old Persian story. A man got stomach-ache because he had eaten some very rotten bread. So he went to the doctor and told him that he had stomach-ache. The doctor said, yes, and he promptly started treating his eyes. Then he said, "What have my eyes got to do with my complaint?" Then the doctor said, "Well, if you had eyes, you would never have got stomach-ache because you would not have eaten rotten bread"

Similarly I would say to the Hon'ble the Home Member, "Have you got eyes? Well, if you had, you would never gave got this stomach-ache". Now, will you open your eyes? Will you have a little more imagination? Have you got any statesmanship left? Have you got any political wisdom? This is not the way you are going to solve the root cause of the trouble. You may temporarily, provisionally, get over this particular trial. But now let us see what is the real cause of the trouble.

I ask this House to consider this. Is there today in any part of the globe a civilised government that is engaged, day in and day out, week in and week out, month in and month out, in prosecuting their people? You have read the daily papers for the last six, eight months. You will find prosecutions in Bengal, prosecutions in Madras, prosecutions in the Punjab, prosecutions all over the country. In fact I am afraid you will soon have to open a new department and to have an additional Member to manage these prosecutions if you go on at this rate and in this way. Do you think that any man wants to go to jail? Is it an easy thing? Do you think any man wants to exceed the bounds of law for the purpose of making a speech which your law characterises as a seditious speech, knowing full well the consequences, that he may have to go to jail for six months or a year? Do you think that this springs out of a mere joke or fun or amusement? Do you not realise yourself, if you open your eyes, that there is resentment, universal resentment, against your policy, against your programme?

Then, Sir, what has happened so far as this House is concerned? What have you done since 1924 with regard to the protests that we have made session after session? Have you accepted the proposal or suggestion of any reasonable section of this House? I do not wish to go into the details, Sir, but what has been the attitude of the Government towards this House and the country outside over the constitutional reforms since 1924, leave alone the past prior history? The reply is: "We have appointed the Simon Commission and we must must await its Report." Well, the Simon Commission was not accepted by this House—but that does not matter. What is the answer in regard to the Indianisation of the Army? You appointed a Committee to go into that very important question; I attach more importance to it than to any other question. What have you done with the unanimous Report of the Skeen Committee which was endorsed by this House, without a division, the responsible House as you call it today and to which you appeal today in the name of "responsibility"? This House endorsed that Report without a division. What have you done with it? The attitude of Government has been an amazing one. The Army Secretary stood there on the floor of this House last session and said: "We cannot get even 20 suitable candidates". Sir, the apparent untruth of that statement is enough to condemn the Government. You cannot get 20 young men out of 300 odd millions of people, who are suitable candidates for the King's Commission?

Then, there are many other matters. What has been your attitude always?

Don't you think that, instead of trying to proceed with an iron hand and pursuing a policy of repression against your own subjects, it would be better if you realised the root causes of the resentment and of the struggle that the people are carrying on? Don't you think that it is high time that you made your position more clear? I understand that there is something in the atmosphere— I hope it is true—that some satisfactory announcement is going to be made in Parliament very soon, when it meets next, which I trust will satisfy this House and the people. Do you want to prepare an atmosphere for it, or you do not? Do you want reconciliation between the Government and the people or you do not? Don't you think that these difficulties and troubles of yours are of a temporary character? They are an obstruction in the trial of this particular case which can be managed by other methods, but that is a very small matter when you compare it with the bigger issues which are awaiting the decision of the Government, this House and the country.

Sir, the Hon'ble Member asked, what are the Government to do? I think I understood the Hon'ble Member aright when he said that the Government have no other course. What are the Government to do? They are, therefore, compelled to bring this Bill. Now, let me tell you that your course is to open your eyes, have more imagination, do not be guilty of bankruptcy of statesmanship, do not merely sit there as if the wheels of the Secretariat must not be clogged at any cost, but try and understand the root cause and deal with the situation as politicians, as statesmen and not as bureaucrats, who can see no other way but to come forward before this House and ask for more statutory powers the moment any difficulty arises. You have got several courses open to you. The first and the foremost course open to you is this. Give these men decent treatment, and I think you will get over your difficulty. At least I hope so. If you do not, you will, at any rate, be exonerated in the eyes of the public and at the Bar of public opinion. Behave as a humane and decent Government, and that is enough for you. I am not going to urge upon the Government to withdraw prosecution cases against men if they have evidence enough to bring home to them their guilt. So try that better treatment first. Secondly, if you do not succeed, split up the trials. Try those with whose trial you can proceed, and leave the rest. After you have made it clear to them that you stand for a decent treatment being given to them and they still wish to torture themselves and follow that course, then you cannot help it; and I venture to say that it will not last very long or indefinitely. And the last words I wish to address the Government are, try and concentrate your mind on the root cause and the more you concentrate on the root cause the less difficulties and inconveniences there will be for you to face, and thank Heaven that the money of the taxpayer will not be wasted in prosecuting men, nay citizens, who are fighting and struggling for the freedom of their country.

Legislative Assembly Debates. Vol. IV, Part I, pp. 752-55 and 757-65.

Appendix IV

"Lahore Conspiracy Case Prisoners Threaten Hunger-strike"

Sir,

With reference to our telegram, dated the 20th June, 1930, reading as follows, we have not been favoured with the reply:—

Home Member, India Government, Delhi—Under-trial, Lahore Conspiracy Case and the other political prisoners suspended hunger-strike on the assurance that the India Government was considering the Provincial Jail Committee's Reports. All-India Jail officials' Conference is over. No action yet taken. As vindictive treatment to political prisoners still continues we request we be informed within a week final Government decision—Lahore Conspiracy under-trials.

As briefly stated in the above telegram we beg to bring to your kind notice that the Lahore Conspiracy Case under-trial and several other political prisoners, confined in the Punjab Jails suspended Hunger-strike on the assurance given by the members of the Punjab Jail Enquiry Committee that the question of the treatment of the political prisoners was going to be finally settled to our satisfaction within a very short period. Further, after the death of our great martyr Jatendra Nath Dass the matter was taken up in the Legislative Assembly and the same assurance was given publicly by Sir James Crerar. It was then pronounced that there had been a change of heart and the question of the treatment of the political prisoners was receiving the utmost sympathy of the Government. Such political prisoners who were still on hunger-strike in jails of the different parts of the country then suspended their hunger-strike on the request being made to this effect in an A.I.C.C. resolution passed in view of the said assurance and the critical condition of some of these prisoners.

DILATORY ATTITUDE

Since then all the local Governments have submitted their reports, a meeting of the I.G. Prisons of different provinces has been held at Lucknow and the deliberations of the All-India Jail officials' Conference have been concluded at Delhi. The All-India Conference was held in the month of December last. Over one month has passed by and still the Government of India has not carried into effect any final recommendations. By such dilatory attitude of the Government we no less than the general public have begun to fear that perhaps the question has been shelved. Our apprehension has been strengthened by the vindictive treatment meted out to the hunger-strikers and other political prisoners during the last four months. It is very difficult for us to know the details of the hardships and sufferings to which the political prisoners are being subjected. Still the little information that has trickled out of the four walls of the Jails is sufficient to furnish us with glaring instances. We give below a few such instances which, we cannot but feel, are not in confirmity with the Government assurances.

1. Sj. B.K. Banerji undergoing five years' imprisonment in connection with the Dakshiveshwar Bomb case in the Lahore Central Jail joined the general hunger-strike last year. Now as a punishment for the same, for each day of his period of hunger-strike two days of remission, so far earned by him, had been forfeited. Under usual circumstances, his release was due in December last but now it will be delayed by full 4 months. In the same Jail similar punishment has been awarded to Baba Sohan Singh, an old man of about 70, now undergoing his sentence of life transportation in connection with the Lahore Conspiracy Case. Besides among others S. Kabul Singh and S. Gopal Singh confined in the Mianwali Jail, Master Mota Singh, in the Rawalpindi Jail, have also been awarded vindictive punishment for joining the general hunger-strike. In most of these cases the period of imprisonment have been enhanced while some of them have been even removed from special class.

KAKORI PRISONERS

2. For the same offence, i.e., joining the general hunger-strike, Messrs Sachindra Nath Sanyal, Ram Kishen Khatri and Suresh Chandra Bhattacharya confined in Agra Central Jail, Rajkumar Sinha, Monmotha Nath Gupta, Sachindra Nath Bakshi and several others Kakori Conspiracy Case prisoners have been severely punished. It is reliably learned that Mr. Sanyal was given bar-fetters and solitary cell confinement and as a consequence there has been a breakdown in his health. His weight has gone down by 18 pounds. Mr. Bhattacharya is reported to be suffering from tuberculosis. The three Bareilly Jail prisoners have also been punished. It is learnt that all their privileges were withdrawn. Even their usual rights of interviewing relatives and communicating with them were forfeited. They have all been considerably reduced in their weight. Two press statements were issued in this connection in Sept., 1929 and January 1930 by Pt. Jawaharlal Nehru.

3. After the passing of the A.I.C.C. resolution regarding hunger-strike,

copies of the same, which were wired to different political prisoners, were withheld by the Jail authorities. Further the Govt. even refused Congress deputation to meet the prisoners in this connection.

CONSPIRACY CASE PRISONERS

The Conspiracy Case under-trials were assaulted brutally on the 23rd and 24th October, 1929. Full details have appeared in the Press. The copy of the statement of one of us, as recorded by the Special Magistrate Pt. Sri Krishna, has been duly forwarded to in a communication dated 16th December 1929. Neither the Punjab Government, nor the Government of India felt it necessary to reply or acknowledge receipt of our communication, praying for enquiry. While, on the other hand, the local Government has felt the imperative necessity of prosecuting us in connection with the same incident for offering non-violent resistance.

In the last week of December 1929 Sj. Kiron Chandra Dass and 8 others, confined in the Lahore Borstal Jail, while produced in the Magistrate's Court, were found handcuffed and chained together in flagrant breach of the unanimous recommendations of the Punjab Jail Enquiry Committee and also of the Inspector-General Prisons Punjab. It is further noteworthy that these prisoners were undertrials charged with a bailable offence. A long statement issued by Doctor Mohd. Alam, L. Duni Chand of Lahore and L. Duni Chand of Ambala in this connection was published in the *Tribune*.

CANNOT WAIT INDEFINITELY

While we learnt of these and other sufferings of the political prisoners we refrained from resuming hunger-strike though we were much grieved, as we thought the matter was going to be finally settled at an early date. But in the light of the above instance are we now to believe that all the untold sufferings of the hunger-strikers and the supreme sacrifice made by Jatindra Nath Dass have all been in vain? Are we to understand that the Government gave its assurance only to check the growing tide of public agitation and to avert a crisis. We hope you will agree with us when we say that we have waited patiently for a sufficiently reasonable period of time. But we cannot wait indefinitely. The Government by its dilatory attitude and continuation of vindictive treatment of political prisoners, have left us no other option but to resume the struggle. We realize that to go on hunger-strike and to carry it on is no easy task. But let us at the same time point out that the revolutionaries can produce many more Jatins and Wazias, Ram Rakhas and Bhan Singhs (the last two named laid down their lives in the Andaman in 1917—the first breathed his last after 92 days of hunger-strike, while the other died the death of a great hero after silently undergoing hardship for full six months).

QUESTION OF MOTIVE

Enough has been said by us and the members of the public in justification of a better treatment of political prisoners and it is unnecessary here to repeat the same. We would, however, like to say a few words as regards the inclusion of motive as the basis and the most important factor in the matter of classification. Great fuss has been created on the question of criteria of classification. We find that motive has altogether been excluded so far from the criteria suggested by different Provincial Governments. This is really a strange attitude. It is through motive alone that the real value of any action can be decided. Are we to understand that the Government is unable to distinguish between a robber who robs and kills his victim and a Kharak Bahadur who killed a villain and saves the honour of a young lady and redeems the society of a most licentious parasite? Are both to be treated as two men belonging to the same category? Is there no difference between two men who commit the same offence, one guided by the selfish motive and the other by a selfless one? Similarly, is there no difference between a common murderer and a political worker,—even if the latter resorts to violence? Does not his selflessness elevate his place amongst those of the ordinary criminals? In these circumstances we think that motive should be held as the most important factor in the criteria for classification.

Last year at the beginning of our hunger-strike, when public leaders, including Doctor Gopichand and L. Duni Chand of Ambala—the last named being one of the signatories to the Punjab Jail Enquiry Committee Report aproached us to discuss the same thing and when they told us that the Government considered it impossible to treat the political prisoners convicted of offences of violent nature as special class prisoners, then by way of compromise we agreed to the proposal to the extent of excluding those actually charged with murder. But later on the discussion took a different turn. And the *communique* containing the terms of reference for the Punjab Jail Enquiry Committee was so worded that the question of motive seemed to be altogether excluded, and whole classification was based on the two things:

1. Nature of Offence.
2. The Social status of the offenders.

This criteria instead of solving the problem made it all the more complicated.

We could understand two classes amongst the political prisoners—those charged with non-violent offences and those charged with violent ones. But then there creeps in the question of social status in the report of the Punjab Jail Enquiry Committee. As Choudary Afzal Haq has pointed out, and rightly too, in his note of dissent to this report, what would be the fate of those political workers who have been reduced to pauperism due to their honorary services in the cause of freedom? Are they to be left at the mercy of a Magistrate who will always try to approve the *bona fide* of his loyalty by classifying everyone as an ordinary convict? Or is it expected that a non-co-operator will stretch his hand before the people against whom he is fighting as an opponent, begging for better treatment in the jail? Is this the reforms that are demanded of the nature of luxury? Are they sifying them? It might be argued that people living in poverty outside the jails should not expect luxuries inside the Jail where they are detained for the purpose of punishment. But are the reforms that are demanded of nature of luxury? Are they not the bare necessities of life? In spite of all the facilities that can possibly be demanded, jails will ever remain a jail. The prison in itself does not contain and can never contain any magnetic power to attract the people from outside. Nobody will commit to come to Jail. Moreover, may we venture to say that it is very poor argument on the part of the Government to say that its citizens have been driven to such extreme destitution that their standard of living has fallen even lower than of that of their Jails? Does not such an argument cut at the very root of that Government's right of existence? Anyhow, we are not concerned with that at present. What we want to say is that the best way to remove the prevailing dissatisfaction would be to classify political prisoners as such into a separate class which may further be sub-divided, if need be, into two classes, one for those convicted of non-violent offences and the other for persons whose offences include violence. In that case, motive will become one of the deciding factors. To say that motive cannot be ascertained in political cases is not correct. What is it that today leads the Jail authorities to deprive the "politicals" even of the ordinary privileges? What is it that deprives them of the special grades or numberdaries, etc? What makes the authorities keep them aloof and separated from all other convicts? The same things can help in the classification also.

As for the specific demands, we have already stated them in full in our memorandum to the Punjab Jail Enquiry Committee. We would, however, particularly emphasize that no political prisoner, whatever his offence may be, should be given any hard and undignified labour for which he may not have aptitude. All of them confined in any one jail should be kept together in the same ward. At least one standard daily newspaper in vernacular or English should be given to them. Full and proper facilities for study should be granted. Lastly they should be allowed to supplement their allowance for diet and clothing from their private sources.

We still hope that the Government will carry into effect, without further delay, its promise made to us and to the public, so that there may not be another occasion for resuming the nunger-strike. Unless and until we find a definite move on the part of the Government to redeem its promise, in the course of the next 7 days, we shall be forced to resume hunger-strike.

The Magistrate has forwarded the letter to the executive authorities.

—*The Tribune*, January 30, 1930.

Appendix V

Text of the Press Communique on New Jail Rules

February 19, 1930.
New Delhi

Important decisions of the Government of India regarding the Jail Rules are announced in a Press Communique which runs:

The Government of India have for some time had under consideration the amendment of jail rules in certain respects. The matter had been referred to Local Govenments who have formulated their views after extensive consultation of unofficial opinion. A conference of the provincial representatives was thereupon held and the Government of India have also had discussions with some prominent members of the Legislative Assembly. The problems under examination have been found difficult and complex and have led to the expression of widely divergent opinions. The Government of India have endeavoured to give due weight to these even when they have not been able to accept in full the representations made. The conclusions at which they have arrived on the more important points and which are designed to secure on matters of principle substantial uniformity throughout India, are now announced.

Three Classes of Prisoners

Convicted prisoners will be divided into three divisions or classes, A, B and C. Prisoners will be eligible for Class 'A' if (1) they are non-habitual prisoners of good character (2) they, by social status, education and habit of life, have been accustomed to a superior mode of living and (3) they have not been convicted of (a) offences involving elements of cruelty, moral degradation or personal greed; (b) seditious or premeditated violence; (c) seditious offences against property; (d) offences relating to possession of explosives, fire-arms and other dangerous weapons with the object of committing an offence or of enabling an offence to be committed; (e) abetment or incitement of offences falling within these sub-clauses.

Prisoners will be eligible for class 'B' who, by social status, education or habit of life have been accustomed to a superior mode of living. Habitual prisoners will not be excluded automatically. The classifying authority will be allowed discretion to suggest their inclusion in this class, having regard to their character and antecedents, subject to confirmation of revision by the Local Government.

Class 'C' will consist of prisoners who are not classified in classes 'A' and 'B'.

The classifying authorities are High Courts, Sessions Judges, District Magistrates, Stipendiary Presidency Magistrates, Sub-divisional Magistrates and Magistrates of the first class (the two latter through the District Magistrate) in cases tried by them originally or in any other case. The District Magistrate should make an initial recommendation for classification in classes A or B to the Local Government, by whom these recommendations will be confirmed or reviewed.

Privileges of 'A' and 'B' Class Prisoners

Certain forecasts of their decisions which have been brought to the notice of the Government of India indicate considerable misapprehension in regard to this tripartite division and its effect upon the existing classes of prisoners. It should be clearly understood that all prisoners within the 'A' class are eligible for the privileges of that class. No class of prisoners will be eligible for any additional privileges on grounds of race. All privileges now given to special class prisoners will be continued to 'A' class prisoners, such as separate accommodation, necessary articles of furniture, reasonable facilities for association and exercises, and suitable sanitary and bathing arrangements.

In other matters, the following decisions have been arrived at:

The diet of classes 'A' and 'B' will be superior to the ordinary prison diet given to prisoners in class C and will be based on a flat rate of cost per prisoner, within the limits of which the actual food may vary. The cost of the superior diet provided in the classes A and B should be borne by the Government as special class prisoners are under the existing rules permitted to suplement prison diet at their own expense. This privilege will be retained as at present as regards 'A' class prisoners.

The existing rules regarding privileges of special class prisoners to wear their own clothes will continue. As regards 'A' class pr: ' r:rs, if they desire to have clothing at Government expense, they will be provided with that prescribed for 'B' class prisoners. 'B' class prisoners will wear prison clothing modified in certain respects and of a better type than that worn by C class prisoners.

A separate jail in each Province for classes A and B is desirable, and its provision though it must depend on the available financial resources of the

Local Governments, should be regarded as the goal to be aimed at. Meanwhile, the Government of India hope that Local Governments will carefully review the resources of the jails now existing in the Provinces and endeavour, by such measures as are within their power, to secure the end in view.

In addition to separate accommodation, the Government of India desire to emphasise the necessity of a special staff to deal with 'A' and 'B' class prisoners and are of opinion that this matter should receive the earliest possible attention.

In accordance with the principle already applied, the importance of which is reaffirmed, the tasks allotted to prisoners in 'A' and 'B' classes should be assigned after due consideration on medical grounds, and with careful regard to the capacity, character, previous modes of life and antecedents of the prisoners.

The Government of India accept the principle that reasonable facilities, subject to safeguards, should be provided by the Government for the intellectual requirements of the educated and literate prisoners. Local Governments will be requested to examine the condition of jail libraries in the Provinces and in cases where those are non-existent or defective, to take early steps to establish or improve them. Literate prisoners may be allowed to read books and magazines from outside subject to the approval of the Jail Superintendent.

Newspapers will be allowed to 'A' class prisoners on the same conditions as under the existing rules, they are allowed to special class prisoners, that is, in special circumstances and with the approval of Local Government. As regards literate prisoners generally, where the Local Governments publish a jail newspaper or where they intend to publish it, this publication will be available once a week for literate prisoners. Where the Local Governments are unable to publish a weekly newspaper, the Government of India have decided that a few copies of a weekly paper approved by the Local Government should be provided at Government expenses for 'A' and 'B' classes of prisoners.

'A' class prisoners will be allowed to write and receive one letter and have one interview a fortnight, instead of once a month as at present. 'B' class prisoners will be allowed to write and receive one letter and have an interview once a month instead of at the considerably longer intervals now permitted under the various jail manuals. Publication of matters discussed at interviews or of the substance of the letters received from prisoners may entail the withdrawal or curtailment of the privilege.

Under-Trial Prisoners

The Government of India accept the principle that some differentiation of treatment is desirable in the case of under-trial prisoners who, by social status, education or habit of life, have been accustomed to a superior mode of living. There will, therefore, be two classes of under-trial prisoners based on the previous standard of living only. The classifying authority will be one trying court, subject to the approval of the District Magistrate. The diet provided for 'A' and 'B' class convicted prisoners will be given to the former and the diet of 'C' class prisoners to the latter. Under-trial prisoners in either class, will be allowed to supplement this diet by private purchase through the jail authorities. Under the existing rules, they are allowed to wear their own clothing. The suggestion has been made that in cases where under-trial prisoners are inadequately clad or are unable to obtain clothing from outside, suitable clothing, which should not be prison clothing, should br provided by jail authorities. The Government of India commend this suggestion for adoption to the Local Governments.

The Government of India are of opinion that the interpretation of the existing rules in a liberal spirit, together with the modifications now proposed and the provision of better cellular accommodation, will effect improvements in the directions which enquiry has indicated as desirable. They, therefore, hope that Local Governments will make every effort to improve the existing accommodation and will at once utilize and adapt their existing resources to the best possible advantage. In many of the opinions received by the Government of India, stress had been laid on the desirability of separating under-trial prisoners, who are habituals or charged with grave offences, from those who have not been previously convicted. On this subject, the Government of India consider that no further orders are necessary as they understand that this is the existing practice.

The local Governments are now being invited to amend their jail manuals in the light of these principles, and to frame rules where necessary under Section 60 of the Prisoners Act. Pending such revision they are being requested as far as possible to give immediate practical effect to these changes—A.P.I.

—*The Tribune*, February 21, 1930.

Appendix VI

Ordinance No. III of 1930

An Ordinance to make provision for the trial of the persons accused in the Lahore conspiracy case.

Whereas an emergency has arisen which makes it necessary to provide specially for the trial of the accused in the cases known as the Lahore conspiracy case;

Now, therefore, in exercise of the power conferred by section 72 of the Government of India Act, the Governor General is pleased to make and promulgate the following Ordinance:

Short Title

1. This Ordinance may be called the Lahore Conspiracy Case Ordinance, 1930.

Definitions.

2. In this Ordinance—
   (a) the "Code" means the Code of Criminal Procedure, 1898; V of 1896
   (b) the "High Court" means the High Court of Judicature at Lahore; and
   (c) the "said cases" mean the cases specified in section 3.

Trial of Lahore Conspiracy cases by Special Tribunal

3. Notwithstanding anything contained in the Code, all cases pending in the Court of Rai Sahib Pandit Sri Kishan, Magistrate of the First Class, Lahore, against any or all of the persons named in the Schedule shall be tried by the Tribunal to be constituted under section 4.

Constitution of the Tribunal

4. (1) As soon as may be after the commencement of this Ordinance, the Chief Justice of the High Court shall constitute a Tribunal for the trial of the said cases consisting of three persons who at the time of such constitution are

Judges, Additional Judges or officiating Judges of the High Court.

(2) The Chief Justice shall appoint one of the members of the Tribunal to be President of the Tribunal.

Appointment of New Member where Member Unable to Attend

5. (*1*) If, for any reason, any member of the Tribunal is unable to discharge his duties, the Chief Justice shall appoint another Judge, Additional Judge, or officiating Judge of the High Court to be member of the Tribunal.

(2) Notwithstanding any change in the composition of the Tribunal, it shall not be incumbent on the Tribunal to re-call or re-hear any witness who has already given evidence, and it may act on any evidence already recorded by or produced before it.

Procedure of the Tribunal

6. (*1*) When the Tribunal has been constituted it shall have cognisance of the said cases and the jurisdiction of the aforesaid Magistrate shall cease.

(2) The Tribunal shall, subject to the provisions of this Ordinance, follow the procedure prescribed in Chapter XXI of the Code for the trial of warrant cases by Magistrates.

(*3*) In matters not coming within the scope of sub-seciton (2), the provisions of the Code, so far as they are not inconsistent with this Ordinance, shall apply to the proceedings of the Tribunal; and for the purpose of applying the said provisions, the proceedings already taken before the aforesaid Magistrate shall be deemed to be proceedings under Chapter XVIII of the Code whereunder the accused persons have been committed to the Tribunal for trial, and the Tribunal shall be deemed to be a Court of Session to whom the accused persons have been duly committed by the aforesaid Magistrate.

(*4*) In the event of any difference of opinion among the members of the Tribunal, the opinion of the majority shall prevail.

Conduct of the Prosecution

7. (*1*) The Local Government may appoint a person to be prosecutor for the conduct of the prosecution of the said cases, and such other persons to assist him as it may think fit.

(2) The prosecutor appointed under this section shall have the powers and shall discharge the duties of a Public Prosecutor under the Code.

Powers of the Tribunal

8. The Tribunal may pass upon any person convicted by it any sentence authorised by law for the punishment of the offence of which such person is convicted and no order of confirmation shall be necessary in respect of any sentence passed by it.

Special Powers of the Tribunal

9. (*1*) The Tribunal shall have powers to take such measures as it may think necessary to secure the orderly conduct of the trial; and where any accused by his voluntary act has rendered himself incapable of appearing before the Tribunal, or resists his production before it, or behaves before it in a persistently disorderly manner, or in any other way wilfully conducts himself to the serious prejudice of the trial, the Tribunal may, at any stage of the trial, dispense with the attendance of such accused for such period as it may think fit and proceed with the trial in his absence.

(2) Where a plea is required in answer to a charge from an accused whose attendance has been dispensed with under sub-section (*1*), such accused shall be deemed not to plead guilty.

(3) An order under sub-section (*1*) dispensing with the attendance of an accused shall not affect his right of being represented by a pleader at any stage of the trial.

Special Rule of Evidence

10. Notwithstanding anything contained in the Indian Evidence Act, 1872, (I of 1872) when the statement of any person has been recorded by a Magistrate, such statement may be admitted in evidence before the Tribunal if such person is dead or cannot be found or is incapable of giving evidence, and the Tribunal is of opinion that such death, disappearance or incapacity has been caused in the interests of any accused.

Finality of Proceedings of Tribunal

11. The judgment of the Tribunal shall be final and conclusive and, notwithstanding the provisions of the Code or of any other law for the time being in force, or of anything having the force of law by whatsoever authority made or done, there shall be no appeal from any order or sentence of the Court, and the High Court shall not have authority to revise any such order or sentence or to transfer any case from the Tribunal, or to make any order under section 491 of the Code or have any jurisdiction of any kind in respect of any proceedings under this Ordinance.

Powers of the President in Ancillary Matters

12. (*1*) The President may make all necessary orders for the transfer to the custody of the Tribunal of all records, documents, exhibits and other things connected with the said cases.

(2) The President may also, from time to time, make orders consistent with this Ordinance to provide for the place and conduct of the trial, and all other ancillary matters which he may deem necessary to carry into effect the provisions of this Ordinance.

SCHEDULE

1. Sukh Dev *alias* Dyal *alias* Swami *alias* Villager, son of Ram Lal, Thaper Khatri, of Mohalla Arya Samaj, Lyallpur.

2. Agya Ram *alias* Masterji, son of Nand Lal, Brahman, of Lalla, police station Killa Sobha Singh, District Sialkot.

3. Kishori Lal Rattan *alias* Deo Datt Rattan *alias* Mast Ram Shastri, son of Raghbar Dutt, Brahman, of Dharampur, police station Hajipur, District Hoshiarpur.

4. Des Raj, son of Ram Kishan, Khatri, of Balgan, police station Sambrial, District Sialkot.

5. Prem Dutt *alias* Master *alias* Amrit Lal, son of Ram Datt, Khatri, of Gujrat.

6. Surindra Nath Pandey *alias* Stone, son of Hira Lal Pandey, Brahman, resident of Mohalla Sabzimandi, Cawnpore.

7. Jai Dev *alias* Harish Chander, son of Babu Salig Ram, Khatri Kapur, Sadar Bazaar, Hardoi.

8. Sheo Varma *alias* Parbhat *alias* Harnarain *alias* Ram Narain Kapur, son of Kanhiya Lal Varma, Khatri, of Hardoi.

9. Gaya Parshad *alias* Dr. B.S. Nigam *alias* Ram Lal *alias* Ram Nath *alias* Desh Bhagat, Kurmi, resident of Khajuri Khurd, police station Billhaur, District Cawnpore.

10. Mahabir Singh *alias* Partab, of Shahpore Tehla, post office Raja ke Rampur, District Eta.

11. Bhagat Singh, son of Kishan Singh of Khawasrian, Lahore.

12. Batukeshwar Dutt *alias* Battu *alias* Mohan, son of G.D. Dutt, of Bedwan, Bengal.

13. Ajoy Kumar Ghosh *alias* Negro-General, son of Dr. Ghosh, of Cawnpore.

14. Jatin Sanyal (Jatindra Nath Sanyal), son of Hira Nath Sanyal, of Allahabad.

15. Bijoy Kumar Sinha *alias* Bachu, son of Markando Kumar Sinha, of Mohalla Karachi Ganj, Cawnpore.

16. Shivram Rajguru *alias* "M", son of Hari Raj Guru, of Sadashiv Peth, Poona.

17. Kundan Lal *alias* Partap *alias* No. 1, of Fyzabad.

18. Kanwal Nath Trivedi, *alias* Kanwal Nath Tewari, son of Pandit Surej Nath Tewari, of Sarya, police station Govindagunj, Champaran (student Vidya Sagar College, Calcutta).

19. Bhagwan Dass *alias* Gunthala, of Jhansi.

20. Chander Shekar Azad *alias* Panditji, son of Baij Nath Ram *alias* Sita Ram, Brahman, of Baij Nath Tula, police station Bhilopur, Benares.

21. Kelash Patti *alias* Kali Charan, son of Harde Narain, Kayasth, of Mongranwan, police station Chamirpur, District Azamgarh.

22. Bhagwati Charan *alias* B.C. Vohra, son of Rai Sahib Shiv Charan Dass, Brahman, of Lahore.

23. Yashpal, son of Hira Lal, Khatri, of Nidhon, police station Hamirpur, District Kangra, and of Wachhowali, Lahore.

24. Satgurdyal, son of Pandit Sukhbasi Lal Avasthi, Brahman, of Mohalla Bama Khori, Cawnpore.

Simla   IRWIN
1st May, 1930.   Viceroy and Governor-General.

STATEMENT

On the 11th July 1929 the enquiry in the proceedings known as the Lahore Conspiracy Case commenced before a Magistrate, who was for this purpose relieved of all other duties. The accused in the case number 24, of whom 5 are still absconding. The offence alleged against the accused are both in their own nature and in their relation to the public security of unusually serious character. They include the murder of Mr. Saunders, Assistant Superintendent of Police, and head constable Chanan Singh in Lahore, on the 17th December 1928, the establishment of bomb factories at Lahore and Saharanpur, the conspiracy leading to the throwing of two bombs in the Legislative Assembly on the 8th April 1929, and various other revolutionary activities. For the purpose of establishing these charges which were concerned with many different places and with events occurring over a considerable period of time, the prosecution considered it would be necessary to produce about 600 witnesses.

2. Two of the accused had resorted to hunger strike before the commencement of the enquiry. A number of others followed the same course shortly afterwards with the result that by the 26th July 1929, the case had to be adjourned owing to some of the accused being unfit to attend the Court. The case had to be successively adjourned on the same ground until the 24th September. It was then resumed, but there were numerous interruptions owing to defiant and disorderly conduct by some of the accused or demonstrations by members of the public. On February 4th, 1930, most of the accused again went on hunger strike, and the case was on this account adjourned from the 8th February till the 8th March.

3. The enquiry has now been in progress for more than 9 months and during that time it has been possible to examine about 230 witnesses, only out of a probable total of 607. The spectacle of these proceedings, obstructed by unprecedented delays, and repeatedly disturbed by disorderly conduct and revolutionary demonstrations, has tended to bring the administration of justice into contempt, and it is impossible to count upon obtaining a conclusion by the normal methods of procedure within any calculable period.

4. After anxious consideration I have come to the conclusion that neither

the ends of justice nor the interests of the accused are served by allowing these proceedings to drag out to a length which cannot at present be foreseen. Public policy clearly demands that the grave charges against the accused should be thoroughly scrutinised and finally adjudicated upon with the least possible delay, by a tribunal of indubitable impartiality and authority, and that the preliminary proceedings which have already extended over nine months and the end of which is not yet in sight should be terminated. It is also necessary to ensure that obstructions shall not further interrupt the course of justice. I have accordingly decided to avail myself of the authority conferred upon the Governor General under section 72 of the Government of India Act and to issue an Ordinance which has the effect of entrusting the trial of this case to a tribunal to be constituted by the Chief Justice of the High Court of Judicature at Lahore, and consisting of three Judges of the High Court and to invest this tribunal with powers to deal with wilful obstruction. By these means the accused will be assured of a trial before a Court of the highest possible authority and it may be expected that a final and just decision will be reached with no unnecessary delay. I am convinced that the action which I have thought it right to take will best secure the achievement of the true ends of justice and re-establish respect for the administration of the law.

Simla   IRWIN
1st May, 1930.   *Viceroy and Governor-General.*

Appendix VII

The Lahore Conspiracy Case Ordinance, Lahore High Court Bar Association Report, June 19, 1930

By a resolution of the High Court Bar Association a sub-committee consisting of Dr. Sir Motisagar, Lala Jagan Nath Aggarwal and the undersigned was appointed to consider and report on the validity and propriety of Ordinance No. 3 of 1930, dated 1st May 1930, designed to make provisions for the trial of certain persons accused in the Lahore conspiracy case. Dr. Sir Motisagar and Lala Jagan Nath were not present in the deliberations of the committee.

No Justification

The undersigned, having carefully gone into the matter, are unanimously of the opinion that the said Ordinance is *ultra vires* of the Governor-General and, therefore, invalid; that, in any case, its promulgation was inexpedient and inadvisable; and that there was no justification whatsoever for depriving the High Court of its power of hearing the appeal from the final order of the Special Tribunal constituted under the Ordinance.

The Ordinance purports to have been promulgated in exercise of the powers conferred upon the Governor-General by section 72 of the Government of India Act.

A perusal of the Section would show that before the Governor-General can promulgate an Ordinance (*a*) an emergency must exist, and (*b*) the Ordinance must be for the peace and good Government of India or any part of it.

QUESTION OF EMERGENCY

Statement Examined

(A) On the question of emergency we are clearly of the opinion that the emergency contemplated in section 72 of the Government of India Act does not exist at all. Emergency, as defined in Webster Dictionary and as generally understood, means "an unforeseen occurrence creating a combination of circumstances which call for an immediate action." Even the statement of reasons and facts issued by His Excellency the Governor-General in justification of the Ordinance promulgated by him does not constitute or disclose any case of emergency justifying this extraordinary measure.

The Statement refers (a) to the murder of Mr. Saunders, Assistant Superintendent of Police, and Head Constable Chanan Singh, which tragic incident took place on the 17th of December 1928; (b) to the establishmen of bomb factories at Lahore and Saharanpur; (c) to the conspiracy resulting in the throwing of bombs in the Legislative Assembly on the 8th of April 1929; (d) to the hunger-strike of two of the accused, which had been resorted to before the commencement of the enquiry; (e) to the joining of a number of other accused in the hunger-strike necessitating the adjournment of the case from time to time owing to some of the accused being unfit to attend the court; and (f) to interruptions caused by the defiant and disorderly conduct of some of the accused, which, in the words of His Excellency, "tend to bring the administration of justice into contempt."

Just Decision

After referring to the constitution of the proposed Tribunal, His Excellency says at the conclusion of his statement that "by these means the accused will be assured of a trial before a court of the highest possible authority, and it may be expected that a final and just decision will be reached with no unnecessary delay. I am convinced that the action which I have thought it fit to take will best secure the achievement of the true ends of justice and re-establish respect for the administration of the law."

We have sought in vain to find in this statement any facts which would lead to the conclusion that there was any emergency for the promulgation of the Ordinance in question, for none of the facts summarized above constitute an unforeseen occurrence calling for immediate action.

The only objects of the Ordinance which we have been able to gather from His Excellency's statement are the prevention of delay in the trial of the Lahore conspiracy case and the re-establishment of respect for the administration of the law. In our opinion these objects in relation to the conduct of one individual case do not justify the promulgation of an Ordinance under section 72 for the peace and good Government for India.

No Emergency

Coming to the facts of the case itself, we are confirmed in our opinion that no emergency whatsoever has been established.

The case was started on the 11th of July 1929, and a short time after an application was made on behalf of the Crown to the High Court asking for an authoritative pronouncement whether a counsel could be appointed to represent an absent accused against his will. This application was decided by the High Court of Judicature at Lahore on the 26th of July 1929 (vide 11 Lahore, page 220) in which it was held that counsel could not be forced upon an accused against his will.

Again, an application was made by the Crown asking for the opinion of the High Court as to whether the evidence originally proposed to be produced against the accused could be curtailed. The High Court refused to give any direction or advice.

Home Member's Bill

On the 6th of September, Sir James Crerar, Home Member of the Government of India, drafted Bill No. 29 of 1929, which was published in the *Punjab Gazette*, dated 20th September 1929. It was proposed in this Bill to amend the Criminal Procedure Code in such a way as to allow the enquiry or trial of an accused to proceed in his absence where the absence was due to the accused's own action. This Bill was, however, withdrawn.

These circumstances show that the Government was fully aware of the delay of the necessity, if any, of the trial being allowed to proceed in the absence of the accused. Nevertheless no action was taken until the 1st of May when this Ordinance was promulgated. In addition to the facts mentioned above, it is admitted that some of the accused had started hunger-strike before the commencement of the enquiry before the committing Magistrate, and it is well-known that the hunger-strike was suspended on an assurance conveyed to them by certain gentlemen who had been appointed by the Government to make an enquiry into the condition of political prisoners and make recommendations with a view to having certain rules framed with respect to the treatment of political prisoners.

Hunger-strike

The accused had definitely intimated to the Government that in case the grievances of political prisoners were not satisfactorily settled they would resume the hunger-strike on a certain date and. as a matter of fact, as His Excellency's own statement shows, the hunger-strike was resumed on the 4th day of February 1930. creating the difficulty which this Ordinance seeks to remove.

It is also important to note that when the rules relating to the treatment of political prisoners were published and were considered satisfactory by those accused who had gone on hunger-strike the hunger-strike was abandoned, and from the 8th of March to the 1st of May 1930, the case went on in the Magistrate's court without any interruption or undesirable incident.

It is also clear that the Government itself did not consider that there was any emergency; otherwise it would not have waited so long from the 26th of July 1929, up to 1st of May 1930, or in any case from the 20th of September 1929, when the Bill for the amendment of the Criminal Procedure Code referred to above was published. to 1st of May 1930. Even if the alleged defiant and disorderly conduct of the accused could be considered any justificatiou for the promulgation of the Ordinance, it had ceased to exist long before the Ordinance was actually promulgated.

GOOD GOVERNMENT

Faith in Justice Shaken

(B) On the question of peace and good Government of India for which alone an ordinance can be promulgated we are of opinion that the Ordinance instead of promoting peace and good government has jeopardised both. Far from restoring respect for law this Ordinance, being most unprecedented and allowing the trial of a large number of persons accused of the most serious crimes in their absence and without any right of appeal, has brought not only the administration of law and justice into contempt but has also gone a great way in making the Government unpopular.

We are further of the opinion that even if it was necessary for the prevention of delay to resort to an Ordinance there was no justification whatsoever for depriving the accused of the right of appeal to the High Court, and depriving the High Court of its powers of superintendence over the Tribunal. In our opinion the taking away of the right of appeal from the highest tribunal of the province has dealt a most fatal blow to the prestige and dignity of the High Court and has further considerably shaken the confidence of the people in the unpartiality of the present trial.

Appeal in High Court

It will be at once admitted that the question of delay caused by any defiant or obstructive conduct of the accused does not arise at all in relation to an appeal in the High Court. Once this appeal is filed the course of the appeal is entirely in the hands of the High Court and cannot possibly be deflected or delayed by any conduct of the accused. The hearing of the appeal unlike the trial does not require the presence of the appellants at all.

In our opinion the Ordinance is not only invalid in view of Section 72 of the Government of India Act but is a most ill-advised measure, which goes much beyond the necessities of the case, and is utterly unjustifiable so far as it takes away the right of appeal from the High Court.

(Sd.) GOKAL CHAND NARANG
(Sd.) BARKAT ALI
(Sd.) NANAK CHAND
(Sd.) MOHD. IQBAL

Note.—The report has been sent to Sir Motisagar and Mr. Jagan Nath for signature.

—*The Tribune*, June 21, 1930.

Kishen Singh's Petition to the Tribunal

Petition of Sardar Kishen Singh, father of B ʰagat Singh, accused:
   In this case, the accused persons wanted to produce defence evidence after the perusal of the prosecution evidence. They wanted time to find out the material from the prosecution evidence because they could not produce the defence evidence without fully knowing what they had to meet. The time asked for was about a week, but the Hon'ble Members of the Tribunal, for the reasons best known to them, refused to allow the time. I, therefore, beg to submit the following points for the consideration of the Hon'ble Judges:
   1. No reliance should be placed on the evidence of the alleged eye-witnesses, for when Bhagat Singh was brought from Delhi to Lahore during the course of the investigation of this murder case of Mr. Saunders, he was not taken to the Central Jail or the Borstal Institution where the prosecution witnesses could have no opportunity to see him before the formal identification parade held by the Magistrate at the Lahore Cantonment police station. The distance between the Lahore Cantonment Police Station and the Central Jail is only 2 miles. Bhagat Singh could very easily have been brought to the Central Jail, and the identification parade could have been held there. At the Cantonment Police Station, the witnesses were procured by the investigating staff, and the Magistrate, who had to hold the identification parade was also sent by the investigating staff. There could be no other object of the police to go out of the way, and to arrange the identification parade at the Cantonment Police Station than to give an opportunity to the witnesses to see Bhagat Singh before the farce of an identification parade. I at once made an application to the District Magistrate, Lahore that the identification parade was of no value and referred 21 P.W.R. 19, 1917 (Cr. Ruling) in that application drawing the attention of the learned District Magistrate to this abnormal conduct of the investigating officer. It has been clearly laid down by the Punjab High Court that the evidence of identification is considerably decreased, if the witnesses get an opportunity to see the accused person before holding the identification

parade. That application of mine was published in the local newspapers *Milap* and very probably in *The Tribune*. No weight, therefore, should be attached to the evidence of those witnesses, who identified Bhagat Singh at the identification parade. You, yourselves, are great Judges and presumably read the newspapers. Photos of Bhagat Singh were published in almost all the newspapers of India after the 'Assembly Bomb Case', and the witnesses should be presumed to have seen these photographs of Bhagat Singh before the present identification parade took place.

2. There is no manner of doubt that Mr. Fearne, European gentleman and Traffic Inspector of Police, who had plenty of opportunity to see the real criminals, could not identify the culprits. This man being a Traffic Inspector had developed his sense of identifying the natives by virtue of his profession and calling in life. He could not pick out Bhagat Singh but it is curious that Ganda Singh, Head Constable, and a Naib Court Police Constable and other witnesses, who were accidentally present on the spot, could spot Bhagat Singh. It means that accused was shown to those witnesses before the identification parade.

3. No reliance be placed on the evidence of the approvers in this case, because the provisions of Sec. 167, Clause (iii) of the Cr. P. Code have been abused by the Magistrate in remanding the accused persons to police custody. Bhagat Singh and other persons, who have been admitted or likely to be admitted as approvers were kept in the police custody in the Lahore Fort and other different police lock-ups for about 3 months continuously. They were not shown the air of the world. Magistrates extraordinarily went over to the lock-ups and remanded the accused persons for fortnights. Instead of being the governors of the police, they were at the beck and call of the police. The object of taking remands in this extraordinary way was that the public might not come to know what grievances the accused persons, who were confined in the strange lock-ups, made before the Magistrate at the time of the remands. Presumably, the police did not want any legal practitioner to contend before the Magistrate at the time of the remands that there are no sufficient reasons for further remanding the accused persons to police custody. The accused persons had no opportunity to know the reasons for which the British subjects were being detained by the police. In 90 days, any amount of evidence can be prepared, the accused persons confined can be made to talk by the notorious methods of the police well known to courts. In Z.C.W.N. page 457, the Hon'ble Judges of the Calcutta High Court have held that the evidence of the accused person, who has confessed and has been admitted or is likely to be admitted as approver, and who has been detained in the police custody up to the time of the trial, is open to the greatest suspicion that the police have arranged his statements so as to fit in with any evidence that they may have obtained elsewhere.

About 100 persons, including the Superintendent Police, Deputy Superintendent, Inspectors, were on the investigating staff in this case. They were the officers of the C.I.D. and the local Police Board vying with one another to contribute some material evidence in this case. It is for the protection of the accused persons and to prevent the fabrication of false evidence in this case that Sec. 167 Cr.P.C. and other similar sections were enacted. In 90 days, even stones can be pulverized into smooth powder. In this case, the accused persons were boys of easy living habits and delicate nature. They could be very easily rehearsed and drilled for a theatrical representation. The C.I.D. keeps record of suspicious persons and their activities, they are in possession of the seditious literature, and have got inter-provincial communications in the country. They could very easily get the seditious literature and the prescriptions (formulae) for bomb-making and fit them in the statements of approvers purchasing their immunity at the sacrifice of the lives of others. And the fiction appears to be more real than the truth. The officers investigating the case, like the experienced craftsmen and engineers, have built up a structure by violations of the remand law. I, therefore, pray that the orders of the remands may kindly be perused at the time of weighing the evidence of the approvers. These persons were certainly kept and detained by the police without any sufficient reasons against the Punjab Chief Court Ruling No. 24 of 1902 Cr. No person can be detained in police custody without the commencement of the trial for more than 15 days. The law protects the accused persons.

4. The witnesses for the prosecution appeared at a very late stage of the investigation and in this country witnesses can be procured and they come forward to give evidence in order to achieve their own private ends, and the police officer investigating big cases did get witnesses from their friends and hangers-on to corroborate the approvers. Sec. 179 Cr.P. Code has been made to take the assistance of the Police diaries to find out the dates on which their statements were recorded by the police. It is also essential for the prosecution to reveal before the Tribunal, how all the witnesses were traced out. I, therefore pray to the court to see whether it had been done or not.

It is, therefore, in this case that the accused persons have not cross-examined the prosecution witnesses, but the bench is composed of judges of experience. They themselves should apply the tests for testing the veracity of the witnesses. Bhagat Singh was in Calcutta on the day of the occurrence and he actually wrote and despatched a letter to one, Ram Lal, Manager of the *Khaddar Bhandar*, Pari Mahal, Lahore, which was duly received by him. There are respectable gentlemen to swear that Bhagat Singh was in Calcutta on the day of the occurrence. I can produce them if I am given an opportunity, according to justice, or they may be called as court witnesses in the interest of justice, equity and good conscience. The question in this case is of life and death. The right of defence is to be jealously preserved for the accused. If an opportunity of defence would have been given, I would have exposed, according to the Evidence Act Sec. 155, who the witnesses for the prosecution are, and what is their position in life, and what are their objects in giving the evidence, when and how they were made witnesses. I still humbly pray that Bhagat Singh may be given an opportunity to produce his defence.

KISHEN SINGH
20th September, 1930   Father of Bhagat Singh, Accused
Bradlaugh Hall, Lahore

Appendix IX

Bhagat Singh's Letter to his father

The letter reads:

"I was astounded to learn that you had submitted a petition to the members of the Special Tribunal in connection with my defence. This intelligence proved to be too severe a blow to be borne with equanimity. It has upset the whole equilibrium of my mind. I have not been able to understand how you could think it proper to submit such a petition at this stage and in these circumstances. In spite of all the sentiments and feelings of a father, I don't think you were at all entitled to make such a move on my behalf without even consulting me. You know that in the political field, my views have always differed with those of yours. I have always been acting independently, without having cared for your approval or disapproval.

"I hope you can recall to yourself that since the very beginning you have been trying to convince me to fight my case very seriously and to defend myself properly. But you also know that I was always opposed to it. I never had any desire to defend myself, and never did I seriously think about it, whether it was a mere vague ideology or that I had certain arguments to justify my position, is a different question and that cannot be discussed here.

"You know that we have been pursuing a definite policy in this trial. Every action of mine ought to have been consistent with that policy, my principles and the programme. At present the circumstances were altogether different, but had the situation been otherwise, even then I would have been the last man to offer defence. I had only one idea before me throughout the trial, i.e., to show complete indifference towards the trial in spite of the serious nature of the charges against us. I have always been of opinion that all the political workers should be indifferent and should never bother about the legal fight in the law courts and should boldly bear the heaviest possible sentences inflicted upon them. They may defend themselves but always from purely political considerations and never from a personal point of view. Our policy in this trial has always been consistent with this principle. Whether we were successful in that or not is not for me to judge. We have always been doing our duty quite disinterestedly.

"In the statement accompanying the text of the Lahore Conspiracy Case Ordinance, the Viceroy had stated that the accused in this case were trying to bring both law and justice into contempt. The situation afforded us an opportunity to show to the public whether we were trying to bring law into contempt or whether others were doing so. People might disagree with us on this point. You might be one of them. But that never meant that such moves should be made on my behalf without my consent or even without my knowledge. My life is not so precious—at least to me—as you may probably think it to be. It is not at all worth buying at the cost of my principles. There are other comrades of mine whose case is as serious as mine. We had adopted a common policy, and have so far stood shoulder to shoulder, so shall we stand to the last no matter how dearly we have to pay individually for it.

"Father, I am quite perplexed. I fear I might overlook the ordinary principles of etiquette, and my language may become a little bit harsh while criticizing or rather censuring this move on your part. Let me be candid. I feel as though I have been stabbed in the back. Had any other person done it, I would have considered it to be nothing short of treachery. But, in your case, let me say that it has been a weakness—a weakness of the worst type.

"This was the time when everybody's mettle was being tested. Let me say, father, you have failed. I know you are as sincere a patriot as one can be. I know you have devoted your life to the cause of Indian Independence, but why at this moment have you displayed such a weakness? I cannot understand.

"In the end I would like to inform you and my other friends and all the people interested in my case, that I have not approved of your move. I am still not at all in favour of offering my defence. Even if the Court had accepted that petition submitted by some of my co-accused regarding defence, etc., I would have not defended myself. My applications submitted to the Tribunal regarding my interview during the hunger-strike were misinterpreted and it was published in the press that I was going to offer defence, though in reality I was never willing to offer any defence. I still hold the same opinion as before. My friends in the Borstal Jail will be taking it as a treachery and betrayal on my part. I shall not even get an opportunity to clear my position before them.

"I want that the public should know all the details about this complication and, therefore, I request you to publish this letter."

—*The Tribune*, October 4, 1930.

Appendix X

Bhagat Singh's last Petition

To
The Punjab Governor

Sir,

With due respect we beg to bring to your kind notice the following:

That we were sentenced to death on 7th October 1930 by a British Court, L.C.C. Tribunal, constituted under the Sp. Lahore Conspiracy Case Ordinance, promulgated by the H.E. The Viceroy, the Head of the British Government of India, and that the main charge against us was that of having waged war against H.M. King George, the King of England.

The above-mentioned finding of the Court pre-supposed two things:

Firstly, that there exists a state of war between the British Nation and the Indian Nation and, secondly, that we had actually participated in that war and were therefore war prisoners.

The second pre-supposition seems to be a little bit flattering, but nevertheless it is too tempting to resist the desire of acquiescing in it.

As regards the first, we are constrained to go into some detail. Apparently there seems to be no such war as the phrase indicates. Nevertheless, please allow us to accept the validity of the pre-supposition taking it at its face value. But in order to be correctly understood we must explain it further. Let us declare that the state of war does exist and shall exist so long as the Indian toiling masses and the natural resources are being exploited by a handful of parasites. They may be purely British Capitalist or mixed British and Indian or even purely Indian. They may be carrying on their insidious exploitation through mixed or even a purely Indian bureaucratic apparatus. All these things make no difference. No matter, if your Government tries and succeeds in winning over the leaders of the upper strata of the Indian Society through petty concessions and compromises and thereby cause a temporary demoralization in the main body of the forces. No matter, if once again the vanguard of the Indian movement, the Revolutionary Party, finds itself deserted in the thick of the war. No matter if the leaders to whom personally we are much indebted for the sympathy and feelings they expressed for us, but nevertheless we cannot overlook the fact that they did become so callous as to ignore and not to make a mention in the peace negotiation of even the homeless, friendless and penniless of female workers who are alleged to be belonging to the vanguard and whom the leaders consider to be enemies of their utopian non-violent cult which has already become a thing of the past; the heroines who had ungrudgingly sacrificed or offered for sacrifice their husbands, brothers, and all that were nearest and dearest to them, including themselves, whom your government has declared to be outlaws. No matter, if your agents stoop so low as to fabricate baseless calumnies against their spotless characters to damage their and their party's reputation. The war shall continue.

It may assume different shapes at different times. It may become now open, now hidden, now purely agitational, now fierce life and death struggle. The choice of the course, whether bloody or comparatively peaceful, which it should adopt rests with you. Choose whichever you like. But that war shall be incessantly waged without taking into consideration the petty (illegible) and the meaningless ethical ideologies. It shall be waged ever with new vigour, greater audacity and unflinching determination till the Socialist Republic is established and the present social order is completely replaced by a new social order, based on social prosperity and thus every sort of exploitation is put an end to and the humanity is ushered into the era of genuine and permanent peace. In the very near future the final battle shall be fought and final settlement arrived at.

The days of capitalist and imperialist exploitation are numbered. The war neither began with us nor is it going to end with our lives. It is the inevitable consequence of the historic events and the existing environments. Our humble sacrifices shall be only a link in the chain that has very accurately been beautified by the unparalleled sacrifice of Mr Das and most tragic but noblest sacrifice of Comrade Bhagawati Charan and the glorious death of our dear warrior Azad.

As to the question of our fates, please allow us to say that when you have decided to put us to death, you will certainly do it. You have got the power in your hands and the power is the greatest justification in this world. We know that the maxim "Might is right" serves as your guiding motto. The whole of our trial was just a proof of that. We wanted to point out that according to the verdict of your court we had waged war and were therefore war prisoners. And we claim to be treated as such, i.e., we claim to be shot dead instead of to be hanged. It rests with you to prove that you really meant what your court has said.

We request and hope that you will very kindly order the military department to send its detachment to perform our execution.

Yours[1]
BHAGAT SINGH

---

[1] Bejoy Kumar Sinha, pp. 68-71.

Appendix XI

Sukh Dev's Letter

Copy of Secret Letter No. 11763-S.B. dated 9th October 1930, from the Punjab C.I.D. to the D.I.B. Home Dept., Government of India.

On the 7th October after judgment in the Conspiracy Case had been pronounced, Sukh Dev, who had been sentenced to death, was searched on being taken into police custody for transfer from the Borstal to the Central Jail, Lahore. In his possession was found a lengthy manuscript document in Hindi, of which I enclose a translation. It will be seen that Sukh Dev was interrupted, while preparing this staement, by the news that judgment had been pronounced a day earlier than was expected.

About the same time as the recovery of this document was taking place, the Punjab C.I.D. received information that a certain man who is said to be one, Des Raj, alias Swami, at present living in the Tilak School of Politics, Lahore, had arranged to obtain a statement from one of the accused for purposes of propaganda.

The translation of the statement is sent to you by order of the Punjab Government for the information of the Government of India.

Translation of Hindi Letter

Dear Brother,

Since long certain feelings (currents) were arising in my mind which, I owing to some reasons, suppressed up till now, but I cannot do so any longer nor do I consider their suppression appropriate. I cannot say how you would take the expression of my thoughts in this manner whether in good or bad (light), whether they will receive your attention, whether they will be in accordance with your views and whether they will be agreeable to you or not. But I am doing what I feel is proper. You may act upon them if you like, that rests with you. If you reply to this letter it would be a good thing. Its advantage would be that my thoughts would be cleared up and I would know whether the four walls of the jail have deprived me of my power of judgment and I am only apt to think of idle and vain schemes, being cut off from the field of practical life.

Since the time we have been jailed the atmosphere outside is becoming heated. So far as actions (revolutionary acts) are concerned, it is gleaned through papers that in almost every province especially in the Punjab and Bengal the things are going to extremes. There the *bomb* has become a simple affair. So many actions (outrages) were hardly committed in the past. It is about these actions that I wish to tell you something and what our policy was in regard to these I shall place before you. After that I shall express my own views regarding 'actions'

We people did only two actions (perpetrated two outrages), one Saunders Murder and the other Bomb in the Assembly. Prior to that we made two or three attempts but did not succeed. In this connection I can say this much that our actions were of three kinds: (1) Propaganda, (2) Money, and (3) Special. Out of these three our main attention was centred towards actions for Propaganda. The other two were regarded (as auxiliiary). By this I do not mean to detract their importance, but at any rate the aim of our existence was to foster action for propaganda (To do) the other two kinds of actions was not our agenda (*sic*). To clear all these three points I place before you (1) the Assembly action, (2) Punjab National Bank Dacoity, and (3) Attempt to release Jogesh Chatterjee.

Leaving aside the latter two kinds of *action* I wish to discuss here action about propaganda. The word propaganda perhaps does not properly signify these actions. In fact these actions used to be in accordance with the wishes of the people. For instance take the case of Saunders' Murder. When Lala received lathi blows we saw that there was a great unrest in the country. Moreover the attitude of the Government added fuel to the fire. The people became much annoyed. This was a very good opportunity for us to attract public attention towards the revolutionaries. First of all we thought that one man should be sent with a pistol and after killing Scott, should there and then give him up. Then in the statement he should give out that the revenge for national insult so long the revolutionaries exist could be taken in that way. It was however thought better to send three men as manpower was believed to be deficient in the people. In this too the object of making good our escape was not predominating. It was not so much wished. Our idea was that after the murder if the police followed us we should face them. He who survived and was arrested should make his statement. With this in view we ran away and got over the roof of the D.A.V. College Hostel. At the time of action it was so arranged that BHAGAT SINGH who could recognize Scott, was to fire the first shot, RAJ GURU was to stand at a little distance and protect Bhagat Singh and if anyone attacked Bhagat Singh, then Raj Guru was to face the opponent.

After this both Bhagat Singh and Raj Guru were to run away and as while running away they could not turn back to shoot those who chased them. Pandit Jee was made to stand behind them for their protection. At the same time we were determined to pay more attention to kill him rather than to save our lives. We did not like that the person we aimed at should die in hospital. For this reason even after Raj Guru had fired a shot, Bhagat singh did not cease firing till he was satisfied that he (Saunders) was dead.

To run away after the murder was not our plot. We wished to enlighten the public that it was a political murder and that its perpetrators were revolutionaries and not the associates of Malangi. We therefore affixed posters after that and sent some for publication. Alas, neither our leaders nor the Press rendered any assistance at that stage, and in order to deceive the Government they deceived their countrymen. We desired that they should write in roundabout way that it was a political murder and was the result of Government's policy and that it was responsible for such an action. But they (the leaders and the Press) knowing all this and in spite of my repeatedly saying did not dare to say so. It was a good thing that we were arrested and everything came to light to the police. Dear brother, I consider my arrest as good luck only for this reason. After clearing the nature of this action I want to dwell on the policy (underlined).

(*Note.* Just at the moment we have côme to know that judgment will be delivered today. To enquire whether we would like to go or not (to hear the judgment) Khan Sahib and Bakshi Ji came to us but we all refused.)

Our idea was that our actions should fulfil the wishes of the public and should only be in response to those grievances (not redressed by) the Government so that they might attract public sympathy and support. With this in view we wanted to infuse revolutionary ideals and tactics in the public and the expression of such ideas looks more glorified from the mouth of one who stands on the gallows for the cause. Our idea was that by coming in direct conflict with the Government we would be able to frame a definite programme for our organisation.

I do not want to say much regarding the other two kinds of *actions*. In regard to 'money action' so much attention and energy was not necessary to be put in the commission of dacoities as the Bengalis did. All the same several petty dacoities have not been successful and we after consideration prepared ourselves for 'gambling' so that if we escaped we would do the work properly and solve the problem of money taking the risk once. After Saunders' murder we had not to think much about money. The dacoities did not yield so much money as we used to collect quietly. Today it is far easier (to get money). Special *actions* should only be done when absolutely necessary and their number should be very limited.

Now I want to say something in regard to those actions *which happened after us (after we wre jailed). After the attempt to bomb the Viceregal Special*

Train, many outrages have taken place. Out of these some actions were of special type, viz. placing a bomb in the way or just those actions which occurred simultaneously at four or five places in the Punjab. I do not understand what was the significance of these actions. So far as I think such actions have not caused special awakening in the public. If it was ony for the purpose of terrorising, I would like you to let me know how far have these actions been successful. In the connection I would not praise the Chittagong action.

Certified to be true translation

Sd/- HARBANS LAL
Senior Clerk, Special Branch,
Punjab C.I.D. Office

PRESS COMMUNIQUE

Prior to their conviction in the Lahore-United Provinces Conspiracy Case all the accused persons except Bhagat Singh, who, being already a convict in the Assembly Bomb Case, was confined in the Lahore Central Jail, were in cutody in a Secion of the Borstal Institution, which is ordinarily used for the custody of under-trial prisoners. On the 7th October, 1930 after judgment had been pronounced the transfer to the Central Jail of all who had been convicted was ordered according to normal procedure. Such transfers are carried out under Police escort; consequently in this case a Police escort was summoned to the Borstal Institution. The officer in command of this escort proceeded as usual to search the prisoners who were being made over to him. SUKH DEV was found to have in his hand an unfinished letter in Hindi which he endeavoured to destroy, but which was taken from him. This document in original has been kept in the personal custody of a responsible officer of Government since it was recovered. Publicity could not be given to it till after the final decision of any appeal that might be made by the writer. A careful translation of the first part of the letter is reproduced below for public information:

Dear Brother,

Since long certain feelings were arising in my mind which, owing to some reasons, I suppressed up till now, but I cannot do so any longer nor do I consider their suppression appropriate. I cannot say how you would take the expression of my thoughts in this manner whether in good or bad light; whether they will receive your attention; whether they will be in accordance with your views and whether they will be agreeable to you or not. But I am doing what I feel is proper. You may act upon them if you like, that rests with you. If you reply to this letter it would be a good thing. Its advantage would be that my thoughts would be cleared up and I would know whether the four walls of the jail have deprived me of my power of judgment and I am only apt to think of idle and vain schemes, being cut off from the field of practical life . . . .

. . . I do not want to say much regarding the other two kinds of *actions*. In regard to 'money action' so much attention and energy was not necessary to be put in the commission of dacoities as the Bengalis did. All the same several petty dacoities have not been successful and we after consideration prepared ourselves for "gambling" so that if we escape we would do the work properly and solve the problem of money taking the risk once. After Saunders' murder we had not to think much about money. The dacoities did not yield so much money as we used to collect quietly. Today it is far easier. Special *actions* should only be done when absolutely necessary and their number should be very limited.

Lahore,   F.H. PUCKLE
26th March 1931   *Offg. Chief Secretary to Government, Punjab*

—F.139/1931 Home Department Political

Gandhi and Bhagat Singh

D.P. Das

Gandhi and Bhagat Singh had in their life-time no occasion to meet each other. The young Bhagat Singh went underground after the assassination of British Police officer Saunders in Lahore in December 1928. He came to Calcutta when the Congress was holding its annual session under the chairmanship of Motilal Nehru. Gandhi was of course there. Bhagat Singh also attended the session incognito and then melted with the crowd. He must have seen Gandhi from a distance and formed opinion about Gandhi which he expressed with revolutionary candour later as an under-trial prisoner in the Delhi Bomb case. To him Gandhi was just a Utopian visionary nursing a futile hope that the mighty British would leave India under the moral pressure of *Ahimsa*.

If Gandhi created the Cult of Ahimsa, Bhagat Singh was also a true symbol of the Cult of the Bomb. They had chosen diametrically opposite paths of service to the motherland, then under the shackles of an alien power. Although they had opposite ideologically, Gandhi had much to do with Bhagat Singh after Bhagat was condemned to death along with two of his comrades, Sukh Dev and Rajguru. The Special Tribunal of the Lahore Conspiracy Case which tried them, pronounced judgement in October 1930.

It was the period when the Civil Disobedience Movement was in full swing. The famous Delhi Pact reached between Gandhi and Viceroy of India, Lord Irwin was concluded in March 1931. During this period Gandhi had to remember Bhagat Singh many times over. The question of securing the release of the condemned prisoners of the Lahore Conspiracy Case (or at least the commutation of the death sentence) was one of the burning issues before the public mind.

Karachi Congress

Bhagat Singh and his comrades were executed on March 23, 1931, just before the opening day of the Congress session in Karachi. There were country-wide demonstrations not only against the Government but also against Gandhi. Charges were levelled against him that he did little to save the lives of the condemned prisoners.

Addressing the Congress delegates in Karachi two days after the execution, Gandhi declared that he had pleaded hard with Lord Irwin for the commutation of the death sentence of the condemned prisoners. "I pleaded with Viceroy as best as I could. I brought all the persuasion at my command to bear upon him." (Tendulkar, *Mahatma Gandhi*, Vol. III, p. 72)

The account of his hard pleading was also confirmed by Lord Irwin in his farewell speech delivered at the Chelmsford Club on March 26.

There should be no doubt that the criticism of Gandhi by the uninformed public was unfair. Gandhi had said that he pleaded hard with Lord Irwin to save the lives of prisoners; and the latter corroborated the statement. But that was not all.

Irwin's Version

Neither Gandhi nor Irwin had told the whole truth. There is a gulf of difference between the public statements of the two principal actors and the whole truth. More than two decades later, remembering the whole episode, Irwin (then Viscount Halifax) wrote the following in his autobiography:

"Mr. Gandhi said that he greatly feared that unless I could do something, the effect would be to destroy our pact. I said that I would regret that no less than he but would be clear to him there were only three possible courses. The first was to do nothing and let the execution proceed, the second was to change the order and grant Bhagat Singh reprieve, the third was to hold up any decision till after the Congress meeting was over. I told him that I thought he would agree that it was impossible from my point of view to grant him his reprieve and that merely to postpone decision and encourage people to think that there was such a chance of remission was not straight forward and honest, the first course alone was possible in spite of attendant evils."

Halifax wrote how the subject was discussed by Gandhi who at one stage told him:

"If the young man was hanged, said Mr. Gandhi, there was likelihood that he would become a national martyr and general atmosphere would be seriously prejudiced."

Halifax then concluded his observations on the episode, giving out some more details of the interview, at the conclusion of which Gandhi asked him:

"Would your Excellency see any objection to my saying that I tried for the young man's life? I said that I saw none, if he would also add that from my point of view he did not know what other course I could have taken. He thought for a moment, then finally agreed and on that basis went to Karachi . . . and I was told afterwards that he was roughly received. But when he had opportunity he spoke in the sense agreed between us." (The preceding extracts are from the book *Fullness of Days*, pp. 149-150.)

Can the testimony of a reminiscing Viceroy, who remembered all these almost thirty years after the event be relied upon without disrespect to him?

Campbell Johnson's Reference

Then there is the testimony of another competent observer. Allan Campbell Johnson in his book *Lord Halifax*, written and published in London in 1943, referred to an understanding between Gandhi and Irwin that Bhagat Singh should not get any reprieve. This is certainly a grave charge which has so far gone unchallenged in books on Gandhi, published later in India. Johnson wrote:

"Sir Herbert Emerson, the Home Member who was called upon to play a prominent role in Delhi negotiations, records listening with amazement to Irwin and Gandhi, after the agreement had been reached by them that Bhagat Singh must be executed, engaged in a prolonged discussion not as between two statesmen on political implication of terrorism but as between two saints on the sanctity of human life." (*Lord Halifax*, p. 313)

The evidence of Johnson is also very nebulous; it is also somebody else's reminiscences orally tendered to the author of Halifax's biography many years after the event. It is very strange that the account given by him has not been rebutted.

All the known biographers of Gandhi have accepted the story of Gandhi's intercession with Irwin for Bhagat Singh and his comrades on the basis of public statements of Gandhi and Irwin and the contemporary newspaper reports. There is Dr. Sitaramayya's *History of Congress*, Nehru's *Autobiography*, Tendulkar's biography of Gandhi, Mira Behn's autobiography. In none of these books is there anything to disprove Johnson. In fact, the gossip of the English journalist has been ignored, probably as contemptuous slander meriting no serious scrutiny.

If we dismiss the evidence of Johnson on the ground that it was mere hearsay, how could we accept the contention of the Indian authors? The Indian authors also depend either upon the public pronouncements of Gandhi and Irwin or upon the gossip of their friends who might have heard from close associates of Gandhi about the attempts by him to save the life of Bhagat Singh. Surely one gossip does not disprove another.

What is the evidence now left out, yet to be examined? The Gandhi-Irwin negotiations which culminated in the formulation of the Delhi Pact were started in February 1931. The terms of the settlement were published in the Gazette of India of March 6. Usually none else was present when the two spoke to each other in close confidence in the Viceregal House in Delhi. Sometimes Herbert Emerson, Home Secretary (not the Home Member as Johnson mentioned him to be), would be called in for drafting the clauses of the settlement.

(It was this Emerson who gossiped to Johnson.) Lord Irwin had left a detailed account of the day-to-day discussions he had with Gandhi. The minutes are a valuable guide to future historians who would write on this aspect of our national liberation movement. The Bhagat Singh question was raised by Gandhi on February 18 with Irwin. Irwin wrote in his minute:

"In conclusion, not connected with above (talks of Delhi Pact), he mentioned the case of Bhagat Singh. He did not plead for commutation (of the death sentence). But he did ask for the postponement in the present circumstances." (*File No -5-45/1931 KW 2 Home Department, Political Branch, National Archives of India*)

On March 19 Gandhi had again some discussion with Irwin in the course of which he mentioned the case of Bhagat Singh. This is Irwin's minute:

"As he (Gandhi) was leaving he asked me if he might mention the case of Bhagat Singh that he had seen in the press the intimation of his execution for March 24. This was an unfortunate day as it coincided with arrival of the new president (of Congress) in Karachi and there would be much popular excitement. I told him that I had considered the case with most anxious care but could find no grounds on which I could justify to my conscience commuting the sentence . . . He appeared to appreciate the force of this argument and said no more." (*Ibid.*, Minute dated March 19)

On March 20 Gandhi had a meeting with Herbert Emerson who, in his note to the Viceroy, recorded what were Gandhi's feelings in the Bhagat Singh case. He wrote that Gandhi "did not seem to me to be particularly concerned in the matter. I told him that we should be lucky if we got through without disorder and I asked all that he could to prevent meetings being held in Delhi during the next few days and to restrain violent speeches. He promised to do all he could." (*File No. 33-1/1931, Home Department Political Branch*, National Archives)

Problem of Evaluation

How should one evaluate the archival documents now available to the scholars? The public posture of Gandhi and Irwin is at variance with the facts contained in the files of the Home Department of the time. Irwin noted that Gandhi did not plead for the commutation of death sentence but pleaded for the postponement of the execution. How is it that while in private they discussed a question with a particular motivation, quite a different impression was sought to be created in the public mind? Was not there any scope of misunderstanding between the two? Moreover, Emerson's evidence is highly coloured by his assessment of a subjective nature. Is it not possible that his one-sided versions were the result of Gandhi's general reticence maintained in some points of fruitless discussion with a British bureaucrat not to budge an inch from the official position? These questions are natural and logical.

Gandhi assured Emerson that he would do all he could in restraining "violent speeches" of Congressmen criticising the Government's obstinacy in Bhagat Singh issue. They talked on March 20 morning. A letter from Emerson on that very day requested Gandhi to restrain Subhas Bose from holding a public meeting in the evening of the same day. This is Gandhi's reply in full:

1, Daryaganj,
Delhi, March 20,1931

My dear Emerson,
   Thank you for your letter just received. I know of the meeting you refer to. I have taken every precaution possible and hope that nothing untoward will happen. I suggest that there should be no display of police force and no interference in the meeting. Irritation is likely to be there. It will be better to allow it find vent through meetings, etc.

Yours sincerely,
Sd/- M.K. Gandhi

   (F4/21/1931 Home Department, Political Branch, National Archives)

Now, how to interpret the letter of Gandhi? It was a communication sent to Emerson advising him how best Government could overcome the difficult situation of their creation. Again this letter was written with full knowledge of the intention of the Government regarding the fate of Bhagat Singh. In fact, he had advised them as to how they should play cool with the agitation.

   Now let us turn to the reference made by Halifax and Johnson in their books which cannot be dismissed off hand. The memoir of the reminiscing Viceroy stands a viable comparison with the main trends of discussion recorded in the contemporary records of the Home Department.

Dual Role

   It will be rash to run into a cynical conclusion about Gandhi. What was his motive in playing a dual role in the crucial days of February-March 1931? The Civil Disobedience Movement launched in 1930 had reached a high peak which disturbed the British power. They offered to negotiate with Gandhi, which Gandhi reciprocated. Their negotiation culminated in the Delhi Pact which he wanted to save at any cost. It was the period when the Tories in Britain launched a tirade against Gandhi (Churchill's Naked-Fakir epithet was flung at Gandhi at this time) and also against Irwin as the capitulator to Congress Party. Similarly, Gandhi was under pressure from Leftist elements in the Congress for disowning the Pact.

   Gandhi wanted to save the Pact from being wrecked. He genuinely believed that the Delhi Pact was much more important than the lives of one revolutionary here or another there. Bhagat Singh and his comrades were the tragic cases that arose at the time which almost stood between a settlement with Irwin by Gandhi.

Gandhi had no difficulty in making his choice or option. In the light of his understanding, the course he took was the only one available in the circumstances. It is true it led him to the path of small deception for a cause which he considered to be noble and patriotic. Moreover, there was no serious reason for him to be particularly concerned with the Lahore Case which was the symbol of the cult of violence quite inimical to the principle he cherished.

There is no lack of precedents in ancient Indian history and our religion of taking resort to small lying or deception for the sake of noble objectives. There was the case of Yudhisthira of *Mahabharata* before him. Yudhisthira applied a phonetic variation in uttering a truth which amounted to worse than a most blatant lie to undo the Kuru Commander-in-Chief, Dronacharya. If this could be excused by the ancient Hindus including the modern purists, Gandhi's public statements on the Bhagat Singh case should not be taken seriously. Take the case of the murder of Bali, the monkey king of *Ramayana*, by Rama. Even the murder was justified on ground of policy of statecraft.

So Gandhi's deception should not make us cynical about him. Nor should the discovery of his deception for a cause considered noble by him be taken as an indication of any absence of nobility in him. He was indeed a great Indian. Let Bhagat Singh episode be just a spot in his career and a condonable spot. Have not we condoned the spot in the moon, Yudhisthira and Rama?

—*MAINSTREAM*, Independence Day, 1970.

Punjab Act IV of 1930 and Related Papers

Secret Letter from the Government of the Punjab, No. 13569-A. S.B., dated the 2nd October 1930.

I am directed to forward a copy of a Bill to supplement the ordinary Criminal Law in the Punjab, together with a Statement of Objects and Reasons and to ask for the sanction of the Governor-General under section 80-A of the Government of India Act to the consideration of this Bill by the Punjab Legislative Council.

Twenty copies of the Bill will follow in due course.

2. The circumstances which make it advisable to introduce such legislation are doubtless known to the Government of India, but for the sake of convenience may be briefly recapitulated.

On the 23rd of December 1929, an attempt was made by the explosion of a bomb to wreck His Excellency the Viceroy's train as it was entering Delhi. On the 2nd of June 1930, bombs exploded in a house on Bahawalpur Road in Lahore. On the 19th June 1930, occurred a series of six simultaneous murderous outrages against police officers by means of the explosion of bombs, which had been so arranged as to explode on the arrival of the police attracted in each case to the scene by a previous explosion. As the result of this outrage two police officers lost their lives, and several others were seriously injured. On the 20th July 1930, an explosion of chemicals occurred in a suit-case in the possession of a young Sikh in Said Mitha Bazaar in Lahore city. In addition to these four cases there have within the last few months been numerous explosions of bombs in different parts of the Province, but in practically all cases the explosions were accidental and the only damage done was suffered by the persons who were in possession of the bombs or in one or two instances by innocent passers-by. Finally, on the 27th September 1930, an attempt was made to bomb a party of about 50 policemen in a bazaar in Rawalpindi city. Fortunately the bomb, which was of a very dangerous nature, failed to explode.

Altogether within the last twelve months there have been over 30 explosions of bombs in different localities in the Punjab.

3. From this brief recital it will be clear that the manufacture and possession of explosive missiles intended for murderous outrages have become a comparatively common form of crime. Careful investigations into the various incidents have resulted in establishing that several of the most serious cases form part of a carefully organized revolutionary conspiracy. The Punjab Government are in possession of information which shows that the absconders of the Lahore Conspiracy case, which is now drawing to a close, have gathered round them a large number of Hindu and Sikh youths, who are committed to the perpetration of terrorist outrages. Some 25 of these youths are now under arrest in connection with the four cases mentioned in the beginning of paragraph 2. Sixteen others are definitely "wanted" in these cases and information in the possession of the Criminal Investigation Department indicates that there is a large but probably distinct gang of a similar type in Rawalpindi, members of which are probably responsible for the outrage of the 27th September already mentioned. Apart from these two gangs, which are believed to be branches of the organization directed by the all-India revolutionary group, dangerous groups of young men are constantly coming to notice in different localities. One such gang, which was arrested in possession of arms, now under trial in Amritsar for planning political dacoities; a second gang in Jullundur and a third in Ludhiana, both now under trial and both brought to book just in time to forestall bomb outrages at the residences of the local Superintendents of Police; the Ahmadgarh train dacoity gang detected and convicted early in 1930, are all examples of groups formed locally either in emulation of or with the intention of eventually joining forces with the central party.

4. The situation with which the Punjab Government is confronted as the result of this serious growth of revolutionary crime may be summarized as follows:

(1) A determined and well organized movement to terroise the police of all ranks by actual and threatened outrage has been established.

(2) Owing to similar terrorisation and owing also to the exaltation of revolutionary crime as a high form of patriotism, increasing difficulty is being found in inducing witnesses to give evidence and in protecting them while trials are in progress.

(3) A considerable portion of the staff qualified for the investigation of revolutionary crime, necessarily very limited, will under the ordinary procedure be immobilized for prolonged periods in the conduct of cases in the courts and will thus not be available for driving home attacks on the movement by further investigations and preventive action.

These statements may be reinforced by illustration:

(*i*) *Terrorisation of the police.*—Besides the cases mentioned in paragraphs 2 and 3 of this letter, there have been in the past twelve months no less than fourteen concrete cases of bombs being used or of the discovery of bombs intended to be used against the police. In one of these cases the European Superintendent of Police of Multan was severely injured. In addition, threats of terrorist outrages on police officers have been widely broadcasted through the medium of leaflets and threatening letters on numerous occasions.

(*ii*) *Difficulty in obtaining evidence.*—In the Lahore Conspiracy case, in spite of protective measures on a most elaborate scale necessitating the whole-time employment for some eighteen months of a number of police officers of the rank of Sub-Inspector and Assistant Sub-Inspector, two approvers resiled from their original statements. In the Amritsar case mentioned in paragraph 3 above another approver has resiled. In a case in Lahore, in which a gang of Railway employees were discovered to be making bombs, a number of eye-witnesses of the accidental explosion, which revealed the plot, have refused to give evidence. In the Said Mitha Bazaar explosion case persons known to be able to identify the culprit with certainty have declined to come forward. Such examples could be multiplied.

(*iii*) *Immobilization of specialist detective staff.*—There can be no doubt that, had not all the best officers of the Punjab C.I.D., including a number of picked men from districts, been occupied from the early summer of 1929 to the autumn of 1930 in efforts to bring the Lahore-U.P. Conspiracy case to a successful conclusion, they would have been able to prevent the revolutionary movement from spreading as it has done. As things are, these officers are now faced, immediately after the prolonged strain, mental and physical, of the conspiracy trial, with the task of investigating a fresh series of incidents in a widespread and intricate conspiracy, while further incidents are adding almost daily to the complexity and magnitude of their task. The difficulties of investigation will, of course, be faced, but if to them is to be added the task, which experience has shown can be prolonged almost indefinitely, of steering cases of this nature through all the stages of normal committal, trial and appeal, there is a grave risk of a breakdown both of individual officers and of the machinery for fighting the revolutionary movement.

5. For the foregoing reasons it is, in the opinion of the Governor in Council, essential that special legislative measures should be taken to expedite the disposal of these trials. But there is another and even more important consideration. The protracted and abortive proceedings in the committing Magistrate's court in the Lahore Conspiracy trial are within the knowledge of the Government of India. These proceedings lasted for 9 months and were the occasion for almost daily scenes of disgraceful disorder and defiance of the authority of the Court. The Magistrate, the investigating staff and the witnesses were exposed to constant intimidation and in at least one case to actual violence. The prestige of the Courts was seriously lowered, and outside the courts the principal accused were applauded as popular heroes and as exponents of the highest form of patriotism. Their portraits were continually published in the press or

exhibited in public meetings and processions. Their successful defiance of the law excited general admiration among all the disorderly elements of the population, and undoubtedly contributed greatly to the revival of the cult of terrorism. It is impossible in the opinion of the Governor in Council to contemplate a repetition of such proceedings, and he, therefore, proposes that legislation should be undertaken to provide for the trial of those accused of terrorist outrages by special Tribunals, without the necessity for commitment proceedings. The proposed legislation will follow closely the lines of the Bengal Criminal Law Amendment Act, 1925, as amended by Bengal Act III of 1930, and will remain in force for a term of five years.

6. The Punjab Government have carefully considered the possibility of prosecuting the persons concerned in the four outrages mentioned in the beginning of paragraph 2 of this letter in four separate cases in preference to having a single trial in which all would be charged with conspiracy; but the objections to separate cases are, in the opinion of the Governor in Council, overwhelming. If such a course were adopted, it would be necessary to produce the approvers and a large number of other witnesses in each of four separate trials. This would obviously increase the risk of their being prevented from giving true evidence either by means of bribery or intimidation or by actual violence. The time occupied in four separate trials would be excessive and the expense would be greater. For these reasons the Governor in Council has accepted the view of the investigating agency that it is preferable that the four cases in question should be put in court in the form of a single conspiracy case. It is hoped that they will be ready for trial by the middle of November and by that time other cases, *e.g.*, that of the Rawalpindi gang, may well be in an advanced stage of preparation. Measures to provide for the speedy trial of these cases and others which may follow are, therefore, a matter of great urgency and it is the intention of the Punjab Government, if the Government of India approve and the sanction of the Governor-General to the Bill now forwarded is received, to convene a session of the Legislative Council shortly after the middle of October.

7. The Bill now submitted reproduces the Bengal Criminal Law Amendment Act, 1925, as extended and modified by Bengal Act III of 1930, the only change of substance being contained in clause (7), which makes provision for appointment to replace members of the Tribunal who may for any reason become unable to function.

8. In order to supplement this provincial legislation, I am to ask that, as foreshadowed in the penultimate paragraph of the Statement of Objects and Reasons, the Government of India should undertake central legislation on the lines of the first three sections of the Bengal Criminal Law Amendment (Supplementary) Act, 1925, in order—(a) to give the right of appeal to the accused to the High Court, and (b) to make capital sentences subject to confirmation by the High Court. Since it will probably not be possible for the

Government of India to introduce this legislation until some time after the session of the Punjab Legislative Council, I am to ask that the Punjab Government may be authorized to give an assurance in the Legislative Council that the Government of India will undertake this legislation.

9. The question of including in the Bill provision against the adoption of obstructive tactics by the accused, such as hunger-strikes or refusal to attend the court, has been considered; but as such a provision might be opposed on the ground that there is no evidence of the intention of any accused persons to adopt such tactics and might seriously prejudice the chances of the Bill being passed by the Legislative Council, the idea of its inclusion has been abandoned. If, however, subsequent events prove it to be necessary, it would be possible to convene an urgent session of the Council and introduce amending legislation later.

10. The attempt against the Viceregal train actually occurred within the limits of Delhi Province and in order to obviate any legal difficulties which may exist with regard to the trial of that offence in the proposed conspiracy case, I am to suggest that the Punjab Act, when passed, should be extended to the Delhi Province by notification of the Government of India under the Delhi Laws Act.

Whereas it is expedient to supplement the ordinary Criminal Law in the Punjab;

And Whereas the previous sanction of the Governor General under section 80-A, of the Government of India Act has been obtained;

It is hereby enacted as follows:—

1. *Short title, extent, commencement and duration.*—(1) This Act may be called the Criminal Law (Punjab Amendment) Act, 1930.

(2) It extends to the Punjab.

(3) It shall come into force on such date as the Local Government may by notification appoint in this behalf.

(4) It shall continue in force for five years from the date of commencement.

2. *Definition.*—In this Act unless there is anything repugnant in the subject or context "the Code" means the Code of Criminal Procedure, 1898.

3. *Power of Local Government to direct trial by Commissioners in certain cases.*—(1) The Local Government may, by order in writing, direct that any person accused of any offence specified in the schedule shall be tried by Commissioners appointed under this Act.

(2) No order under sub-section (1) shall be made in respect of, or be deemed to include, any person who has been committed under the Code for trial before a High Court, but save as aforesaid an order under that sub-section may be made in respect of, or may include, any person accused of any offence specified in the schedule whether such offence was committed before or after the commencement of this Act.

4. *Appointment and qualification of Commissioners.*—(1) Commissioners for the trial of persons under this Act shall be appointed by the Local Government.

(2) Such Commissioners may be appointed for the whole of the Punjab or for any part thereof, or for the trial of any particular accused person or persons.

(3) All trials under this Act shall be held by three Commissioners, of whom at least two shall be persons who at the time of appointment under this section are serving as, and have for at least three years served as or exercised the powers of Sessions Judges or Additional Sessions Judges, or are persons qualified under sub-section (3) of section 101 of the Government of India Act, for appointment as Judges of a High Court.

5. *Procedure of Commissioners.*—(1) Commissioners appointed under this Act may take cognizance of offences without the accused being committed to them for trial, and in trying accused persons, shall record evidence in the manner prescribed in section 356 of the Code and shall, in other respects also, subject to this Act and to any rules made thereunder, follow the procedure prescribed by the Code for the trial of warrant cases by Magistrates.

(2) In the event of any difference of opinion among the Commissioners, the opinion of the majority shall prevail.

6. *Powers of Commissioners.*—(1) The Commissioners may pass upon any person convicted by them any sentence authorised by law for the punishment of the offence of which such person is convicted.

(2) If in any trial under this Act it is found that the accused person has committed any offence, whether such offence is or is not an offence specified in the schedule. the Commissioners may convict such person of such offence and pass any sentence authorised by law for the punishment thereof.

7. *Special powers of Commissioners.*—(1) If for any reason any one of the Commissioners appointed under this Act is unable to discharge his duties, the Local Government shall appoint, subject to the qualifications required by clause (3) of section 4, another person to be a Commissioner in his place.

(2) Notwithstanding any change among the Commissioners it shall not be incumbent on the Commissioners to recall or rehear any witness who has already given evidence and the Commissioners may act on any evidence already recorded by or produced before them.

8. *Application of Code of Criminal Procedure to proceedings of Commissioners.*—The provisions of the Code, so far only as they are not inconsistent with the provisions of, or the special procedure prescribed by or under, this Act shall apply to the proceedings of Commissioners appointed under this Act, and such Commissioners shall have all the powers conferred by the Code on a court of session exercising original jurisdiction.

9. *Tender of pardon.*—(1) Commissioners trying an offence under this Act may, with a view to obtaining the evidence of any persons supposed to have been directly concerned in, or privy to, the offence, tender a pardon to such

person on condition of his making a full and true disclosure of the whole circumstances within his knowledge relative to the offence and to every other person concerned whether as principal or abettor in the commission thereof.

(2) Where, in the case of any offence for the trial of which by Commissioners an order has been made under sub-section (1) of section 3, a pardon has, before the passing of such order, been tendered to and accepted by any person under section 337 of the Code, the provisions of sub-section (2) and (3) of that section of the Code shall apply as if the accused person had been committed for trial to the Commissioners.

(3) For the purposes of sections 339 and 339-A. of the Code pardons tendered under sub-section (1) and sub-section (2) shall be deemed respectively to have been tendered under sections 338 and 337 of the Code.

10. *Special rule of evidence.*—Notwithstanding anything contained in the Indian Evidence Act, 1872, when the statement of any person has been recorded by any Magistrate, such statement may be admitted in evidence in any trial before Commissioners appointed under this Act, if such person is dead or cannot be found or is incapable of giving evidence, and the Commissioners are of opinion that such death, disappearance, or incapacity has been caused in the interests of the accused.

11. *Rule making powers of local Government.*—The local Government may, by notification in the Gazette, make rules consistent with this Act to provide for all or any of the following matters, namely:—

(i)   the times and places at which Commissioners appointed under this Act may sit;

(ii) the procedure of such Commissioners, including the appointment and powers of their President, and the procedure to be adopted in the event of any Commissioner being prevented from attending throughout the trial of any accused person;

(iii) the conduct of and the procedure at trials, the manner in which prosecutions before such Commissioners shall be conducted and the appointment and powers of persons conducting such prosecutions;

(iv) the execution of sentences passed by such Commissioners;

(v)   the temporary custody or release on bail of persons referred to or included in any order made under sub-section (1) of section 3, and the transmission of records to the Commissioners; and

(vi) any matter which appears to the local Government to be necessary for carrying into effect the provisions of this Act relating or ancillary to trials before Commissioners.

THE SCHEDULE
(See sections 3 and 6)

Any of the following offences, if in the opinion of the local Government there are reasonable grounds for believing that such offence has been committed by a member, or a person controlled or instigated by a member, of any association of which the objects or methods include the commission of any of such offences, namely:—

(a) any offence punishable under any of the following sections of the Indian Penal Code, namely, sections 148, 302, 304, 326, 327, 329, 332, 333, 385, 386, 387, 392, 394, 395, 396, 397, 398, 399, 400, 401, 402, 431, 435, 436, 437, 438, 440, 454, 455, 457, 458, 459, 460 and 506;

(b) any offence under the Explosive Substances Act, 1908;

(c) any offence under the Indian Arms Act, 1878;

(d) any attempt or conspiracy to commit, or any abetment of, any of the above offences.

STATEMENT OF OBJECTS AND REASONS ATTACHED TO THE BILL

The increase in the Punjab during recent months of murderous outrages and conspiracies to commit crimes of violence has, in the opinion of the Punjab Government, rendered necessary special legislation to amend the law relating to the procedure for the trial of criminal cases.

The ordinary commitment procedure provided in the Criminal Procedure Code involves in practice a double hearing and a protracted trial frequently extending over many months. The resulting delay in obtaining a final decision and the risks to which witnesses are exposed by frequent appearances in court require the abolition of commitment proceedings and its substitution by a special procedure for the trial of such cases.

The Bill which, with the exception of one provision, reproduces the Bengal Criminal Law Amendment Act, 1925, as extended and modified by Bengal Act III of 1930, enables the local Government to appoint Commissioners for the trial of certain specified offences. The Commissioners thus appointed are invested with the powers of a court of session and are empowered to take cognizance of specified cases direct without commitment. Their procedure will be regulated by the provisions in the Criminal Procedure Code relating to the trial of warrant cases.

The Bill introduces one special provision, not embodied in the corresponding Bengal Act, which will enable the special court to dispense with the necessity of *de novo* proceedings in the event of anyone of the Commissioners being unable to continue to sit after the commencement of the trial. In the interests of expedition in the disposal of cases, which it is the object of the Bill to secure, the Punjab Government feel that such special powers are essential.

It is not intended to deprive the accused in these cases of the right of appeal to the High Court or of the safeguard of requiring confirmation by the High Court of capital sentences; but as the Punjab Legislature is not empowered to confer additional jurisdiction on the High Court, the necessary provisions have not been incorporated in this Bill. Following the precedent of the corresponding Bengal legislation of 1925, the Government of India will in due course undertake special legislation to provide for appeals to, and confirmation of death sentences by, the High Court.

It is proposed that the Act shall be in force for five years only.

—File No. 4/26 of 1931 K.W. Home Ministry Political.

Whereas it is expedient to supplement the Criminal Procedure (Punjab Amendment) Act, (Punj. Act IV of 1930); It is hereby enacted as follows:

Short Title

1. This Act may be called the Punjab Criminal Procedure Amendment (Supplementary) Act, 1931.

Definitions

2. In this Act,—

(*a*) "Code" means the Code of Criminal Procedure, 1898 (V of 1898); and

(*b*) "local Act" means the Criminal Procedure (Punjab Amendment) Act, 1930 (Punj. Act IV of 1930).

Appeals and confirmations

3. (1) Any person convicted on a trial held by Commissioners under the local Act may appeal to the High Court of Judicature at Lahore, and such appeal shall be disposed of by the High Court in the manner provided in Chapter XXXI of the Code.

(2) When the Commissioners pass a sentence of death, the record of the proceedings before them shall be submitted to the High Court and the sentence shall not be executed unless it is confirmed by the High Court which shall exercise, in respect of such proceedings, all the powers conferred on the High Court by Chapter XXVII of the Code.

STATEMENT OF OBJECTS AND REASONS

An Act has been passed under the title of the Criminal Procedure (Punjab Amendment) Act, 1930 (Punjab Act IV of 1930), which enables the Local Government to appoint Commissioners for the trial of certain specified offences. When the Bill was introduced in the Punjab Legislative Council on 27th October, 1930, an explicit undertaking was given on the authority of the Government of India, that legislation would in due course be undertaken in the Central Legislature to provide for an appeal to the High Court by any person convicted on a trial held by Commissioners under the local Act, and for the submission to the High Court for confirmation of any sentence of death passed by the Commissioners, and the present Bill is intended to effect these objects.

J. CRERAR

New Delhi
2nd December, 1930

—File No. 194 of 1931, Home Department, Pol.

Index